Personality, Development and Learning

A Reader

Edited by Peter Barnes, John Oates,
John Chapman, Victor Lee and Pam
Czerniewska *at the Open University*

HODDER AND STOUGHTON

in association with
The Open University

British Library Cataloguing in Publication Data

Personality, development and learning.
 I. Educational psychology
 I. Barnes, Peter, *1946–*   II. Open University
 370.15   LB1051

  ISBN 0-340-35955-2

First published 1984
Fourth Impression 1989

Photoset by Rowland Phototypesetting Ltd,
Bury St Edmunds, Suffolk

Printed and bound in Great Britain
for Hodder and Stoughton Educational,
a division of Hodder and Stoughton Ltd,
Mill Road, Dunton Green, Sevenoaks, Kent,
by Athenaeum Press Ltd., Newcastle upon Tyne

CoL. B 0769 /6.50. 9.90

Contents

Preface

This Reader is published in connection with the Open University course E206, 'Personality, Development and Learning'. The course is intended for those interested in psychology and education.

Because this Reader is only part of a total learning package, it does not claim to be a complete picture of the issues with which it deals. Nevertheless, it does present a wide ranging and integrated collection of papers arranged in four separately introduced sections.

It is not necessary to become an undergraduate of the Open University in order to take E206. Further information about the course may be obtained by writing to: The Admissions Office, The Open University, PO Box 48, Walton Hall, Milton Keynes, MK7 6AB.

General introduction

The past century has seen a great expansion of the science of psychology and of its application to many aspects of our lives. And as it has grown so its methods, its claims and its emphases have changed and many, perhaps, have revised their expectations of what it can reasonably be expected to achieve. As with other sciences, trends have come and gone, paradigms have changed; the sacred truths of one generation have become the myths of the next. Alongside this have run changes in education and social policy and practice which, if not the direct result of the findings of research, have at least an association with them.

This mixture of theory, research and practice set against a historical backdrop characterises the collection of readings in this volume. It has been assembled to accompany the Open University course E206: 'Personality, Development and Learning' which is an introductory course about psychology and education approached from two directions – the basic psychology which is thought to inform and influence educational practice and the consideration of educational issues to which psychology and psychologists have, in their various ways, contributed.

Some of the readings present important debates within psychology, some recount specific pieces of research and others describe and evaluate practice. They span, albeit selectively, the three areas of personality, development and learning which are the prime concerns of the course, and they are arranged here in three sections, each with its own introduction. The fourth and final section emphasises practice.

The scene is set by one of the founding fathers of modern psychology, William James, who, in an elegant piece written at the turn of the century, raises many of the questions about the relationship between psychology and education which remain with us today. Though addressed to teachers, the issues that it raises – like those in the rest of this book – are of far wider relevance.

Psychology and the teaching art

William James

[. . .] Psychology ought certainly to give the teacher radical help. And yet I confess that, acquainted as I am with the height of some of your expectations, I feel a little anxious lest, at the end of these simple talks of mine, not a few of you may experience some disappointment at the net results. In other words, I am not sure that you may not be indulging fancies that are just a shade exaggerated. That would not be altogether astonishing, for we have been having something like a 'boom' in psychology in this country. Laboratories and professorships have been founded, and reviews established. [. . .] 'The new psychology' has become a term to conjure up portentous ideas withal; and you teachers, docile and receptive and aspiring as many of you are, have been plunged in an atmosphere of vague talk about our science, which to a great extent has been more mystifying than enlightening. Altogether it does seem as if there were a certain fatality of mystification laid upon the teachers of our day. The matter of their profession, compact enough in itself, has to be frothed up for them in journals and institutes, till its outlines often threaten to be lost in a kind of vast uncertainty. Where the disciples are not independent and critical-minded enough (and I think that, if you teachers in the earlier grades have any defect – the slightest touch of a defect in the world – it is that you are a mite too docile), we are pretty sure to miss accuracy and balance and measure in those who get a license to lay down the law to them from above.

As regards this subject of psychology, now, I wish at the very threshold to do what I can to dispel the mystification. So I say at once that in my humble opinion there *is* no 'new psychology' worthy of the name. There is nothing but the old psychology which began in Locke's time, plus a little physiology of the brain and senses and theory of evolution, and a few refinements of introspective detail, for the most part without adaptation to the teacher's use. It is only the fundamental conceptions of psychology which are of real value to the teacher; and they, apart from the aforesaid theory of evolution, are very far from being new – I trust that you will see better what I mean by this at the end of all these talks.

I say moreover that you make a great, a very great mistake, if you think that psychology, being the science of the mind's laws, is something from which you can deduce definite programmes and schemes and methods of instruction for immediate schoolroom use. Psychology is a science, and teaching is an art; and sciences never generate arts directly out of

Source: JAMES, W. (1899) *Talks to Teachers on Psychology: and to Students on some of Life's Ideals* (ch. 1). London: Longmans Green.

themselves. An intermediary inventive mind must make the application, by using its originality.

The science of logic never made a man reason rightly, and the science of ethics (if there be such a thing) never made a man behave rightly. The most such sciences can do is to help us to catch ourselves up and check ourselves, if we start to reason or to behave wrongly; and to criticize ourselves more articulately after we have made mistakes. A science only lays down lines within which the rules of the art must fall, laws which the follower of the art must not transgress; but what particular thing he shall positively do within those lines is left exclusively to his own genius. One genius will do his work well and succeed in one way, while another succeeds as well quite differently; yet neither will transgress the lines.

The art of teaching grew up in the schoolroom, out of inventiveness and sympathetic concrete observation. Even where (as in the case of Herbart) the advancer of the art was also a psychologist, the pedagogics and the psychology ran side by side, and the former was not derived in any sense from the latter. The two were congruent, but neither was subordinate. And so everywhere the teaching must *agree* with the psychology, but need not necessarily be the only kind of teaching that would so agree; for many diverse methods of teaching may equally well agree with psychological laws.

To know psychology, therefore, is absolutely no guarantee that we shall be good teachers. To advance to that result, we must have an additional endowment altogether, a happy tact and ingenuity to tell us what definite things to say and do when the pupil is before us. That ingenuity in meeting and pursuing the pupil, that tact for the concrete situation, though they are the alpha and omega of the teacher's art, are things to which psychology cannot help us in the least.

The science of psychology, and whatever science of general pedagogics may be based on it, are in fact much like the science of war. Nothing is simpler or more definite than the principles of either. In war, all you have to do is to work your enemy into a position from which the natural obstacles prevent him from escaping if he tries to; then to fall on him in numbers superior to his own, at a moment when you have led him to think you far away; and so, with a minimum of exposure of your own troops, to hack his force to pieces, and take the remainder prisoners. Just so, in teaching, you must simply work your pupil into such a state of interest in what you are going to teach him that every other object of attention is banished from his mind; then reveal it to him so impressively that he will remember the occasion to his dying day; and finally fill him with devouring curiosity to know what the next steps in connection with the subject are. The principles being so plain, there would be nothing but victories for the masters of the science, either on the battlefield or in the schoolroom, if they did not both have to make their application to an incalculable quantity in the shape of the mind of their opponent. The mind of your own enemy, the pupil, is working away from you as keenly and eagerly as is the mind of the commander on the other side from the scientific general. Just what the respective enemies want and think, and what they know and do not know, are as hard things for the teacher as for the general to find out. Divination and perception, not psychological pedagogics or theoretic strategy, are the only helpers here.

But, if the use of psychological principles thus be negative rather than positive, it does not follow that it may not be a great use, all the same. It certainly narrows the path for experiments and trials. We know in advance, if we are psychologists, that certain methods will be wrong, so our psychology saves us from mistakes. It makes us, moreover, more clear as to what we are about. We gain confidence in respect to any method which we are using as soon as we believe that it has theory as well as practice at its back. Most of all, it fructifies our independence, and it reanimates our interest, to see our subject at two different angles – to get a stereoscopic view, so to speak, of the youthful organism who is our enemy, and, while handling him with all our concrete tact and divination, to be able, at the same time, to represent to ourselves the curious inner elements of his mental machine. Such a complete knowledge as this of the pupil, at once intuitive and analytic, is surely the knowledge at which every teacher ought to aim.

Fortunately for you teachers, the elements of the mental machine can be clearly apprehended, and their workings easily grasped. And, as the most general elements and workings are just those parts of psychology which the teacher finds most directly useful, it follows that the amount of this science which is necessary to all teachers need not be very great. Those who find themselves loving the subject may go as far as they please, and become possibly none the worse teachers for the fact, even though in some of them one might apprehend a little loss of balance from the tendency observable in all of us to over-emphasize certain special parts of a subject when we are studying it intensely and abstractly. But for the great majority of you a general view is enough, provided it be a true one; and such a general view, one may say, might almost be written on the palm of one's hand.

Least of all need you, merely *as teachers*, deem it part of your duty to become contributors to psychological science or to make psychological observations in a methodical or responsible manner. I fear that some of the enthusiasts for child-study have thrown a certain burden on you in this way. By all means let child-study go on – it is refreshing all our sense of the child's life. There are teachers who take a spontaneous delight in filling syllabuses, inscribing observations, compiling statistics, and computing the per cent. Child-study will certainly enrich their lives. And, if its results, as treated statistically, would seem on the whole to have but trifling value, yet the anecdotes and observations of which it in part consist do certainly acquaint us more intimately with our pupils. Our eyes and ears grow quickened to discern in the child before us processes similar to those we have read of as noted in the children – processes of which we might otherwise have remained inobservant. But, for Heaven's sake, let the rank and file of teachers be passive readers if they so prefer, and feel free not to contribute to the accumulation. [. . .] I cannot too strongly agree with my colleague, Professor Münsterberg, when he says that the teacher's attitude toward the child, being concrete and ethical, is positively opposed to the psychological observer's, which is abstract and analytic. Although some of us may conjoin the attitudes successfully, in most of us they must conflict.

The worst thing that can happen to a good teacher is to get a bad conscience about her profession because she feels herself hopeless as a psychologist. Our teachers are overworked already. Every one who adds a jot or tittle of unnecessary weight to their burden is a foe of education. A bad conscience increases the weight of every other burden; yet I know that child-study, and other pieces of psychology as well, have been productive of bad conscience in many a really innocent pedagogic breast. I should indeed be glad if this passing word from me might tend to dispel such a bad conscience, if any of you have it; for it is certainly one of those fruits of more or less systematic mystification of which I have already complained. The best teacher may be the poorest contributor of child-study material, and the best contributor may be the poorest teacher. No fact is more palpable than this.

So much for what seems the most reasonable general attitude of the teacher toward the subject which is to occupy our attention.

Section One

Human development

The theme of the first section of this Reader is human psychological development. The papers included cover a range of related topics and give a flavour of the variety of different approaches that developmental psychologists take to their subject matter. To a large extent, the particular methods a psychologist chooses reflect the sort of questions to which answers are being sought. This specialisation of enquiry needs to be tempered by a broad understanding of general principles of development including the effects of the cultural context in which development takes place.

The first paper in this section, by Lawrence Stone, takes as its starting point a critical analysis of three major contributions in the field of 'psychohistory' – the study of historical changes in society and their relationship to the psychological development of individuals. Stone is critical of the assumption, which he traces to psychoanalytic roots, that the 'critical period' for the formation of personality is to be found in the earliest years of life, in the early interactions of parents and children. Rather, he believes, we should acknowledge that the psychological conditions of family life are closely linked with broader cultural trends. So, according to Stone, traumas such as those Freud associated with weaning and toilet training depend entirely upon how these areas are viewed by a culture and by groups within a culture at different points in history. Stone is arguing, in effect, that the psychology of child development gives too little attention to external influences on the dynamics of families and their consequent effects on children. He alerts the reader to historical changes in the way that functions originally confined to the family have been variously taken over or renounced by state institutions, so that the role of the family has become narrower at times, and broader again at others. These changes, Stone argues, have profound implications for the psychological conditions of family life and hence for the connections that psychologists pursue between early experiences and the development of personality.

These far-reaching criticisms can usefully be applied to Melanie Klein's exposition of her classic theory of the links between the infant's earliest experiences of feeding and the development of adult personality. For Klein, a pivotal influence on character formation is the balance between the 'good breast' and the 'bad breast' in the baby's early fragmented perceptions of the world. Klein, echoed later by Piaget, believed that some months of a baby's life passed before the 'concept of object' was formed. Prior to that, she proposed, each experience is seen anew as a 'part-object', each with associated good or bad feelings projected on to it by the baby. The resolution of this phase, when the developing child comes to see that whole objects are made up of both good and bad parts, is, according to Klein, a key point in determining adult personality. The sources of positive adult feelings such as altruism, sympathy and caring, and negative feelings such as greed, envy and selfishness can be found, Klein argues, in the way the child handles the emotions of loss and betrayal that arise when 'good' part-objects have to be relinquished for the more ambivalent whole objects of the real world.

Jean Piaget's work is one of the most important influences on modern developmental psychology. He provided a conceptual framework, a way of thinking about cognitive development, that has informed a whole tradition of research. His methods and his key experiments have prompted countless replication studies, and have been used to explore many questions about development both within and across cultures. The third paper is one of Piaget's clearest expositions of his theory. In it, he first describes the theory's central concepts of the processes by which intelligent thought develops. He also gives examples that show his distinctive approach to exploring children's thought, and then goes on to outline his famous stage theory of the course of cognitive development. In this, he sees the child progressing from a self-centred preoccupation with learning the results of bodily actions, through a sequence of progressively more complex and abstract representations, to the adult stage of abstract thought. This final stage brings the child to the possibilities of forming general hypotheses and making abstract deductions.

Piaget's theory has served as a guiding principle for many of the changes that have come about in Western schools, particularly at the nursery and primary levels. This application of Piagetian principles has often been made with little critical analysis. Charles Brainerd, in the fourth paper in this section, sets out to provide such a review of the educational implications of Piagetian theory and their validity. He focuses mainly on two areas: first, the Piagetian notion that assisting children's mental development can only be done if close account is taken of the stage they have already reached and if teaching is aimed at a level only slightly above this; second, the idea that active, self-discovery learning is far more effective than passive tutorial type learning. After discussing these two axioms and how they can be experimentally examined, Brainerd traces some of the lines of research that have been carried out in these two areas. While much of the earlier research produced equivocal or conflicting results, Brainerd suggests that more recent research has raised serious doubts about the validity of the two prescriptions. (The second half of this paper, which deals specifically with the application of Piaget's theory in the preschool, can be found in Section 4 of this Reader, pages 323–37.)

One of Piaget's legacies to nursery and primary education has been a strong belief in the importance of play in mental development. The fifth paper, by Kathy Sylva, Jerome Bruner and Paul Genova, reports an experiment that examined whether play can assist children in solving problems, and whether adult instruction can be equally effective. This study compared the effects on problem-solving of allowing children to play with the experimental materials beforehand with the effects of an adult showing the children the components in the problem solution. The authors found that the children's self-directed activity with the materials seemed much better at helping them to find a solution than the adult's demonstration.

The final paper in this section, by Michael Lamb, Ann Frodi, Majt Frodj and Carl-Philip Hwang, is a report of a study in a somewhat neglected area of child development: mothers always seem to figure prominently in psychological theories of the role of early interactions, while fathers seem to remain, at best, shadowy figures in the background. This study concentrated on the analysis of interactions between parents and their sixteen-month-old children. The comparisons were between mothers and fathers, and between 'traditional' families in which the mother had the primary responsibility for childcare, and 'non-traditional' families in which the father took this responsibility. The data were collected by observing the parents and children during normal activity in their homes. Despite the 'non-traditional' fathers' much greater involvement with their children, the mothers in these families were still rated higher than the fathers on the range of measures of interactions used in the study. Although these were Swedish families, the differences that were found were very similar to those found in another study of American families. The authors suggest that these differences are either biologically determined or that they reflect the potent effects of the socialization of the parents.

John Oates

1.1 Children and the family

Lawrence Stone

Although three-quarters of a century have passed since Freud first drew attention to the crucial effect of childhood events in determining adult character and behavior patterns, it was not until the 1950s that there appeared the first general history of childhood in the West. Of the four significant studies of this phenomenon, all have been written by non-historians, persons who, with respect to the profession, are marginal men.

In 1955 J. H. van den Berg, a Dutch psychologist, published *Metabletica, of Leer der veranderingen (The Changing Nature of Man)*, a bold, overarching, psychohistorical study of parental relations to children, based mainly on philosophical sources like Rousseau (van den Berg, 1955). In 1960 Philippe Ariès, a French director of publications at the Institute for Applied Research for Tropical and Subtropical Fruits, published his now famous *Centuries of Childhood* (Ariès, 1960). In 1970 David Hunt, an American historian who has also worked as a psychologist with disturbed children, reinterpreted some of Ariès's French seventeenth-century material in *Parents and Children in History*, using a modified Eriksonian model of ego-development (Hunt, 1970). And in 1974 Lloyd deMause, an American academic dropout, a successful businessman and self-taught psychohistorian, produced a collective volume, *The History of Childhood*, the key essay in which was his own lengthy general survey of 'The Evolution of Childhood' ranging from the Greeks and Romans to the present day (deMause, 1974).

The first problem in studying the history of childhood is how to choose the appropriate psychological model. Nothing in the historical record disproves Freud's theory about how at different stages of infantile development different erogenous zones become the foci of sexual stimulation, thus providing a logical explanation of the later relationship between oral, anal, and genital pleasure. Nor does the historical record do anything to belittle the importance of sublimation, or of the unconscious operating with a secret dynamic of its own. What it does do, however, is to cast very great doubt upon the assumption that the particular kinds of infantile traumas upon which Freud laid so much stress have been suffered by the whole of the human race at all times and in all places. It is now fairly clear that four of the main traumas Freud looked for and found among his patients, and therefore assumed to be universal, are dependent on particular experiences which did not happen to the vast majority of people in

Source: STONE, L. (1981) *The Past and the Present* (ch. 13). London: Routledge and Kegan Paul.

most of the recorded past, but which were peculiar to middle-class urban culture of late Victorian Europe. Provided that it was carried out slowly, as it apparently was in many cases, the oral trauma of weaning can hardly have been a serious one when it occurred as late as fifteen to eighteen months after birth. The anal trauma of toilet training is unlikely to have existed in a population which lived amid its own excrement, which hardly ever washed, and whose women and children wore no underpants.

The only detailed historical example of toilet training in the past that we have is, unfortunately, that of a less than typical person, a future king, the young Louis XIII in the early years of the seventeenth century. His training apparently did not begin until he was sixteen months or so, and was not internalized before about three years. He, at any rate, cannot have been traumatized by pressure to control his sphincters at an early age. We just do not know about how other children were toilet trained, but there is the strong negative evidence that contemporary child-rearing manuals do not even discuss the matter.

Although children in the past, as we shall see, had to endure far worse things, the passage through the oral and anal stages of childhood, in the purely technical sense, does not seem to have been particularly traumatic. As for the genital stage, the one example we have—again that of Louis XIII – suggests that no one was bothered by infantile and childhood sexual autoeroticism, sexual display, or sexual curiosity. Louis could get courtiers to kiss his penis, and was allowed to poke his little fist up the vaginas of several ladies-in-waiting. We also know that most families slept in one room, while even if they did not, houses were poorly constructed with thin board partitions through which it was easy to see or hear – as Fanny Hill soon found out. Consequently, from a very early age most children must have witnessed their parents and others – to say nothing of animals – engaged in sexual intercourse.

There is also the negative evidence that childhood and adolescent masturbation was not regarded as a mortal sin in the eighteenth-century Catholic confession manuals (although it was in the Middle Ages), and that although the paranoid drives to suppress all hints of autoeroticism began in 1710, it did not catch on before the early nineteenth century. Finally, we know that half of all children would have lost one parent before completing adolescence, and that in England a majority of them left home anyway between the ages of seven and fourteen, to act as servants in other people's houses, to serve apprenticeships, or to go to boarding school. Under such circumstances the conflict of wills between parents and their adolescent children, which rips apart so many modern homes today, can have had little opportunity to develop. The identity crisis of puberty was normally passed away from home.

It is now possible to provide alternatives to these historically inappropriate traumas advanced by Freud as self-sufficient explanations of adult personality problems. As David Riesman has put it:

There has been a tendency in current social research, influenced as it is by psychoanalysis, to over-emphasize and overgeneralize the importance of very early childhood in character formation. Even within this early period, an almost technological attention has sometimes been focused on what might be called the tricks of the child-rearing trade: feeding and toilet training schedules.

This 'assumes that once the child has reached, say, the weaning stage, its character structure is so formed that, barring intensive psychiatric intervention, not much that happens afterward will do more than bring out tendencies already set' (Riesman, 1950).

No one doubts that child-rearing practices affect the adult personality, but acceptance of the theories of more recent ego-psychologists like Erikson and Hartmann opens up a new range of possibilities for the historian (Erikson, 1959, 1963; Hartmann, 1964). These theories involve hypotheses about the continued plasticity of the ego far into adulthood as it responds, through a series of crises, to the twin challenges of maturation and the influences of the family, the culture, and the environment. Not only do these theories have a strong ring of truth about them in the light of common experience, but they have the enormous advantage to the historian that they admit ego-development into periods of the life cycle when historical data become more readily available.

Second, since these developmental theories admit the influence of the social and cultural environment in affecting the nature, timing, and resolution of the recurring crises, they allow the historian to view the problem of ego-development in a broad historical frame. Clear evidence of distinctive features of national character, and fundamental shifts in character over time, for example from the other-directed to the inner-directed personality, can be explained in broader terms than those internal to the family itself.

This does not mean, however, that childhood experience in the past was without its effects on the adult personality. On the contrary, the experiences of the average child were so damaging that I believe that a large number of adults, at any rate of the gentry class in the period with which I am most familiar, namely, the sixteenth and seventeenth centuries, were emotionally stunted and found it extremely difficult to establish warm personal relationships with other people.

[. . .]

Given the validity of 'psychohistory' as a legitimate enterprise, which is the most profitable field in which this research can be pursued? In my opinion, it will not be in the application of this or that psychological theory to the analysis of some particular person in history – Luther or Leonardo da Vinci or Woodrow Wilson or Hitler or Gandhi. What can more fruitfully be done is to study changes in family patterns and structures of specific classes or status groups in particular places. These changes will include relations of the nuclear core to the kin and the community, and economic and social power and affective relations between both husbands and wives and parents and children.

In that sense van den Berg, Ariès, and deMause are pursuing a far more promising line of historical inquiry than those who have tried to use psychology to interpret the behavior of individual figures in the past. I just do not think that such things as the extermination of six million Jews can be explained by the alleged fact that Hitler's mother was killed by treatment given her by a Jewish doctor in an attempt to cure her cancer of the breast; or that Luther's defiance of the Roman church can be explained by the brutal way he was treated by his father or by his chronic constipation.

These things may perhaps be necessary causes, but they certainly are not sufficient, and the result of such work to date has been disappointing, partly because of the flimsiness of the evidence of childhood experience, partly because of the speculative nature of the causal links with adult behavior, partly because of the neglect of the influence of the great processes of historical change in religion, economics, politics, society, and so on. As Malinowski pointed out in 1927, 'Man disposes of a body of material possessions, lives within a type of social organization, communicates by language, and is moved by systems of spiritual values' (Malinowski, 1927). Any explanation of his history which ignores these cultural facts is not likely to be very convincing.

The first general model of childhood development in the West was that of Philippe Ariès. It is a pessimistic one of degeneration from an era of freedom and sociability to an era of oppression and isolation. According to him the Middle Ages and the sixteenth century were a period of happy social polymorphism, in which there were no divisions of ranks or ages, no separation of the child from the adult, no privacy, no external pressures from the state or the needs of an industrial economy, no internalized work ethic. Children and adults mixed together easily and naturally, wearing the same clothes, playing the same games, and working together on the same jobs. They also shared from the beginning a common knowledge of both sex and death. This easy egalitarian familiarity was one in which child abuse could not occur. It all sounds too good to be true – as indeed it is.

In the seventeenth century, as a result of the spread of new kinds of Christianity into both Protestant and Catholic regions, a new attitude toward children developed, an event he describes as 'the discovery of childhood.' This was not the work of Renaissance humanists but of seventeenth-century clergy. There was a rising concern for the child, which took two forms. First, there was a tightening of family bonds, along with the isolation of the family from external influences and a growing concern by the parents for their children; and second, there was a growing fear of the inherent corruptibility of the child by sin, leading to severity toward him in the home and to his isolation in schools regimented by age groups and disciplined to suppress all signs of moral backsliding. Medieval sociability was replaced not by Enlightenment individualism but by the isolated child-centered family and by the school, in both of which the prime concern was the taming of the will.

The rise of the repressive boarding school is the significant feature of this development, involving as it did a progressive extension of the period of childhood into adolescence and even beyond: 'The central event is quite obvious: the extension of school education.' This transformation of attitudes toward childhood preceded demographic change, and indeed became itself the cause of demographic change when in the late eighteenth and nineteenth centuries it inspired a deliberate policy of contraception.

Ariès's book has had a dazzling success and has been the *primum mobile* of Western family history in the last two decades. As a pioneer work, erudite, imaginative, and inventive, it deserves all the praise and attention it has received. It is the kind of pathbreaking book no traditional historian could have written, and without it our culture would be the poorer. But for all its seminal brilliance, there remain unanswered certain basic questions. Is its methodology sound? Are its data reliable? Is its causal hypothesis valid? Are the alleged facts and alleged consequences true? In short, is the model correct, and if so, for what areas and for what classes?

In the first place, Ariès omits to point out the undeniable fact that between the Middle Ages and the nineteenth century the institution of the family lost many of its older functions to a series of impersonal institutions, such as poorhouses for the indigent, alms houses for the old, hospitals for the sick, schools for the children, banks for credit, and insurance companies for protection against catastrophe. Its legal, political, and economic functions declined before the ever-encroaching march of the institutions of the modern state. This functional erosion enhanced the prominence of the last area of family concern, the nurturance and socialization of the infant and young child.

Furthermore, the power of the state undermined the influence of the kin, and thus increased the isolation and privacy of the nuclear family. This process can hardly be called the rise of the family, but rather its reorientation to serve a narrower, more specialized function. The rise of the school is best seen not as part of the same process as the growth of the child-oriented family, but as its very antithesis, the transfer to an impersonal institution of a socializing function previously performed by the family. Moreover, although the repressive school was based on the theory of original sin, it was only in its first stage, in the seventeenth century, that the more child-centered family was also repressive and there is clear evidence that by the eighteenth century among the English upper classes it was loving, affectionate, and nurturant.

Thus Ariès's model is broken-backed, for his two agents of change, the child-centered family and the repressive school, were pulling in different directions and were caused by different ideas and influences. It thus lacks explanatory cohesion, as both Hunt and deMause point out. Moreover, its use of evidence, particularly iconographic evidence from art, to prove that the 'discovery of childhood' actually happened, is not very convincing. For example, we now know for certain that although the Florentine bourgeoisie of the fifteenth and sixteenth centuries decorated their houses with painted and sculptured putti, they emptied them of flesh and blood babies, who were all sent out to wet-nurses in the countryside. Putti, which Ariès uses as evidence of the discovery of childhood, are therefore really not evidence at all.

In addition, the thesis has a unilinear view of historical evolution which is contrary to the known facts. Children were more harshly treated in the sixteenth and seventeenth centuries and again in the nineteenth century at the two peaks of religious zeal for moral reform than they were in the eighteenth or twentieth centuries, and perhaps also than in the fifteenth century. Ariès's chronology is very vague. One can never be quite sure whether one is dealing with the sixteenth or the seventeenth or the eighteenth century, and the book dodges about from century to century in a most confusing and indeed ahistorical way.

It is as vague in its geography as it is in its chronology, ranging casually from Italy to France to England for its evidence. For example, the presence of effigies of long-dead babies on tombs was relatively rare in France, but extremely common in England in the late sixteenth and early seventeenth centuries – a distinction whose significance Ariès completely ignores. Flogging died out in French schools in the eighteenth century but persisted in English schools into the twentieth. Wet-nursing died out in eighteenth-century England but persisted well into the nineteenth century in France on a very large scale. Geography clearly matters.

There is also too little attention paid to the particular class which is being dealt with. Ariès deduces the attitudes to infantile sexuality of the society as a whole from that of the entourage of the future Louis XIII. The development of the boarding school teaching the classics, which affected only a tiny minority of the population, becomes a key event in early modern history. And finally, the powerful historical forces that affected the family so profoundly, changes in religion, political power, industrialization, urbanization, and poverty, are virtually ignored. Ariès's book is in fact a history of French schools, and of upper-class and middle-class parents and children, that lacks the necessary historical context of time, place, class, and culture. A fascinating pioneering book, it is now recognized to be badly flawed in both its methodology and its conclusions.

David Hunt's book is a psychological gloss on that by Ariès. It begins with a brilliant critique of Eriksonian ego-psychology, pointing out that the latter's optimism is ill-founded, for generativity is a fragile cultural artefact, not an instinctive human response. Consequently, in reality children have often been neglected and abused. Hunt also criticizes Ariès's historical model for its nostalgic, even reactionary, *Gemeinschaft-Gesellschaft* Durkheimian view of change, and for its exaggerated stress on the school.

He then settles down to a detailed analysis of Dr Héroard's account of the upbringing of the infant Louis XIII. He stresses the child's very close relation to his father, the all-powerful and virile Henry IV, and his very distant relations with his mother; and the way the child's will was deliberately broken from the age of two by frequent whippings in order to instill the basic principle of obedience. He points to Louis's later life as an unhappy, semi-impotent husband and, by a great leap of the imagination, attributes this to the experiences of his upbringing: knowing the physical facts of sex but not their psychological meaning, confused by contradictory signals about what was permitted and what was not, cowed by frequent whippings, and more or less isolated from his mother. Hunt further stresses the traumatic nature of the break at the age of seven, when he put on adult clothes, and was transferred from the control of women to that of men. His conclusion is that not sex, not anality, but 'infantile autonomy was the major child-rearing problem in seventeenth-century society,' and that this was linked to anxieties about status in a hierarchical law-and-order society.

Hunt is correct to stress that the breaking of the will was the key element in child-rearing in the sixteenth and seventeenth centuries, but it has to be pointed out that his evidence is in many respects less than satisfactory. In the first place (as I have mentioned), he is dealing with the son and heir of a king, and it is probably not legitimate to extrapolate the education of such an exalted person to that of, say, the middle-class child at the same period. Second, he has worked exclusively from the printed record of Dr Héroard's diary, which was published in the mid-nineteenth century, and which contains only a relatively small part of the whole text. It appears that in the manuscript the doctor's main preoccupation was neither sexuality nor discipline, but the child's health, and that much of it is therefore a detailed record of the daily input-output flow of food and excreta respectively. Until the total diary has been published, any conclusions based upon the published Victorian extract must remain suspect. Finally, the link between the adult personality traits and the infantile experience remains no more than an interesting speculation.

DeMause's model of historical change is the exact opposite of that of Ariès's, for it is optimistic. It is based on the following five propositions: (1) Parent-child relations are an independent variable in history. (2) There are only three possible adult reactions to children: projective, reversal, and empathic; the first two resulting in hatred and cruelty, and the third in love and affection. (3) Changes in parent-child relations are not affected by religious, social, political, economic, or any other factors, but operate by 'psychogenesis', a process by which the parents' capacity to regress to the psychic age of the child has improved slowly over the centuries. Thus from generation to generation parents do a little better each time, until we reach the present when the perfect child is just around the corner. It is apparently as inevitable and self-contained a process as

Darwinian evolution, 'a powerful private force for change in historical personality,' operating 'wholly independent of public events, economic, social, whatever.' (4) There has been an upward linear progression in the history of childhood for the last two thousand years, from the Infanticide Mode of classical antiquity to the Abandonment Mode of the early Middle Ages to the Ambivalent Mode of the late Middle Ages and early modern period to the Intrusive Mode of the eighteenth century – the great watershed – to the Socialization Mode of 1800–1950 to the Helping Mode of 1950 onward. (5) Child-rearing practices provide the key to the transmission of all other cultural traits visible in the adult.

Prodded by critics, deMause asserts that his model is not unilinear but multilinear, and involves 'methodological individualism' – whatever that means – not 'psychological reductionism'. These disclaimers do nothing to solve the problem of how to regard so bold, so challenging, so dogmatic, so enthusiastic, so perverse, and yet so heavily documented a model. For deMause child-rearing has replaced Marx's control of the means of production and the class war as the key element around which the whole of history has to be conceived: our task as historians is to construct 'a scientific history of human nature'. Are we dealing here with what Clifford Geertz has described as 'the natural tendency to excess of seminal minds' or with a hopelessly unscholarly aberration, hanging loosely in the void between history and psychology, and lacking the methodological rigor of either discipline?

DeMause's essay undoubtedly makes enthralling, if horrifying, reading. One learns about the way the writers of antiquity treated infanticide as a normal and sensible way to dispose of unwanted children; of how they amused themselves by using little children for fellatio or anal intercourse; of how the bones of child sacrifices are to be found in the foundations of buildings ranging from 7000 BC to 1843 AD; of how seventeenth-century nurses played catch-ball with the tightly swaddled infants and sometimes dropped them, with lethal consequences; of how infants were dipped in ice-cold baths, in order to harden them, or perhaps merely to baptize them, but in practice sometimes killing them; about how the doorsteps and dunghills of eighteenth-century European towns were littered with bodies of infants, dead, dying, or just abandoned; how some wet-nurses systematically starved their charges to death to save money or simply because they had accepted too many babies for their milk supply; of how children were ferociously beaten, shut up in the dark, deprived of food, terrified by bogeymen, taken to see hangings and corpses, sold into prostitution, blinded and otherwise mutilated to attract alms, castrated to supply testicles for magic, had their teeth ripped out to supply dentures, and in the nineteenth century suffered clitoridectomy, the attachment of toothed penile rings, and even nightly imprisonment in straitjackets to prevent masturbation – and so on, and so on, and so on.

What is one to make of this catalogue of atrocities? One obvious problem is the extent to which deMause is generalizing from the particular in constructing his linear model of child care. He clearly has a special taste for the macabre, and often grossly exaggerates, but in general it looks as if some of his basic conclusions are probably well founded. Antiquity undoubtedly regarded infanticide as casually as many of us regard abortion today, and certainly Christianity changed attitudes on this subject. There can also be no doubt that children were often neglected and exploited in the past, and there is growing evidence that the critical change to a more affectionate parent-child relationship took place in the eighteenth century.

The first question is whether this adds up to a linear theory of progress. The eighteenth-century change occurred mainly in England and America, and was largely confined to the professional and gentry classes. But middle and upper-class parent-child relations worsened again significantly in the nineteenth century, before improving in the twentieth. The middle-class Victorian father was a terrifying, and often cruel, authority figure. As for the children of the poor, their condition probably deteriorated during the demographic, urban, and industrial explosion of the late eighteenth and early nineteenth centuries. But during the nineteenth century, contraception, humanitarian legislation, slowly improving economic conditions, welfare services, and schools probably improved the lot of the children of the poor, just at the time when that of the rich was worsening. The theory of linear progress is thus clearly a false one, and the story of change will have to be traced country by country and class by class, since each has its own individual life history.

Second, the 'psychogenic' causal theory of change in parental attitudes is mere mystical nonsense. The reaction of parents to children is far from being limited to the projective, reversal, and empathic, as proposed by deMause. Everything suggests that in the past most parents have treated their children as inevitable by-products of sexual pleasure, sometimes bitterly unwelcome, sometimes barely tolerated, sometimes useful to be exploited economically, and sometimes cherished and loved. Most frequently, however, the response seems to have been one of relative indifference. The cruel truth – crueller, perhaps, than anything deMause has suggested – may be that most parents in history have not been much involved with their children, and have not cared much about them. Hence the staggering infant mortality rates – between a quarter and a third were dead before the age of one – were caused not by deliberate parental hostility, as he suggests, but rather by ignorance, poverty, and indifference. Most children in history have not been loved or hated, or both, by their parents; they have been neglected or ignored by them.

For all its brilliance, deMause's model is thus defective in certain critical respects. There is no unilinear upward progression of childhood felicity, different stages apply to different classes in different countries, while there are huge time lags between different countries at the same period; the psychogenic theory of parental evolution is an unproven and implausible hypothesis; parent-child relations have altered in response to cultural determinants such as religious beliefs, economic pressures, customary practices, state power, etc.; parents have not normally had intense relations with their children but rather have regarded them with some indifference; and finally, it is an oversimplification to argue that 'the child is father to the man' and that brutalized children automatically result in brutalized adults, who then take out their frustrations in war, violence, and murder. Unfortunately, neither modern ego-psychology nor modern genetics nor modern anthropology suggests so simplistic a chain of causation.

[. . .]

In view of the weaknesses as well as the brilliant insights of the models presented by Ariès and deMause, what are we to put in their place? One of the many problems of studying childhood in isolation is that it lends itself to passionate polemics – all the authors have an obvious axe to grind. Another more serious objection is that it is impossible to study children in isolation from those who killed them off or fed them, neglected them or nurtured them, beat them or fondled them, namely, their parents. The history of childhood is in fact the history of how parents treated children. [. . .] The proper unit of historical studies in this area is thus neither children nor women nor men, but the family, the institution within which all these personal interactions take place.

[. . .]

References

ARIES, P. (1960; translated BALDICK, R., 1962) *Centuries of Childhood: A Social History of Family Life*. London: Cape.

DeMAUSE, L. (ed.) (1974) *The History of Childhood*. New York: The Psychohistory Press.

ERIKSON, E. (1959) 'Identity and the Life Cycle', *Psychological Issues, Vol. 1*. New York: International Universities Press.

ERIKSON, E. (1963) *Childhood and Society*. New York: Norton.

GEERTZ, C. (1975) *The Interpretation of Cultures*. London: Hutchinson.

HARTMANN, H. (1964) *Ego Psychology and the Problem of Adoption*. New York: International Universities Press.

HUNT, D. (1970) *Parents and Children in History: The Psychology of Family Life in Early Modern France*. New York: Harper and Row.

MALINOWSKI, B. (1927) *Sex and Repression in Savage Society*. London: Kegan Paul.

RIESMAN, D. (1950) *The Lonely Crowd*. New York: Doubleday.

VAN DEN BERG, J. H. (1955; translated CROES, H. F., 1961) *The Changing Nature of Man: Introduction to a Historical Psychology (Metabletica)*. New York: Norton.

1.2   Our adult world and its roots in infancy

Melanie Klein

[. . .]

The play technique that I developed in the psychoanalysis of very young children, and other advances in technique resulting from my work, allowed me to draw new conclusions about very early stages of infancy and deeper layers of the unconscious. Such retrospective insight is based on one of the crucial findings of Freud, the transference situation, that is to say the fact that in a psychoanalysis the patient re-enacts in relation to the psychoanalyst earlier – and, I would add, even very early – situations and emotions. Therefore the relationship to the psychoanalyst at times bears, even in adults, very childlike features, such as over-dependence and the need to be guided, together with quite irrational distrust. It is part of the technique of the psychoanalyst to deduce the past from these manifestations. We know that Freud first discovered the Oedipus complex in the adult and was able to trace it back to childhood. Since I had the good fortune to analyse very young children, I was able to gain an even closer insight into their mental life, which led me back to an understanding of the mental life of the baby. For I was enabled by the meticulous attention I paid to the transference in the play technique to come to a deeper understanding of the ways in which – in the child and later also in the adult – mental life is influenced by earliest emotions and unconscious phantasies. It is from this angle that I shall describe with the use of as few technical terms as possible what I have concluded about the emotional life of the infant.

I have put forward the hypothesis that the newborn baby experiences, both in the process of birth and in the adjustment to the post-natal situation, anxiety of a persecutory nature. This can be explained by the fact that the young infant, without being able to grasp it intellectually, feels unconsciously every discomfort as though it were inflicted on him by hostile forces. If comfort is given to him soon – in particular warmth, the loving way he is held, and the gratification of being fed – this gives rise to happier emotions. Such comfort is felt to come from good forces and, I believe, makes possible the infant's first loving relation to a person or, as the psychoanalyst would put it, to an object. My hypothesis is that the infant has an innate unconscious awareness of the existence of the mother. We know that young animals at once turn to the mother and find their food from her. The human animal is not different in that respect, and this instinctual knowledge is the basis for the infant's primal relation to his mother. We can also observe that at an age of only a few weeks the baby already looks up to his mother's face, recognizes her footsteps, the touch of

Source: KLEIN, M. (1959) *Human Relations*, **12**, 4, pp. 291–303.

her hands, the smell and feel of her breast or of the bottle that she gives him, all of which suggest that some relation, however primitive, to the mother has been established.

However, he not only expects food from her but also desires love and understanding. In the earliest stages, love and understanding are expressed through the mother's handling of her baby, and lead to a certain unconscious oneness that is based on the unconscious of the mother and of the child being in close relation to each other. The infant's resultant feeling of being understood underlies the first and fundamental relation in his life – the relation to the mother. At the same time, frustration, discomfort and pain, which I suggested are experienced as persecution, enter as well into his feelings about his mother, because in the first few months she represents to the child the whole of the external world; therefore both good and bad come in his mind from her, and this leads to a twofold attitude toward the mother even under the best possible conditions.

Both the capacity to love and the sense of persecution have deep roots in the infant's earliest mental processes. They are focused first of all on the mother. Destructive impulses and their concomitants – such as resentment about frustration, hate stirred up by it, the incapacity to be reconciled, and envy of the all-powerful object, the mother, on whom his life and well-being depend – these various emotions arouse persecutory anxiety in the infant. *Mutatis mutandis* these emotions are still operative in later life. For destructive impulses towards anybody are always bound to give rise to the feeling that that person will also become hostile and retaliatory.

Innate aggressiveness is bound to be increased by unfavourable external circumstances and, conversely, is mitigated by the love and understanding that the young child receives; and these factors continue to operate throughout development. But although the importance of external circumstances is by now increasingly recognized, the importance of internal factors is still underrated. Destructive impulses, varying from individual to individual, are an integral part of mental life, even in favourable circumstances, and therefore we have to consider the development of the child and the attitudes of the adults as resulting from the interaction between internal and external influences. The struggle between love and hate – now that our capacity to understand babies has increased – can to some extent be recognized through careful observation. Some babies experience strong resentment about any frustration and show this by being unable to accept gratification when it follows on deprivation. I would suggest that such children have a stronger innate aggressiveness and greed than those infants whose occasional outbursts of rage are soon over. If a baby shows that he is able to accept food and love, this means that he can overcome resentment about frustration relatively quickly and, when gratification is again provided, regains his feelings of love.

Before continuing my description of the child's development, I feel that I should briefly define from the psychoanalytic point of view the terms *self* and *ego*. The ego, according to Freud, is the organized part of the self, constantly influenced by instinctual impulses but keeping them under control by repression; furthermore it directs all activities and establishes and maintains the relation to the external world. The self is used to cover the whole of the personality, which includes not only the ego but the instinctual life which Freud called the *id*.

My work has led me to assume that the ego exists and operates from birth onwards and that in addition to the functions mentioned above it has the important task of defending itself against anxiety stirred up by the struggle within and by influences from without. Furthermore it initiates a number of processes from which I shall first of all select *introjection* and *projection*. To the no less important process of *splitting*, that is to say dividing, impulses and objects I shall turn later.

We owe to Freud and Abraham the great discovery that introjection and projection are of major significance both in severe mental disturbances and in normal mental life. I have here to forgo even the attempt to describe how in particular Freud was led from the study of manic-depressive illness to the discovery of introjection which underlies the superego. He also expounded the vital relation between superego and ego and the id. In the course of time these basic concepts underwent further development. As I came to recognize in the light of my psychoanalytic work with children, introjection and projection function from the beginning of post-natal life as some of the earliest activities of the ego, which in my view operates from birth onwards. Considered from this angle, introjection means that the outer world, its impact, the situations the infant lives through, and the objects he encounters, are not only experienced as external but are taken into the self and become part of his inner life. Inner life cannot be evaluated even in the adult without these additions to the personality that derive from continuous introjection. Projection, which goes on simultaneously, implies that there is a capacity in the child to attribute to other people around him feelings of various kinds, predominantly love and hate.

I have formed the view that love and hate towards the mother are bound up with the very young infant's capacity to project all his emotions on to her, thereby making her into a good as well as dangerous object. However, introjection and projection, though they are rooted in infancy, are not only infantile processes. They are part of the infant's phantasies, which in my view also operate from the beginning and help to mould his impression of his surroundings; and by introjection this changed picture of the external world influences what goes on in his mind. Thus an inner world is built up which is partly a reflection of the external one. That is to say, the double process of introjection and projection contributes to the interaction between external and internal factors. This interaction continues throughout every stage of life. In the same way introjection and projection go on throughout life and become modified in the course of maturation; but they never lose their importance in the individual's relation to the world around him. Even in the adult, therefore, the judgement of reality is never quite free from the influence of his internal world.

I have already suggested that from one angle the processes of projection and introjection that I have been describing have to be considered as unconscious phantasies. As my friend the late Susan Isaacs put it in her paper on this subject:[1]

Phantasy is (in the first instance) the mental corollary, the psychic representative of instinct. There is no impulse, no instinctual urge or response which is not experienced as unconscious phantasy . . . A phantasy represents the particular content of the urges or feelings (for example, wishes, fears, anxieties, triumphs, love or sorrow) dominating the mind at the moment.

Unconscious phantasies are not the same as day-dreams (though they are linked with them) but an activity of the mind that occurs on deep unconscious levels and accompanies every impulse experienced by the infant. For instance, a hungry baby can temporarily deal with his hunger by hallucinating the satisfaction of being given the breast, with all the pleasures he normally derives from it, such as the taste of the milk, the warm feel of the breast, and being held and loved by the mother. But unconscious phantasy also takes the opposite form of feeling deprived and persecuted by the breast which refuses to give this satisfaction. Phantasies – becoming more elaborate and referring to a wider variety of objects and situations – continue throughout development and accompany all activities; they never stop playing a great part in mental life. The influence of unconscious phantasy on art, on scientific work, and on the activities of everyday life cannot be overrated.

I have already mentioned that the mother is introjected, and that this is a fundamental factor in development. As I see it, object relations start almost at birth. The mother in her good aspects – loving, helping, and feeding the child – is the first good object that the infant makes part of his inner world. His capacity to do so is, I would suggest, up to a point innate. Whether the good object becomes sufficiently part of the self depends to some extent on persecutory anxiety – and accordingly resentment – not being too strong; at the same time a loving attitude on the part of the mother contributes much to the success of this process. If the mother is taken into the child's inner world as a good and dependable object, an element of strength is added to the ego. For I assume that the ego develops largely round this good object, and the identification with the good characteristics of the mother becomes the basis for further helpful identifications. The identification with the good object shows externally in the young child's copying the mother's activities and attitudes; this can be seen in his play and often also in his behaviour towards younger children. A strong identification with the good mother makes it easier for the child to identify also with a good father and later on with other friendly figures.

As a result, his inner world comes to contain predominantly good objects and feelings, and these good objects are felt to respond to the infant's love. All this contributes to a stable personality and makes it possible to extend sympathy and friendly feelings to other people. It is clear that a good relation of the parents to each other and to the child, and a happy home atmosphere, play a vital role in the success of this process.

Yet, however good are the child's feelings towards both parents, aggressiveness and hate also remain operative. One expression of this is the rivalry with the father which results from the boy's desires towards the mother and all the phantasies linked with them. Such rivalry finds expression in the Oedipus complex, which can be clearly observed in children of three, four, or five years of age. This complex exists, however, very much earlier and is rooted in the baby's first suspicions of the father taking the mother's love and attention away from him. There are great differences in the Oedipus complex of the girl and of the boy, which I shall characterize only by saying that whereas the boy in his genital development returns to his original object, the mother, and therefore seeks female objects with consequent jealousy of the father and men in general, the girl to some extent has to turn away from the mother and find the object of her desires in the father and later on in other men. I have, however, stated this in an over-simplified form, because the boy is also attracted towards the father and identifies with him; and therefore an element of homosexuality enters into normal development. The same applies to the girl, for whom the relation to the mother, and to women in general, never loses its importance. The Oedipus complex is thus not a matter only of feelings of hate and rivalry towards one parent and love towards the other, but feelings of love and the sense of guilt also enter in connection with the rival parent. Many conflicting emotions therefore centre upon the Oedipus complex.

We turn now again to projection. By projecting oneself or part of one's impulses and feelings into another person, an identification with that person is achieved, though it will differ from the identification arising from introjection. For if an object is taken into the self (introjected), the emphasis lies on acquiring some of the characteristics of this object and on being influenced by them. On the other hand, in putting part of oneself into the other person (projecting), the identification is based on attributing to the other person some of one's own qualities. Projection has many repercussions. We are inclined to attribute to other people – in a sense, to put into them – some of our own emotions and thoughts; and it is obvious that it will depend on how balanced or persecuted we are whether this projection is of a friendly or of a hostile nature. By attributing part of our feelings to the other person, we understand their feelings, needs, and satisfactions; in other words, we are putting ourselves into the other person's shoes. There are people who go so far in this direction that they lose themselves entirely in others and became incapable of objective judgement. At the same time excessive introjection endangers the strength of the ego because it becomes completely dominated by the introjected object. If projection is predominantly hostile, real empathy and under-standing of others is impaired. The character of projection is, therefore, of great importance in our relations to other people. If the interplay between introjection and projection is not dominated by hostility or over-dependence, and is well balanced, the inner world is enriched and the relations with the external world are improved.

I referred earlier to the tendency of the infantile ego to split impulses and objects, and I regard this as another of the primal activities of the ego. This tendency to split results in part from the fact that the early ego largely lacks coherence. But – if envy is strong, goodness cannot be assimilated, become part of one's inner life, and so give rise to gratitude. By contrast, the capacity to enjoy fully what has been received, and the experience of gratitude towards the person who gives it, influence strongly both the character and the relations with other people. It is not for nothing that in saying grace before meals. Christians use the words, 'For what we are about to receive may the Lord make us truly thankful.' These words imply that one asks for the one quality – gratitude – which will make one happy and free from resentment and envy. I heard a little girl say that she loved her mother most of all people, because what would she have done if her mother had not given birth to her and had not fed her? This strong feeling of gratitude was linked with her capacity for enjoyment and showed itself in her character and relations to other people, particularly in generosity and consideration. Throughout life such capacity for enjoyment and gratitude makes a variety of interests and pleasures possible.

In normal development, with growing integration of the ego, splitting processes diminish, and the increased capacity to understand external reality, and to some extent to bring together the infant's contradictory impulses, leads also to a greater synthesis of the good and bad aspects of the object. This means that people can be loved in spite of their faults and that the world is not seen only in terms of black and white.

The superego – the part of the ego that criticizes and controls dangerous impulses, and that Freud first placed roughly in the fifth year of childhood – operates, according to my views, much earlier. It is my hypothesis that in the fifth or sixth month of life the baby becomes afraid of the harm his destructive impulses and his greed might do, or might have done, to his loved objects. For he cannot yet distinguish between his desires and impulses and their actual effects. He experiences feelings of guilt and the urge to preserve these objects and to make reparation to them for harm done. The anxiety now experienced is of a predominantly depressive nature; and the emotions accompanying it, as well as the defences evolved against them, I recognized as part of normal development, and termed the 'depressive position'. Feelings of guilt, which occasionally arise in all of us, have very deep roots in infancy, and the tendency to make reparation plays an important role in our sublimations and object relations.

When we observe young infants from this angle, we can see that at times, without any particular external cause, they appear depressed. At this stage they try to please the people around them in every way available to them – smiles, playful gestures, even attempts to feed the mother by putting a spoon with food into her mouth. At the same time this is also a period in which inhibitions over food and nightmares often set in, and all these symptoms come to a head at the time of weaning. With older children, the need to deal with guilt feelings expresses itself more clearly; various constructive activities are used for this purpose and in the relation to parents or siblings there is an excessive need to please and to be helpful, all of which expresses not only love but also the need to make reparation.

Freud has postulated the process of *working through* as an essential part of psychoanalytic procedure. To put it in a nutshell, this means enabling the patient to experience his emotions, anxieties, and past situations over and over again both in relation to the analyst and to different people and situations in the patient's present and past life. There is, however, a working through occurring to some extent in normal individual development. Adaptation to external reality increases and with it the infant achieves a less phantastic picture of the world around him. The recurring experience of the mother going away and coming back to him makes her absence less frightening, and therefore his suspicion of her leaving him diminishes. In this way he gradually works through his early fears and comes to terms with his conflicting impulses and emotions. Depressive anxiety at this stage predominates and persecutory anxiety lessens. I hold that many apparently odd manifestations, inexplicable phobias, and idiosyncrasies that can be observed in young children are indications of, as well as ways of, working through the depressive position. If the feelings of guilt arising in the child are not excessive, the urge to make reparation and other processes that are part of growth bring relief. Yet depressive and persecutory anxieties are never entirely overcome; they may temporarily recur under internal or external pressure, though a relatively normal person can cope with this recurrence and regain his balance. If, however, the strain is too great, the development of a strong and well-balanced personality may be impeded.

Having dealt – though I am afraid in an over-simplified way – with paranoid and depressive anxieties and their implications, I should like to consider the influence of the processes I have described on social relations. I have spoken of introjection of the external world and have hinted that this process continues throughout life. Whenever we can admire and love somebody – or hate and despise somebody – we also take something of them into ourselves and our deepest attitudes are shaped by such experiences. In the one case it enriches us and becomes a foundation for precious memories; in the other case we sometimes feel that the outer world is spoilt for us and the inner world is therefore impoverished.

I can here only touch on the importance of actual favourable and unfavourable experiences to which the infant is from the beginning subjected, first of all by his parents, and later on by other people. External experiences are of paramount importance throughout life. However, much depends, even in the infant, on the ways in which external influences are interpreted and assimilated by the child; and this in turn largely depends on how strongly destructive impulses and persecutory and depressive anxieties are operative. In the same way our adult experiences are influenced by our basic attitudes, which either help us to cope better with misfortunes or, if we are too much dominated by suspicion and self-pity, turn even minor disappointments into disasters.

Freud's discoveries about childhood have increased the understanding of problems of upbringing, but these findings have often been misinterpreted. Though it is true that a too disciplinarian upbringing reinforces the child's tendency to repression, we have to remember that too great indulgence may be almost as harmful for the child as too much restraint. The so-called 'full self-expression' can have great disadvantages both for the parents and for the child. Whereas in former times the child was often the victim of the parents' disciplinarian attitude, the parents may now become the victims of their offspring. It is an old joke that there was a man who never tasted breast of chicken; for when he was a child, his parents ate it, and when he grew up, his children were given it. When dealing with our children, it is essential to keep a balance between too much and too little discipline. To turn a blind eye to some of the smaller misdeeds is a very healthy attitude. But if these grow into persistent lack of consideration, it is necessary to show disapproval and to make demands on the child.

There is another angle from which the parents' excessive indulgence must be considered: while the child may take advantage of his parents' attitude, he also experiences a sense of guilt about exploiting them and feels a need for some restraint which would give him security. This would also make him able to feel respect for his parents, which is essential for a good relation towards them and for developing respect for other people. Moreover, we must also consider that parents who are suffering too much under the unrestrained self-expression of the child – however much they try to submit to it – are bound to feel some resentment which will enter into their attitude towards the child.

I have already described the young child who reacts strongly against every frustration – and there is no upbringing possible without some unavoidable frustration – and who is apt to resent bitterly any failings and shortcomings in his environment and to underrate goodness received. Accordingly he will project his grievances very strongly on to the people around him. Similar attitudes are well known in adults. If we contrast the individuals who are capable of bearing frustration without too great resentment and can soon regain their balance after a disappointment with those who are inclined to put the whole blame on to the outer world, we can see the detrimental effect of hostile projection. For projection of grievance rouses in other people a counter-feeling of hostility. Few of us have the tolerance to put up with the accusation, even if it is not expressed in words, that we are in some ways the guilty party. In fact, it very often makes us dislike such people, and we appear all the more as enemies to them; in consequence they regard us with increased persecutory feelings and suspicions, and relations become more and more disturbed.

One way of dealing with excessive suspicion is to try to pacify the supposed or actual enemies. This is rarely successful. Of course, some people can be won over by flattery and appeasement, particularly if their own feelings of persecution make for the need to be appeased. But such a relation easily breaks down and changes into mutual hostility. In passing, I would mention the difficulties that such fluctuations in the attitudes of leading statesmen may produce in international affairs.

Where persecutory anxiety is less strong, and projection, mainly attributing to others good feelings, thereby becomes the basis of empathy, the response from the outer world is very different. We all know people who have the capacity to be liked; for we have the impression that they have some trust in us, which evokes on our part a feeling of friendliness. I am not speaking of people who are trying to make themselves popular in an insincere way. On the contrary, I believe it is the people who are genuine and have the courage of their convictions who are in the long run respected and even liked.

An interesting instance of the influence of early attitudes throughout life is the fact that the relation to early figures keeps reappearing and problems that remain unresolved in infancy or early childhood are revived though in modified form. For example, the attitude towards a subordinate or a superior repeats up to a point the relation to a younger sibling or to a parent. If we meet a friendly and helpful older person, unconsciously the relation to a loved parent or grandparent is revived; while a condescending and unpleasant older individual stirs up anew the rebellious attitudes of the child towards his parents. It is not necessary that such people should be physically, mentally, or even in actual age similar to the original figures; something in common in their attitude is enough. When somebody is entirely under the sway of early situations and relations, his judgement of people and events is bound to be disturbed. Normally such revival of early situations is limited and rectified by objective judgement. That is to say, we are all capable of being influenced by irrational factors, but in normal life we are not dominated by them.

The capacity for love and devotion, first of all to the mother, in many ways develops into devotion to various causes that are felt to be good and valuable. This means that the enjoyment which in the past the baby was able to experience because he felt loved and loving, in later life becomes transferred not only to his relations to people, which is very important, but also to his work and to all that he feels worth striving for. This means also an enrichment of the personality and capacity to enjoy his work, and opens up a variety of sources of satisfaction.

In this striving to further our aims, as well as in our relation to other people, the early wish to make reparation is added to the capacity for love. I have already said that in our sublimations, which grow out of the earliest interests of the child, constructive activities gain more impetus because the child unconsciously feels that in this way he is restoring loved people whom he has damaged. This impetus never loses its strength, though very often it is not recognized in ordinary life. The irrevocable fact that none of us is ever entirely free from guilt has very valuable aspects because it implies the never fully exhausted wish to make reparation and to create in whatever way we can.

All forms of social service benefit by this urge. In extreme cases, feelings of guilt drive people towards sacrificing themselves completely to a cause or to their fellow beings, and may lead to fanaticism. We know, however, that some people risk their own lives in order to save others, and this is not necessarily of the same order. It is not so much guilt which might be operative in such cases as the capacity for love, generosity, and an identification with the endangered fellow being.

I have emphasized the importance of the identification with the parents, and subsequently with other people, for the young child's development and I now wish to stress one particular aspect of successful identification which reaches into adulthood. When envy and rivalry are not too great, it becomes possible to enjoy vicariously the pleasures of others. In childhood the hostility and rivalry of the Oedipus complex are counteracted by the capacity to enjoy vicariously the happiness of the parents. In adult life, parents can share the pleasures of childhood and avoid interfering with them because they are capable of identifying with their children. They become able to watch without envy their children growing up.

This attitude becomes particularly important when people grow older and the pleasures of youth become less and less available. If gratitude for past satisfactions has not vanished, old people can enjoy whatever is still within their reach. Furthermore, with such an attitude, which gives rise to serenity, they can identify themselves with young people. For instance, anyone who is looking out for young talents and who helps to develop them – be it in his function as teacher or critic, or in former times as patron of the arts and of culture – is only able to do so because he can identify with others; in a sense he is repeating his own life, sometimes even achieving vicariously the fulfilment of aims unfulfilled in his own life.

At every stage the ability to identify makes possible the happiness of being able to admire the character or achievements of others. If we cannot allow ourselves to appreciate the achievements and qualities of other people – and that means that we are not able to bear the thought that we can never emulate them – we are deprived of sources of great happiness and enrichment. The world would be in our eyes a much poorer place if we had no opportunities of realizing that greatness exists and will go on existing in the future. Such admiration also stirs up something in us and increases indirectly our belief in ourselves. This is one of the many ways in which identifications derived from infancy become an important part of our personality.

The ability to admire another person's achievements is one of the factors making successful team work possible. If envy is not too great, we can take pleasure and pride in working with people who sometimes outstrip our capacities, for we identify with these outstanding members of the team.

The problem of identification is, however, very complex. When Freud discovered the superego, he saw it as part of the mental structure derived from the influence of the parents on the child – an influence that becomes part of the child's fundamental attitudes. My work with young children has shown me that even from babyhood onwards the mother, and soon other people in the child's surroundings, are taken into the self, and this is the basis of a variety of identifications, favourable and unfavourable. I have above given instances of identifications that are helpful both to the child and to the adult. But the vital influence of early environment has also the effect that unfavourable aspects of the attitudes of the adult towards the child are detrimental to his development because they stir up in him hatred and rebellion or too great submissiveness. At the same time he internalizes this hostile and angry adult attitude. Out of such experiences, an excessively disciplinarian parent, or a parent lacking in understanding and love, by identification influences the character formation of the child and may lead him to repeat in later life what he himself has undergone. Therefore a father sometimes uses the same wrong methods towards his children that his father used towards him. On the other hand, the rebellion against the wrongs experienced in childhood can lead to the opposite reaction of doing everything differently from the way the parents did it. This would lead to the other extreme, for instance to over-indulgence of the child, to which I have referred earlier. To have learnt from our experiences in childhood and therefore to be more understanding and tolerant towards our own children, as well as towards people outside the family circle, is a sign of maturity and successful development. But tolerance does not mean being blind to the faults of others. It means recognizing those faults and nevertheless not losing one's ability to co-operate with people or even to experience love towards some of them.

In describing the child's development I have emphasized particularly the importance of greed. Let us consider now what part greed plays in character formation and how it influences the attitudes of the adult. The role of greed can be easily observed as a very destructive element in social life. The greedy person wants more and more, even at the expense of everybody else. He is not really capable of consideration and generosity towards others. I am not speaking here only of material possessions but also of status and prestige.

The very greedy individual is liable to be ambitious. The role of ambition, both in its helpful and in its disturbing aspects, shows itself wherever we observe human behaviour. There is no doubt that ambition gives impetus to achievement but, if it becomes the main driving force, co-operation with others is endangered. The highly ambitious person, in spite of all his successes, always remains dissatisfied, in the same way as a greedy baby is never satisfied. We know well the type of public figure who, hungry for more and more success, appears never to be content with what he has achieved. One feature in this attitude – in which envy also plays an important role – is the inability to allow others to come sufficiently to the fore. They may be allowed to play a subsidiary part as long as they do not challenge the supremacy of the ambitious person. We find also that such people are unable and unwilling to stimulate and encourage younger people, because some of them might become their successors. One reason for the lack of satisfaction they derive from apparently great success results from the fact that their interest is not so much devoted to the field in which they are working as to their personal prestige. This description implies the connection between greed and envy. The rival is not only seen as someone who has robbed and deprived one of one's own position or goods, but also as the owner of valuable qualities which stir up envy and the wish to spoil them.

Where greed and envy are not excessive, even an ambitious person finds satisfaction in helping others to make their contribution. Here we have one of the attitudes underlying successful leadership. Again, to some extent, this is already observable in the nursery. An older child may take pride in the achievements of a younger brother or sister and do everything to help them. Some children even have an integrating effect on the whole family life; by being predominantly friendly and helpful they improve the family atmosphere. I have seen that mothers who were very impatient and intolerant of difficulties have improved through the influence of such a child. The same applies to school life where sometimes only as few as one or two children have a beneficial effect on the attitude of all the others by a kind of moral leadership which is based on a friendly and co-operative relation to the other children without any attempt to make them feel inferior.

To return to leadership: if the leader – and that may also apply to any member of a group – suspects that he is the object of hate, all his antisocial attitudes are increased by this feeling. We find that the person who is unable to bear criticism because it touches at once on his persecutory anxiety is not only a prey to suffering but also has difficulties in relation to other people and may even endanger the cause for which he is working, in whatever walk of life it may be; he will show an incapacity to correct mistakes and to learn from others.

If we look at our adult world from the viewpoint of its roots in infancy, we gain an insight into the way our mind, our habits, and our views have been built up from the earliest infantile phantasies and emotions to the most complex and sophisticated adult manifestations. There is one more conclusion to be drawn, which is that nothing that ever existed in the unconscious completely loses its influence on the personality.

A further aspect of the child's development to be discussed is his character formation. I have given some instances of how destructive impulses, envy and greed, and the resulting persecutory anxieties disturb the child's emotional balance and his social relations. I have also referred to the beneficial aspects of an opposite development and attempted to show how they arise. I have tried to convey the importance of the interaction between innate factors and the influence of the environment. In giving full weight to this interplay we get a deeper understanding of how the child's character develops. It has always been a most important aspect of psychoanalytic work that, in the course of a successful analysis, the patient's character undergoes favourable changes.

One consequence of a balanced development is integrity and strength of character. Such qualities have a far-reaching effect both on the individual's self-reliance and on his relations to the outside world. The influence of a really sincere and genuine character on other people is easily observed. Even people who do not possess the same qualities are impressed and cannot help feeling some respect for integrity and sincerity. For these qualities arouse in them a picture of what they might themselves have become or perhaps even still might become. Such personalities give them some hopefulness about the world in general and greater trust in goodness.

I have concluded this paper by discussing the importance of character, because in my view character is the foundation for all human achievement. The effect of a good character on others lies at the root of healthy social development.

[. . .]

Reference

1 ISAACS, S. (1952) 'The Nature and Functions of Phantasy', in KLEIN, M., HEIMANN, P., ISAACS, S. and RIVIERE, J. *Developments in Psycho-Analysis.* London: Hogarth Press.

1.3 The stages of the intellectual development of the child

Jean Piaget

A consideration of the stages of the development of intelligence should be preceded by asking the question, What is intelligence? Unfortunately, we find ourselves confronted by a great number of definitions. For Claparède, intelligence is an adaptation to new situations. When a situation is new, when there are no reflexes, when there are no habits to rely on, then the subject is obliged to search for something new. That is to say, Claparède defines intelligence as groping, as feeling one's way, trial-and-error behavior. We find this trial-and-error behavior in all levels of intelligence, even at the superior level, in the form of hypothesis testing. As far as I am concerned, this definition is too vague, because trial and error occurs in the formation of habits, and also in the earliest established reflexes: when a newborn baby learns to suck.

Karl Bühler defines intelligence as an act of immediate comprehension: that is to say, an insight. Bühler's definition is also very precise, but it seems to be too narrow. I know that when a mathematician solves a problem, he ends by having an insight, but up to that moment he feels, or gropes for, his way; and to say that the trial-and-error behavior is not intelligent and that intelligence starts only when he finds the solution to the problem, seems a very narrow definition. I would, therefore, propose to define intelligence not by a static criterion, as in previous definitions, but by the direction that intelligence follows in its evolution, and then I would define intelligence as a form of equilibration, or forms of equilibration, toward which all cognitive functions lead.

But I must first define equilibration. Equilibration in my vocabulary is not an exact and automatic balance, as it would be in *Gestalt* theory; I define equilibration principally as a compensation for an external disturbance.

When there is an external disturbance, the subject succeeds in compensating for this by an activity. The maximum equilibration is thus the maximum of the activity, and not a state of rest. It is a mobile equilibration, and not an immobile one. So equilibration is defined as compensation; compensation is the annulling of a transformation by an inverse transformation. The compensation which intervenes in equilibration implies the fundamental idea of reversibility, and this reversibility is precisely what characterizes the operations of the intelligence. An operation is an internalized action, but it is also a reversible action. But an

Source: *Bulletin of the Menninger Clinic* (1962) 26, pp. 120–8. Reprinted in MUNSINGER, H. (1975) *Readings in Child Development* (2nd edn). New York: Holt, Rinehart and Winston.

operation is never isolated; it is always subordinated to other operations; it is part of a more inclusive structure. Consequently, we define intelligence in terms of operations, co-ordination of operations.

Take, for example, an operation like addition: addition is a material action, the action of reuniting. On the other hand, it is a reversible action, because addition may be compensated by subtraction. Yet addition leads to a structure of a whole. In the case of numbers, it will be the structure that the mathematicians call a 'group'. In the case of addition of classes which intervene in the logical structure it will be a more simple structure that we will call a grouping, and so on.

Consequently, the study of the stages of intelligence is first a study of the formation of operational structures. I shall define every stage by a structure of a whole, with the possibility of its integration into succeeding stages, just as it was prepared by preceding stages. Thus, I shall distinguish four great stages, or four great periods, in the development of intelligence: first, the sensori-motor period before the appearance of language; second, the period from about two to seven years of age, the pre-operational period which precedes real operations; third, the period from seven to 12 years of age, a period of concrete operations (which refers to concrete objects); and finally after 12 years of age, the period of formal operations, or propositional operations.

Sensori-motor stage

Before language develops, there is behavior that we can call intelligent. For example, when a baby of 12 months or more wants an object which is too far from him, but which rests on a carpet or blanket, and he pulls it to get to the object, this behavior is an act of intelligence. The child uses an intermediary, a means to get to his goal. Also, getting to an object by means of pulling a string when the object is tied to the string, or when the child uses a stick to get the object, are acts of intelligence. They demonstrate in the sensori-motor period a certain number of stages, which go from simple reflexes, from the formation of the first habits, up to the co-ordination of means and goals.

Remarkable in this sensori-motor stage of intelligence is that there are already structures. Sensori-motor intelligence rests mainly on actions, on movements and perceptions without language, but these actions are co-ordinated in a relatively stable way. They are co-ordinated under what we may call schemata of action. These schemata can be generalized in actions and are applicable to new situations. For example, pulling a carpet to bring an object within reach constitutes a schema which can be generalized to other situations when another object rests on a support. In other words, a schema supposes an incorporation of new situations into the previous schemata, a sort of continuous assimilation of new objects or new situations to the actions already schematized. For example, I presented to one of my children an object completely new to him – a box of cigarettes, which is not a usual toy for a baby. The child took the object, looked at it, put it in his mouth, shook it, then took it with one hand and hit it with the other hand, then rubbed it on the edge of the crib, then shook it again, and gave the impression of trying to see if there were noise. This behavior is a way of exploring the object, of trying to understand it by assimilating it to schemata already known. The child behaves in this situation as he will later in Binet's famous vocabulary test, when he defines by usage, saying, for instance, that a spoon is for eating, and so on.

But in the presence of a new object, even without knowing how to talk, the child knows how to assimilate, to incorporate this new object into each of his already developed schemata which function as practical concepts. Here is a structuring of intelligence. Most important in this structuring is the base, the point of departure of all subsequent operational constructions. At the sensori-motor level, the child constructs the schema of the permanent object.

The knowledge of the permanent object starts at this point. The child is not convinced at the beginning that when an object disappears from view, he can find it again. One can verify by tests that object permanence is not yet developed at this stage. But there is there the beginning of a subsequent fundamental idea which starts being constructed at the sensori-motor level. This is also true of the construction of the ideas of space, of time, of causality. What is being done at the sensori-motor level concerning all the foregoing ideas will constitute the substructure of the subsequent, fully achieved ideas of permanent objects, of space, of time, of causality.

In the formation of these substructures at the sensori-motor level, it is very interesting to note the beginning of a *reversibility*, not in thought, since there is not yet representation in thought, but in action itself. For example, the formation of the conception of space at the sensori-motor stage leads to an amazing decentration if one compares the conception of space at the first weeks of the development with that at one and one-half to two years of age. In the beginning there is not one space which contains all the objects, including the child's body itself; there is a multitude of spaces which are not co-ordinated: there are the buccal space, the tactilokinesthetic space, the visual and auditory spaces; each is separate and each is centered essentially on the body of the subject and on actions. After a few months, however, after a kind of Copernican evolution, there is a total reversal, a decentration such that space becomes homogenous, a one-and-only space that envelops the others. Then space becomes a container that envelops all objects, including the body itself; and after that, space is mainly co-ordinated in a structure, a co-ordination of positions and displacements, and these constitute what the geometricians call a 'group'; that is to say, precisely a reversible system. One may move from A to B, and may come back from B to A; there is the possibility of returning, of reversibility. There is also the possibility of making detours and combinations which give a clue to what the subsequent operations will be when thought will supersede the action itself.

Pre-operational stage

From one and one-half to two years of age, a fundamental transformation in the evolution of intelligence takes place in the appearance of symbolic functions. Every action of intelligence consists in manipulating significations (or meanings) and whenever (or wherever) there are significations, there are on the one hand the 'significants' and on the other the 'significates'. This is true in the sensori-motor level, but the only significants that intervene there are perceptual signs or signals (as in conditioning) which are undifferentiated in regard to the significate; for example, a perceptual cue, like distance, which will be a cue for the size of the distant object, or the apparent size of an object, which will be the cue for the distance of the object. There, perhaps, both indices are different aspects of the same reality, but they are not yet differentiated significants. At the age of one and one-half to two years a new class of significants arises, and these significants are differentiated in regard to their significates. These differentiations can be called symbolic function. The appearance of symbols in a children's game is an example of the appearance of new significants. At the sensori-motor level the games are nothing but exercises; now they become symbolic play, a play of fiction; these games consist in representing something by means of something else. Another example is the beginning of delayed imitation, an imitation that takes place not in the presence of the original object but in its absence, and which consequently constitutes a kind of symbolization or mental image.

At the same time that symbols appear, the child acquires language; that is to say, there is the acquisition of another phase of differentiated significants, verbal signals, or collective signals. This symbolic function then brings great flexibility into the field of intelligence. Intelligence up to this point refers to the immediate space which surrounds the child and to the present perceptual situation; thanks to language, and to the symbolic functions, it becomes possible to invoke objects which are not present perceptually, to reconstruct the past, or to make projects, plans for the future, to think of objects not present but very distant in space – in short, to span spatio-temporal distances much greater than before.

But this new stage, the stage of representation of thought which is superimposed on the sensori-motor stage, is not a simple extension of what was referred to at the previous level. Before being able to prolong, one must in fact reconstruct, because behavior in words is a different thing from representing something in thought. When a child knows how to move around in his house or garden by following the different successive cues around him, it does not mean that he is capable of representing or reproducing the total configuration of his house or his garden. To be able to represent, to reproduce something, one must be capable of reconstructing this group of displacements, but at a new level, that of the representation of the thought.

I recently made an amusing test with Nel Szeminska. We took children of four to five years of age who went to school by themselves and came back home by themselves, and asked them if they could trace the way to school and back for us, not in design, which would be too difficult, but like a construction game, with concrete objects. We found that they were not capable of representation; there was a kind of motor-memory, but it was not yet a representation of a whole – the group of displacements had not yet been reconstructed on the plan of the representation of thought. In other words, the operations were not yet formed. These are representations which are internalized actions; but actions still centered on the body itself, on the activity itself. These representations do not allow the objective combinations, the decentrated combinations that the operations would. The actions are centered on the body. I used to call this egocentrism; but it is better thought of as lack of reversibility of action.

At this level, the most certain sign of the absence of operations which appear at the next stage is the absence of the knowledge of conservation. In fact, an operation refers to the transformation of reality. The transformation is not of the whole, however; something constant is always untransformed. If you pour a liquid from one glass to another there is transformation; the liquid changes form, but its liquid property stays constant. So at the pre-operational level, it is significant from the point of view of the operations of intelligence that the child has not yet a knowledge of conservation. For example, in the case of liquid, when the child pours it from one bottle to the other, he thinks that the quantity of the liquid has changed. When the level of the liquid changes, the child thinks the quantity has changed – there is more or less in the second glass than in the first. And if you ask the child where the larger quantity came from, he does not answer this question. What is important for the child is that perceptually it is not the same thing any more. We find this absence of conservation in all object properties, in the length, surface, quantity, and weight of things.

This absence of conservation indicates essentially that at this stage the child reasons from the configuration. Confronted with a transformation, he does not reason from the transformation itself; he starts from the initial configuration, then sees the final configuration, compares the two but forgets the transformation, because he does not know how to reason about it. At this stage the child is still reasoning on the basis of what he sees because there is no conservation. He is able to master this problem only when the operations are formed and these operations, which we have already sensed at the sensori-motor level, are not formed until around seven to eight years of age. At that age the elementary problems of conservation are solved, because the child reasons on the basis of the transformation *per se*, and this requires a manipulation of the operation. The ability to pass from one stage to the other and be able to come back to the point of departure, to manipulate the reversible operations, which appears around seven to eight years of age, is limited when compared with the operations of the superior level only in the sense that they are concrete. That is to say, the child can manipulate the operations only when he manipulates the object concretely.

Stage of concrete-operations

The first operations of the manipulation of objects, the concrete-operations, deal with logical classes and with logical relations, or the number. But these operations do not deal yet with propositions, or hypotheses, which do not appear until the last stage.

Let me exemplify these concrete-operations: the simplest operation is concerned with classifying objects according to their similarity and their difference. This is accomplished by including the subclasses within larger and more general classes, a process that implies inclusion. This classification, which seems very simple at first, is not acquired until around seven to eight years of age. Before that, at the pre-operational level, we do not find logical inclusion. For example, if you show a child at the pre-operational level a bouquet of flowers of which one half is daisies and the other half other flowers and you ask him if in this bouquet there are more flowers or more daisies, you are confronted with this answer, which seems extra-ordinary until it is analyzed: the child cannot tell you whether there are more flowers than daisies; either he reasons on the basis of the whole or of the part. He cannot understand that the part is complementary to the rest, and he says there are more daisies than flowers, or as many daisies as flowers, without understanding this inclusion of the subclass, the daisies, in the class of flowers. It is only around seven to eight years of age that a child is capable of solving a problem of inclusion.

Another system of operation that appears around seven to eight years of age is the operation of serializing; that is, to arrange objects according to their size, or their progressive weight. It is also a structure of the whole, like the classification which rests on concrete operations, since it consists of manipulating concrete-objects. At this level there is also the construction of numbers, which is, too, a synthesis of classification and seriation. In numbers, as in classes, we have inclusion, and also a serial order, as in serializing. These elementary operations constitute structures of wholes. There is no class without classification; there is not symmetric relation without serialization; there is not a number independent of the series of numbers. But the structures of these wholes are simple structures, group-ings in the case of classes and relations, which are already groups in the case of numbers, but very elementary structures compared to subsequent structures.

Stage of formal-operations

The last stage of development of intelligence is the stage of formal-operations or propositional-operations. At about eleven to twelve years of age we see great progress; the child becomes capable of reasoning not only on the basis of objects, but also on the basis of hypotheses, or of propositions.

An example which neatly shows the difference between reasoning on the basis of propositions and reasoning on the basis of concrete-objects comes from Burt's tests. Burt asked children of different ages to compare the colors of the hair of three girls: Edith is fairer than Susan, Edith is darker than Lilly; who is the darkest of the three? In this question there is seriation, not of concrete-objects, but of verbal statements which supposes a more complicated mental manipulation. This problem is rarely solved before the age of 12.

Here a new class of operations appears which is superimposed on the operations of logical class and number, and these operations are the propositional-operations. Here, compared to the previous stage, are fundamental changes. It is not simply that these operations refer to language, and then to operations with concrete-objects, but that these operations have much richer structures.

The first novelty is a combinative structure; like mathematical structures, it is a structure of a system which is superimposed on the structure of simple classifications or seriations which are not themselves systems, because they do not involve a combinative system. A combinative system permits the grouping in flexible combinations of each element of the system with any other element of that system. The logic of propositions supposes such a combinative system. If children of different ages are shown a number of colored disks and asked to combine each color with each other two by two, or three by three, we find these combinative operations are not accessible to the child at the stage of concrete-operations. The child is capable of some combination, but not of all the possible combinations. After the age of 12, the child can find a method to make all the possible combinations. At the same time he acquires both the logic of mathematics and the logic of propositions, which also supposes a method of combining.

A second novelty in the operations of propositions is the appearance of a structure which constitutes a group of four transformations. Hitherto there were two reversibilities: reversibility by inversion, which consists of annulling, or cancelling; and reversibility which we call reciprocity, leading not to cancellation, but to another combination. Reciprocity is what we find in the field of a relation. If A equals B, by reciprocity B equals A. If A is smaller than B, by reciprocity B is larger than A. At the level of propositional operations a new system envelops these two forms of reversibility. Here the structure combines inversion and reversibility in one single but larger and more complicated structure. It allows the acquisition of a series of fundamental operational schemata for the development of intelligence, which schemata are not possible before the constitution of this structure.

It is around the age of 12 that the child, for example, starts to understand in mathematics the knowledge of proportions, and becomes capable of reasoning by using two systems of reference at the same time. For example, if you advance the position of a board and a car moving in opposite directions, in order to understand the movement of the board in relation to the movement of the car and to other movement, you need a system of four transformations. The same is true in regard to proportions, to problems in mathematics or physics, or to other logical problems.

The four principal stages of the development of intelligence of the child progress from one stage to the other by the construction of new operational structures, and these structures constitute the fundamental instrument of the intelligence of the adult.

1.4 Modifiability of cognitive development

Charles J. Brainerd

A perennial question about human intelligence, one that has befuddled educators and developmental researchers alike, concerns the extent to which the normal course of intellectual development can be altered by appropriate learning experiences. There are two opposing doctrines, which are sometimes called the *interventionist* position and the *horticulturalist* position.

Extreme interventionists believe that cognitive development is largely controlled by learning. In everyday life, we are all familiar with newspaper accounts of parents who read great works of literature to newborn infants in the belief that it will foster genius. In modern psychology, behaviorism is usually taken as the textbook illustration of an interventionist theory, though behaviorists themselves are inclined to reject this interpretation (e.g., Skinner, 1974). Interventionism's philosophical roots are in the British empiricist and utilitarian traditions.

Extreme horticulturalists believe that learning can modify cognitive development in only minor respects and that attempts at such modification, though well intentioned, may do more harm than good. An everyday illustration of horticulturalism is provided by parents who avoid any direct teaching of basic skills such as bladder control, walking, speech, etc., to their offspring and, instead, wait for such skills to emerge 'spontaneously'. Philosophically horticulturalism is easily recognizable as a Rousseauian doctrine (e.g., Brainerd, 1978a, 1978b). Piaget's stage model of cognitive development (e.g., Piaget, 1970a; Piaget and Inhelder, 1969) is the standard example of a horticulturalist theory in psychology, though Piagetians, like behaviorists, are inclined to disagree (e.g., Sinclair, 1973).

We know, of course, that neither extreme interventionism nor extreme horticulturalism is correct. Research has shown that there are maturational limits on what can be taught to children of given ages, which argues against interventionism. For example, bladder and bowel control cannot be trained until certain areas of the motor cortex have been myelinated (McGraw, 1940). But research has also shown that the effects of learning on cognitive development are far from trivial, which argues against horticulturalism. Here, the most compelling illustrations come from cross-cultural studies, wherein subjects from cultures with different levels of literacy tend to perform very differently on standardized cognitive tests (Cole and Scribner, 1974).

Although interventionism and horticulturalism, in their pure forms, are wrong, a question of considerable scientific interest lies between these

---

Source: MEADOWS, S. (ed.) (1983) *Developing Thinking* (ch. 2). London: Methuen.

poles, namely, what are the exact constraints under which learning operates during cognitive development? Historically, developmental researchers have studied this question in many ways. For the past two decades, however, such research has been closely connected to Piaget's theory. In particular, there are two topics which are especially relevant to the problem of just how modifiable cognitive development is. The first is the series of laboratory-style learning experiments in which investigators have sought to teach conceptual skills from Piaget's stages to children who do not yet possess them. The second is a group of experimental pre-school curricula in which early-childhood educators have attempted to implement Piaget's ideas about the relationship between learning and development.

[. . .]

Teaching Piagetian concepts in the laboratory

Piaget proposed that cognitive development consists of four global stages – the sensori-motor stage (roughly birth to two years), the pre-operational stage (roughly two to seven years), the concrete-operational stage (roughly seven to 11 years), and the formal-operational stage (roughly 11 years and beyond). During each stage, there is a fundamental control program, or underlying competence system, which Piaget called 'cognitive structures'. The cognitive structures of a stage, which are comprised of mental entities called 'operations', define the basic characteristics of intelligence during that stage and are supposed to set certain constraints on learning (see Inhelder, Sinclair and Bovet, 1974; Inhelder and Sinclair, 1969; Piaget, 1970a). This section is concerned with research on these constraints.

[. . .]

Conservation concepts

The cognitive skills that are most often associated with Piaget's theory are the well-known conservation concepts. According to the theory, most types of conservation appear during the concrete-operational stage, though some complex versions of it do not emerge until the formal-operational stage. Broadly speaking, conservation refers to children's understanding that quantitative relationships among objects remain invariant (are 'conserved') across changes in irrelevant perceptual aspects of the objects. A particular conservation concept (say, conservation of number) refers to children's understanding that some specific quantitative property (number in this case) remains invariant in the face of some specific type of perceptual transformation (changes in length in this case).

The standard paradigm of assessing a conservation concept involves presenting the child with two familiar objects. Depending on the particular concept that is being measured, the objects are such things as rows of plastic chips, clay balls, glasses of water, lengths of string, etc. Following the terminology in an early paper by Elkind (1967), one of the objects in the pair is called the *standard stimulus* (S) and the other object is called the *variable stimulus* (V). This emphasizes the fact that one object, S, will remain unchanged throughout the assessment, whereas the other object, V, will undergo certain perceptual deformations. After the variable stimulus has been deformed in some way, it is then denoted V' rather than V.

At the start of a conservation problem, S and V are perceptually identical. The assessment begins by establishing to the child's satisfaction that S and V are also equal with respect to some familiar quantitative dimension (e.g., length, height, number, weight, mass). Next, the experimenter transforms V in such a way that the perceptual identity is destroyed but the quantitative equivalence is preserved. The experimenter then asks one or more questions that are designed to determine whether the child understands that S = V' despite the fact that they no longer look the same. For example, suppose that it is number conservation that is being measured. The first step would be to construct two parallel rows of familiar objects (e.g., poker chips) which (a) contain the same number of items and (b) are of exactly the same length. After the subject has agreed that the two rows have the same number, the experimenter destroys the perceptual identity by lengthening or shortening one of the rows. The experimenter then poses questions such as, 'Do the two rows still have the same number of chips, or does one of them have more chips now?' Remarkably, children younger than about five or six are strongly inclined to say that the longer row has more (Piaget, 1952).

Although there are as many forms of conservation as there are dimensions of quantitative variation, the types that have been studied in most conservation-learning experiments are number conservation, length conservation, mass conservation, quantity conservation, and weight conservation. For the sake of clarity, the assessment procedures for four of these concepts are summarized in Table 1 (page 42).

There is an extensive data base on the normative course of development of conservation concepts in Western children. At least three conclusions appear to be unarguable. First, the earliest conservation concepts do not spontaneously appear in most children's thinking until about age six or so. Second, there appears to be a definite sequence in the emergence of some of them. For example, number conservation is usually the first form of conservation for most children. Length conservation normally appears sometime after number, while concepts such as quantity and weight conservation are later still. Third, the development of conservation takes quite a long time. Although the normative data show that the average seven- or eight-year-old child understands number and length conservation (e.g., Brainerd and Brainerd, 1972), these same data show that concepts such as volume conservation, density conservation, and area

Table 1   Four types of conservation that have frequently been studied in learning experiments

Length conservation	Two wooden or metal rods of the same length	(1) The experimenter places the rods close together so the child can see that they are the same length. (2) The experimenter places one of the rods so that it is perpendicular to the other rod. (3) The experimenter poses questions of the form, 'Are the two rods still the same length or is one of them longer now?'
Mass conservation	Two clay balls of the same size	(1) The experimenter presents the two clay balls so the child can see that they have the same amount of clay. (2) The experimenter flattens one of the clay balls into a 'pancake'. (3) The experimenter poses questions of the form, 'Do the ball and the pancake have the same amount of clay or does one of them have more?'
Number conservation	Some red and blue poker chips	(1) The experimenter builds a row of blue chips and a row of red chips side-by-side so the child can see that they contain the same number of chips. (2) The experimenter lengthens one of the rows. (3) The experimenter poses questions of the form, 'Is there still the same number of red and blue chips, or does one of the rows have more now?'
Quantity conservation	Two identical glasses, plus a third glass that is taller and thinner than the other two	(1) The experimenter fills the two identical glasses with water in such a way that they contain the same amount of water. (2) The experimenter pours the contents of one of the identical glasses into the tall, thin glass. (3) The experimenter poses questions of the form, 'Is there the same amount of water in the two glasses now, or does one of them have more?'

conservation are not understood by the average junior high school (12 to 14 years old) student (e.g., Brainerd, 1971; Brainerd and Allen, 1971b).

The Piagetian view of learning

Piaget (e.g., 1970a) proposed that children's ability to learn the concepts from his stages via programs of direct instruction is constrained in two general ways. First, whether or not learning occurs hinges on children's current stages of cognitive development. Second, it also depends on the teaching methods that we use. To set the stage for the discussion of experimental findings, I summarize what the theory has to say on each of these matters.

The when of learning

The key idea here is that learning, in the sense of coming to understand a concept such as conservation as a consequence of direct instruction, is under the control of development. [. . .]

To begin with, a general process called 'cognitive development' is posited in the theory, and this process is said to be governed by its own special laws and principles (e.g., assimilation, accommodation, equilibration, decentration). It is cognitive development that supposedly determines when and under what conditions an instructional program will be effective: 'Learning is no more than a sector of cognitive development which is facilitated by experience' (Piaget, 1970a, page 714). The rule of thumb is that children's capacity to profit from learning experiences will be 'subject to the general constraints of the current developmental stage' (Piaget, 1970a, page 713). If a group of children is trained on a concept from one of Piaget's stages, the amount of learning that is obtained in individual children is expected to 'vary very significantly as a function of the initial cognitive levels of the children' (Piaget, 1970a, page 715). Other things being equal, the higher a child's current stage of cognitive development, the better his or her learning is likely to be. From statements such as these, it is obvious that the Piagetian view of learning is a classical readiness doctrine.

To see why Piaget made such statements, it is necessary to delve into the infrastructure of his theory. Cognitive development is described as a stage-like process in the theory. As I have mentioned, each of these stages is defined by its own unique set of cognitive structures. The concepts that are associated with a given stage are thought to be 'deduced' from these structures or 'generated' by them in a manner that is vaguely analogous to the way in which a logician deduces or generates theorems from a small set of axioms (see Brainerd, 1978c). According to the theory, a target concept (say, conservation) cannot be expressed by a child unless the relevant structures for that concept (in this case, the so-called grouping structures of the concrete-operational stage) have been laid in. These structures are acquired as a by-product of the process of cognitive development, not as a consequence of learning. Therefore, learning experiences designed to induce a particular concept can only be effective to the extent that the structures which are necessary for the expression of that concept *have already developed*. This means that training will not be successful whenever the child's current stage is far below the one at which the pertinent structures appear. Successful training requires that the current stage be the same as or very near to the one at which the target concept 'spon-taneously' appears. These claims were aptly summarized in Piaget's statement that 'teaching children concepts that they have not acquired in their spontaneous development . . . is completely useless' (Piaget, 1970b, page 30).

At first glance, it would not seem difficult to test the validity of such proposals. Naively, we should only have to conduct a learning experiment in which, first, we train children at various stages of cognitive develop-ment on some given concept and, second, we determine whether or not learning is better in children who are at more advanced stages. For example, imagine a hypothetical experiment in which we attempt to train the concept of number conservation in a group of children who do not yet possess it. Suppose that the children in our experiment are of two types, concrete-operational children (i.e., the stage at which conservation 'spon-taneously' develops) and pre-operational children (i.e., the stage preced-ing the emergence of conservation). Suppose that we assign each child to one of two conditions, a training condition in which the child receives some sort of direct instruction that should enhance conservation knowl-edge and a no-training control group. In other words, our experiment is a simple two × two factorial design, with the two factors being stage of cognitive development (concrete-operational or pre-operational) and amount of training (some or none). It is obvious what Piagetian theory anticipates in this situation: there should be a large stage × training interaction. Specifically, the training procedure should produce larger improvements in conservation knowledge among the concrete-operational children than among the pre-operational children.

Unfortunately, it is impossible to conduct experiments of this sort. The reason is that one of the two factors in the design, stage of cognitive development, cannot be measured. Although Piaget and his collaborators have often spoken of stages as though they were objective characteristics of children (e.g., Inhelder, 1956; Piaget, 1960), they are not. Unlike height, weight, eye color, gender, and so forth, we do not have any way of telling exactly what a child's 'current stage of cognitive development' is. This is because stages are not objective things at all but, rather, they are what theoreticians call *hypothetical constructs* or *intervening variables* (cf., Brainerd, 1981, 1982a and b). That is, they are *assumptions* that Piaget introduced in the hope of explaining certain kinds of data, not things that he actually measured in children's behavior. Hence, our simple two × two experi-ment cannot be conducted because we have no way of knowing precisely which children are pre-operational and which are concrete-operational.

Assuming that we still wish to investigate Piaget's views on learning after discovering this problem, the only solution is to seek other, objective variables in terms of which children can be classified and which should be related to stage of cognitive development in a sensible way. Ideally, we should rely on variables that can be assumed to be *monotonically related* to stage of cognitive development – i.e., children who have more of the variable are always at higher stages than children who have less of it. To date, two such variables have been used in attempts to evaluate the hypothesis that children's concept learning depends on their stages of cognitive development: (a) levels of pretraining performance on tests for the to-be-trained concept and (b) chronological age.

Concerning (a), suppose that all the children in our hypothetical experiment received an extensive battery of tests for conservation concepts before they participated in the training phase of the research. When performance on these pre-tests is inspected, suppose that we find that the children tend to fall into two groups, namely, those who fail all the tests across the board and those who pass some tests while failing others. In other words, some children appear to know nothing about conservation, whereas others have some slight grasp of it. We still do not know which of these children are preoperational and which are concrete-operational. However, Piaget did tell us this much: conservation concepts first develop during the concrete-operational stage, which means that children in the second group are more likely to be concrete-operational than children in the first group. Therefore, we can conduct a two × two experiment in which the factors are level of pretraining performance (none or some) and amount of training (some or none). In this study, level of pretraining performance substitutes for stage of cognitive development in the original design.

In such an experiment, there are two findings that would tend to support the hypothesis that concept learning is constrained by stage of cognitive development. First, since the hypothesis anticipated a stage × training interaction in the original design, it anticipates a pretraining performance × training interaction here such that children who show some understanding of conservation learn better than children who show none. Second, since children who fail conservation pre-tests across the board should be primarily pre-operational, this group should be especially difficult to train (because pre-operational children do not yet possess the cognitive structures whereby conservation is expressed).

Concerning (b), the standard age norms given for the pre-operational and concrete-operational stages are two to seven and seven to 11, respectively. Although these are said to be only averages, they can be used to divide children into groups that are more likely to be at a given stage than other groups. For example, suppose we selected a group of normal children, all of whom were in the four- to five-year-old age range (i.e., older preschoolers and kindergarteners). All of these children come from the nominal age range for the pre-operational stage. Hence, except for an occasional precocious child, the age norms indicate that this is a pre-operational sample. If we were to attempt to train concrete-operational concepts with such children, the theory tells us that we should fail. In short, chronological age can be used to test the hypothesis that concept learning is constrained by cognitive development as follows. First, use the age norms for the stages to select a sample that, by and large, can be assumed to be operating at a given stage. Second, attempt to train concepts from some more advanced stage, with poor learning being the expected outcome.

The how of learning

The other type of constraint that cognitive development is said to impose on learning is concerned with the nature of the learning experiences themselves. Suppose, for the sake of discussion, that we obey the first constraint and select a sample of children whom we have reason to suppose have attained a stage that is appropriate for whatever it is that we wish to teach. The theory now tells us that not just any training procedure will work. Instead, our training must take account of what happens in everyday cognitive development to be effective. For example, Inhelder, Sinclair and Bovet (1974) explain the rationale for the training methods used in Genevan learning research as follows: 'We started with the idea that under certain conditions an acceleration of cognitive development would be possible, but that this could only occur if the training resembled the kind of situations in which progress takes place outside the experimental set-up' (page 24).
[. . .]
The specific type of learning experiences that Piagetians favor are those that involve *active self-discovery* of the concept that is being trained. These methods are usually contrasted in Genevan writings with procedures that involve *passive reception of information*, which are not supposed to work very well (e.g., Sinclair, 1973). For example, Inhelder and Sinclair (1969) described Genevan learning methods by noting that 'in all of them we avoid imposing definite strategies on the child . . . the child is encouraged to make his own co-ordinations . . . the child is asked to anticipate the likely outcome of certain transformations and then to observe the actual outcome of the transformation. . . . In other cases, we aim at a step-by-step circumscription of the problem destined to make the child aware of contradictions in his arguments.' [. . .]
To see why active self-discovery learning is favored by Piagetians, it is necessary to delve into the theory's infrastructure again. The general principle that is supposed to govern cognitive development in everyday life is called *construction*. According to this principle, it is children's active manipulations of their environments (building things, tearing them down, transforming things) that produce cognitive growth. Of course, we all know that children, especially young children, spend considerable time in such activity. Piaget believed that children's active manipulation of things in their environments leads to cognitive changes via a disequilibrium/ equilibrium process. The general idea is that the child's current stage of cognitive development leads him or her to anticipate that a manipulation will produce certain results. When results do not conform to expectations, the child's cognitive structures are thrown into a state of disequilibrium.

Ultimately, the disequilibrium is resolved by acquiring new cognitive structures which will make correct predictions about the results of manipulations.

[. . .]

Following earlier terminology (Brainerd, 1978a), I shall refer to the active, manipulative training experiences emphasized by Piagetians as *self-discovery* training and to the passive-reception procedures that they eschew as *tutorial* training. Common illustrations of tutorial instruction include: (a) observational learning, where children who lack a certain concept observe the performance of children or adults who possess the concept (e.g., Rosenthal and Zimmerman, 1978); (b) rule instruction, where children who lack a certain concept are taught a rule or rules that are critical to correct performance (e.g., Beilin, 1965; Goldschmid, 1968; Hamel and Riksen, 1973); (c) corrective feedback, where children who lack a certain concept are given direct training on the correct answers to the items on tests for that concept (e.g., Brainerd, 1972a and b; Bucher and Schneider, 1973). Generally speaking, Piagetians claim that self-discovery training is successful and tutorial training is not. The reason, naturally, is that the former mirrors the principle of construction but the latter does not.

It is much easier to evaluate these proposals about the 'how' of children's learning than it is to evaluate the earlier proposals about the dependence of learning on stage of cognitive development. This is because our training methods are objective variables that we can control and measure, not hypothetical constructs as stages are. If we conduct learning experiments in which the type of training that children receive is varied, then there are several results that bear on the claim that training must reflect the construction principle if it is to be effective. To begin with, children should be able to learn concepts such as conservation via self-discovery, but they should not show much improvement as a result of tutorial training. Second, suppose that we conducted experiments in which specific varieties of self-discovery training were compared to specific varieties of tutorial training. We would expect consistently better learning with the former. Finally, suppose that we conducted experiments in which subjects received several types of training, with training procedures differing in the amount of self-discovery that they incorporate. Here, we would expect some sort of monotonic increase in amount of learning as the amount of self-discovery in a training method increases. All these predictions presuppose that we have taken account of the first constraint and have selected groups of children who can be assumed to have attained whatever stage is required for the concepts being trained.

Experimental findings

Now that Piaget's basic proposals about learning have been considered, we can turn to what research has shown about their validity. As mentioned, the bulk of this research consists of experiments in which investigators have attempted to train one or more conservation concepts. [. . .]

Basic design

Most experiments have involved three steps, namely, a pre-test phase, a training phase, and a post-test phase. During the pre-test phase, tests are administered for one or more concepts from some Piagetian stage (e.g., tests for certain conservation concepts). A decision as to whether a given child is to continue to the second phase is rendered on the basis of his or her performance on these pre-tests. In some experiments, only children who fail all the pre-tests are retained for training. In other experiments, children are permitted to pass some minimum proportion of items (say, up to fifty per cent). In all instances, however, subjects who pass all or nearly all the items are discarded.

At the beginning of the training phase, the remaining children are assigned to treatment groups. The minimum design consists of two conditions, a treatment group whose members all receive the same type of training and a control group whose members receive no training. More elaborate designs involve multiple treatment groups, with the members of each group receiving different types of training, plus a control condition. The subjects who are assigned to a given treatment condition may either receive a fixed amount of training or they may be trained until they reach a performance criterion of some sort (criterion training).

The post-test phase begins sometime after the subject has completed training. There are two important post-test variables, namely, the types of post-tests that are administered and the time interval between the completion of training and the beginning of the post-tests. On the former point, Piaget and his collaborators have emphasized that 'true learning' of a concept demands that the improvements produced by training should generalize across variations in the way that a concept is measured. For example, if we conducted a conservation-learning experiment in which we attempted to train *number* conservation during the second phase, we would probably administer post-tests for both number conservation and some other types of conservation (e.g., length, weight). On the latter point, Piaget and his collaborators have also emphasized that 'true learning' has occurred only if improvements are retained for a long time after training. Thus, in the experiment just mentioned, we would probably administer conservation post-tests immediately after training and a week or two later as well. We might even administer conservation post-tests several months later (see Gelman, 1969; Goldschmid, 1968).

Early findings: 1959–71

It is convenient to divide Piagetian learning research into two historical periods, an early period running from 1959 to 1971 and a recent period running from 1972 to the present. As we shall see, the questions investigators have been concerned with during these periods have been somewhat different.

The nominal starting point for the early period was the publication of two pilot experiments conducted in Geneva (Smedslund, 1959; Wohlwill, 1959), though the investigators themselves were not Genevans. The early period concluded with the publication within a few months of each other of three independent reviews of experiments that had been reported through 1970 (Beilin, 1971; Brainerd and Allen, 1971a; Goldschmid, 1971). The main question throughout this period was whether it was possible to produce *any* learning of Piagetian concepts, especially conservation. It was widely believed at this time that Piagetian theory simply predicted no learning. Although we have already seen that this interpretation is not accurate, the results of some of the earliest experiments appeared to support it.

In Smedslund's (1959) and Wohlwill's (1959) original pilot studies, Wohlwill attempted to train conservation of number and Smedslund attempted to train quantity conservation. Wohlwill subsequently replicated his study with a larger sample (Wohlwill and Lowe, 1962), and Smedslund expanded his study into a series of experiments (Smedslund, 1961a, b, c, d, e and f). In the Wohlwill and Lowe (1962) experiment, children were trained on number conservation with three different procedures: corrective feedback, rule instruction, and perceptual-set training. The key result was no evidence of learning – i.e., the post-test conservation performance of the children in each of these conditions was not measurably better than that of the children in the no-treatment condition. In the initial experiments in the Smedslund series, children were trained on weight conservation with three different techniques: training of weighing operations (Smedslund, 1961b), teaching an addition-subtraction rule (Smedslund, 1961b), and perceptual-set training (Smedslund, 1961d). Like Wohlwill, Smedslund found no significant improvement in conservation as a consequence of such training.

At the time, these findings [. . .] were thought to show that Piagetian concepts are extremely difficult for children to learn, a conclusion that obviously favors the theory's claim that learning is sharply limited by development. For example, Flavell's (1963) early book on Piaget's theory contains the following commentary:

What can be concluded from all these experiments? Perhaps the most certain conclusion is that it can be a surprisingly difficult undertaking to manufacture Piagetian concepts in the laboratory. Almost all the training methods reported impress one as sound and reasonable and well-suited to the educative job at hand. And yet most of them have had remarkably little success in producing cognitive change. It is not easy to convey the sense of disbelief that creeps over one in reading these experiments . . . there is more than a suspicion from present evidence that when one does succeed in inducing some behavioral change through this or that training procedure, it may not cut very deep.   (page 377)

Investigators outside Geneva, primarily in North America, did not allow this conclusion to go unchallenged. During the next few years, several experiments were reported in which various tutorial methods were used to train concrete-operational concepts. Priority for the first successful experiment following Flavell's book goes to Wallach and Sprott (1964). They reported a study in which number conservation was trained by giving children instruction on a reversibility rule. On number conservation post-tests, trained children performed much better than controls. In subsequent experiments, various other tutorial procedures produced large differences in the post-test conservation performance of trained and untrained children. [. . .]

Although some unsuccessful experiments were also reported after 1963 (e.g., Mermelstein and Meyer, 1969), by 1970 most of the basic varieties of conservation had been successfully trained in more than one experiment. [. . .]

It was clear [. . .], first, that laboratory-style learning experiments could produce large improvements in certain concrete-operational and formal-operational concepts; second, that the tutorial-type training which Piagetians criticize actually works rather well; and third, that the same tutorial procedures that appeared to fail in the early Smedslund and Wohlwill studies could be made to succeed (Hatano, 1971; Hatano and Suga, 1969). By 1971, therefore, there appeared to be some consensus that it was not necessarily a 'difficult undertaking to manufacture Piagetian concepts in the laboratory'. However, many questions remained to be answered about the limits of children's susceptibility to training.

Although the issue of whether Piagetian concepts are, in principle, trainable dominated early research, we have already seen that the theory does not actually predict untrainability. Instead, it merely restricts learning in two general ways. The early literature, perhaps because of its emphasis on mere trainability, did not provide definitive evidence on either of these limitations.

Concerning the first limitation (learning depends on stage of cognitive development), some data appeared to favor this assumption and others argued against it. I noted earlier that there have been three experimental strategies for investigating the hypothesis that stage constrains concept learning. The first strategy (determine the relationship between pretraining knowledge of a concept and susceptibility to training) was adopted in conservation-learning experiments by Beilin (1965) and by Strauss and Langer (1970). These investigators classified children as being either pre-operational or in transition between the pre-operational and concrete-operational stages on the basis of conservation pre-tests. Following training, the subjects were reclassified as pre-operational, transitional, or concrete-operational. A correlation was observed between the children's pre-training and post-training stage classification. In line with Piagetian theory, Beilin interpreted this result as showing that 'the group most likely to profit from training is that group whose members have at least some . . .

conservation ability' (1965, page 335). The second strategy (determine the trainability of children who fail pre-tests across the board) was adopted in several experiments. In fact, most of the conservation-learning experiments reported between 1964 and 1970 were concerned with children who showed no pre-training knowledge of conservation. In contrast to the results from the first strategy, most of these experiments produced clear evidence of learning, a result which suggests that pre-operational children can learn concrete-operational concepts. Finally, data from experiments involving the third strategy (determine trainability of very young children), like those from experiments involving the first strategy, seemed to favor Piagetian theory. Except for a study by Emrick (1967), conservation-learning experiments with preschool children that were published up to 1970 were consistently unsuccessful (e.g., Bruner, 1964; Halford, 1970; Mermelstein and Meyer, 1969).

Concerning the second constraint on learning (self-discovery training is best), the early literature also presented a mixed picture. On the one hand, the fact that procedures such as observational learning, rule instruction, and corrective feedback had proved effective in teaching children Piagetian concepts made the hypothesis that tutorial procedures do not work untenable. On the other hand, virtually nothing was known about the effects of self-discovery training. Genevan investigators (e.g., Inhelder and Sinclair, 1969; Inhelder, Sinclair, Bovet and Smock, 1966) had reported some pilot studies with small numbers of children in which self-discovery procedures were used to train conservation. Although these results suggested that self-discovery training might be effective, the data were too thin to conclude that such training was actually successful and, more important, to assess the relative effectiveness of self-discovery and tutorial training.

Recent findings: 1972 – present

Fortunately, subsequent experimentation has delivered reasonably unambiguous answers to the questions that were left open in the early literature. In particular, studies published after 1971 provide rather strong disconfirmation of both of the constraints that Piaget imposed on learning. I summarize the data bearing on each constraint separately.

Does learning depend on stage of cognitive development?   It has been noted that early studies which adopted either the first or third approach to this question produced data that seemed favorable to the theory, whereas those that adopted the second strategy produced unfavorable data. In later studies, however, both the first and third strategies produced unfavorable data.

With respect to the first strategy, a fairly large number of experiments accumulated during the early 1970s in which children with differing pre-test levels of conservation knowledge received conservation training.

This literature included several experiments conducted in Geneva by three of Piaget's collaborators (Inhelder, Sinclair and Bovet, 1974). Those experiments that had been published as of 1977 were reviewed with a view toward deciding whether or not they supported the hypothesis that concept learning improves as pre-test knowledge of trained concepts increases (Brainerd, 1977). Most of these experiments followed Beilin's (1965) design in the sense that subjects were classified as pre-operational or transitional on the basis of pre-tests, were then trained, and finally were reclassified as pre-operational, transitional, or concrete-operational on the basis of post-tests. As in Beilin's (1965) and Strauss and Langer's (1970) original studies, it was generally found that the pre- and post-test stage classifications correlated with each other. In particular, children classified as pre-operational on the pre-test tended to be classified either pre-operational or transitional on the post-test, whereas children classified as transitional on the pre-test tended to be classified either transitional or concrete-operational on the post-test. This datum was usually interpreted as supporting the hypothesis that stage constrains learning. For example: 'the nature and extent of the subjects' progress was always, in fact strikingly so, dependent on their initial developmental level' (Inhelder *et al.*, 1974, page 244). In fact, however, this conclusion does not follow. As long as the pre- and post-tests on which the stage classifications are based are reliable, a positive correlation between pre- and post-test classifications is virtually guaranteed. What we really need to know is whether *the amount of pre- to post-test improvement* in performance (i.e., the amount of learning) is different for children with different stage classifications. What we anticipate, of course, is that the amount of pre- to post-test improvement should be smaller for children with a pre-operational classification than for children with a transitional classification. However, when the amount of improvement was calculated for studies published up to 1977, it turned out that conservation training produced just as much improvement in pre-operational children as in transitional children (see Brainerd, 1977, Table 1). This finding has been replicated in later experiments (e.g., Brainerd, 1979). It has even been found that under some conditions, children who know less about a concept learn *more* than children who know more about that concept (Brainerd, 1982a)!

Turning to the third strategy, although early experiments generally failed to produce learning in preschoolers, several successful experiments with preschool samples have been reported since 1971. As usual, most of them were concerned with conservation learning, and all of them relied on forms of training that Piagetians would regard as tutorial. So far, the particular techniques that have proved to be effective with preschoolers are attentional training (Emrick, 1967), verbal rule instruction (Denney, Zeytinoglu and Selzer, 1977; Field, 1981), observation of skilled models (Rosenthal and Zimmerman, 1972; Zimmerman and Lanaro, 1974), behavior modification (Bucher and Schneider, 1973), and corrective feedback (Brainerd, 1974). In most studies, the amount of learning obtained with a given method is smaller for preschoolers than for elementary schoolers. However, it is clear that it is possible to produce substantial pre- to post-test improvements with preschoolers, that these learning effects will generalize to untrained concepts (e.g., Denney *et al.*, 1974), and that they are stable for several months following training (e.g., Field, 1981).

Is self-discovery training best?   We saw that the early literature left some doubt as to whether self-discovery training is an effective approach to training Piagetian concepts, and if it is, whether self-discovery training is more effective than tutorial training. The subsequent literature indicates that although self-discovery training can produce learning, it is generally *less* effective than tutorial training.

Concerning the ability of self-discovery training to produce learning, Inhelder *et al.* (1974) reported a series of experiments in which conservation and class inclusion were trained with self-discovery methods. In these experiments, the children were encouraged to manipulate various types of apparatus that were designed to lead them to discover a certain rule that is critical to the concept being trained. As an illustration, consider the first experiment that they reported. The object was to train liquid quantity conservation. In the liquid quantity task (see Table 1, page 42), non-conservers think that the amount of liquid in a glass depends on its height: when confronted with two glasses of liquid of different heights, they claim that the taller column of liquid is more than the shorter column, regardless of the true quantities involved. One problem that such children appear to have is that they do not understand that heights and widths are compensatory. Hence, Inhelder *et al.* (1974, Chapter 1) devised an apparatus consisting of different-size beakers. Non-conservers of liquid quantity were encouraged to pour a fixed amount of liquid from one beaker to another in the hope that they would notice that the amount of liquid stays the same regardless of the beaker in which it is contained. The fact that this procedure, and analogous methods, produced improved performance on tests for concrete-operational concepts suggests that children can benefit from self-discovery instruction. Similar findings have been obtained in experiments conducted outside Geneva (e.g., Cantor, Dunlap and Rettie, 1982).

On the other hand, there is no evidence that self-discovery training works better than tutorial training and, in fact, the weight of evidence favors the opposite conclusion. It has been pointed out elsewhere (Brainerd, 1978a) that the size of improvements observed in Genevan self-discovery experiments has been smaller than those observed in tutorial experiments. Also, the subjects in Genevan self-discovery experiments were older (seven years and above) than those in most tutorial experiments (kindergarteners and preschoolers). Last, Inhelder *et al.* (1974) found very little evidence of learning in children who showed no knowledge of the target concept during the pre-test phase. As we have seen, however, various types of tutorial training are known to produce learning in children who fail pre-tests across the board.

There have also been a few experiments in which a given type of tutorial training was compared to a given type of self-discovery training. To date, the outcome has either been no difference in relative effectiveness (e.g., Botvin and Murray, 1975) or a difference in favor of tutorial training (Cantor, Dunlap and Rettie, 1982). All of these findings argue against the view that self-discovery training is the royal road to learning Piagetian concepts.

Synopsis

To sum up the implications, two decades of research, most of it on concrete-operational concepts, has failed to provide any definitive support for the two developmental constraints that Piagetian theory imposes on learning. With respect to the first constraint (learning depends on pre-training stage of cognitive development), there is converging evidence from three experimental strategies, and each type of evidence says the same thing, namely, that there do not seem to be strong stage limits on learning. With respect to the second constraint (self-discovery training works best), there is overwhelming evidence that tutorial procedures are effective, even with preschool children. In addition, there is growing evidence that the amount of learning produced by self-discovery learning is normally smaller than that produced by comparable tutorial methods.

The second part of this paper and the references can be found on pages 323–37.

1.5 The role of play in the problem-solving of children 3–5 years old

Kathy Sylva, Jerome S. Bruner and Paul Genova

The essence of play is in the dominance of means over ends. This is not to say that play is without goals – witness the toddler building a tower of blocks – but in play the process is more important than the product. Freed from the tyranny of a tightly held goal, the player can substitute, elaborate and invent. Eibl-Eibesfeldt (1970) describes the play of animals as bits of behaviour borrowed from non-play modes, e.g., defence or reproduction, and strung together in unusual sequence. With a slightly different emphasis, Bruner (1972) describes the human infant playing with an object, say a cup, by fitting it into a variety of action programmes. He raises it to the lips, bangs it on the table, then drops it to the floor. In both the human and non-human examples, we see play as practice in assembling bits of behaviour (or means) into unusual sequences.

Because play behaviours are so often borrowed from non-play sequences, Reynolds (1976) describes it as taking place in the 'simulative mode'. A young baboon simulates attack; a child simulates meal preparation. These acts share with other simulations, e.g., wind tunnels for aircraft and dress rehearsals for drama, the lessening or elimination of risk. The second characteristic of play, then, is its lessening the risk of failure.

A third characteristic of play is the temporary moratorium on frustration that it affords the player. Because process takes precedence over product, an obstacle that would be deplored if met while problem-solving is met in play with equanimity or even glee (Miller, 1973).

Play offers still another freedom, this one being the peculiar vulnerability of the player to the world around him. Robert White (1959) hints at this in his contrast between the busy man rushing off to an appointment and the man strolling leisurely for pleasure. One is unaware of the streets, trees and people whereas the other is alert to both detail and novelty. The person at play shares with the strolling man his openness to the surrounding world. He has 'free attention'. The fourth characteristic of play, then, is its invitation to the possibilities inherent in things and events. It's the freedom to notice seemingly irrelevant detail.

The fifth characteristic of play, and the one underlying all others, is its voluntary nature. The player is free from environmental threats and urgent needs. Play behaviour is self-initiated. The sulky child forced to 'play' a maths game by his teacher is not really at play.

Source: BRUNER, J., JOLLY, A. and SYLVA, K. (eds) (1976) *Play: its role in development and evolution* (ch. 24). Harmondsworth: Penguin.

The fruits of play stem from its characteristics outlined above. The person who plays with objects and actions gains practice in assembling them in unusual ways. He pays attention to their details and possibilities. Because play's 'low risk' nature allows for experiment and reduces frustration, he sustains activity over a long period of time. [Writers in this field have often] argued that the animal with a rich history of play has prepared himself to be an 'opportunist'. He is able to solve the problems he encounters in both an organized and flexible way.

The work to be described investigates the relationship between play and the solving of mechanical problems. There is a long and rich literature on the ways that humans and other creatures go about solving such problems. The chimpanzee Sultan was an early star in the field because of his clever solutions to the problems set before him by Köhler (1925). When a banana was placed beyond his reach outside his cage, Sultan grabbed a stick and used it as a rake. If the sticks in the cage were too short to reach the banana, Sultan joined together two bamboo sticks (one end telescoped into the other), thereby constructing a tool long enough to reach the goal. Köhler attributed Sultan's success at both the single and double stick problems to *sudden insight* into the functional relations inherent in the problem situation. In other words, Köhler saw no need to study the relation between problem solving and *prior* experience because of his claim that the solution derived from the perceptual present.

Others thought differently. Birch (1945) argued that insight such as Sultan's depended on the animal's prior experience with sticks. Sultan's clever acts might have been the consequence of prior manipulation of sticks and not sudden 'perceptual re-organization of the visual field'. Birch experimented with six young chimpanzees by presenting them the single-stick-as-rake problem. Unlike Sultan, detailed histories of these chimps were on hand and only one of them, Jojo, had ever been seen to manipulate sticks. When confronted with an attractive lure outside the test cage, Jojo immediately seized a nearby stick and used it effectively as a rake. Only one other chimp solved the problem, and this animal's solution occurred after he 'accidentally' touched the banana with the stick and noticed it move towards him. The remaining four chimps in Birch's experiment spent thirty minutes in frustrated efforts to get the banana. Following the initial presentation of the problem, all the chimps were provided with sticks in the home cage and they were seen to manipulate them for three days. When tested again, all six chimps solved the stick problem within twenty seconds. Thus it appears that prior experience with sticks led to problem solution whereas lack of it was most often associated with failure.

Reported next are the results of a study in which children were presented with the stick-as-rake problem. The study examines the contribution of play, as well as other forms of prior experience, to the child's subsequent approach to the stick problem.

Method

The task

The child sat at a low table in a quiet room. Directly in front of him, but out of reach, was a transparent plastic box approximately 14 × 8 × 6 inches. The box opened on the side facing the child, although its door was held closed by a 'J' shaped hook. A piece of coloured chalk was placed inside the box and the child's task was to retrieve it.

In front of the child were three bright blue sticks (15 × 1¼ × ¼; 13 × 1¼ × ¼; 5 × 1¼ × ¼ inches) and two 'G' clamps (4¼ inches at longest part). Figure 1 shows the mechanical aspects of the problem. All children were given the following instructions:

See the coloured chalk? That's the prize in a game you're going to play. Your job is to figure out a way to get the chalk. If you do, you can take it home and keep it. You can take as much time as you wish to play the game and can use any object you think will help you. There's only one rule to the game. You can't get out of your chair.

The sticks and clamps were the only objects within the child's reach. The box was placed at a distance such that the longest stick would not reach it. The straightforward solution to the problem is, of course, for the child to construct an elongated tool by rigidly joining two long sticks with a clamp. He needs such a tool to open the latch and rake the chalk towards him.

The adult sat quietly at the table with a stop-watch and notepad on his lap. Each child worked at his own pace, although the adult gave hints under the following circumstances: (a) if a child got up from the chair and walked toward the door, (b) if a child ignored the problem for at least one minute, e.g., stared at hands in lap, sang a song, gazed out of the window, (c) if a child repeatedly asked to leave. Hints were standardized and given in the following sequence.

#1   Have you used everything you can think of that might help you?
#2   Can you think of a way that you can use the clamp to help you?

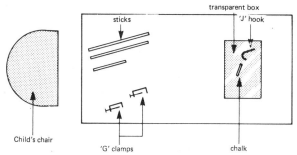

Figure 1   Schematic view of the task

#3   Can you think of a way that you can use both the clamp and the sticks to help you?

#4   You could clamp the two long sticks together and make a longer stick.

#5   I will hold these two sticks together here. Can you clamp them tightly together with this clamp? (Direct physical assistance given if child unable to follow this instruction.)

Subjects

There were 180 children tested in the two experiments that follow. All participants were tested at the day-care centres they attend in towns surrounding Boston. With a very few exceptions, children were middle-class and white.

Experiment 1: treatment conditions

In this experiment, we compare three kinds of experience prior to presentation of the stick problem. There were thirty-six children in each treatment condition, six boys and six girls at 3, 4, 5 years of age. The treatments are summarized in Table 1 below.

Table 1   Treatment conditions in Experiment 1

Name	Nature of experience prior to presentation of problem	Duration of prior experience	Manipulation of sticks and clamps?
Play	Adult demonstrates one clamp tightened on to middle of one long stick Child allowed free play with 10 blue sticks and 7 clamps	10 minutes	yes
Observe principle	Adult demonstrates one clamp tightened on to middle of one long stick Adult demonstrates construction of elongated tool by rigidly joining two long sticks with clamps	2 minutes	no
No treatment	Adult demonstrates one clamp tightened on to middle of one long stick	1 minute	no

Experiment 1: results

A *Spontaneous solutions*. The number of children in each group who constructed the tool and used it to retrieve the chalk is shown in Table 2.* These solutions are 'spontaneous' in that the children required no hints from the adult. The various treatments led to different performances ($x^2 = 11.73$, $df = 2$, $p < 0.01$). For example, *play* and *no treatment* are significantly different from one another ($x^2 = 9.32$, $df = 1$, $p < 0.01$).

Table 2   Spontaneous solutions according to treatment condition

	Play	Observe principle	No treatment
Solve	14	15	3
No solve	22	21	33

B *Effective use of hints*. By comparing children in the *play* and *observe principle* groups, it is clear that those given opportunity to play make more effective use of the early hints. Each child received a score (0–5) for the number of hints required to solve the problem. The Mann-Whitney U test, corrected for ties, shows that children in the *play* group required fewer hints than those in the group that observed the principle. ($U = 4.246$, $p < 0.01$).

C *Various approaches to the problem as a function of treatment*. A most suggestive finding of the study is that the various treatments prior to presentation of the problem led children to approach the task in different ways. When confronted with the chalk in the distant box, the children who played first were eager to begin, continuous in their efforts to solve the problem, and flexible in their hypotheses. In contrast, children who observed the principle first were prone to an 'all or nothing' approach.

Children chose a variety of means for retrieving the chalk, some more complex than others. In analysing problem-solving behaviour, we confined ourselves to the child's use of hands. If a behaviour that involved the hands seemed directed towards the goal, we called it a *means* towards the end of chalk retrieval.

Table 3 lists the most common means. Its categories encompass about 80 per cent of the children's manual responses.

Table 4 shows the total number of all responses (according to treatment condition) made by children when presented with the problem. These include goal-directed actions (here called means) as well as those that are not, e.g., toying with the clamp, stacking the sticks in a pile, or arranging the sticks to form alphabet patterns on the table.

* One-way analysis of variance showed that there were no significant differences in the times it took children to solve the problem or to construct the tool. Differences among groups appear in frequencies of solvers in each group.

Table 3   Six means to obtain goal (chalk)

Means	Description	Object Configuration (if any)
I	Use of hands/arm to attain goal	
II	Use of a single object as tool to extend the arm. (This is always one stick or clamp.)	
III	Use of two unco-ordinated tools. (Usually child held stick in either hand.)	
IV	Assembly and use of an elongated but disjointed tool construction. (Usually child used one stick to push the other forward.)	
V	Assembly and use of rigidly jointed tool but one which is not sufficiently elongated.	
VI	Assembly and use of an elongated tool consisting of two long sticks, rigidly joined by clamp at point of overlap.	

Table 4   Total number of (a) responses and (b) goal-directed responses in each group

	Play	*Observe principle*	*No treatment*
Total number of all manual responses	68 mean = 1.89	48 mean = 1.33	51 mean = 1.42
Total number of goal-directed manual responses	62 mean = 1.72 N = 36	31 mean = 0.86 N = 36	33 mean = 0.92 N = 36

Although the children who had played first appeared slightly more active in the problem-solving situation, the differences among groups are not statistically significant (two-way analysis of variance, age × treatment: $F_{treatment} = 2.34$, $df = 2$). The groups are notably different, however, when we look at goal-directed responses. Children given a prior chance to play are significantly more goal-directed (two-way analysis of variance, age × treatment: $F_{treatment} = 7.27$, $df = 2$, $p < 0.01$) once the problem is presented.

The data of Table 4 indicate that a playful experience prior to problem-solving encourages children towards more goal-directed behaviour. It does more than that, however. The six means described in Table 3 comprise a hierarchically ordered sequence. Children whose prior experience consisted of play observation of the principle worked their way 'up' from simple to more complex means. In contrast, children in the control group chose means in an apparently random order. Both play and observation of the principle led children to approach the problem in an orderly (simple to complex) manner; play, however, produced more goal-directed behaviour than observing the principle.

It is interesting to note the number of children in each group who 'opted out' or 'opted into' solving the problem. Table 5 shows the number of children in each group who demonstrated at least one goal-directed behaviour. Comparing children in the *play* and *observe principle* groups, it is clear that the latter tend to 'opt out' more frequently (Fisher exact test, $p < 0.04$).

Table 5   Frequency in each group of children who demonstrate at least one means

	Play	*Observe principle*	*No treatment*
Use one or more means	28	21	23
Absence of means	8	15	13

Table 6   Frequency of children in each group who begin with simple means
(I–II) or complex means (III–VI)

	Play	Observe principle	No treatment
Begin simple (Means I–II)	21	9	16
Begin complex (Means III–VI)	7	12	7

Although the *play* children characteristically attempt solution, they
tend to begin their problem-solving efforts with simple means, e.g., using
the arm or just one stick. Table 6 shows the number of children in each
group whose first attempt at solution was Means I or II, contrasted with
those whose initial means was III, IV, V, or VI. (Note that children who
show no means at all have been eliminated from analyses that follow in
Tables 6, 7, 8.) Comparison between the *play* and *observe principle* groups
shows that the former tend to begin with simple means whereas the latter
begin with complex ones that include at least two objects ($x^2 = 5.22$,
$df = 1, p < 0.05$).

It has been shown that the *play* children engage in more goal-directed
behaviour, yet they begin with simple means. How do they manage to
solve the problem? They do so by using means of increasing complexity,
step-by-step. We define 'learners' as those children who begin lower than
Means III but eventually reach Means IV or higher. This means that they
began *at best* with one stick but reached a means that includes two
co-ordinated objects. 'Non-learners' are of two types: those who remain at
the level of simple means or those who begin with very complex ones.
Table 7 shows the number of 'learners' in each group. Again, comparing
play and *observe principle* groups we find more 'learners' in the former
(Fisher exact test, $p = 0.05$).

Table 7   Frequency of children in each group who are Learners and
Non-learners

	Play	Observe principle	No treatment
Learners	12	4	1
Non-learners	16	17	22

To complete the examination of differences between *play* and *observe
principle* groups, we focused only on children who solved the problem
(without hints) and then counted the number in each group whose first
goal-directed action was the correct one. We called these children 'immediate solvers' and found significantly more of them in the *observe principle*
group than in the *play* group ($x^2 = 4.44$, $df = 1, p < 0.05$). Table 8 shows
again that the children who had observed are of the 'all or nothing'
variety. They tend to opt out of the problem or go directly to the solution.

Table 8 Frequency of children in each group who are Immediate and Eventual solvers

	Play	*Observe principle*	*No treatment*
Immediate solvers	3	9	2
Eventual solvers	11	6	1

On the other hand, children allowed to play reach solution more often by the step-by-step route.

Experiment 2: treatment conditions

The second experiment holds constant duration of prior experience and once again varies the nature of the experience prior to presentation of the stick problem described in Experiment 1. Table 9 describes its treatment conditions.

Table 9 Treatment conditions in Experiment 2

Name	*Nature of experience prior to presentation of the problem*	*Duration of prior experience*	*Manipulation of sticks and clamps?*
Observe components	Adult and child sit at table and adult creates a 'puppet show' in which sticks and clamps become characters in a drama. Mr Clamp and his brothers 'eat' members of the Stick Family by clamping their 'jaws' around the 'waists' of the Sticks.	10 minutes	no
Training on components	Training consists of demonstration, specific commands (e.g., 'Turn the handle the other way') and verbal encouragement (e.g., 'You're getting it tightened; don't give up')	10 minutes	yes

As in the previous experiment, there were thirty-six children in each group, six boys and six girls at ages 3, 4, 5 years. To test for the effect of configurational richness on subsequent problem-solving, children in both groups of Experiment 2 were yoked to the *play* children in Experiment 1. An example of the yoking will clarify. Subject #31 in the *play* group was a five-year-old girl named Ginny. She made five distinct configurations in her ten minutes of free play. Three of them consisted of simple clampings

of a single clamp to one stick. Two of Ginny's play configurations were
more complex: twice she clamped two sticks together to make a longer,
double-stick object. Her yoke mates in the two conditions of Experiment 2
were five-year-old girls like Ginny. They experienced the identical configurations constructed by Ginny – except that one of the new girls
observed the adult build Ginny's configurations while the other new girl
was trained by the adult to construct Ginny's configurations. One might
say that the child in the *observe components* condition watched Ginny
whereas the child in the *training on components* condition was instructed by
the adult to copy Ginny's configurations.

One of the questions asked in Experiment 2 concerned the effect of
richness of configuration on subsequent problem-solving performance. If
all three children in the yoked trio experienced complex configurations,
would their performance be similar to one another and different from the
performances of another trio who had experienced simple configurations?

Experiment 2: results

A *Spontaneous solution.* Table 10 shows that the two groups did not differ
significantly in the number of children who spontaneously solved the
problem.

Table 10   Frequency of spontaneous solutions according to treatment condition
in Experiment 2

	Observe components	*Training on components*
Solve	6	7
No solve	30	29

Although the two treatments produced roughly equal numbers of
solvers, there is a slight trend showing that children who received training
made better use of hints. In general, however, the children in the two
conditions of the second experiment acted similarly.

B *Various approaches to the problem as a function of treatment.* Another way that
children in the two groups are similar is in their characteristic approach to
the problem. They both tend to start with simple means, e.g., Means I or
II. Although there were about the same number of 'learners', in the two
groups, there were many fewer than in the *play* condition of the first
experiment. Those who did discover the solution did so in the 'eventual'
style rather than going 'immediately' to the correct solution.

C *Effect of configurational richness.* Did the yoking make a difference? More
precisely, were the scores of children in the two yoked conditions correlated with the scores of their yoke mates in the *play* group of Experiment 1?
Each child's score for number of hints (0–5) was correlated with the score
of his yoke mate in the free play condition. The correlations were all

statistically significant. Spearman rank correlations between *play* and *observe components* were $rs = 0.673$, $p < 0.05$; between *play* and *training on components* $rs = 0.672$, $p < 0.05$. We conclude that the richness of the configuration to which the child is exposed affects his subsequent performance in problem-solving.

D *Comparison between Experiments 1 and 2*. Having established that the two groups in Experiment 2 were very similar in problem-solving performance, we compare them to the *play* group of Experiment 1. Table 11 shows the number of spontaneous solvers in both experiments. It is difficult to make direct statistical comparisons between the two groups since most tests required independence that the yoking procedure does not allow.

Table 11 Frequency of spontaneous solutions in Experiments 1 and 2

	Play	Observe principle	No treatment	Observe components (yoked to play)	Training on components (yoked to play)
Solve	14	15	3	6	7
No solve	22	21	33	30	29

However, one can compare the two groups in the second experiment with the earlier *play* group by assigning scores for number of hints (0–5) and then applying to them tests for matched pairs. *Play* is superior to *observe components* (Wilcoxon test for two matched samples, $T = 41.5$, $p < 0.05$, two-tailed and also superior to *training on components*, $T = 90.0$, $p < 0.05$, two-tailed).* This is an especially interesting finding because the three children in each trio experienced identical configurations. One 'invented' a configuration in free play, one observed construction of the same configuration, and one was trained to construct it by the adult. Only the behaviour of the *play* child, of course, was self-initiated.

Discussion and conclusion

Which aspects of the *play* treatment contributed to its efficacy as preparation for problem-solving? Clearly manipulation of the actual sticks and clamps will not, by itself, lead to problem solution. In the training session of Experiment 2 the children who handled the materials (but not with their own plans of operation) did not perform well when later presented

* Some caution must be exercised in proclaiming the *play* children superior to those in Experiment 2. Although children were yoked on age and sex, they were not yoked on intelligence since these data were not available. However, although it's true that a very bright child in the second experiment might have been constrained by being exposed to a barren stick-and-clamp configuration, a duller child might well have been helped by exposure to an especially rich one. Children were randomly assigned to their yoke mates.

with the problem. Nor was a long experience with the adult (10 minutes as in the original *play* condition) sufficient to explain the results since both groups in Experiment 2 experienced this and yet they did not perform as well on the problem.

We look for clues to the benefits of play in the characteristic approach demonstrated by the children who had played prior to testing. Although there are no differences in total number of responses made by children in the various groups, the *play* children engage in many more goal-directed ones. *Play* children, moreover, tend to begin with simple means but progress systematically towards complex ones. In other words, a failed attempt (e.g., using one stick to try to reach the box) did not frustrate them. They neither persevered nor gave up. Used to playing, they more often used the information from a failure to arrive at the next hypothesis, which was usually to combine two sticks. But play produced more than enthusiasm; the *play* children were productive and organized in their problem-solving as well.

The children with prior play experience did as well in solving the problem as those children who had been shown the principle of making a tool appropriate to the task. It is a nice question to ask why those children who had been shown the principle did not outperform the players. In a sense, their problem was easier: to apply a general principle in a specific task. The playing children had also to *discover* the principle. Obviously the experiment cannot shed direct light on this issue, for it was not designed with it in mind. All that can be said is that it might be worthwhile in future research to explore whether play with the application of general principles to specific problems is of help in problem-solving of this order. It may also be the case that observing the application of a principle creates a rather monolithic view of the procedure – with the means–end structure appearing too fixed for easy adaptation to later tasks. If this were the case, then one can understand why some of the observer children did not succeed, and why prior play may have been a real advantage to the other group.

In sum, then, those who play before attempting problem-solving seem to do better for the following reasons. (1) Solving problems required self-initiation and our playing children were the only ones in the experiments whose actions were self-initiated. (2) Tool invention (like other forms of problem-solving) requires serial ordering of the constituent acts involved. The players were the only ones who had an opportunity to explore alternative serial orders. (3) Play reduces the stress of anticipating success and failure. Our players, less stressed, were able to proceed with less frustration and fear of failure – they were more goal-directed. They could benefit from hints and could approach the solution gradually without breaking off. To reiterate the point with which we started, the effect of prior play seems to be not only in combinatorial practice, but also in shifting emphasis in a task from ends to means, from product to process.

References

BIRCH, H. G. (1945) 'The relation of previous experience to insightful problem-solving.' *Journal of Comparative and Physiological Psychology*, **38**, 367–83.

BRUNER, J. S. (1972) 'The nature and uses of immaturity.' *American Psychologist*, **27**, 1–28.

EIBL-EIBESFELDT, I. (1970) *Ethology: the Biology of Behavior*. New York: Holt, Rinehart and Winston.

KOHLER, W. (1925) *The Mentality of Apes*. London: Routledge and Kegan Paul.

MILLER, S. (1973) 'Ends, means and galumphing: some leitmotifs of play.' *American Anthropologist*, **75**, 87–98.

REYNOLDS, P. C. (1976) 'Play, language and human evolution', in BRUNER, J., JOLLY, A. and SYLVA, K. (eds) *Play: its role in development and evolution*. Harmondsworth: Penguin.

WHITE, R. W. (1959) 'Motivation reconsidered: the concept of competence.' *Psychological Review*, **66**, 297–330.

1.6 Characteristics of maternal and paternal behavior in traditional and non-traditional Swedish families

Michael E. Lamb, Ann M. Frodi, Majt Frodj and Carl-Philip Hwang

[. . .] The descriptive study of developing parent–child relationships has become extremely popular in the last decade. Many of the relevant studies have focused on the development of infant–mother and infant–father attachments (e.g., Cohen and Campos, 1974; Kotelchuck, 1976; Lamb, 1977a and b). Others have been designed to specify characteristic differences between maternal and paternal behavior (Lamb, 1976; 1977b; Yogman *et al.*, 1977). The present study was designed to explore the effects of nontraditional family patterns on maternal and paternal interactional styles.

Several researchers have shown that mothers and fathers in traditional families (i.e., families in which mothers are primary caretakers and fathers are minimally involved in childcare) interact with their infants in characteristically distinct ways. When engaged in face-to-face interaction with young infants, for example, mothers tend to provide rhythmic stimulation interspersed with attempts to contain the infants' arousal within tolerable limits. Fathers, by contrast, provide more unpredictable, arhythmic, and physical stimulation in this context (Yogman *et al.*, 1977). Home observations of seven- to 13-months-olds have revealed similar differences: fathers engaged in more physically stimulating and unpredictable play than mothers do whereas mothers are more likely to initiate conventional games (Lamb, 1976, 1977b). Fathers are more likely to hold their infants to play with them, whereas mothers are more likely to pick up their infants in the course of caretaking routines (Lamb, 1976, 1977b; Belsky, 1979). Other studies have confirmed the association of fathers with play – especially robust, physically-stimulating play (Clarke-Stewart, 1978; Parke and Tinsley, 1981). In addition, mothers are more likely to smile at and vocalize to their infants than fathers are (Yogman, 1982).

Recently, researchers have begun speculating about the origins of these characteristic differences in behavioral style. Some have suggested that the behavioral differences reflect biologically-based sex differences, whereas others see them as products of the differential socialization of men and women (Brazelton, 1977; Lamb and Goldberg, 1982). Unfortunately (for researchers), biological gender and caretaking role are usually confounded, making it difficult to determine whether mothers (fathers) be-

Source: LAMB, M. E., FRODI, A. M., FRODJ, M. and HWANG, C.-P. (1982) *International Journal of Behavioral Development*, **5**, pp. 131–41.

have as they do because they are women (men) or because they are primary caretakers (non-caretakers). However, by studying nontraditional families – that is, families in which fathers are more and mothers less involved in childcare – it may be possible to assess the relative importance of biological and social influences on behavioral style. If the characteristic behavioral differences disappear when fathers are unusually involved in childcare, for example, it would suggest that the differences were sociocultural rather than biological in origin. Two recent studies have followed this logic in attempts to explore the origins of sex differences in parental behavior.

In the first study, Field (1978) compared the behavior of primary caretaking fathers, primary caretaking mothers, and 'secondary' caretaking fathers engaged in face-to-face interaction with their four-month-old infants. Field reported that the primary caretaking fathers and mothers emitted more smiling, imitative grimaces, and high-pitched imitative vocalizations than did secondary caretaking fathers, whereas the primary and secondary caretaking fathers engaged in more 'poking' and game playing and less holding of the infants' limbs than did primary caretaking mothers. Unfortunately, only three minutes of behavior was recorded per subject and no secondary caretaking mothers were studied, making it impossible to assess the effects of gender and parental role in a factorial design.

Analyses of data gathered in earlier observations of the present subjects revealed that parental gender was a much more important predictor of behavioral style than was parental role (Lamb *et al.*, 1982a, 1982b). Analyses of data gathered when the infants were eight months of age yielded especially clear results (Lamb *et al.*, 1982b). Mothers were more likely to hold, tend to display affection toward, smile at, and vocalize to their infants than fathers were, regardless of relative involvement in caretaking. The same results were obtained whether we considered involved fathers to be those who had been primary caretakers for at least one (the average was nearly three) of the preceding eight months, or those who had been primary caretaker in the three months immediately preceding the eight-month home observations. A major goal of the present study was to see whether the same conclusions were suggested by analyses of the parents' behavior when their infants were 16 months old.

A second goal was to attempt a replication of several unexpected results obtained in the earlier analyses. On five of the six major measures employed, the less involved mothers (i.e., those whose partners were highly involved) had the highest scores. These results suggested that the less involved mothers attempted to compensate for their daily unavailability by being especially active with their children when at home, while the highly involved fathers happily took breaks when their wives were present. These findings and this explanation were consistent with those reported by Pedersen and his colleagues (1982), but unfortunately the reverse pattern was evident on analyses of the frequency of play (total) and of several of the subcategories of play. Consequently, it seemed important to determine whether either of the patterns was evident in later observations of these subjects.

Method

Subjects

The subjects were 51 Swedish couples and their firstborn 16-month-old infants (± 2 weeks). The families were all residents of Göteborg, Sweden, and were recruited prenatally through childbirth preparation classes to take part in a longitudinal study to end when their children were 16 months old. Nontraditional families ($n = 17$) were defined as those in which fathers had spent more than one month ($x = 2.82$ months) at home alone with the baby as primary caretaker. These fathers were designated. Highly Involved, and their partners were labelled Less Involved. Most of these fathers (14) took their leave beginning when their infants were five months old. Traditional families ($n = 34$) were defined as those in which fathers took little if any parental leave ($x = 10$ days) and were never primary caretakers. These men were considered Less Involved and their partners were designated Highly Involved. The average age of the mothers at the time of their children's births was 27.2 years; the average age of the fathers was 30.2 years. All of the families were middle to upper class in socio-economic characteristics. There were no significant group differences in maternal and paternal age or on the Education and Occupation Scales of Hollingshead's Four Factor Index of Social Status (1975). One couple divorced, another family left the city, and four observational records were lost due to technical malfunctions. Thus the present data are derived from observations of 45 families (15 non-traditional, 30 traditional). There were 26 girls and 19 boys.

Procedure

The families were all observed at home at a time convenient to the parents. Since we wanted to conduct observations at times when both parents were present, most took place in the evenings: the average one involved 115 minutes ($SD = 12.40$ minutes) of observation. The parents were asked to behave as naturally as possible, and were free to leave the room at will, although they were encouraged to remain in the same room as the child most of the time. Following Lamb's (1976, 1977b) procedure, each visit was made by two investigators. One of them, the Visitor, interacted with parents and the infant in an effort to make them feel comfortable about being observed. The other investigator, the Observer, retreated to a corner of the room and recorded an account of the social interaction using a keyboard-recorder device that automatically encoded the time of each entry (Stephenson *et al.*, 1975). The observer recorded each time an adult *picked up and held* or *played* with the infant, as well as the type of play or the purpose of the hold, using Lamb's categories and definitions. The observer also noted when the hold or bout of play ended, so that we could obtain measures of the duration of the activities. Unfortunately, there was much more disagreement about the termination of activities than about their initiation so the duration measures were not adequately reliable ($r <$ 0.75). All our results are based on analyses of frequency measures. This is not problematic because Lamb (1976, 1977b) obtained similar results from analyses of duration and frequency measures of play and physical contact.

For descriptive and analytic purposes, we distinguished among seven reasons for *holding* the infant. *Caretaking* holds were cases when the infant was picked up to feed it or carry it to or from a changing table, high chair, bath, etc. *Discipline* was coded when the child was moved away from some forbidden site (e.g., electrical outlets, ashtrays) or activity. *Play* was coded when the child was picked up simply for social interaction; *affection* when the child was picked up to cuddle, kiss, or hug it; *soothing* when the child was distressed and thus needed comforting; and *respondent* when the adult picked up the child in response to a clear request to be held. If none of these reasons applied, the hold was counted under a miscellaneous category, *other*.

As far as *play* was concerned, we distinguished among seven types of play. There were three categories of play that usually involved toys: *co-ordinate* play, when the child and adult engaged in a reciprocal game in which each took turns (e.g., alternately adding blocks to a tower); *parallel* play, in which the child and adult played side-by-side on similar activities with little direct interaction (e.g., parent and child each built separate block structures); and *stimulus* play, which involved attempts by the parent to stimulate the infant and attract/hold its attention. Two types of play involved physical stimulation: *minor physical*, which involved limited degrees of physical contact (e.g., tickling the infant or pretending to nibble it); and *physical*, which involved robust, vigorous, physical stimulation (e.g., rough and tumble play). *Conventional* play involved ritualized activities like peek-a-boo and pat-a-cake. Any other types of play were classified in a miscellaneous category, *idiosyncratic*.

Four other types of parental behavior (in addition to play and holding) were recorded. *Affectionate* behaviors involved kissing, hugging, or cuddling. *Vocalizing* was recorded each time the parent spoke to or made vocal noises directed to the infant. *Touch* was scored when the adult touched the infant with his/her hand. *Tend* was scored whenever the adult engaged in some form of caretaking – wiping the nose, feeding, burping, etc.

Reliability

All observations were conducted by two observers. Prior to conducting home observations for the project, they trained to criterion agreement

($r > 0.80$) using first videotapes and then live observations of infants and parents who were not in the study. During the course of the study, the observers periodically undertook reliability checks during which the two simultaneously recorded the interaction. A total of eight such checks (18% of the total) were conducted. As noted earlier, the termination of play of physical contact was not reliably recorded, but reliability regarding the frequency of each behavior or event consistently remained above $r = 0.80$. Thus all analyses are based on frequency measures.

Results

To control for variations in the length of the observations, all scores were converted into rates per hour of observation before analysis. The primary analyses were designed to assess the effects of parent sex and relative involvement in caretaking by means of two-way ANOVAs with Sex of Parent and Relative Involvement as the two factors. Means, standard deviations, and the results of these analyses are presented in Table 1. Inspection of this table reveals significant effects for Parent Sex on five of the six major measures. All differences were in the predicted direction: regardless of their relative involvement in caretaking, mothers were more likely to vocalize, display affection toward, engage in caretaking, touch, and hold their infants than fathers were. Although the difference was not significant, fathers were more likely to play with their infants. Analyses of the subcategories within the measures hold and play were less informative: mothers were more likely to hold their infants to soothe them or for 'other' reasons than fathers were, but there were no significant differences in the types of play initiated by mothers and fathers.

There were no significant main effects for relative involvement on any of the major measures or on any of the subcategories within the measures of play and hold. Further, there were statistical interactions on only one major and one subcategory measure. Involved mothers vocalized to their infants more and played less than Less Involved mothers did, whereas Involved fathers vocalized less and played more than Less Involved fathers.

Inspection of group means revealed that the Involved mothers scored highest on all six of the major measures ($p < 0.05$ by sign test). However, there was no apparent tendency for Involved fathers to score lower than the Less Involved fathers on the play subcategory measures while the Involved mothers scored higher than the Less Involved mothers (cf., Lamb *et al.*, 1982b). Parental behavior was unaffected by the infants' sex.

Discussion

These analyses confirm that parents' sex has a much more powerful influence on parental behavior than does their relative involvement in

Table 1 Effects of parent sex and involvement in caretaking on parental behavior

Behavior	Mothers		Fathers		Parent (F)	Involvement (F)	Interaction (F)
	Involved	Less involved	Involved	Less involved			
Vocalize	47.55 (26.53)	32.86 (14.94)	27.17 (20.47)	33.11 (26.53)	3.57[b]		3.75[c]
Tend	1.73 (1.15)	1.08 (0.83)	0.93 (1.02)	0.92 (0.85)	4.85[a]		
Affection	1.95 (2.26)	1.12 (1.25)	0.66 (1.16)	0.63 (1.03)	5.83[a]		
Touch	3.23 (2.40)	2.27 (1.97)	1.53 (1.35)	1.87 (1.75)	5.28[a]		
Play (total)	3.53 (2.49)	2.74 (2.32)	3.01 (2.82)	3.31 (2.32)			
Stimulus	2.38 (2.02)	1.61 (1.56)	1.96 (1.34)	2.02 (1.54)			
Parallel	0.11 (0.31)	0.07 (0.18)	0.04 (0.13)	0.10 (0.24)			
Coordinate	0.38 (0.46)	0.18 (0.25)	0.39 (0.51)	0.37 (0.43)			
Minor Physical	0.47 (0.57)	0.48 (0.60)	0.57 (0.83)	0.44 (0.68)			
Physical	0.14 (0.30)	0.21 (0.42)	0.42 (0.85)	0.22 (0.49)			
Conventional	0.33 (0.59)	0.54 (1.06)	0.42 (0.84)	0.51 (0.81)			
Idiosyncratic	0.17 (0.50)	0.04 (0.14)	0.04 (0.14)	0.05 (0.21)			
Hold (total)	3.82 (2.39)	3.81 (1.67)	2.53 (1.59)	3.12 (2.44)	3.85[a]		
Caretaking	2.63 (8.64)	1.29 (1.04)	0.90 (1.18)	1.01 (1.23)			2.63[c]
Play	0.50 (0.43)	0.88 (0.96)	0.98 (1.03)	0.75 (0.94)			
Affection	1.12 (2.91)	0.83 (0.87)	0.55 (0.53)	0.40 (0.62)			
Discipline	0.33 (0.70)	0.23 (0.34)	0.22 (0.69)	0.28 (0.51)			
Soothing	0.78 (1.16)	0.61 (0.81)	0.26 (0.27)	0.37 (0.53)	4.09[a]		
Respondent	0.02 (0.10)	0.0 (0.0)	0.0 (0.0)	0.02 (0.09)			
Other	1.01 (1.13)	0.78 (1.12)	0.44 (0.53)	0.59 (0.70)	3.20[b]		

Note In all cases, $df = 1,86$. Standard deviations are presented in parentheses. Means represent rates per hour of observation.
[a] $p < 0.02$ by 1-tailed test; [b] $p < 0.05$ by 1-tailed test; [c] $p < 0.10$ by 2-tailed test.

childcare. Specifically, five of six measures revealed significant effects for parent sex, and on only one was there a significant interaction with relative involvement. On none of the measures was there a significant main effect for relative involvement. Furthermore, all of the significant effects for parents' sex revealed differences similar to those observed in traditional American families (Lamb, 1981; Yogman, 1982) and in previous observations of these traditional and nontraditional Swedish families (Lamb *et al.*, 1982b). In all cases, mothers (regardless of their relative involvement in childcare) vocalized to, displayed affection toward, touched, tended to (engaged in caretaking), and held their infants more than fathers did. Not all measures, however, revealed the expected differences between mothers and fathers. Unlike American fathers, these Swedish men did not initiate more play (especially physically stimulating and idiosyncratic play) than mothers; nor did they hold their infants predominantly to play with them.

Overall, these results suggest that the differences between maternal and paternal behavior are remarkably robust, remaining stable inter- and intra-culturally despite variations in the relative involvement of mothers and fathers in childcare. This suggests either that these behavioral differences are biologically-based (Brazelton, 1977) or that they are deeply internalized during years of socialization. We will not be able to evaluate these alternative explanations until we are able to study parents who were themselves reared in a nonsextyped fashion and assign primary parental responsibilities to the fathers. Unfortunately, such families are very rare – which may be significant in itself. Although the present subjects (especially, but not only, the nontraditional families) divided household and childcare responsibilities more equitably than traditional American parents do, they were all raised in a sextyped society, and in every case mothers had major responsibility for childcare. Further, even though the Involved fathers had stayed home as primary caretakers for an average of three months, this occurred several months before these observations took place. In the intervening time, the mothers were primary caretakers. This, of course, limits the types of conclusions we can draw from these analyses. At the very least, however, these findings suggest that gender differences in parental behavior are much less amenable to social/experiential influences than many psychologists currently believe (Field, 1978; Lamb and Goldberg, 1982; Nash and Feldman 1981), although we are not yet able to say whether gender differences in parental style have some biological basis.

On the other hand, it is possible that the sex-typical behavior of these parents was accentuated by the fact that they were being observed. Berman (1980) has reported that American men and women behave in a more sextyped fashion in public contexts, and it is conceivable, therefore, that the parents in this study responded to the observers in the same way. By its nature, this possibility is hard to assess empirically, but its viability is weakened by the fact that fathers did not engage in much of the vigorous playful interaction which is viewed as typically masculine or paternal.

Whereas these findings were consistent with those obtained in observations of these parents when the infants were eight months old, some of the findings at 16 months differed from those obtained in the earlier observations. Specifically, our earlier observations, like those of Pedersen *et al.* (1982), indicated that less involved mothers (the partners of primary caretaking fathers and employed mothers respectively) were most active when observed with their children. We did not obtain similar findings in the present study. On the contrary; we found that the more involved mothers attained the highest scores on all of the major behavioral measures. Our failure to replicate the earlier findings is probably attributable to the fact that our assessment of low or high involvement referred to behavior in the first year of the infants' lives, rather than the recent allocation of parental responsibilities. It is understandable that employed mothers and mothers who are currently leaving their infants with their husbands daily should attempt to compensate for their daily unavailability by being especially interactive when they are at home. The less involved mothers in the present study had no need to compensate in this way because, like the more involved mothers, most were with their infants all day. However, while this might explain why the less involved mothers were not most active, it does not explain why the more involved mothers (i.e., those who had been primary caretakers throughout their infants' lives) should be most active instead. Perhaps it is because these women are the most traditional, and hence tend to emit more of the parental behaviors which we know from previous studies to characterize mothers more than fathers (Lamb, 1981; Parke and Tinsley, 1981; Yogman, 1982). This would at least explain the tendencies on five of the six measures: it would not explain the equivalent trend in the frequency of play, which should be the predominant behavior of traditional fathers.

References

BELSKY, J. (1979) 'Mother-father-infant interaction: a naturalistic observational study.' *Developmental Psychology*, **15**, 601–7.

BERMAN, P. W. (1980) 'Are women more responsive than men to the young? A review of developmental and situational variables.' *Psychological Bulletin*, **88**, 668–95.

BRAZELTON, T. B. (1977) 'Mother-father-infant interaction.' Presentation to the Conference on Family Interaction, Educational Testing Service, Princeton, NJ, December.

CLARKE-STEWART, K. A. (1978) 'And daddy makes three: the father's impact on mother and young children.' *Child Development*, **49**, 466–75.

COHEN, L. J. and CAMPOS, J. J. (1974) 'Father, mother, and stranger as elicitors of attachment behaviors in infancy.' *Developmental Psychology*, **81**, 207–17.

FIELD, T. (1978) 'Interaction patterns of primary versus secondary caretaker fathers.' *Developmental Psychology*, **14**, 183–4.

HOLLINGSHEAD, A. B. (1975) 'The four factor index of social status.' Unpublished manuscript (Department of Sociology, Yale University, New Haven, CT 06520).

KOTELCHUCK, M. (1976) 'The infant's relationship to the father: experimental evidence', in LAMB, M. E. (ed.) *The Role of the Father in Child Development*. New York: Wiley.

LAMB, M. E. (1976) 'Interactions between eight-month-old children and their fathers and mothers', in LAMB, M. E. (ed.) *The Role of the Father in Child Development*. New York: Wiley.

LAMB, M. E. (1977a) 'The development of mother-infant and father-infant attachments in the second year of life'. *Developmental Psychology*, **13**, 637–48.

LAMB, M. E. (1977b) 'Father-infant and mother-infant interaction in the first year of life'. *Child Development*, **48**, 167–81.

LAMB, M. E. (1981) 'The development of father-infant relationships', in LAMB, M. E. (ed.) *The Role of the Father in Child Development* (revised edition). New York: Wiley.

LAMB, M. E., FRODI, A. M., HWANG, C.-P., FRODI, M. and STEINBERG, J. (1982a) 'Effect of gender and caretaking role on parent-infant attachment', in EMDE, R. N. and HARMON, R. J. (eds) *The Development of Attachment and Affiliative Systems*. New York: Plenum.

LAMB, M. E., FRODI, A. M., HWANG, C.-P., FRODI, M. and STEINBERG, J. (1982b) 'Mother-and-father-infant interaction involving play and holding in traditional and non-traditional Swedish families.' *Developmental Psychology*, **18**, 215–21.

LAMB, M. E. and GOLDBERG, W. A. (1982) 'The father-child relationship: a synthesis of biological, evolutionary, and social perspectives', in HOFFMAN, L. W., GANDELMAN, R. and SCHIFFMAN, H. R. (eds), *Parenting: its causes and consequences*. Hillsdale, NJ: Erlbaum.

NASH, S. C. and FELDMAN, S. S. (1981) 'Sex-role and sex-related attributions: constancy and change across the family life cycle', in LAMB, M. E. and BROWN, A. L. (eds) *Advances in Developmental Psychology*, Vol. 1. Hillside, NJ: Erlbaum.

PARKE, R. E. and TINSLEY, B. A. (1981) 'The father's role in infancy: determinants of involvement in caregiving and play', in LAMB, M. E. (ed.) *The Role of the Father in Child Development* (revised edition). New York: Wiley.

PEDERSEN, F. A., CAIN, R. L. and ZASLOW, M. (1982) 'Variation in infant experience associated with alternative family roles', in LAOSA, L. and SIGAL, I. (eds) *Families as Learning Environments for Children*. New York: Plenum.

STEPHENSON, G. R., SMITH, D. P. and ROBERTS, T. W. (1975) 'The SSR system: an open-format event recording system with computerized transcription.' *Behavior Research Methods and Instrumentation*, **7**, 497–515.

YOGMAN, M.-W. (1982) 'Development of the father-infant relationship', in FITZGERALD, H., LESTER, B. and YOGMAN, M.-W. (eds) *Theory and Research in Behavioral Pediatrics, Vol. 1*. Yew York: Plenum.

YOGMAN, M., DIXON, S., TRONICK, E., ALS, H. and BRAZELTON, T. B. (1977) 'The goals and structure of face-to-face interaction between infants and fathers.' Paper presented to the Society for Research in Child Development, New Orleans, March.

Section Two

Learning – theoretical and practical issues

In this section we look at some of the theory and application of ideas about the nature of learning, a subject which has attracted the attention and energies of countless psychologists for decades and continues to provide many puzzles and challenges.

Robert Borger and A. E. M. Seaborne begin the section with an attractive account of some of the classic experimental work of the early Behaviourists and the descriptions and analysis of simple learning situations that were derived from it. The legacy of this work remains in many contemporary accounts of learning.

It is a big step from these comparatively simple situations to the complex learning environment of institutions like schools. Stephen Castles and Wiebke Wustenberg's short account of the secondary element of the Tvind schools in Denmark illustrates a conscious attempt to create an environment of a particular sort based on a model of co-operative learning centred around useful productive work. Concrete experience, rather than books, is the medium through which learning takes place and the knowledge thereby gained is seen, first and foremost, as a tool for improving society. The ideology which supports such a system is quite clear.

Teaching takes place in many aspects of our lives, not merely in schools. Adults teach children; children teach adults; adults teach adults; children teach children. One significant influence on this teaching is (or ought to be) the individual teacher's idea of how it is that people learn. John Parsons, Norman Graham and Terry Honess describe one way of investigating such implicit models of learning and explore in detail how this worked for one particular person. Such an understanding is of relevance to attempts to improve teaching skills, whoever the audience.

The processes of memory are of obvious central significance to the study of learning. Psychologists studying memory have tended to fall into two camps, those searching for the basic mental mechanisms involved by means of closely controlled laboratory experiments and those – perhaps a growing band – who seek to understand the way memory manifests itself in everyday life. Henry Bennett's article straddles both of these by investigating, under controlled and semi-artificial conditions, the memory skills of cocktail waitresses whose work (and income) requires them to be highly accurate in recalling and matching both orders and customers. Though the subject matter may appear trivial at first sight, this article raises some interesting questions about human memory.

Another component part of the puzzle of learning is the concept of intelligence and its relation to thinking. For psychologists a long-standing question has been whether intelligence can be measured, and, if so, how.

W. E. C. Gillham's article charts the changing fortunes of the mental testing movement and provides an interesting critique of the psychometric tradition.

The remaining two articles focus on related areas of learning in action – the early acquisition of language by young children and the nature of the process of learning to read. Catherine Snow is a prominent researcher in the fast changing field of children's language and in this article she focuses on the linguistic environment of the language-learning child – particularly as that is provided by mothers' speech – and language acquisition. Perhaps surprisingly, detailed investigation of this topic has come late, restrained by the belief in a large innate component in linguistic ability. Snow considers the available research on adult speech to children and shows how, in their desire to communicate, they tend to modify their style of speech in consistent ways. Whether or not this facilitates language learning – and if so, how – is a much more difficult question to answer.

The changing emphasis of research can also be seen in Jessie Reid's account of learning to read. The emphasis on visual perception which characterised the 1950s has been replaced by an increasing awareness of the importance of an understanding by the child of the nature of written alphabetic language and its communicative function. This change has brought with it changes in thinking about the ways that reading should be taught, thus nicely illustrating the potential for linking research to practice.

John Chapman

2.1 An analysis of simple learning situations

Robert Borger and A. E. M. Seaborne

One of the authors has a cat that scratches at the kitchen window to be let in – not through the window itself but through a door some distance away. The sequence of events usually runs something like this: cat scratches window – runs to door and waits – door is opened (sometimes) – cat comes in. From here on things are more variable; she may head straight for a comfortable chair, or hang around her plate on the floor, or just sit down and wash.

This cat has another, equally unremarkable characteristic: anyone handling a newspaper is likely to be followed around with much miaowing, purring and rubbing against legs. Quite often the newspaper is subsequently put down on the floor with a plate of food on top of it.

This sort of thing will be familiar to anyone who has ever had a domestic animal. Dogs, even more noticeably than cats, will, over time, develop patterns of behaviour that are in various ways adapted to how things work in their particular surroundings: from 'begging' for biscuits to fetching leads or walking sticks as a preliminary to going for a walk. How do we explain this sort of behaviour?

Suppose that a visitor who has just opened *The Guardian* asks, 'Why is your cat getting so excited?' If we tell him that the paper frequently serves as a kind of feeding mat, he is likely to be quite satisfied with this explanation. Clearly the cat thinks she is going to be fed. What puzzles the visitor is not the general and very familiar fact that repeated experience gives rise to expectations, or that expectations lead to various forms of appropriate behaviour, but simply the way this particular animal is behaving. For this purpose, and in this context, the explanation given is perfectly adequate. But if we are making a study of learning, we may want to ask questions precisely about those familiar facts and relationships in terms of which we just explained the individual case, and which we normally – quite rightly – take for granted. *How* does experience lead to expectation, or expectation to behaviour? And just what is expectation? Since, especially in the case of a cat, expectations may be difficult to identify in their own right, can we perhaps dispense with such an intermediary stage altogether, and simply investigate the relationship between experience and behaviour?

These are general questions, and just to ask them in this form leads very naturally to setting up the inquiry in a corresponding way. Thus we may try to identify and arrange a number of prototypical learning situations,

Source: BORGER, R. and SEABORNE, A. E. M. (1982) *The Psychology of Learning* (2nd edn). Harmondsworth: Penguin.

intended to represent and emphasize features that are common to a wide variety of individual cases – hoping (or assuming) that their study will provide general insights into the 'nature of learning'. Consider two well-known early experiments on animal learning.

Conditioning

The Russian physiologist Pavlov, in the course of investigations on the digestive system in dogs, decided to examine in detail the 'anticipatory' behaviour of his animals. He had noticed that some features of their behaviour which at first occurred only when the dogs were being fed, began to make their appearance when they were *about to be* fed, apparently in response to the feeding preparations. Instead of taking this familiar phenomenon as self-evident and simply labelling it 'expectation of food', he set about a detailed examination of what this expectation amounted to, and on what features of the situation it depended.

Dogs were placed in a harness, in a sound-proof room with constant temperature and constant illumination. The reason for taking these precautions was to ensure that accidental variations of position, noise, etc., would not affect the course of the experiment. A small operation made it possible to tap one of the salivary ducts in the dog's mouth and to obtain an accurate measure of the amount of saliva being secreted. Salivation is one aspect of an animal's eating behaviour and Pavlov singled it out for scrutiny because it was comparatively easy to quantify.

When the animals had acclimatized themselves to the experimental situation, the following sequence of events was introduced. A bell was sounded, and after a short interval, with the bell still sounding, a small measured quantity of dry food was delivered to the animal. The bell–food sequence was presented over and over again. Gradually the amount of saliva produced began to increase as soon as the bell sounded, anticipating the arrival of the food. The animal could now be said to salivate in response to the bell, whereas at the start of the experiment it had not done so.

Pavlov called the presentation of the food the *unconditioned stimulus* (UCS) and the salivation which it evoked the *unconditioned response* (UCR). The repeated pairing of the bell with food turned the originally 'neutral' stimulus into a *conditioned stimulus* (CS) which now evoked salivation as a *conditioned response* (CR). The whole process was called conditioning, now usually known as *classical* or *respondent conditioning*. The essence of conditioning came to be seen as the gradual *transfer* of responses, which at the outset occurred only in conjunction with one stimulus – the UCS – to another, originally neutral, stimulus – the CS; Pavlov and his students examined in great detail the effects of such CS–UCS pairings on experimental subjects, using different conditioned and unconditioned stimuli, varying the relative time of occurrence, duration, intensity, etc.

Changes in the animal's response pattern were observed, but normally did not affect the course of stimulus presentation.

Instrumental conditioning

At about the same time, E. S. Thorndike in America used cats in another simple, though differently structured, learning experiment. He put a hungry cat into a cage, food being available outside and visible through the bars. The cage was so constructed that a given operation, such as the pulling of a loop of wire hanging from the top, or the pressing of a lever, would open the door of the cage. At first the animal would struggle against the sides of the cage, reaching out paws towards the food, biting the bars – i.e., it would behave in a way that we call 'trying to get out', 'trying to get at the food'. In the course of its activity the cat would sooner or later work the escape mechanism 'by accident', leave the cage and eat.

After an interval, the cat was put back into the cage, escaped, and so on. Thorndike observed that as time went on, the animal's general activity shifted increasingly towards the vicinity of the 'door latch', and that the period between arriving in the cage and getting out got progressively shorter. After a large number of trials the cat would operate the escape mechanism as soon as it was put in the box, struggling, reaching, etc., having completely stopped.

A more modern version of Thorndike's experimental situation is provided by a 'Skinner box', a flexible type of laboratory device named after Harvard psychologist B. F. Skinner who first developed it. Such a box is constructed so that we can arrange for a selected piece of behaviour (pressing a lever, pushing a door open, pecking at a key) to be followed by a consequence (such as the delivery of a food pellet, access to water, the turning on or off of lights, sounds, etc.). Usually it also incorporates a provision for the automatic and timed recording of any stimuli that are presented, of responses made and of their consequences. While the overall way in which the box works is of course arranged by the experimenter, it is a characteristic feature of this type of experimental situation that the animal's activity forms an integral link in the sequence of events which it experiences.

Thorndike expressed the results of his experiments in terms of his 'Law of Effect': 'Acts followed by a state of affairs which the individual does not avoid, and which he often tries to preserve or attain, are selected or fixated.' He called such desirable states of affairs *satisfiers* and the learning process *Trial-and-error learning*. The term *reinforcer* is now normally used, corresponding to Thorndike's satisfier, and *instrumental* or *operant conditioning* replaces trial-and-error learning.

Many of the subsequent developments in learning theory rest on these two types of experiment, and the way in which they represent learning as taking place; it will be useful therefore from the outset to have some appreciation of their similarities and differences, as well as of the particular features of our interaction with the world to which they draw attention. Here we will be concerned with these basic models, some of their later elaborations, and the way they have been applied to analyse both artificial and naturally occurring learning situations. There has also been much controversy about whether classical and instrumental conditioning involve different learning *processes*, and not just different experimental procedures; whether there are one, two, or indeed more basic learning processes.

Classical and instrumental conditioning compared

Both classical and instrumental conditioning experiments essentially present the subject with an environment in which there is a simple relationship between two events, A and B. In the examples that we have considered, the occurrence of B depends on the (slightly) earlier occurrence of A. Typically the second event B is chosen to be 'of significance' to the subject – i.e., it is an event, like the presentation of food to an animal, to which there tends to be a definite response. The object of the experiment is to examine in detail the changes in the subject's behaviour as a result of being exposed to this relationship, or *contingency*.

[. . .]

Change of behaviour and the UCS/reinforcer

There is a good reason for choosing something 'significant' as the second event – we are more likely to be affected by a sequence of happenings, or by an action and its consequence, if the final outcome is in some way interesting or important. In the case of animals, we can regard an event as being important if it evokes some well-established response. The presentation of food has been one of the favourite choices, as being of obvious importance in this sense, and has been used in both classical and instrumental conditioning. However, the role that it is regarded as playing is very different in the two cases.

[. . .]

Classical and instrumental conditioning experiments investigate the behaviour changes that result when a subject is exposed to a contingent relationship between events in its environment: classical conditioning focuses attention on the effects of 'announcing' something important, while instrumental conditioning examines what happens when a subject is provided with different kinds of opportunity for bringing about (or avoiding) some important event. In classical conditioning, if it is food (as

UCS) that is signalled in advance by the CS, the experimenter is usually on the lookout for some anticipatory occurrence of reactions *to* food. By contrast, if food is used as the reinforcer in instrumental conditioning, generally there is little interest in the detailed reactions to the food itself (and hence in any similarity that this might have to the 'instrumental' behaviour that eventually develops); instead, we follow the animal's progress in meeting the (arbitrary) conditions which must be met before food is provided. This also means that the *kinds* of responses that are highlighted in the two types of experiment are different: 'involuntary' reactions in classical conditioning, actions, operations on the environment, in instrumental learning. This difference is reflected in the Skinnerian terms 'respondent' and 'operant' in place of 'classical' and 'instrumental' conditioning.

Applying the learning models

Let us now see how we can use these models to describe the case of the domestic cat with which we started. The development of the window-scratching habit looks like a case of instrumental conditioning. The opening of the door, and the opportunities that this presents, are the consequences of the animal's behaviour and we may therefore suppose that the habit has developed because of this relationship. On the other hand, the circumstances leading up to the cat's excited reaction to paper-rustling have the structure of classical conditioning: over a period of time, this kind of sound has been followed (though not invariably) by the provision of food, and this sequence has (to the best of our knowledge) been unaffected by the cat's behaviour during the interval between the two events.

We can, however, in this last situation, also find features that fit an instrumental pattern. Although feeding does not *in fact* depend on the cat's reactions and behaviour after she has heard the sound of paper, it does nevertheless usually follow, and, from the cat's point of view, this may be indistinguishable from a 'real' consequence. The animal is affected by the arrival of food in a particular context, not by someone's intention that it should be a reinforcer, unconditioned stimulus, or whatever. Again, in the window-scratching–door-opening sequence we have to remember that the response that came to be reinforced, i.e., scratching, was in the first instance provided by the cat, it was something she did 'spontaneously', and this suggests that it could be something like an unconditioned response made to an obstacle.

Earlier we drew attention to the fact that the *types* of response that are usually given prominence in the two kinds of experiment are different: movements, operations in one case, reactions like salivation or sweating in the other. These types of response are also differentiated by some of their physiological characteristics, and for a long time it was thought that each was modified exclusively by the corresponding kind of learning contingency. More recently it has become clear that there is overlap: heart rate, for example, can be influenced by its consequences – this is the basis of the therapeutic use of *bio-feedback*; on the other hand, movement-type responses do occur purely as a result of CS–UCS sequences, as will be discussed in the next chapter. Meanwhile, in our domestic example, although the first analysis probably isolates the dominant learning influences we are left with some uncertainties. For example, is the excited miaowing before being fed like the anticipatory salivation in Pavlov's experiments, or more like the operation of a lever in a Skinner box? Clearly in such naturally occurring circumstances there are going to be complexities and ambiguities which a traditionally designed classical or instrumental experiment might avoid or conceal.

We have been looking at just a few among the very many, more or less stable features that characterize the world as it affects one particular cat. In the world of most infants we would find that raising their arms was often followed by their being picked up, and that the sound of the mother's voice occurred in frequent conjunction with particular kinds of visual and tactual experiences. For every one of us, whether human or animal, the environment provides a whole network of such experiential patterns. Many of the relationships involved are complicated; they overlap, interact, and will often be a great deal more variable than any described so far – but they are not chaotic. If learning is a process of adaptation to the environment, then we should find clues to the learning process by paying attention to the *structure* of the environment in which a given individual lives – more precisely, to the way in which that environment impinges on him. We could even approach the study of learning by concentrating *exclusively* on the relationships and pattern of events in the environment of the learner, and try to explain any variations in the course of behaviour by reference to corresponding differences in these patterns.

This has been the very influential, and, within limits, successful approach associated with Skinner, sometimes called the Experimental Analysis of Behaviour. It is an analysis based on classical and instrumental conditioning, although it gives a great deal more prominence to the latter – to operant conditioning, in Skinner's terminology. It deliberately avoids any reference to what may be going on inside the learner – either in terms of mental or cognitive events, or of physiological processes – and for this reason it has sometimes been referred to as the 'psychology of the empty organism'. Skinner does not of course deny that there are internal stages and happenings, but he believes that because they simply mediate between the impact of the environment and behavioural output, to consider them does not add anything to an account that tries to relate behaviour directly to the environment.

[. . .]

Primary and secondary reinforcers

Often when we want to reward a child for something that he has done, we promise there and then to give him something that he likes. Although the reward itself may be some way off, the promise alone produces an effect at the moment at which it is made, anticipating the impact of the reward itself. We are here dealing with the use of language and an altogether more complex situation than the sort of thing we have been considering, but there is an analogous phenomenon at a more primitive level.

The food delivery mechanism in a Skinner box usually makes a click as it operates. If the experimenter operates it repeatedly, the animal will be exposed to a classical (or respondent) conditioning situation in which a click is followed by the presentation of food. This conditioning can produce an effect which does not show up within the normal classical conditioning procedure: if at this stage we arrange things in such a way that some operation, like pressing a lever, is followed by a click and *nothing else*, there is some limited learning of the bar-pressing response, much as when food is actually presented. The click is thus acting as a reinforcer – a *secondary* or *conditioned* reinforcer, as distinct from a *primary* reinforcer like food. A primary reinforcer is one that requires no special learning to make it effective. A secondary reinforcer – and it is assumed that this could be any event whatever – acquires its special property through being re-peatedly followed by a primary reinforcer.

Obviously we do not want to draw too close a parallel between promises and clicks. They are similar only in the (important) sense of deriving their power from their relationship to another and more fundamental event which they announce. Clicks, like promises, lose their effectiveness if they repeatedly fail to be honoured.

We can see now that the instrumental learning situation inevitably involves secondary as well as primary reinforcers – for example, the sight of food is a secondary reinforcer, even though this property will have been developed outside the experimental situation. We can also make deliber-ate use of secondary reinforcement by pairing a suitable signal with food presentation. The advantage of this is that a signal, like a click, can be made to follow a desired response immediately, whereas there is inevi-tably some delay before the presented pellet of food is seized and eaten. It is in this kind of context, rather than on its own, that the phenomenon of secondary reinforcement is best observed – helping to bridge the time gap between action and primary reinforcement.

Extinction

What happens if learning takes place under a given set of conditions, and there is then a change, so that particular relationships cease to hold? Suppose for example that we have established a conditioned salivary response, and now change the situation so that the CS is no longer followed by food. Since salivation has come to *precede* the arrival of food, it will obviously occur to an undiminished extent the first time the bell sounds under the new rules. As we repeat the presentation of bell without food – CS without UCS – the conditioned response continues to occur, but to a decreasing extent, until it eventually disappears. Like the impact of the original rule, the impact of the changed rule is gradual in its effect. The process is called *extinction*, and has a counterpart in instrumental conditioning, when a response established by reinforcement eventually ceases after repeated non-reinforcement. In both cases, a response comes about gradually when B repeatedly follows A, and ceases gradually when this is no longer the case.

We should not, however, think of extinction as a simple reversal or undoing of the original learning. Although the response may appear to have ceased, it will tend to start off again after an interval such as that separating two experimental sessions. This recurrence is called *spontaneous recovery*. It is only if the extinction procedure is repeated several times that spontaneous recovery finally fails to occur. Even then we do not have a return to the animal's original state, in that the time taken to re-establish the response, if the A–B rule comes once more into operation, tends to be less than on the first occasion.

Continuous and partial reinforcement

Extinction is a gradual process. If a reinforcement is again provided before extinction is complete, this will keep the behaviour going for a while longer, and in this way we can change from an arrangement in which every response is reinforced – *continuous* reinforcement (CRF) – to one in which only some are reinforced – *partial* reinforcement (PRF). This will maintain the response, paradoxically with increased vigour and at an increased rate. Partially reinforced behaviour is also more resistant to extinction, in the sense that the number of responses made after the cessation of all reinforcement is greater than in the continuously reinforced case.

[. . .]

Schedules of reinforcement

When reinforcement is partial, it follows the instrumental response intermittently. The rules which describe just when it does occur define a *schedule* of reinforcement. We may arrange, for example, that there will be a reinforcement after a fixed number of responses have been made – say after every fifth response. This is a *fixed ratio* schedule (FR), and such schedules can produce very high rates of response. Ratios of one reinforcement to a thousand pecks have been maintained with pigeons. On the other hand, we may arrange that after every reinforcement there is a pause of fixed duration during which no reinforcement is given, whether the animal responds or not. This is a *fixed interval* (FI) schedule, producing response pauses after every reinforcement, with a build-up in the response rate as the interval draws to a close. *Variable ratio* (VR) schedules maintain a given average ratio between responses and reinforcements, but the number of responses required to earn a reinforcement varies; similarly, with *variable interval* (VI) schedules, the interval during which no reinforcement is available changes from occasion to occasion, while maintaining a given average value. Both produce a very steady rate of responding, the rate being much higher for VR schedules than for VI schedules. VR schedules are particularly resistant to extinction. Skinner has pointed out that the reinforcement conditions under which gamblers operate are essentially of this kind. Although we may suspect that there are many factors that enter into the behaviour of roulette players which do not apply to pigeons, it is nevertheless interesting to note that their notorious persistence is predicted by their reinforcement schedule.

There are many other types of schedule – their potential number is after all only limited by the experimenter's ingenuity in devising functional relationships between action and consequence – whose effects on behaviour have been studied in detail. Skinner has claimed that even the most complex behaviour is generated and maintained by the interaction of the many schedules into which real life can be analysed – indeed if we cannot account for behaviour in a given instance, this must be because the analysis has not gone far enough. Be that as it may, the deliberate use of this approach has been very successful in developing, maintaining and controlling comparatively simple animal behaviour, suggesting that it is an appropriate analysis at least for this purpose and at this level.

Generalization and discrimination

What happens when we look at behaviour in situations which are different in various ways from those in which the original learning took place? This is obviously an issue of considerable importance, since in 'real life' situations rarely repeat themselves exactly. We normally expect that the effects of a learning experience will not be limited too precisely by the conditions in which it took place – indeed, judging by the great contrast which usually exists between the setting and content of formal education and the circumstances in which we hope to benefit from it, we appear to have great faith in the possibility of a very general extension of learning to new situations, at least when we are dealing with human beings. Are there any parallels to this at a more primitive level?

Although our cat is normally fed on *The Guardian*, it will get just as excited by a tabloid and probably by brown wrapping paper – no exact tests have been carried out. There are in fact a whole variety of events which produce greater or lesser effects that look like anticipation of food, and this is probably because there have been, over the years, a variety of antecedents to feeding, in constantly changing combinations. But even if we establish a conditioned response in controlled conditions, and to a precisely defined stimulus – say, to a particular tone of constant pitch – if we now present a tone of a different frequency, there will still be a response, though usually at a lower intensity. The phenomenon is called *stimulus generalization* and has been extensively investigated. There are of course many dimensions along which stimuli can differ, especially when the original CS is at all complex. [. . .]

Generalization occurs also in instrumental learning. [. . .] Suppose for example that a pigeon has learned to peck at an illuminated key by repeated reinforcement. A change in the colour of the light will not normally make much difference to this behaviour once it has become established. If, however, we arrange that pecking the key is reinforced only when the light is green, and never when it is red, then the response becomes strongly established in the first, and extinguished in the second situation – i.e., the colour of the key becomes a critical factor in the occurrence of the response. The environmental rule has now become: 'Response A is followed by reinforcement B, in the presence of stimulus 1, but not in the presence of stimulus 2.' Skinner uses the symbol S^D to denote a stimulus that signals the occasion for reinforcement, and S^Δ for one that announces non-reinforcement. By means of this sort of *differential* reinforcement we can produce *discrimination* where there would otherwise be a greater degree of generalization.

Stimulus control

Discrimination involves *stimulus control* – in the sense that presenting the S^D, the stimulus associated with reinforcement, brings about the appropriate responses, whereas S^Δ inhibits it. Children learn to recognize the occasions on which requests of different kinds are likely to be met. Our cat, observed from another room, will lie quietly on the kitchen-window ledge, and will begin to 'ask' for admission only when someone enters the kitchen. More generally, discriminative stimuli can mark the transition from one reinforcement schedule to another and in this way produce an appropriate switch of behaviour. Like most of the phenomena in this section, stimulus control is not so much a discovery, as a more explicit recognition of a principle, claimed to have universal application. For Skinner all behaviour sooner or later comes under stimulus control (though usually we don't know what the controlling stimuli are). While this last claim is open to serious objection, the phenomenon of stimulus control undoubtedly *plays a part* in the regulation of behaviour, and can be deliberately utilized in the design of training procedures.

Equally, the identification of controlling stimuli can help in the treatment of unwanted – e.g., compulsive or addictive – behaviour.

Response chains

When a stimulus like the green light in the previous example becomes an S^D it is at the same time increasingly paired with reinforcement. This is because the animal comes to respond regularly in its presence, and these responses are reinforced. A stimulus thus becomes a secondary reinforcer at the same time as becoming an S^D. We can now arrange that the green light – which announces that response A will henceforth be reinforced – will itself be turned on if some other response A′ is first made. In this way we can establish a short *chain* of behaviour: pecking one key, say, turns the light from red to green, which provides the go-ahead for the next response, which leads to reinforcement. Actually the chain is already longer than this. The sound made by the food dispenser, itself a secondary reinforcement for the immediately previous response, has become an S^D for the response of looking in the food tray, where the sight of food reinforces looking, and provides an S^D for pecking and eating. This illustrates the way in which the concepts of secondary reinforcement and stimulus control *can* be used, not only in the deliberate regulation of behaviour but also, by extension, in the description of what takes place 'naturally', without human intervention. Whether such an extension to behaviour regulation in general is justified is another matter.

Shaping

We have mentioned reinforcement schedules involving one reinforcement to a thousand responses. Obviously we cannot arrive at such a performance at one go. If we simply put a pigeon into a situation arranged in such a way that the thousandth peck at a key will produce a grain of food, key pecking will never get established, let alone at a high rate. Nor can we change directly from the continuous reinforcement which is most effective in developing the response, to this sort of ratio. However, it can be achieved by a gradual increase in the response–reinforcement ratio; a gradual shift, that is, in the exact conditions for earning a reward. As this ratio increases, so does the number of unreinforced responses emitted before extinction. The gradual increase in the ratio thus ensures that the behaviour will not extinguish at any stage of the process, and we are able to arrive at a level of performance far removed from the original one.

In this particular example, the change in conditions involved the number of responses required to secure reinforcement. What happens when we change the conditions relating to the *kind* of behaviour that is required?

Skinner has described the process of training two pigeons to play a modified form of table-tennis. This is important, not because there is any particular demand for birds with this sort of skill, but because it illustrates the efficacy of the principles on which the training process is based in a rather dramatic way. The pigeon version of the game involves the two birds standing at the ends of a low table each attempting to propel a ball past its opponent and off the table. Such behaviour is quite a long way removed from what we ordinarily associate with pigeons, and it may at first be difficult to see how the principles of operant conditioning may be used to achieve this sort of result. Since they involve the reinforcement of the behaviour to be learned, the behaviour must occur, before it can be reinforced. If, given a pair of novice pigeons, we simply impose on them the condition that engaging in a fully fledged game will be reinforced, it is unlikely that either of them will even as much as show interest in a ping-pong ball.

Operant conditioning must necessarily utilize such existing behaviour as has a reasonable probability of occurring. Although at the start of training the final achievement aimed at may be quite certain not to occur spontaneously, the animals' 'behavioural repertoire' will contain some components which lie in the direction of this achievement. Thus, if we start with one pigeon wandering about in the presence of a ping-pong ball, it will sometimes be close to, at other times farther away. If we reinforce 'closeness to ball' we soon get a situation in which most of the bird's activity takes place in this area. Under these new circumstances, there is a much better chance than at the beginning that the pigeon will peck at the ball. We can now begin to restrict reinforcement to these occasions – setting at first comparatively loose criteria for what constitutes a peck, but as soon as this behaviour has become established, tightening conditions so as to reinforce only pecks that move the ball in a specified direction. When the process has been repeated with the other animal, we are obviously a great deal nearer the desired end result and can start on selective reinforcement in the competitive situation. Needless to say, a secondary reinforcer such as a click is used to make possible the very precise timing on which success depends.

This process of 'edging' an animal's behaviour towards a goal, by using a gradual change in the conditions for reinforcement, is known as *shaping*. It involves the selection, at consecutive stages, of modified criteria for success, such that they move the behavioural spectrum towards the goal, and at the same time have a good chance of being met. The concept of shaping makes explicit a principle that is used implicitly in many teaching procedures.

When we can, in advance, map the 'space' between the start and the end point of a learning sequence into a number of over-lapping reinforcement conditions, such a sequence of conditions constitutes a *learning program*.

Painful stimulation

In considering the effects of various kinds of A–B relationships to which an animal might be exposed, we have so far concentrated primarily on cases where B – the 'significant' event – was essentially pleasant, something liable to be approached, a reward. What if B is a noxious, an *aversive* stimulus? In the case of classical conditioning, we might expect that, again, some portion of the unconditioned response to the stimulus itself would come to occur earlier, following the 'warning signal'; and that in the instrumental case, the use of an aversive stimulus as consequence for some response – like a punishment – might be thought simply to reverse the learning effects produced by reinforcement, to undo them. This is what Thorndike believed at first; a section within his account of the 'Law of Effect' stated that 'acts followed by states of affairs which the individual avoids or attempts to change, are eliminated.' But things turned out to be more complicated, and that part of the Law had to be abandoned. Skinner also found it difficult to assimilate aversive events within his scheme and tended to minimize their influence in his account of behaviour. [. . .]

Punishment

One form of instrumental conditioning with an aversive stimulus, like its rewarding counterpart, involves making the stimulus contingent on a particular response – the response is *punished*. This is only possible of course with a response that occurs with reasonable regularity, otherwise the effects of the procedure cannot be adequately observed. As an example, consider regular lever pressing in a Skinner box that has been maintained by a variable interval schedule. If these responses are now closely followed a given number of times by some unpleasant consequence, there is, as we might expect, a drop in the response rate; and indeed, responding might stop altogether. But with moderate levels of punishment, the suppression of behaviour is temporary and will pick up again, often as though the aversive consequences had not occurred. In certain circumstances, mild punishment can even enhance the rate and vigour of concurrently rewarded activity. It becomes very important to specify the conditions exactly, the delay between response and punishment, the nature of the stimulus used, its intensity, the animal's previous experience with the stimulus, the amount of previous positive reinforcement of the punished response, and indeed the species we are dealing with. It is not really surprising that Skinner, concerned with finding very general laws of behaviour, should have come to regard punishment as an *unreliable* factor. That does not mean, however, that unpleasant consequences – whether they are deliberately introduced or occur naturally – do not exercise an important influence on behaviour.

Avoidance learning

This phenomenon has produced a great deal of controversy and theoretical difficulty – although, as in so many cases, it is something with which we are quite familiar. Suppose that an unpleasant event is preceded by a 'warning signal' – it might be an actual signal, like a buzzer, or it might simply involve being in a place where the event has previously occurred; and suppose further that a particular response, like 'getting away', not only terminates the event, but, provided it happens in time, avoids it altogether. Such avoidance responses are often maintained for a very long time. The problem is that there appears to be no reinforcement, since the shock, or whatever, is completely avoided. The 'danger' might in fact no longer exist. But without reinforcement, why does the behaviour not extinguish, as all good responses should under such conditions? One favourite explanation has been in terms of two separate processes: one, which establishes a conditioned response of *fear* to the buzzer or situation, which thus itself becomes aversive; and a second, which involves escape from the now aversive *conditioned* stimulus – it is the latter which continues to provide the reinforcement. There are many difficulties with this solution. Why, for example, since there is no more shock, does the warning signal continue to arouse fear? And indeed there is evidence to suggest that after a time it doesn't. In the meantime it may help to think of the situation as involving exposure to two consecutive 'rules' of the environment: (1) stimulus is followed by shock; (2) stimulus-plus-response is not followed by shock. The second rule continues to be confirmed. If confirmation of a rule can maintain behaviour – and these are all ideas which do not fit too easily into the framework that we have presented so far – then we can see that it helps to insulate the individual from certain critical aspects of the environment. As long as avoidance behaviour continues, the *original* rule, which caused all the trouble, is not tested, and continues to hold *for the learner*, even though it may no longer do so in fact.

[. . .]

2.2   The Tvind schools

Stephen Castles and Wiebke Wustenberg

The Tvind schools [at Ulfborg, West Jutland] in Denmark, were started up in 1970 by a group of teachers who were dissatisfied with the abstraction and irrelevance of teaching in the state school system. Tvind runs general courses for young people, a teachers' training seminar and a school for 14- to 18-year-olds. [In the main complex there are] not only school buildings and living accommodation, but also a motor workshop, a building depot, a farm with barns and livestock houses, greenhouses and meeting halls. Most surprising is a huge propeller – Europe's largest wind power-station – as well as solar energy collectors, bio-gas installations and many similar objects. When we realise that virtually everything has been designed and constructed by the students and teachers, then we understand one of the main principles of Tvind: learning is based on necessary, productive work.

The self-sufficiency of the schools does not mean that they form an inward-looking educational island. They are a base from which students go out and study work and life in Denmark and in other countries. A lot of time, effort and finance at Tvind goes into providing transport and making journeys of exploration. 'In the Tvind schools, the classrooms are buses and ships. The group rooms are animal houses and workshops and the place of learning is the world.' The function of the school buildings is to serve as a place for comparing, exchanging and systemising experience. The students make their reports here and discuss them with the teachers. Theoretical work arising from outside experience can be organized and carried out here.

[. . .]

The *Efterskole*

The *efterskole* is a secondary school for young people aged fourteen to eighteen. It has received a certain amount of state support, probably because the authorities hope that it will provide new methods for dealing with unemployment among school-leavers. At the beginning of the course, the pupils are divided (usually by lot) into groups of three, which are the basic learning units. These small groups are linked together in 'occupational groups' embracing nine to eighteen pupils and one teacher. These are responsible for organizing and carrying out daily chores like cooking,

Source: CASTLES, S. and WUSTENBERG, W. (1979) *The Education of the Future.* London: Pluto Press Ltd.

cleaning and washing clothes. There are no classes divided up according to age: the occupational groups include pupils of varying ages. The school year is divided into four 50-day periods, and a one-month travel period. For 50 days an occupational group is responsible for one of the following tasks: printing, food preparation, motor maintenance, journalism, building work, energy technology, farming, office work. The work is not just a trick for motivating pupils – it has a serious character: nobody can travel if the motor mechanics do not repair the buses; there are no eggs if the farmers do not feed the hens; life is uncomfortable if the builders do not keep the accommodation in repair; financial chaos results if the office workers do not keep the books in order. So young people learn not only how to carry out practical work, but also the importance of each task. Each occupational group is responsible for deciding what needs doing and how to do it and they learn to organize their own working and learning processes. The printers produce the school books and works on education which have come out of the Tvind projects. The journalists are concerned with giving information to the outside world, receiving guests, etc.

About half the time is spent on practical work and half on theoretical work. As far as possible, the topics for theoretical work are derived from practice. For instance, the motor mechanics visit a motor factory and a repair workshop. This leads to questions like: why do cars wear out so quickly? To find an answer requires studying both technological and economic problems. The office workers have to improve their reading and writing abilities to do their job properly. They also learn how to organise the administration and economy of a large institution. They do the accounts, using a computer, and provide information in such a way as to allow collective decision-making. The journalists start to wonder why youth problems are dealt with so inadequately by the press, and start learning about the political economy of the mass media. The building workers learn about materials, costs, mathematics and technical draughtsmanship. However, it has been found that certain subjects and capabilities, like reading, writing, mathematics and languages, do require regular, systematic practice. So there are special learning periods called 'fixed doses'. Contact with the outside world plays a big part in the *efterskole*. The journalists follow the mass media and make regular reports on important events. The occupational groups go out and visit people who carry out similar work in everyday life. For instance, those concerned with agricultural work visit farmers, perhaps helping with the work, and learn about methods of production and their economic and historical backgrounds. The energy technicians visit factories, power-stations, oil refineries. The knowledge they gain encourages them to carry out experiments in saving energy through insulation or in producing energy with sun-collectors, through bio-gas or with wind power. The travel period might consist of a visit to England which includes going down a mine and staying in the home of a miner.

At the end of every school year, pupils can take state exams for various school-leaving certificates or for technical qualifications. The collective efforts of pupils and teachers ensure that the success rate is very high.

Principles and Problems

The Tvind schools are based on certain common principles. The first is that education has a political character. School is an important part of society and it should give children the knowledge and capabilities they need to understand reality. School must therefore deal with real things – with the problems of society and of the pupils. Teachers have to understand society and the background of the children. They must take a clear position against domination and exploitation, against nationalism and imperialism. By learning how ordinary people live and work in various countries, the teachers and pupils of Tvind take their side and try to change oppressive social relationships. One example of this is the important role played by Tvind in the ecology movement: through studying the technology and economy of energy production and use, Tvind has provided important material for the struggle against atomic power and other wasteful and dangerous technologies. This is not just a question of theoretical work: Tvind has proved the possibility of cheap decentralized power with its wind power-station, sun-collectors, and the like.

The second principle is that of learning through useful productive work. Technical learning at Tvind is never a purpose in itself, but a means to an end. Working methods are learnt and work carried out because it is necessary for daily life, for travel and for meeting school expenses. This means that pupils learn to respect work, to see its importance and to understand its relevance to social relationships. A third principle is closely related to this: learning through concrete experience rather than just from books. At Tvind, young people learn through work, travel and observation. They also learn through talking to people of all kinds about their life, work and problems. This direct experience helps people to realize the need for systematic theoretical study, which therefore takes on a new relevance.

Fourth, pupils learn to work and to solve problems collectively. Competitiveness is reduced with the realization that an objective can only be achieved through the ideas and efforts of all participants. Solidarity is regarded as the best precondition for the development of the individual personality. This is only possible if everybody takes part in planning and decision-making. The work groups decide on their own methods and objectives. In the event of difficulties, general assemblies are held. Decisions are not made by majority votes, but by discussing a matter until everybody agrees on a solution, however long that may take – one assembly actually lasted five days before general agreement was reached.

Fifth, knowledge should not be collected for its own sake, but because it is useful to pupils in their present and future situation. Knowledge should be passed on to other people and made into a tool for improving society.

All in all, the Tvind schools have shown that it is possible to achieve many principles of polytechnic education within capitalism. Of course, the Tvind model has certain limitations and problems. To start with it is a boarding school, which means that some of its methods are inappropriate to normal day schools. Second, outside pressure has led to certain restrictive rules which are hard to reconcile with free education: for instance, sexual relationships, drinking alcohol and taking any sorts of drugs are forbidden. Transgressions have led to expulsions, although these have been decided upon by general assemblies and not by the teachers alone. Anyone wanting to learn from Tvind must look closely at this kind of problem. A further question is the extent to which the success of Tvind depends on special conditions in Denmark. It is highly unlikely that the West German or the British states would be willing to follow the example of the Danish authorities in recognizing and subsidizing the Tvind schools, and even paying some of the teachers' salaries. Tvind has also received considerable support from the labour movement. In 1976, a second *efterskole* was set up with support from the SID (a trade union for unskilled workers). One third of the pupils are to come from the families of SID members, and there is to be close co-operation between pupils, teachers, parents and other SID members.

[. . .]

2.3 A teacher's implicit model of how children learn

John M. Parsons, Norman Graham and Terry Honess

The problem of bringing advanced psychological knowledge to bear on the practice of teaching in a productive way, as well as of formulating crucial questions in teaching in a way which is susceptible to psychological techniques of enquiry could be expressed in terms of 'mapping'. A map of academic psychological concepts and methods of enquiry, though continually changing, would be comparatively easy to provide. However, in spite of the large number of studies which have focused on the overt behaviour of the teacher in the act of teaching, far fewer investigations have been concerned with the belief and assumptions underlying teachers' behaviour. As a contribution to the mapping required between academic psychology and the practical professional knowledge of the experienced teacher, the research offered is principally concerned with developing a methodological framework to help elaborate and make explicit the practising teacher's implicit model of learning. The terms 'model' and 'implicit' are used advisedly in view of the many studies which have inferred an organized set of rules or principles underlying teaching activity (e.g., Bishop and Whitfield, 1972; Hargreaves, 1976), but which the teachers concerned have much difficulty in describing in a coherent way. Notwithstanding the general importance of such descriptive studies, it is also asserted that a more precise understanding and explicit description of the individual teacher's model of how children learn are invaluable for effective in-service training with regard to application of academic psychology (e.g., Howe's (1980) review on the relationship between learning and the relevance for the subject concerned).

The assumption that teachers, along with other professions, [. . .] operate on typically implicit rules and principles may be usefully elaborated within the context of Schutz's (1971) argument that teachers' assumptions and beliefs constituting their developed, though unarticulated, understanding of the world of children are not easily altered. Schutz (1971) has contended that in societies so insular and tightly knit as the average school, staffs may develop a distinct body of knowledge and attitudes, based upon the pooling of individual and collective teacher experiences. This system of knowledge may take on for the members of this 'in-group' the appearance of coherence, clarity and consistency sufficient to give everybody in it the chance of being understood. Concerning decision-making, for example, it is argued that teachers frequently operate on the basis of a well-established set of 'recipes' which provide

Source: *British Educational Research Journal*, 1983, **9**, 91–101.

ready-made solutions for typical problems available for typical actors. Schutz describes this as 'cookery book knowledge'. Such knowledge serves to 'routinize' decision-making (Bishop and Whitfield, 1972) and hence to mask the existence of possible alternatives in the situation.

Details of just one teacher's protocol are to be presented in the study described here in order to provide a clear demonstration of the interviewing strategy and to provide the necessary details to allow for a non-facile examination of our participant's 'model'. Given the implicit nature of the teacher principles that need elaborating, there is an evident limit on the value of direct questions. Nevertheless, by indirect methods involving tasks which presumably require the recruitment and operation of the subject's systems of knowledge and beliefs we may succeed in revealing some of the characteristics of that system. If additionally, extensive observations of the behaviour in question are carried out under naturalistic conditions, and further, verbatim recordings are made which can be reviewed and discussed by the researchers and teacher in a spirit of mutual enquiry, the resulting rich data from these various sources can be cross-referenced and checked. These considerations determine the overall strategy of the research.

The assumptions underlying the authors' choice of this strategy have diverse roots, and notions relating to individual production practices (viz., ethnomethodological work), account gathering, negotiation, triangulation, thematic analysis and the general under-employment of the psychological case study are all relevant here. A detailed treatment of such methodologies is clearly inappropriate; however, it is necessary to assert that it is fully recognized that the status of any one account (see Harré, 1979) is problematic: it may be mere 'rationalization', an 'excuse', or a 'valid reason for action' and so on. However, we would argue, consistent with a mass of research and theoretical data, that the teacher's expectations, intentions, plans and the like are usually of profound importance with regard to that teacher's practical involvement with his or her pupils in the classroom. What is required, therefore, in any research strategy is a procedure that minimizes the possibility of superficial self-presentation on the part of the participants, and a lack of commitment from participants to the task in hand. In the research described below, an individual's proneness to present particular views is challenged through the use of methodologies that situate the individual within different perspectives.

Method

A teacher, to be referred to as Mrs C., known to the first author (who also acted as interviewer) was invited to be the sole subject of the investigation. This teacher was female, 45 years of age, married, a university graduate in Geography and had 15 years' varied teaching experience. She is a member of the staff of a small primary school in a residential area adjacent to a large West Midlands conurbation. The children in her class were aged eight to nine years old and came from middle and high income families living in privately owned and local authority owned houses.

Fourteen of the children in the class were randomly selected and, on the basis of individual photographs, the teacher was invited to complete a Kellyan repertory grid (Kelly, 1955) using triadic comparison to elicit constructs concerning her ideas about the similarities and differences in the manner in which these children learned. She was asked to state the way in which two of the children were similar in the manner in which they learned (the similarity pole) and different from the third child. She was further asked to state the opposite of this similarity pole [. . .]. The procedure was repeated until Mrs C. could provide no new constructs. Seventeen constructs were elicited:

(1)	Motivated	— Unmotivated
(2)	Tries	— Doesn't try
(3)	Competitive	— Non-competitive
(4)	Retains concept	— Doesn't retain concepts
(5)	Anxious when uncomprehending	— Not anxious when uncomprehending
(6)	Intelligent	— Not intelligent
(7)	Comprehends easily	— Comprehends less easily
(8)	Appears able to order thoughts in written work	— Appears unable to order thoughts in written work
(9)	Independent learner	— Dependent learner
(10)	Good memory	— Poor memory
(11)	Prefers discovery	— Prefers instruction
(12)	Can concretize alone	— Needs help to concretize
(13)	Copes better with uncertainty	— Copes less well with uncertainty
(14)	More able to transfer concepts	— Less able to transfer concepts
(15)	Good concentration	— Poor concentration
(16)	More able to follow logical progression	— Less able to follow logical progression
(17)	Less anxious if wrong	— More anxious if wrong

Mrs C. was then asked to score each pupil in the sample on a seven-point scale (+3 to −3) on each construct.

The repertory grid analysis was used to provide a basic line model of the subject's ideas concerning how children learn. This model was then supplemented by an 'illuminative evaluation' of the teacher's actual behaviour in the classroom (Parlett and Hamilton, 1972). Arrangements were made to observe and record twelve lessons in elementary mathematics taken by Mrs C. with her class in successive weeks over a period of one term. Eight of these lessons were recorded on videotape which required the presence of a technician with the necessary equipment. Four further lessons were recorded on audiotape using a remote control microphone and in two of these the researcher was present. The decision to utilize audio recordings was taken in order to check for any possible distortion in the classroom situation arising from potentially distracting video recording arrangements. Neither the researcher or the teacher felt, or was able to quantify, any difference in the style or content of the video or audio recorded lessons. An effort was also made to reduce such effects by habituating the children to the equipment and the procedures prior to the experimental sessions. During the course of each lesson the researcher made field notes on potential points of interest for later discussion. At the conclusion of each lesson researcher and teacher discussed issues arising from each lesson using the video replay of the lesson as a focus for discussion. These discussions were recorded separately and later transcribed in full. It is important to stress that throughout the discussions the teacher was kept fully informed and of course involved in the researcher's summaries of the evolution of her model. Considerable efforts were made not just to report what was said but to attempt to cross check verbal descriptions with actual practice, and to recheck with the teacher those aspects of the model whose consistency and strength seemed to offer a firm base for analysis.

Stated in more formal terms, focii for discussion and selection of material for inclusion in the model were largely drawn up with reference to guidelines suggested by Bromley (1977, pages 170–3) for developing a 'scientific case study', and Helling's (1975, 1976) hints for a thematic, as opposed to quantitative content analysis. Bromley's guidelines are a general prescription for all psychological case studies, hence not all are relevant here, however, in order to provide a wider context for interpreting the methodology of our own study, a full summary is provided below.

(i)   The aims and objective of the case study should be explicitly stated.

(ii)   The investigator must report truthfully and be accurate in matters of detail. In particular, the importance of any fact must be established by rational argument.

(iii) The simplest explanation of the individual's reports and behaviour must always be given especial consideration, but any lack of fit with available evidence should stimulate further explanations.

(iv)   There must be critical inquiry into the internal coherence, logic and external validity of the whole network of argument.

(v)   A close, fairly long and at times possibly difficult, relationship with the subject should be anticipated

(vi)   The person must be seen in an 'ecological context'; the proper focus of a case study is not so much a 'person' as a 'person in a situation'.

(vii)   The case study should involve a presentation of the subject's point of view in 'good plain English'.

(viii) The case study should contribute to psychological 'case-law' in virtue of the general principles employed (Bromley omits to add 'or inferred') in explaining the individual's adaptations.

It will be recalled that the general principles that we are concerned with relate more to the strategy employed rather than the psychological functioning of the individual. For work with individuals, the identification of pertinent *themes* is at least as appropriate as mere quantification. Here, a particular interview and transcript is listened to and read several times in order to identify any apparent integrative themes (this is close to what Bromley indicates in (iii) above). Such themes, which may have been explicitly stated by participants themselves, are treated as hypothesis, and all statements are listed that refer to them (whether supporting or rejecting) in order to establish the apparent best fit. The strategy is one that Helling describes but since a thematic analysis should encapsulate the participant's own perspective her procedure does not go far enough. It is imperative to re-present such themes to individuals for further commentary as in the case of the research proposed here.

Results

Standard analysis of the grid data [. . .] provided construct means and standard deviations, intercorrelations between the constructs, distances between the pairs of elements (children), factor analysis of construct intercorrelation, and a graphical representation showing the distribution of children relative to the two major factors. From this analysis two factors accounting for 87 per cent of the score variance emerged. As shown in Table 1, 11 of the 17 constructs had high loadings on Factor I which accounted for 67.7 per cent of the variance. Broadly speaking, these all referred to the possession of cognitive skills as opposed to their absence. Several constructs had high loadings for Factor II which accounted for 18.4 per cent of the variance. These constructs were concerned with motivational/affective aspects.

Analysis of the repertory grid data provides a very useful source of counter or confirmatory accounts for further discussions and evaluations which took place during the play back of the video recording at the conclusion of each lesson. Five of those topics were especially important in the view of both teacher and researcher (viz., guidelines for identifying central themes outlined earlier) to the emerging 'model' implicit in the teacher's expressed views and actual behaviour. These were 'work rate', 'rote learning', 'discovery learning', 'risk taking/anxiety', and 'level of achievement'; these are now considered in detail below. However, it may also be noted that there were several albeit peripheral concerns relating to

Table 1   Factor loadings on two principal
components for 17 teacher constructs
about how children learn

Constructs	Factors	
	I	II
1	0.61	−0.71
2	0.54	−0.77
3	0.31	−0.60
4	0.97	−0.07
5	−0.07	−0.85
6	0.93	0.18
7	0.96	0.20
8	0.92	0.05
9	0.94	0.26
10	0.95	0.14
11	0.88	0.18
12	0.98	0.11
13	0.93	0.32
14	0.98	0.07
15	0.74	−0.57
16	0.96	0.04
17	0.14	0.63

such matters as memory search, mental imagery, active and passive learning, indicating an incipient concern with process which Mrs C. found difficult to verbalize but which could also form potential points of articulation with bodies of systematized knowledge in psychology.

The first central theme to be detailed is that of work rate. Within the time available for teaching Mrs C. frequently articulated, and was seen in video to demonstrate, that certain 'amounts' of work must be completed. Work in this quasi-quantitative sense appeared to be thought of in terms of new concepts and skills mastered, new levels of organization of pupils' existing ideas achieved – indexed by correct answers to both oral and written questions and problems. This concern for producing amounts of work in a given time appears to be the teacher's criterion for the concept of productivity. Both teacher and child must have something to show for their time spent in the classroom.

There was also a persistent focus upon the notion of rote learning often initiated by recorded episodes of the teacher taxing a child with not having learnt his/her tables. For example, to the eventual direct question, 'Do you actually encourage children to learn their tables by heart?' Mrs C. responds:

Answer: Oh yes, very much so, every now and again we have a chanting session. I know it's old fashioned but I'm all for it. I mean if it's there it's so much quicker . . . I mean look at Justin writing every single day down. I said, 'Count how many days there are from January 3rd to the end of the month and instead of saying January

3rd, one week, two weeks, and – four times seven equals twenty-eight plus, he wrote down every day from January 3rd onwards. And yet when I said (to Justin), 'Look at those rows of weeks there, can't you think of a quicker way if you've got one, two, three rows of weeks and then a few days?' and he said, 'Yes you could count in sevens.' He could see it when it was pointed out to him.

Question: I wonder whether learning by rote actually causes them to know when they're to be used?

Answer: Well, I don't know whether it has with him, but it does with the good ones, definitely; they do it automatically – it's not something they think about, they just know that four times seven equals twenty-eight, so that if they've got four weeks and it's seven days in a week, which they know as well, they don't consciously think oh, ah! now I must use my seven times table. It just happens.

In discussion revolving around the third central theme, that of discovery learning, Mrs C. initially presented firm negative views on this matter. Although a superficial review of the quantitative analysis would suggest otherwise (construct 11 refers to a preference for discovery), discovery learning did not at that moment form part of her model of how learning takes place. Further discussion, however, revealed that the teacher and interviewer interpreted the term differently. Much of her teaching contained elements of such learning where pupils were set objectives and merely given signposts to guide their progress. It became clear that while she rejected 'pure' discovery learning she certainly believed in and practised forms of guided discovery, asserting its efficacy for some children, but mainly for high achievers. However, for Mrs C., discovery learning must generally be characterized as what teaching does *not* involve, but gives clear indications, by use of contrast, of what Mrs C. evaluates more positively, e.g., 'work rate' and 'structured steps' with regard to new material.

Several recorded incidents had also touched upon the notion of children taking risks when learning. Perhaps the most continuous flow of ideas occurred in a discussion during the seventh session when Mrs C. had occasion to recapitulate her earlier perception that children who tend to be anxious do not take risks in learning if they can avoid it. The less anxious will tend to take risks more often. The emerging 'implicit model' has suggested a relationship between 'risk' and achievement. Hence it was felt appropriate to test this further by the question, 'Do you think, then, that children of different levels of ability take different levels of risk?'

Answer: Yes, I would say so.

Question: In what way?

Answer: Well the ones that normally get it right have a bash, they don't seem to mind if they occasionally go wrong . . . but if they keep getting it wrong, and they don't achieve and they're not very good, they don't want to get it wrong again. And also they don't retain the concept once it has been pointed out to them they're going to get the same thing wrong again, and that worries them more and creates more anxiety.

Question: Does the opposite apply?

Answer: Yes, I suppose so. Except that poor old Alex (recognised as a low-achiever), will sit there and write the most appalling rubbish and not turn a hair when you tell him it's a load of trollop, and go and do it again ... he was completely wasting his time as far as I could see today; what he did bring out was rubbish.

She perceived that those who are naturally anxious tend to take fewer risks, as do those who may or may not be of anxious disposition and who are low achievers. However, with regard to the latter point a third category of pupils emerges whom she sees as being utterly indifferent to achievement or risk taking and fairly content to drift along. Generally speaking she perceived high achievers to be better risk takers not seeming to mind getting the wrong answers occasionally. Poor achievers, in her view of learning, took fewer risks and several episodes were recorded in which children of 'lower' achievement were told off for rubbing out the rough work by which they had supposedly arrived at the answer to the problems.

Finally, from the outset of the research it was emphasized by Mrs C. that her implicit model involved a clear distinction between those she perceived as high and those children she perceived as low achievers. This distinction showed in the seating arrangements. High and low achievers sat in separate groups and interspersed between them sat children whom Mrs C. saw as not being unintelligent, but somewhat indifferent to achievement: fairly content to drift along without achieving success in the traditional pattern of socialization. A very important point is that such groupings were not teacher-directed but occurred through pupil preference, although the teacher's perception and action may well exert an influence upon pupil decisions in this respect after the first few days in the new classroom as Rist (1970) so graphically describes in his study. Indeed there was clear evidence from the video-audio recordings that pupils were treated differently. With high achievers Mrs C. would often adopt a 'working with' approach, i.e., verbalizing what the children had done, with their help. When confronted by low achievers, Mrs C. would more often ask 'why?' they had tackled problems in a certain manner, and wait for an answer.

Analysis of the grid (shown in Figure 1) corresponded to this 'achievement' grouping vividly. In selecting pupils with the lowest distance between each other, pupils whom Mrs C. perceived as being similar, 'achievers' emerge into distinct groups, although not surprisingly some children do appear in more than one group. One exception was Richard P. who failed to be included in any group although he was closer to the high achievers than any other grouping. Perceived by Mrs C. as being extremely intelligent, he was a constant source of behavioural difficulties. Thus although this teacher's judgement of how children learn appears inextricably linked with her perception of their academic potential, she appears to take account of more extraneous factors. The total body of data led to several refinements (reorganizations and renegotiations) of Mrs C.'s model; the final picture that emerged is shown in Figure 2. The dimen-

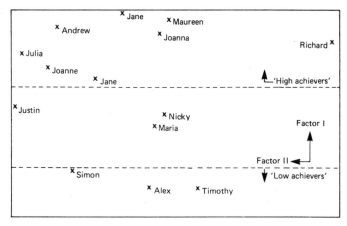

Figure 1   Graphical representation of grid output

sions indicated appear to be relatively fixed signposts for the teacher, although they may be flexibly applied to particular pupils.

In this attempt to elicit a teacher's implicit psychology of learning three further points should be noted. First, the constructs obtained which according to Kelly reflect the individual's personal view of the world and which mediate behaviour, tended to be concerned with the evaluation of

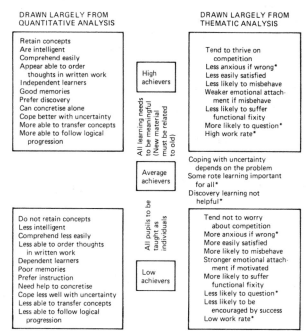

Figure 2   Mrs C.'s model of the manner in which children learn

the child as learner rather than with the manner in which he/she learned. Category knowledge appeared to dominate the model to the virtual exclusion of 'process' knowledge. When pressed on this Mrs C. said in discussion that she did not know what went on inside the pupil's head.

Secondly, it was clear both from the grid data and the prolonged discussions under conditions of stimulated recall, that the teacher's views were not couched in abstract or generalized terms. This raises the question of the form in which the professional knowledge of the teacher is represented psychologically. It appears that much of this knowledge is encapsulated in generalized memories of representative people, objects, incidents and situations.

Thirdly, it was noted above that Mrs C. took up a fairly uncompromising position with regard to several topics but retrospectively stimulated by discussion modified that position. Following the Schutz perspective articulated in the introduction it may be argued that the person's initial explanations, justifications, excuses or whatever are typically a function of a consensus view arrived at in the closed context of micro-society like a school staffroom and subscribed to by its members almost as a condition of that membership. This points to the strong advantage of the present approach involving cross-checking of verbally based judgements against full recordings of actual behaviour and the persistent pressure for clarification presented in a series of face to face interviews, which is close to the ethnomethodologists pursual of their respondents with the question, 'Why?'

Conclusion

The methodology employed appears to afford a means by which the implicit psychology of the teacher with regard to the learning of pupils can be elucidated. However, if further research is to be carried out on any scale within a reasonable period of time then the methods adopted in this study would have to be compressed. The greatest consumption of time occurs in video recording the lessons and it is suggested that this be reduced from eight to four sessions or replaced by the exclusive use of audio recording – a possibility currently being explored with strong positive indications by the authors. Further, limiting the teacher to a sample of 14 children out of 30 in her class may have been a weakness for it may have unduly constrained her opportunity to provide more constructs. However, we wish to assert that the methodological 'package' described here, and the associated rules/theory for interpretation do allow for the development of a sophisticated understanding of any teacher's implicit model.

Too often in research involving teachers, investigators have simply reported teachers' discussions directly without giving them the opportunity to comment on their initial ideas at a later date. If researchers are to make the most of their privileged opportunities they must allow teachers to reflect upon the notions which they are investigating, if they are not to receive somewhat glib and superficial impressions of teacher's thinking. Throughout the study, Mrs C. has given the impression that her ability to comprehend matters relating to the psychology of learning is always greater than her ability to produce them, and her ability to produce them was always far greater the second time the topics were discussed. Finally, we must stress that Mrs C.'s 'model' was developed with the minimum of experimenter influence; that such a model is an extremely valuable if not indispensable starting point for effective and durable in-service teacher education whatever its focus. Furthermore, it is assumed that the process of focused reflection is of value to the teacher. Indeed it is ironic that whereas it is fully recognized that teachers' materials/planning should be geared, wherever possible, to ensure relevance for their pupils, it is not sufficiently acknowledged that similar guidelines ought to operate for the training of teachers as well.

References

BISHOP, A. J. and WHITFIELD, R. C. (1972) *Situations in Teaching.* London: McGraw-Hill.

BROMLEY, D. B. (1977) *Personality Description in Ordinary Language.* London: Wiley.

HARGREAVES, D. H. (1976) 'A phenomenological approach to classroom decision making.' Unpublished manuscript, University of Manchester.

HARRE, R. (1979) *Social Being.* Oxford: Blackwell.

HELLING, I. (1975) 'First order constructs in occupational biography: an attempt to apply the sociology of A. Schutz.' Unpublished BPhil thesis, St Anne's College, University of Oxford.

HELLING, I. (1976) 'Autobiography a self-presentation: carpenters of Konstanz.' In HARRE, R. (ed.) *Life Sentences.* London: Wiley.

HOWE, M. J. A. (1980) *The Psychology of Human Learning.* New York: Harper and Row.

KELLY, G. (1955) *The Psychology of Personal Constructs.* New York: Norton.

PARLETT, M. and HAMILTON, D. (1972) *Evaluation as Illumination: a new approach to the study of innovatory programmes.* Edinburgh: Centre for Research in Educational Sciences, University of Edinburgh.

RIST, R. C. (1970) 'Student social class and teacher expectations: the self-fulfilling prophecy in ghetto education.' *Harvard Educational Review,* **40**, 3.

SCHUTZ, A. (1971) 'The stranger: an essay in social psychology', in COSIN, B. *et al.* (eds) *School and Society.* London: Routledge and Kegan Paul.

2.4 Remembering drink orders: the memory skills of cocktail waitresses

Henry L. Bennett

Some years ago, in a heated discussion in a graduate seminar on memory, I remarked that waitresses can remember far greater amounts of information in short term memory than theories of memory predict they should. [In the face of disbelief by colleagues,] I vowed to investigate the question. This paper is the result: a report of the memory abilities of cocktail waitresses. The project evolved into an empirical field and laboratory study on the interactions between customers and waitresses, memory comparisons with a control group, and, from the waitress's perspective, the determinants of customer satisfaction and tipping.

The cocktail waitress must remember drink orders placed by customers at a number of spatially distinct locations throughout the cocktail lounge. Most cocktail waitresses do not write down drink orders but rely on their skill of remembering. On a busy evening, upwards of fifteen drink orders may regularly be remembered on a trip to the bar, representing orders from more than one table. At many bars, the waitress must combine and mentally rearrange the orders from the tables into the bartender's 'calling order'. The calling order is used by the bartender as a sequence for making drinks quickly, usually beginning with beers, then wines, 'well' drinks (simple combinations using the house liquors, e.g., screwdriver, scotch and soda), on up to more complex mixed and finally blended drinks.

Combining orders from as many as four or five tables, the waitress calls out the orders within this framework. While waiting for the drinks, she may engage in conversation or, on a busy evening, return to the floor for more drink orders. Once the drinks are ready and carried out on to the floor, the waitress places each drink in front of a customer at one table, collects the cost and moves on to the next table. A good cocktail waitress conducts this sequence rapidly and accurately, representing a considerable economic factor in the operation of the cocktail lounge. As one bartender told us, 'Speed and accuracy are so important in this business. A good waitress can make the difference between bringing in $900 or $1700 on a night. They can make or break a place.' On the other hand, customers and waitresses alike have repeatedly told us, 'There's nothing worse than auctioning the drinks at the table.' Auctioning is the practice of asking customers who had what drink.

Reports of waitresses' abilities make reference to their accurate memory developing as a learned skill (Spradley and Mann, 1975; Howe, 1977). The present investigation was meant to systematically explore waitresses'

Source: *Human Learning*, 1983, **2**, 157–69.

memory abilities using empirical methods with hopes of exploring the nature and limits of remembering drink orders on the job.

Within experimental psychology, a great deal of research has been conducted on memory for discrete items. Conducted in laboratory settings, these studies have repeatedly found a serial position effect. The effect describes the likelihood of remembering an item as a function of its position within the list. Initial items are remembered best with performance falling off quickly when there is a delay following learning. In the present case, an adequate sample from a population of waitresses may be studied and compared to the results obtained with an unskilled control group and to results obtained in typical studies of serial memory for discrete items (Norman, 1970). Although there are rare individuals who do not show serial position effects (Luria, 1968; Hunt and Love, 1972), the intent of this paper is to describe differences between populations of waitresses and ordinary individuals, in this case college students.

Results obtained in a pilot study with food waiters and waitresses suggested the design and method for this study. The pilot results showed that observation alone was inadequate for obtaining good quantitative data, though earlier work in a bar had been successful (Sommer, 1965). For this reason, a field and laboratory study using more precise experimental methods was conducted.

Methods

Forty cocktail waitresses from the San Francisco–Sacramento area of Northern California and 40 undergraduate students from the University of California, Davis were selected by (1) surveying drinking establishments where there was sufficient business to suppose that waitresses were kept busy remembering drink orders, and by (2) volunteer sign-up sheets offering extra credit in lower division psychology courses.

A testing kit was assembled consisting of miniature tables, chairs, customers and drinks. Two circular tables, 14 centimetres in diameter, were covered with green felt and mounted on individual 30 × 30 centimetres masonite boards by a small block raising the surface of the table to three centimetres above the masonite. Several varieties of the same plastic doll were selected from a toy store. The flexible dolls measure 9.5 centimetres in length for both male and female versions. Dolls were then clothed with different fabrics and jewellery appropriate to the doll's gender. Hair colour was painted on and some males received beards and/or moustaches so that, as in real life, each doll customer was a unique individual. Each doll was mounted on a two centimetres high white block which served as a chair for that customer. This permitted a unique customer for each of the drink memory locations around each of the two tables.

Drinks consisted of small laboratory rubber stoppers with flag pins mounted into the stoppers. Different drink names were typed onto the flags. Finally a cassette tape was made of the different drink names for each series of seven, 11 and 15 drink orders by recording different male and female voices for each drink name. There was a two second delay on the tape between each order, e.g., 'Bring me a margarita' – two seconds – 'I'll have a Budweiser.' The testing kit then consisted of two felt-covered tables, 33 doll customers, 33 drink names mounted in stoppers, a cassette tape and player, a stopwatch, scoring sheets and interview forms. Two complete kits were constructed and each was contained in a portable case.

Design

All 80 subjects – 40 waitresses and 40 students – had consecutive trials of seven, 11 and 15 drink orders distributed over two tables. Half of the waitresses and students heard all drink orders *in order* sequentially around each table on all trials; the other half heard all drink orders in a *scattered* ordering sequence within each table on all trials.

Procedure

Cocktail waitresses were approached on the job during the early evening hours from Sunday to Thursday when business was slow. Two investigators entered the cocktail lounge, sat at a table, and when approached by the waitress, gave a standard introduction that asked for her participation in a study of memory. This introduction noted that her occupation was of particular interest because of the demands on remembering that were involved. All but one waitress was agreeable to the study. Following a few introductory questions, an experimenter brought out the two tables and the seven doll customers for the first trial. The waitress was asked to listen to drinks being ordered and the tape recorder was started. As each voice on the tape ordered a drink, we would wiggle one of the dolls indicating that doll was ordering that drink. Starting positions were the same and the experimenter wiggled dolls either in order or by the predetermined scattered sequence first at one and then at the other table.

Following drink ordering there was a two minute waiting period when we asked the waitress more questions. This was meant to mimic real life and minimize active verbal rehearsal as she talked with us. Meanwhile, one of us arranged the rubber stoppers with drink name flags on a tray out of the waitress's sight. After the delay we gave the tray to the waitress as one of us started the stopwatch and the other began recording drink placement order on the scoring sheet diagram of customer and table layouts. This was done out of the waitress's view. Following the seven drink trial, the task continued with the eleven and fifteen drink trials. Ordered or scattered sequence of drink ordering was continued throughout the trials for any one waitress.

Finally, the structured interview was completed. This asked for reports of how drinks are remembered, factors influencing waitresses' memory and estimates of memory demands and performance during typical and busy evenings. We also asked waitresses whether tipping and customer satisfaction was affected by remembering abilities.

Undergraduate students were tested in a laboratory setting. A similar introduction was used but students were not told they were serving as a control group. Six female students had cocktail waitress experience and were included in the waitress category. The procedure continued as with waitresses. Interview questions were modified to how students remembered material for tests and, following the trials, how they remembered drinks.

The sample of waitresses had a median length of experience on the job of eight months and a mean age of 23 years. Students averaged 20 years of age. Though both male and female students were used, their performances did not differ on the experimental task.

Results

Accuracy

Of the 33 drink orders presented, waitresses averaged 90 per cent correct whereas students remembered 77 per cent of the drink orders. This was a significant difference in memory performance $(F[1,76] = 27.56$, $MS_e[bet.] = 4.79$, $p < 0.001$). Figure 1 also illustrates the interaction between occupation and drink number $(F[1,152] = 9.14$, $MS_e = 2.96$, $p < 0.001$). Ordered versus scattered sequences were not significantly different by this analysis neither as main effects $(F[1,76] = 1.53)$ nor in

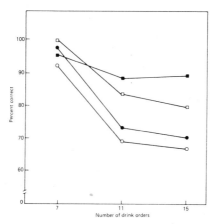

Figure 1   Drink memory by occupation and ordering sequence variables. $N = 80$, $n = 20$ per condition;

■ waitress-ordered; □ waitress-scattered;
● student-ordered; ○ student-scattered

interactions with occupation $(F[1,76] < 1)$ nor number of drinks $(F[2,152] = 2.31)$.

The first trial of seven drink orders was used as a relatively simple task to encourage participation. Both students and waitresses performed at high levels here, 94 per cent and 99 per cent, respectively. Waitresses remembered 84 per cent of 11 drinks and 86 per cent of 15 drinks whereas students correctly placed 70 per cent of 11 and 68 per cent of 15 drinks. Six students with cocktail waitress experience and tested in the lab showed slightly better accuracy and faster drink placement speeds than other waitresses tested in the field.

The high percentage correct for waitresses suggests our task could have been increased to twenty or more drink orders to provide more error data for analysis. The task was effective in showing relatively high levels of accuracy compared to students and to predictions from standard theories of short-term memory which limit capacity in such a task to around five discrete items.

Speed

The time taken to place drinks in front of doll customers was recorded on all trials as an indirect measure of the automaticity of memory processes. Although memory and attention to a novel task require considerable effort and focused attention, a well-developed skill can usually be implemented more automatically and more quickly (Chase and Ericsson, 1981). Our approach to waitress's memory for drink orders is that of a learned skill. The waitress's job is to provide drinks to customers quickly and efficiently. According to our interview data, writing down drink orders is considered inefficient and leads to errors of who ordered what drink. While this skill of remembering large quantities of drink information develops as a normal consequence of the environmental demands of her job, waitresses did not report being taught intentional strategies for remembering. Rather, the nature of the task leads, in most cases, to an efficiency of effort which develops somewhat incidently. Time to place drink orders reflects this skill level.

Table 1 gives the drink placement times for waitresses and students. The statistical analysis is highly significant for occupation $(F[1,76] = 37.84, MS_e[bet.] = 1,789.20, p < 0.001)$ but not for ordering sequence. This result is equivalent to the accuracy data.

Speed of drink placement also demonstrates the skill level of waitresses over that of controls. This fact can be seen in a regression function for the time to place each drink. The slope value gives an indication of the efficiency of remembering achieved by waitresses. For waitresses, the slope value is 0.27 for the time y to place each of x drinks $(y = 0.27x + 1.07$ $[r = 0.996])$. For students the slope value is 0.52 $(y = 0.52x + 0.69$ $[r = 1.00])$. Waitresses were nearly twice as efficient in time to place each drink as were students. The six waitresses who gave perfect perform-

Table 1 Mean speed in seconds for drink placement times for 40 cocktail
waitresses and 40 students. ( ) = standard deviations

Number of drinks	7		11		15	
	Average (s)	Time per drink (s)	Average (s)	Time per drink (s)	Average (s)	Time per drink (s)
Waitress	20.4 (9.2)	2.9	45.7 (25.3)	4.2	76.0 (29.0)	5.1
Student	30.1 (14.9)	4.3	71.0 (40.5)	6.5	126.2 (58.8)	8.4

ances, correctly placing all 33 drink orders, had a slope value of 0·23 ($y =$
$0.23x + 2.58$ [$r = 0.993$]), slightly more efficient in speed than the other
waitresses.

These six waitresses heard the seven, 11 and 15 drink orders at the same
two seconds per drink order as all other participants in the study. Two of
these six received the scattered order sequence. For these two, placement
times following presentation of the drink tray were as phenomenally fast
as they were accurate. The placement times for the orders were 13, 24 and
32 seconds and 13, 19 and 52 seconds for the 7, 11 and 15 drinks. This
works out to drink placement times of 2.09 and 2.55 seconds per drink over
all drinks, about as fast as the drinks could be physically placed in front of
the doll customers. Given that these were drink orders from the scattered
ordering sequence, each customer's drink had to have been held individually in memory as there was no sequence information around the
tables. This speed indicates that rather than holding drink orders in
short-term memory, other memory processes are involved with skilled
cocktail waitresses. These are discussed with the interview data.

Ordered and scattered sequences of ordering

The manipulation of ordering sequence was meant to examine the
specificity of waitresses' abilities. For example, it could be that waitresses
prefer to take the initial order from a particular category of customer such
as the oldest person, the one at the end of the table, or whoever orders the
first drink. From there, the waitress could address customers in order
around the table. Having to remember only one customer to know the
sequence for the remaining drink orders at a table would be efficient for
information stored in memory. Scattered ordering within each table does
not provide this and could lead to less accurate performance.

As mentioned above, however, there were no overall effects of ordering
sequence on accuracy or speed. Figure 1 does show a trend for waitresses

to remember an ordered sequence better. To further examine the data, an ANOVA with trend was performed on the serial position data for waitresses between ordered and scattered ordering sequences. For 12 of the 15 drink orders in the 15 drink condition, waitress accuracy was better in the ordered sequence. The trend analysis gives $F (1,103) = 6.07, p <$ 0.02 showing that for 15 drinks, ordered sequence of drink ordering does provide for more accuracy. This was also true for student data. Examining Figure 2, the data of interest lie in the first three positions of the second table, drink numbers nine, ten and eleven. The ordered sequence leads to each table being considered as a separate list, with serial position effects for each table. For the scattered sequence however, performance on the first orders of the second table is similar to that of the middle of a typical serial position list (Norman and Rumelhart, 1970). Apparently in the scattered sequence, waitresses lose the cues available in sequential ordering for the distinctiveness of each table as a separate list even though all orders were scattered within only one table before ordering began for the second table.

Because this effect was also seen for the student data, and to a greater degree, it must be the structure of the ordering sequence which leads to these differences. Ordered sequences allow for separate lists for each table whereas scattered ordering within each table leads to a continuous list across tables and less accuracy during drink placement.

In summary, the experimental results show that waitresses perform more accurately and more quickly on the task than controls, and they do so particularly well with ordered lists at each table. Given the high degree of accuracy with as many as 15 drink orders in our empirical task, we still need to understand how waitresses manage this incredible load on

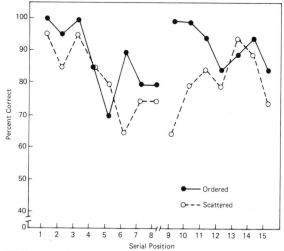

Figure 2   Waitress serial position effects by ordering sequence for the 15 drink condition. $N = 40, n = 20$ per condition

memory. Our task did not mirror what a waitress does on busy nights when she collects up to twenty orders, rearranges them into the bar's calling order, returns to the floor for more orders, pauses for brief conversations, then loads her tray with what the bartender has prepared some minutes later and returns to the floor to place the drinks in front of the customers who ordered them. This is the remarkable fact of waitress memory performance that led us out into the world in the search for a population to assess contemporary theories of memory. Although we were not able empirically to assess the limits of memory on the job, if indeed these exist, we were able to gather interview data on waitresses' experiences and strategies for accurate remembering.

Interview data

All waitresses received the same structured interview designed to first obtain objective data and then to probe for memory strategies. Our sample of waitresses had a median length of job experience of only eight months. The range was from two weeks to five years (standard deviation = 15 months). Of forty waitresses, fifteen managed to remember at least 31 of the 33 orders presented over the three trials, meaning that they confused only one drink order with another over the seven, 11 and 15 drink order trials. These waitresses averaged 16 months of job experience, twice the overall average. However, the overall correlation between length of job experience and memory performance was negligible. Younger waitresses, attending college, were perhaps more familiar with testing procedures whereas older waitresses often seemed more anxious when performing our task.

Waitresses, we found, have good reasons for their outstanding memory abilities. For 93 per cent of our sample (37 of 40), accurate drink memory increases both tipping and customer satisfaction. Not only are drinks more likely to be re-ordered, but accurate memory appears to be a subtle form of flattery to customers. This customer satisfaction means income to the bar and to the waitress. On the other hand, waitresses stated that there was nothing worse than 'auctioning the drinks' at a table, asking who had what drink.

Of considerable interest to us was the fact that 78 per cent of the waitresses (31 of 40) reported that their memories were *more* accurate during especially busy times when there was pressure on the number of drinks to remember and the number of customers to serve. Waitresses' attentional processes at these busy times are deployed exclusively on their jobs, so much so that statements such as, 'Then I'm in the flow', or, 'When you have to remember, you do' were given by these 31 waitresses. This agrees with other findings reported by Csikszentmihalyi (1978) on attentional demands in natural contexts. There may be qualitative differences operating in natural contexts, differences which may be difficult to assess but ones which can inform theories with performance data not found elsewhere.

Two waitresses gave these reports of the maximum number of orders they had remembered. Both incidents occurred during especially busy evenings. A restaurant waitress with 17 years experience was interviewed in our pilot study. She stated:

My memory is much better when the place is busy. My momentum is up and I'm geared for it. When it's slow my mind tends to drift. I perform better under pressure. Regularly I have five tables so there are fifteen to twenty orders to remember. I've always done it without writing down the orders. Five years ago I had a party of 25 people. They all had separate bar and food tabs. I memorized the whole order and later wrote out all the separate checks for the food and from the bar, so I guess 50 is the most I've ever remembered at any one time.

A cocktail waitress with three years' experience told of a particular New Year's Eve at the bar where she was working. The two other waitresses scheduled for that night called in 'sick' and she was left as the only waitress for the approximately 150 customers. 'By the end of the night I knew what every customer was drinking. I'd just stand by the bar, looking for hands, and give the bartender the order. Then I'd take the drinks over to the table. I really don't know how I did it.'

The following discussion attempts to make sense of these abilities, practised every evening by thousands of experienced waitresses. Our interview questions asked for specifics on how the waitress remembered drink orders.

Although waitresses unanimously reported never receiving training in remembering, they did seem to have their own formal systems of remembering that, based on our empirical results, were differentially efficient depending upon the techniques used. There are several steps in processing drink orders which were shared by the waitresses who demonstrated the most accurate memories in our experimental task. It is clear that waitresses make use of complex interactive perceptual images.

The following discussion represents a composite of the attentional and mnemonic strategies reported by skilled waitresses. For the specifics of techniques, Table 2 provides categories of mnemonics which develop spontaneously owing to the demands of the task.

When approaching a group of customers seated at a table, the waitress anticipates what each customer might order. This serves to form an interactive image of drink and customer attributes and occurs automatically after several months on the job. Three waitresses stated that 'after a while customers start looking like drinks'. Even before an order is placed, the attentional processes of the waitress are already focused on the distinctive qualities of the customer which provide cues for remembering.

Approaching a certain category of customer such as the oldest female for the first order from a table allows for use of ordered sequences. After hearing the order, the waitress visually anticipates that customer with that drink, matching features of customer and drink. Colours, drink names and type of drink (e.g. blue collar, executive type) are available as drink cues. More features are available from customers. The interactive perception between drink and customer can range widely but is typically a common rather than a bizarre image. For example, a woman wearing rouge who ordered a strawberry Daiquiri would be easy to remember. A well-dressed gentleman who ordered a 'double Chevas, soda back with lemon' would also provide for interactive perceptions of drink and customer. Although all customers are not so obviously distinctive, wait-resses create distinctiveness by perceiving characteristics provided by the rich stimulus display of the customer. As in the Singular (1982) article, our sample of waitresses did not easily provide their mnemonic strategies. The typical response was, 'I don't know how I remember drinks.' Few waitresses could recall ever talking about remembering drinks except to guess with another waitress what drinks a party would order. However, our interviews were designed to minimize experimenter bias, and they were conducted by several experimenter teams following protocol. It was only after thinking about the drink-order to drink-serving sequence or even acting it out, did waitresses begin to supply these reports of their perceptual awarenesses during the task. It was largely unconscious. We do not have data on the number who were initially unable to describe the sequence but it was not unusual.

The top of Table 2 summarizes the interview data for customer–drink order interactions. Ten of the fifteen more accurate waitresses attend to face and appearance during drink ordering. Only one of the fifteen better waitresses used only verbal techniques as the mnemonic. She repeated the order to herself during drink ordering.

Table 2   Mnemonic strategies reported by all 40 waitresses and by 15 most accurate waitresses (remembered at least 31 of 33 drink orders in empirical test)

Cues reported during order taking	Number using this method	No of drinks remembered out of 33	Used by better waitresses
Face and appearance	22	29.6	10
Position at table	10	28.5	4
Drink name	8	26.8	1
Method and use of verbal rehearsal:			
Repeat to customer and/or on way to bar	18	29.2	7
Rehearse in bar's calling order	11	28.8	5
No rehearsal	7	27.7	1
Write down drinks	4	28.0	2

Verbal mnemonics are used but in addition to the perceptual techniques described above. The bottom of Table 2 gives the categories of verbal rehearsal for the 29 waitresses reporting its use. During particularly busy or noisy times the waitress will repeat the order aloud to the customer to verify the order. More commonly, multiple table orders are rehearsed on the way to the bar, preparing to announce them to the bartender. If a calling order is in use, she will rehearse in that order, combining orders across tables into the categories of the calling order. There are really two memory tasks for the waitress and we have studied only one of them. The other is the verbal report to the bartender which is a quite different process.

Writing down drink orders proved to be the most inefficient method for accurate memory. Only two of the better waitresses wrote down drink orders during busy times. Writing the orders distracts from the attention needed to focus on the customer, leads to more difficulty with drink serving and results in drink auctioning. On the other hand, the task can lead to highly accurate memory using perceptual and verbal skills, especially during very busy times of high drink turnover.

The difference between either accurately remembering multiple drink orders or auctioning them off at each table depends upon the initial attention and perception by the waitress. It is clear that there are two methods that when used together increase the likelihood of accurate memory. Attending to the face and appearance of the customer during drink ordering creates a rich interactive perception of drink and customer attributes. Secondly, verbal grouping prepares the waitress for giving orders to the bartender and may aid in later customer memory.

Comparison to the method of loci

During particularly busy times, waitresses must collect multiple table orders. Surprisingly, nearly 80 per cent of the waitresses we interviewed reported that their memories were more accurate during very busy evenings. With attention to the task increased during these times, the perceptual strategies used by the waitress become particularly important. Owing to the large numbers of customers at multiple tables, the information available to the waitress becomes nested within her area of the lounge or bar. The layout of the tables in the room is nested within the physical space. In these situations, drink orders are then nested within tables. Here, waitresses' memory abilities resemble the method of loci (Yates, 1966; Bower, 1970). This analogy may help to account for the remarkable load on memory that is achieved with accuracy during busy times.

The analogy to the method of loci is fairly direct. The waitress's task is to remember what item is paired with each of fifteen to twenty locations in space, each location defined by a unique customer. During drink ordering, the waitress has perceived the individual customer as transformed, holding the drink or matching drink and customer features. The layout of tables in the lounge becomes the imagined physical layout in the method of loci. With an interactive image for each customer at each of several tables, the waitress uses the known spatial arrangement of the tables as she proceeds through them. The waitress proceeds through physical space; in the method of loci the agent must proceed through a remembered or imagined territory. For the waitress, the tables remain constant and in the same locations from one night to the next. Only the customers change.

The strategies for order taking of the fifteen most accurate waitresses emphasize unique perceptual images at individual customer locations. This helps explain why writing down drink orders is considered inefficient. Laboratory research lends support to this assertion: 'it is much easier to think about something while actually looking at it, even though one may be imagining it transformed' (Avons and Phillips, 1980, page 419). Writing detracts from the visual transformation directed at the customer, takes relatively long periods of time and leads to later confusion and auctioning of drinks.

Conclusions

In the everyday performance on their jobs, skilled cocktail waitresses demonstrate an ability to remember large numbers of drink orders that challenges a limited capacity approach to short-term memory. Their abilities appear to develop somewhat automatically as a consequence of the particular demands of the job. Through the use of interactive perceptions during customer ordering, accurate and efficient drink placements are achieved. Memory loads are challenged during busy evenings when waitresses must remember multiple table orders. At these times waitresses report that their memories are more accurate. The upward boundary of waitress memory capacity for drink orders on the job is not known. Given the more successful remembering strategies of the more accurate waitresses in the empirical trials, our data indicate that such a limit probably does not exist.

These findings appear to conflict with accepted descriptions of short-term memory: only about five discrete items can be held at one time. Other studies of expert memory have developed the concept of intermediate knowledge states. During expert memory performance, this postulates direct access between the stimulus and anticipated future perceptions rather than relying on working short-term memory (Chase and Ericsson, 1981). The postulate relieves the burden on short-term memory by allowing direct encoding and retrieval from the knowledge base without requiring concurrent rehearsal or other active maintenance of the new information. The key is that the information be encoded as an anticipation of a future event, in this case serving the drink to the customer. Though the drink memory task mimics a short-term memory experiment, with waitress experts at work, interference or capacity limitations do not occur due to an anticipated future perception formed at the customer location during drink ordering.

Implications for cocktail lounge managers include selection of the waitress candidate by processing speed abilities. Although skills certainly develop with practice, the correlation between accuracy and length of experience was low. Baseline imagery ability, spatial memory and associative memory will probably predict memory ability on the job. A quick memory task with suggested strategies for accuracy could be administered to the potential waitress. Secondly, encouragement of drink-customer perceptions during drink ordering will lead to increased waitress efficiency, better income for bar and waitress and heightened customer satisfaction. Finally, the practice of writing down drink orders tends to promote auctioning of the drinks especially on busy evenings when the bar's income is potentially maximized. During these times it is important to encourage the 'flow experience' reported by 78 per cent of waitresses who do not write down drink orders. The experience is one of high visual attention to customers' orders and surprisingly accurate memory for drinks.

Further work on waitress' memory skills may elaborate both applied and theoretical issues. Using doll customers, each of whom are unique, more accurately represents actual cognitive situations encountered in the real world than do lists of verbal items. Further work might continue the use of doll customers while expanding the number of drinks to over twenty. Asking waitresses to anticipate what each customer might order could be combined with memory for the actual drink–customer pairing. The study of the calling order of the bar and the waitress' verbal reports to the bartender offers another area of study that we did not assess.

The selection of waitresses as a target population was determined by the close analogy of their work to laboratory list learning and experimentation. However, it is unlikely that subjects in the laboratory have encountered such tasks and their performances may be unrepresentative of more skilled abilities which are active elsewhere. Pairing customers and drink names parallels laboratory experimentation but also exists in a lived context, one which includes a high level of motivation for accuracy. A population of mnemonists awaits you.

References

AVONS, S. E. and PHILLIPS, W. A. (1980) 'Visualization and memorization as a function of display time and poststimulus processing time.' *Journal of Educational Psychology: Human Learning and Memory*, **6**, 407–20.

BOWER, G. H. (1970) 'Analysis of a mnemonic device.' *American Scientist,* **58**, 496–510.

CHASE, W. G. and ERICSSON, K. A. (1981) 'Skilled memory', in ANDERSON, J. R. (ed.) *Cognitive Skills and Their Acquisitions.* Hillsdale, NJ: Erlbaum.

CSIKSZENTMIHALYI, M. (1978) 'Attention and the holistic approach to behavior', in POPE, K. S. and SINGER, J. L. (eds) *The Stream of Consciousness*. New York: Plenum.

HOWE, L. K. (1977) 'The other side of service with a smile.' *Working Woman*, March, 42–9.

HUNT, E. and LOVE, T. (1972) 'How good can memory be?', in MELTON, A. W. and MARTIN, E. (eds) *Coding Processes in Human Memory*. Washington, DC: Winston.

LURIA, A. R. (1968) *The Mind of a Mnemonist*. New York: Basic Books.

NORMAN, D. A. (1970) 'Appendix: Serial position curves', in NORMAN, D. A. (ed.) *Models of Human Memory*. New York: Academic Press.

SINGULAR, S. (1982) 'A memory for all seasonings.' *Psychology Today*, October, 54–63.

SPRADLEY, J. P. and MANN, B. J. (1975) *The Cocktail Waitress*. New York: Wiley.

SOMMER, R. (1965) 'The isolated drinker in the Edmonton beer parlor.' *Quarterly Journal of Studies on Alcohol*, **26**, 95–110.

YATES, F. A. (1966) *The Art of Memory*. Chicago, Ill.: University of Chicago Press.

2.5 Measurement constructs and psychological structure; psychometrics

W. E. C. Gillham

Experimental versus psychometric approaches

Psychologists have typically employed two fundamental strategies in investigating the variety of processes usually subsumed under the heading of thinking, processes which may be as diverse as problem-solving, concept formation, intuition and creative elaboration. One such strategy may be described as the more or less 'experimental' and systematic examination of individual/task parameters to illuminate one aspect of 'thinking'; such investigations are characteristically restricted in scope, complex in conception and organization, and sometimes highly ingenious. [. . .]

A second strategy, which is the concern of the present chapter, is what may be described as the psychometric approach. [. . .] [This] is characterized by a search for definition by measurement so that, for instance, 'intelligence' has been seen as adequately defined by tests that purported to measure it. The first intelligence tests came into widespread use during the second decade of this century at the same time as techniques of correlation and factor analysis were being developed. The application of these techniques to cognitive tests was seen as the ultimate in the scientific exploration of the cognitive domain. In the 1930s the identification of a 'new' factor was regarded as a discovery on a par with other scientific discoveries (Burt, 1940; Vernon, 1950), the definitive charting of unknown territory. The tacit assumption that factors had some kind of 'real' existence led to their being given causal, quasi-explanatory status – like 'ability' constructs in general but with the superimposed gloss of 'objective' measurement. The concept of factors as reflecting basic psychological elements led Burt (1940) to consider the 'metaphysical status of factors', and Guilford (Guilford and Hoepfner, 1971) to construct a 'search' model of the intellect based on an *a priori* assumption of the existence of 120 orthogonal (uncorrelated) abilities whose validity would depend on their independent measurement.

What we have to consider is the extent to which 'thinking' is usefully studied by means of cognitive tests yielding quantitative scores that can subsequently be manipulated in various ways (correlated, factor analysed, and so on). These cognitive tests, usually called intelligence tests, or tests of various abilities, or creativity, may or may not be standardized,

Source: BURTON, A. and RADFORD, J. (eds) (1978) *Thinking in Perspective* (ch. 6). London: Methuen.

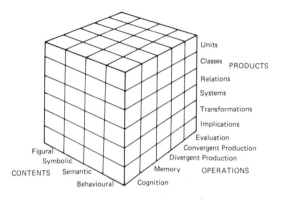

Figure 1   The structure-of-intellect model (from Guilford and Hoepfner, 1971)

i.e., related to population norms. What they have in common is that they are usually assumed to sample 'underlying' or 'latent' abilities, traits or processes, and that the test responses are coded in quantitative, 'equal unit' terms – these being the raw data for further processing.

This is a critical point of departure and one we must consider carefully. The distinction between the experimental and the psychometric approach to the study of thinking is not at the level of the kind of task with which subjects are presented. The experimental investigation of thinking has often involved items from intelligence tests and some cognitive tests have derived their items from experimental psychology. And experimental as well as psychometric psychologists specify test materials and standard instructions. Where they differ is in their reasons for giving the test items and what they do with, and as a consequence of, the subject's responses to the test tasks. The experimental psychologist is using the test tasks to answer questions usually derived from theory. As a result of the subject's responses he may modify the tasks, develop supplementary ones, scrap the whole procedure and work out something better designed, or change his theoretical basis. The psychometric psychologist is more likely to be in search of data that will allow him to rank subjects in terms of presumed abilities or processes, and which may be given inferential support from the factor analysis of the intercorrelation of the test variables. Insofar as he can be said to have a theoretical model it will probably be a factorial one, although few tests (and none of those widely used) are constructed according to a factorial model. Guilford's tests which are so derived, by and large exist in the literature but not in practice. Attempts to construct tests based on Piaget's theory of cognitive development (e.g., Tuddenham, 1970; Pinard and Sharp, 1972; Elliott, 1975) are either not easily accommodated to psychometry where they have sought to preserve qualitative description and exploration in terms of stage-like shifts in ways of reasoning and thinking, or not Piagetian where precise test tasks and score values are specified. Piaget himself rejects psychometrics as a means of investigation (Tuddenham, 1970) and it is worth noting that his interest in cognitive development arose from his experience in using some reasoning tests by Burt in translation: he noted that some children gave the same 'wrong' answers and realized that this reflected how *they* were thinking about the problem.

Piaget advocates the use of exploratory techniques to gain insight into cognitive processes – the 'clinical method' or, latterly, the well-named 'method of critical exploration' (Inhelder *et al.*, 1975) – and his work is testimony to the complicated procedures this sometimes involves. To become aware of this complexity, however, one has to probe for it, otherwise it is possible to see test responses as being simpler or more unitary than they really are; and, indeed, to remain in ignorance of the psychological processes that are actually involved. [. . .] It is in the very nature of conventional cognitive tests with the constraints and prohibitions of standardized administration and scoring of items that psychologists using them inevitably standardize and simplify the data they obtain. That this must be so is apparent in those studies which, using conventional tests, have sought to investigate the strategies of problem solution employed by testees – for example, Donaldson's (1963) study of children's errors on verbal reasoning test items.

Psychometric constructs and psychological structure

Donaldson's study showed that identical or very similar responses or 'products' were sometimes achieved by very different routes. [. . .] If thinking is a product-related process, it is partly defined by its products but not adequately so. An apparently sensible classification of test responses (the 'products') as being of 'the same kind' may be some way from reflecting the nature of the processing that preceded them. [. . .]

But conventional tests do not classify responses so much as pass or fail them, coding them by assigning equal-value scores and thereby obliterating any variety they might display. It is not too much of an exaggeration to say that a great deal of information is discarded (given no score value) and the rest given uniform weight and identified in terms of the title of the test or sub-test variable (verbal comprehension, block design, and so on). For what test constructors usually do is to group together items that they presume will tap vaguely or broadly defined 'processes' or ability traits, and define normative score-ranges which will make it possible to rank individuals on the presumed trait dimension. This coding and classification means that already, within one test variable and before any correlating and factor analysing have taken place, you are a considerable distance from the psychological reality of the processes and strategies involved in producing the overt responses to the items making up the test. No subsequent psychometric magic can put back into the numerical data what has been excluded by the form of coding employed.

In the light of this it is quite surprising what has been expected of (and claimed for) the analysis of the intercorrelations of test variables scored in this fashion, although it is perhaps no more remarkable than what has been claimed for intelligence tests in general. Suffice it to say that the very construct of intelligence has been seen as having its main support via the 'construct validation' provided by factor analysis. Like 'internal consistency' methods of calculating reliability, test validity has often been seen as something to be found within sets of test variables, rather than between tests and real-life competence in what might be considered criterial situations. [. . .]

Observing, as we have done, that test intercorrelation is usually given most attention in construct validation, Levy (1973) comments that, 'Typically, we seem to want to understand the meaning of one test in terms of several other tests whose own "construct validities" may not be well understood. Almost as a consequence of our frustration with the multiple meanings of the mass of data collected, we follow up with a factor analysis which may well confuse the issues more than it illuminates them.'

[. . .]

The nature of factor analysis

The basis of factor analysis is correlation, and linear correlation at that. This means that only linear relationships are reflected in the correlational matrix from which factors are extracted. Levy points out that 'a qualitative structure among variables is not always to be found by a structure of linear equations.' Donaldson (1972) refers to a number of cognitive skills in which qualitative changes result in a performance decrement, at least for a time, when strategies are initially adopted that will ultimately lead to an enhanced level of performance.

The more obvious correlational fallacy is to assume that a numerical relationship necessarily implies a psychological relationship (or lack of it). We are all familiar with anecdotes such as Thouless's observation of a high positive correlation between the rate of increase in the human population and the population of storks in Southern India; we tend to forget that a more plausible correlation may equally be fable. Numerical relationships are neutral and explain nothing: they have themselves to be explained, which is why a zero correlation may still reflect a psychological relationship of a kind which cancelled out or balanced up the numerical values.

But even if we accept that a positive correlation coefficient indicates a genuine psychological relationship there is a limit to a correlation-based statistic which is almost always overlooked. It is well expressed by Burt (1940) in his professorial prose:

It would be truer ... (and) ... more instructive, to think of our tables of measurements, correlations, factor-saturation and the like as comprising a series of mutually equivalent matrices, each capable of being transformed into the other, and to note that each of those matrices, even if ultimately reduced to a single row or vector, can still enumerate only *relations between qualities and not the amounts of those qualities by themselves* ... (my italics).

[. . .] Given a matrix of intercorrelations there are many things you can do with it mathematically – all justifiable although perhaps not equally so – and all affecting the resultant factor pattern, and therefore one's basis for making inferences. And how does one make these inferences?

Factors, like human beings, are born with no name although there is usually one waiting for them, which may not fit their character very well. But as with their human counterparts they soon become assimilated to their name-identity and the initial act of ascription, and perhaps its unsuitability, is often forgotten. Human beings, however, have the advantage over factors in that their meaning does not reside just in their name. Factors, like correlation coefficients, have no intrinsic psychological significance: meaning is ascribed to them by a psychologist with his preferences and presuppositions. And by a more or less careful scrutiny of the test variables which 'load' on a particular factor, the psychologist assigns a 'best-fit' descriptive label which may be of a 'content' or 'process' kind, or possibly both. Some test items appear to invite a process label more readily than others: a factor which loaded heavily on such test variables as repeating digits forward and backwards would be unlikely to escape being labelled as 'memory'. Thurstone (1938) in identifying his (usually) seven Primary Mental Abilities (Verbal, Number, Spatial, Memory, Reasoning, Word-fluency, Perceptual speed) gave some of them content labels and some process labels. Despite the 'illogicality' of this nomenclature, the terms Thurstone uses seem the obvious and sensible ones. What it does call into question is how 'process' these descriptions really are.

Factorial 'models' of psychological processes

More tidy-minded psychologists such as Eysenck (1967) and Warburton (1970) have proposed a two-dimensional content x process 'model', but tidy-mindedness is no guarantee of psychological veracity. If it were then Guilford with his 3-D content x process x product model of 120 discrete abilities (see Figure 1, page 123) would have achieved a unique level of truth. Cattell (1971) criticizes the structure-of-intellect model as involving categories chosen on too rational, philosophic and *a priori* a basis. Cattell's work has largely been directed to the discovery of empirically derived but definitive factor structures which means that he does not entirely escape from his own criticism. However, Guilford's insistence on finding tests that will fit his model is the obverse of discovery: indeed, it is more like psychological invention.

The fundamental assumption of such *a priori* classifications is that, given construct validity, i.e., relatively independent uncorrelated factors, you can virtually guarantee the processes that subjects have employed in solving the test items. This presupposes, firstly, that one can identify definitive tests for a hypothesized factor structure and secondly, that processes can be regarded as a property of test problems rather than test problem solvers.

I am not suggesting that certain test tasks may not constrain, more or less severely, what we can do with them, that is, the kind of mental operations we will find necessary for their solution. But having some experience of investigating problem-solving strategies on a fairly narrow range of tasks, I am impressed by the perverseness and trickiness of the average problem-solver. I am also impressed by the difficulty of finding out how an individual is solving a problem even when he is doing so under your very eyes. To attempt to construct test items that 'require' a certain kind or level of thinking would seem to fly in the face of what cognitive psychology has taught us during the last fifteen years or so; which is presumably why attempts to construct 'Piagetian' tests always seem to peter out. Test items themselves have no psychological properties: they are only so characterized in relation to the cognitive operations of human beings, and individuals are likely to perceive, and process, the 'objectively' identical problem in different ways. Hence the myth of 'unambiguous' test instructions. Whilst some forms of test instructions are more likely to lead to multiple interpretations by testees than others, no test instruction can guarantee a uniform interpretation.

The cumulative significance of all this is that at the level of the factor matrix we are at a considerable distance from the psychological reality of cognitive processes: the chain of inference is long and the transformations in the data have been many. When you are operating at such a distance from your raw material, it is easy to come to believe in the primacy and explanatory power of such statistical abstractions. This seems to be characteristic of those psychologists, like Burt, Cattell, Eysenck and Guilford, who have used factor analysis as the basic technique for 'theory' or 'model' construction. It is not difficult to see the desirability of identifying (or prescribing) a definitive and stable factor structure for psychologists who have sought for their discipline the status and character of the 'discoveries' and 'laws' of the natural sciences. The relativity and reflexive character of psychological organization defeats such aims although it is possible to minimize confrontations with psychological reality by working with more or less restricted populations. P. E. Vernon, for example, has persistently criticized Guilford for using too homogeneous a population in determining factors for his search model of the intellect. Certainly Guilford's factor structure only applied to the test items used *with the test populations he has employed*. In other words, for substantially different populations the same sets of test problems might produce different patterns of interrelationship, different *factorial* patterns.

However, if we are interested in the possibilities of factor analysis as a tool for investigating broad aspects of psychological processing, such relativity immediately starts to look a little more promising.

Factorial relativity and psychological discovery

If factor structure is not objectively defined but defined relative to a population group, then comparative factor analyses of different group performances might tell us something about differences in the processes being employed, even if only at a gross and general level. Instead of a means of achieving a predetermined factor structure, factor analysis then becomes a technique of discovery amongst sets of test items assembled for other reasons, for example because they are educationally important, or culturally valued in some other way.

Even without between group comparisons, the element of discovery in factor analysis has always been in terms of an unexpected factor structure (that is, unexpected correlations). Thus Maxwell (1959) in a factor analysis of the WISC found that some 'performance' subtests loaded more heavily on a verbally referenced factor than they did on a 'space-performance' factor. This suggested that linguistic processes *might* be involved in the successful solution of these subtests. Such an inference would seem justified, but note that it is only possible because subtests of verbal content formed part of the correlation matrix. If factors, as Burt has pointed out, at the most reflect *relations* between qualities (rather than the qualities themselves), then the presence of a factor merely indicates that this is a source of variation (or co-variation) for the population producing the scores being analysed, since two or more variables have to vary together for correlation to be possible. A factor is only available for interpretation if such co-variation exists in the matrix.

Balinski (1941) carried out a factor analysis of the standardization data obtained for the Wechsler-Bellevue at the different (mainly adult) age-levels sampled. Overall the factor structure obtained was very similar but at two age-levels a factor appeared which Balinski identified as a *memory* factor. But this does not mean that recall processes were not involved at those age-levels where no memory factor was apparent – it is simply that they were not a major source of *variation* for that age population. This is one step further back from our earlier observation that factor analysis (necessarily) neglects non-correlational data: for correlation to be possible there has to be variation attributable to the inferred quality. We recall Vernon's (1970) observation that 'for the psychometrist an ability must be something on which people vary'; without variation it cannot be measured, although operative.

Balinski was comparing factorial patterns of ability at different age levels; this poses some problems as to the continuity of the qualities involved in intellectual performance. There is some evidence that older people learn and solve problems somewhat differently from young adults, although performances may be comparable until that last, more or less dramatic declension into infantile forms of thinking. But if we consider the beginning of the life-span and the qualitative ascent of intellectual growth, it is clear that in comparing factor analytic patterns of adults and children we are up against discontinuity in many of the variables that might interest us. Being intelligent at the age of five or seven or ten is different in *kind* from being intelligent at twenty. Thus what may look like the same factors at different age-levels may be nothing of the sort. But this doesn't prevent your making comparisons with such cautions in mind.

Factorial complexity and individual differences in cognitive organization

One very general finding is that fewer factors are apparent in analyses of children's test performances, the 'general' factor in particular being larger. Why this is so is not clear but it is reasonable to assume that in part it may be due to a qualitative differentiation in ways of thinking. Biological considerations apart it is evident that children have a much more standardized intellectual environment than adults: for purposes of comparison one would have to give all adults the same kind of job. The great variation in adult work experiences would seem likely to increase differences in ways of thinking and areas of attainment between individuals. The more complex factor patterns obtained when adults are given similar sets of tests as have been given to children may reflect greater process and strategy variations in the adult population as a result of their varying training and work experiences.

French (1965) makes a similar point for reasons that themselves merit our consideration. French has this to say:

It seems possible that the factorial composition of test problems involving higher mental processes often appears complex, not only because the problems require several different kinds of abilities in their solution, *but also because they measure something different for examinees who solve them by using different methods* . . . an investigation of this situation (seems) likely to lead to worthwhile information about individual differences in problem-solving styles, an appreciation of the different things a test measures for different subjects, and an understanding of the extent to which factor analysis reflects qualitative differences in individuals' reactions to a test as well as to differences in the nature of the tests themselves [my italics].

French's comments are made in the introduction to a study in which subjects were grouped on the basis of their identified problem-solving styles and their performances on the *same* set of fifteen cognitive tests subsequently factor-analysed. Different factorial patterns were found for the groups pre-identified in this fashion. The styles of approach identified were broadly of the systematizing versus scanning and the analytic versus global way of perceiving problems. French's study is of interest because he identifies these as *characteristics* of cognitive operations rather than as 'ability' or 'operations' constructs *per se*.

[. . .]

The origins of factors

In order to test any hypotheses one might have as to the origins of observed factors, several conditions need to be met. Anastasi (1970) stipulates that 'The investigator must administer a fairly large number of suitable tests to sufficiently large groups; he must employ appropriate factor-analytic techniques: and he must have access to at least some data regarding relevant cultural and other experimental variables.' Anastasi's paper constitutes a substantial review of the factor analytic literature relating to the identification of psychological traits and she observes that in such studies the meaning of ability traits 'becomes essentially an inquiry into the causes of correlation among different behavioural samples, as represented . . . by test scores.'

Anastasi quotes Tryon(1935) as proposing three mechanisms to account for correlation among different psychological measures, such as test scores. Firstly, the extent to which they 'sample similar universes of conceptual components'; secondly, the correlation between the environmental fields in which the different psychological components originated, e.g., educational advantage enhancing performance on a range of different attainments; thirdly, the correlation of 'independent gene blocks' attributed to assortative mating. Such a breakdown would seem to be difficult to make in practice. [. . .] But 'accounting' for the correlation is not the same as knowing the nature of the interrelating behaviours that make up the correlation; the 'causes' of behaviour (including co-varying sets of test responses) do not determine the detail of their operation, either the form of the response or the nature of the processes involved.

Factor analytic comparison of groups: three studies

Up to now this chapter has been rather abstract – necessarily so because we were considering the nature of psychometric abstractions. Coming down to the level of practical research we have suggested that comparative factor analyses (same tests, different populations) might indicate differences in the way these groups handle test problems; it might even indicate what kind of tasks are most 'open' in this respect. It is not suggested that such factor studies would ever be adequate on their own for the elucidation of the processes involved, but that they might provide a point of reference for other kinds of investigations. I shall describe three comparative studies to illustrate the possible uses of such a psychometric perspective.

Dockrell (1965) (cited by Anastasi, 1970) administered a battery of ten tests dealing with verbal and non-verbal ability, linguistic and numerical skills, and practical/spatial ability to groups of children aged ten, twelve and fourteen years. He classified these children according to their social class as determined by the Registrar-General's classification of their father's occupation and (for the secondary school age children) the type of school they attended: grammar, technical or secondary modern.

Dockrell had hypothesized that there would be differences in the kind of factors and the degree of their differentiation as a function of social class and type of secondary school. He found, as have other research workers (e.g., Mitchell, 1956) that middle-class children are more differentiated in their abilities than working-class children; he also found that this differentiation occurred earlier in middle-class children. [. . .]

In his comparison of the different secondary school groups Dockrell found generally greater differentiation amongst those attending grammar and technical schools, but in the former verbal abilities were more clearly differentiated whilst spatial and numerical skills were more highly differentiated in the technical school children. It is interesting to compare these sorts of findings with small-scale experimental studies of the effects of practice upon factor patterns – presumably a micro-version of what happens in social and educational settings. For example Fleishman and his associates have investigated the factor make-up of sets of perceptual-motor tasks at different stages of practice, revealing regular and progressive changes suggesting an increasing differentiation of function as learning proceeds (Fleishman, 1972). This is in accord with Ferguson's transfer theory referred to earlier since he concludes that 'as the learning of a particular task continues, the ability to perform it becomes gradually differentiated from . . . other abilities' (Ferguson, 1954).

It is possible to relate this increasing differentiation to Piaget's concept of operations which develop through the organism's interaction with his environment into a hierarchy of increasing complexity. However, the data that Dockrell presents allow no more precise inference than that.

Two important cross-cultural studies are those of Irvine (1969a) and Vernon (1969).

Irvine's investigation involved a large number of subjects – over 5000 children in a variety of elementary and secondary schools in Kenya, Zambia and Rhodesia. He used a large test battery classified as: reasoning in English; reasoning with low verbal content; language skills (English); numerical and mathematical skills; spatial and perceptual tests; information and knowledge. It is immediately obvious that there are two qualifications as to how far this can be regarded as a cross-cultural study: in the first place the sample, although large, was a selected one (by definition of school attendance) and therefore more westernized than those not attending school; secondly, the choice of tests designed to sample the skills and values of Western culture necessarily restricted the extent to which they sampled vernacular linguistic and cognitive styles. Irvine was, of course, well aware of these limitations and attributed the broad cross-cultural uniformity of the main factor loadings to the standardized English-model education in these African schools. The greatest degree of uniformity was in overlearned drill skills such as spelling and arithmetic. There was less factorial uniformity in tests where the materials were non-verbal but where internal verbalization was of some importance. Irvine followed up some of these differences with individual interviews, and comments that 'students reported switching back and forth from vernacular to English in working through items in tests of a "nonverbal" kind'. Irvine pursues the implications of this in relation to 'the common belief that verbal tests are more potent sources of culture differentiation than figural and nonverbal tests' and suggests that the nature of verbal problems is such that cultural bias is more easily identified. Irvine observes that, 'In symbolic and figural tests, the limits of individual perceptual and verbal strategy differences . . . seem to be considerably extended, and are correspondingly the more difficult to map.' In a further study (Irvine, 1969b) of the performance of African students on Raven's Progressive Matrices he found individual variation in strategies when achieving the same score, a degree of item-group interaction across cultures, significant item-difficulty changes between cultural groups, and at least five factors. He concludes that 'figural tests may offer open-ended situations where between-groups differences in perceptual organization and learning opportunity operate in a complex fashion.'

Irvine's work is of particular interest to psychologists concerned with the study of thinking because he got behind the test performance and factorial patterns and took account of the educational and social milieu and the strategies that individuals brought to bear on the test problems. This is also characteristic of one of the most extensive cross-cultural studies carried out on school-children, that of P. E. Vernon (1969).

The size of the groups studied by Vernon was smaller than in Irvine's investigation but more geographically widespread, including schoolboys in England, the Hebrides, Jamaica, Uganda, and Indian and Eskimo boys in Canada. The range of tests used was also unusually diverse including a variety of tests aimed at assessing basic concepts and perceptual skills as well as tests developed as 'creativity' measures. The factor patterns obtained by Vernon were notable for their cross-cultural similarity but there were some interesting variations. Thus the verbal-educational factor ($v:ed$), which usually emerges as a broad group factor (i.e., loading on most but not all test variables) when a wide range of tests is used, was actually a general factor in the Hebrides and Jamaica having substantial loadings on tests other than those sampling conventional educational attainments. Vernon thought that this was because the cultural stimulus for all the skills tested was derived from school experience.

In Uganda, by comparison, no general factor was found, the largest group factor being *v:ed* loading mainly on school-type subjects and apparently distinct from other cognitive tests, notably Raven's Matrices, the Draw-a-Man Test and Kohs Blocks. Vernon comments (1969, page 186) that this means that such tests 'would have even less predictive value for school work than they do in Western cultures, since education depends so heavily on the specialized ability of acquiring the English language.' Vernon identified an additional group factor in his Uganda data which loaded on figural, perceptual and performance tests. He suggested that 'This factor may be interpreted as an ability for coping with perceptual analysis, concrete operations and the world of objects, quite distinct from educational attainments' [page 187].

The three studies that have been described represent some of the best work using comparative factor analytic techniques to elucidate the organization of 'abilities'. Although they could perhaps have been improved by the use of more recent techniques for making factor comparisons across groups (Jöreskog, 1971; Sorbom, 1974), they do make clear the limitations of the factorial approach: without good information about the educational and social experiences of the testees and some insight into the strategies they employ in solving the test problems, the factor patterns themselves are almost meaningless. A belief in the construct validity provided by factor patterns alone, is one dimension of the myth of 'objective' testing which has persisted for so long.

It seems that only now (1978), in the late seventies, are we able to get the mental testing movement into perspective. We can see it as remarkable in vigour, confidence and unselfconsciousness, which it maintained almost undiminished for half a century. Even as late as 1965 Holtzman, writing about the concept of intelligence, could say that 'one of the most significant accomplishments of psychology has been the development of tests for measuring intelligence' (Holtzman, 1966). But at the time, such a claim seemed to many people, including the writer, perfectly reasonable; a decade later it is obvious that intelligence tests and their analysis by traditional psychometric manipulations obscure more than they reveal about the nature of intelligent behaviour and the processes that underlie it. Our expectations of psychometric constructs in terms of clarifying psychological functioning now seem rather curious, having the difficult-to-explain character of one's own personal recent past: it is hard to understand why we were not more critical. In contrast, it is now possible to see what needs to be done, even if we are unsure how to achieve it: to develop a psychometry – which may not look much like traditional psychometry – that reflects the qualitative aspects of our psychological data. Perhaps the writer with the clearest view of this is Guttman (1971), who provides a suitable concluding paragraph. He comments:

Just as we have learnt not to be subservient to the normal distribution, and just as we have begun to learn to treat qualitative observations with the same respect as numerical observations, let us try to be free of other *a priori* mathematical and statistical considerations and prescriptions . . . Instead, let us try to think substantively during the initial stages of a problem of measurement, and focus directly on the specific universe of observations with which we wish to do business.

References

ANASTASI, A. (1970) 'On the formation of psychological traits.' *American Psychologist*, **25**, 899–910.

BALINSKI, B. (1941) 'An analysis of the mental factors of various age groups from nine to sixty.' Genetic Psychology Monographs, **23**, 191–234.

BURT, C. (1940) *The Factors of the Mind*. London: University of London Press Ltd.

CATTELL, R. B. (1971) *Abilities: Their Structure, Growth and Action*. New York: Houghton Mifflin.

DOCKRELL, W. B. (1965) 'Cultural and educational influences on the differentiation of ability', in Proceedings of the 73rd Annual Convention of the American Psychological Association. Washington, DC.

DONALDSON, M. (1963) *A Study of Children's Thinking*. London: Tavistock Publications.

DONALDSON, M. (1972) 'Preconditions of inference', in COLE, J. K. (ed.) *Nebraska Symposium on Motivation 1971*. Lincoln, NB: University of Nebraska Press.

ELLIOTT, C. D. (1975) 'The British Intelligence Scale: final report before standardization 1975–6.' Paper presented at the Annual Conference of the British Psychological Society: Nottingham, England.

EYSENCK, H. J. (1967) 'Intelligence assessment: a theoretical and experimental approach.' *British Journal of Educational Psychology*, **37**, 81–98.

FERGUSON, G. A. (1954) 'On learning and human ability.' *Canadian Journal of Psychology*, **8**, 95–112.

FLEISHMAN, E. A. (1972) 'On the relation between abilities, learning, and human performance.' *American Psychologist*, **27**, 1018–32.

FRENCH, J. W. (1965) 'The relation of problem-solving styles to the factor composition of tests.' *Educational and Psychological Measurement*, **25**, 9–28.

GUILFORD, J. P. and HOEPFNER, R. (1971) *The Analysis of Intelligence*. New York: McGraw-Hill.

GUTTMAN, L. (1971) 'Measurement as a structural theory.' *Psychometrika*, **36**, 329–48.

HOLTZMAN, W. H. (1966) 'Intelligence, cognitive style and personality: a developmental approach', in BRIM, O. G. JR, CRUTCHFIELD, R. S. and HOLTZMAN, W. H. *Intelligence: Perspectives 1965*. New York: Harcourt Brace and World.

INHELDER, B., SINCLAIR, H. and BOVET, M. (1975) *Learning and the Development of Cognition*. London: Routledge and Kegan Paul.

IRVINE, S. H. (1969a) 'Factor analysis of African abilities and attainments: constructs across cultures.' *Psychological Bulletin*, **71**, 1, 20–32.

IRVINE, S. H. (1969b) 'Figural tests of reasoning in Africa.' *International Journal of Psychology*, **4**, 3, 217–28.

JORESKOG, K. G. (1971) 'Simultaneous factor analysis in several populations.' *Psychometrika*, **36**, 4, 409–4.

LEVY, P. (1973) 'On the relation between test theory and psychology', in KLINE, P. (ed.) *New Approaches in Psychological Measurement*. London: Wiley.

MAXWELL, A. E. (1959) 'Factor analysis of the Wechsler Intelligence Scale for Children.' *British Journal of Educational Psychology*, **29**, 237–41.

MITCHELL, J. V. (1956) 'A comparison of the factorial structure of cognitive functions for a high and low status group.' *Journal of Educational Psychology*, **47**, 397–414.

PINARD, A. and SHARPE, E. (1972) 'I.Q. and point of view.' *Psychology Today*, **6**, 1, 65–8.

SORBOM, D. (1974) 'A general method for studying differences in factor means and factor structure between groups.' *British Journal of Mathematical and Statistical Psychology*, **27**, 229–39.

THURSTONE, L. L. (1938) 'Primary mental abilities'. *Psychometric Monographs*, 1.

TRYON, R. C. (1935) 'A theory of psychological components – an alternative to "mathematical factors".' *Psychological Review*, **42**, 425–54.

TUDDENHAM, R. (1970) 'A "Piagetian" test of cognitive development', in DOCK-RELL, W. B. (ed.) *On Intelligence*. London: Methuen.

VERNON, P. E. (1950) *The Structure of Human Abilities*. London: Methuen.

VERNON, P. E. (1969) *Intelligence and Cultural Environment*. London: Methuen.

VERNON, P. E. (1970) 'Intelligence', in DOCKRELL, W. B. (ed.) *On Intelligence*. London: Methuen.

WARBURTON, F. W. (1970) 'The British Intelligence Scale', in DOCKRELL, W. B. (ed.) *On Intelligence*. London: Methuen.

2.6   Conversations with children

Catherine E. Snow

Only ten years ago it was thought possible to study language acquisition without studying the language addressed to children. All the research done before the late 1960s on the nature of linguistic input to children was carried out by linguists and anthropologists studying 'baby talk'; i.e., they collected data on the special lexicon used with babies, and several noted that the baby talk words could be analysed as simplified forms of adult words (reviewed in Ferguson, 1977). Other features of baby talk noted fairly generally were high pitch and exaggerated intonation contours (see, e.g., Blount and Padgug, 1977). This research on baby talk was done primarily with the purpose of describing a certain speech register, not with any specific interest in the relevance of baby talk to language acquisition (though several papers noted that the informants justified using baby talk with a didactic motive, 'to make the language easier to learn'). Much more recently, psychologists and linguists interested in language acquisition have started studying the nature of the speech addressed to children. They have concentrated on syntactic and semantic rather than lexical or phonological aspects of that speech, and have tended not to use the term 'baby talk' to refer to their object of study. Other terms have been coined, such as 'motherese', which gives the misleading impression that only mothers talk in a special way to children. [. . .]

This article will be primarily concerned with the nature of speech addressed to children as a factor in acquisition. Until very recently, children's acquisition of language was studied without considering the speech addressed to children because it was assumed that the nature of that speech made very little difference to the course of language acquisition. It was thought that there was a large innate component in linguistic ability which buffered language acquisition against sparseness, complexity and confusion in the primary linguistic data. Two positions on the nature of this innate linguistic component can roughly be identified: the notion that the innate component supplied knowledge of linguistic universals such as the existence of word classes and the importance of order of elements (McNeill, 1966), and the position that the innate component supplied procedures for discovering the grammar of the language to be learned (Fodor, 1966). Under the assumption of either innate grammatical knowledge or innate grammar discovery procedures, it could be argued that only a minimum of linguistic input was adequate to enable the

Source: FLETCHER, R. and GARMAN, M. (eds) (1979) *Language Acquisition*. Cambridge: Cambridge University Press.

child to learn language, and that both a high level of complexity and a large amount of misinformation (e.g., ungrammatical utterances, slips of the tongue) in this linguistic input could easily be tolerated.

I will attempt to present the current position regarding the relationship between the linguistic environment of the language learning child and language acquisition. Since the present position is the result of several major shifts of emphasis within a relatively short time, it is perhaps useful to review the research which has been done on this topic historically.

1 Stage I: simple, well-formed, redundant

The first analyses of speech addressed to children were undertaken in response to the view that such input was ill-formed (characterized by mistakes, garbles, ungrammaticalities, false starts, mispronunciations and stutters; see, for example, Miller and Chomsky, 1963, and McNeill, 1966) and that it was very complex. This description assumed that the 'primary linguistic data' available to the child did not differ in any important way from the language used among adults (Fodor, 1966). It was a fairly simple matter to disconfirm that view. Various investigators collected and analysed samples of speech addressed to children in the age range 18 to 36 months by their mothers (Broen, 1972; Drach, 1969; Kobashigawa, 1969; Phillips, 1973; Remick, 1976; Sachs *et al.*, 1976; Snow, 1972a). Every measure used in these studies for grammatical complexity (mean length of utterance, incidence of subordinate clauses, mean preverb length, incidence of conjunction, etc.) or for well-formedness (incidence of hesitations, disfluencies, within constituent pauses, false starts, etc.) revealed that the speech addressed to children aged 18 to 36 months was much simpler and much more grammatical than the speech addressed to adults. Not only was speech to children found to be simple and well-formed, but it was also found to be highly redundant. Mothers repeated phrases and whole sentences and paraphrased their own utterances frequently (Snow, 1972a). Individual mothers used certain 'sentence frames' (e.g. *'That's* NP'; *'Where's* NP'; *'See* NP') quite frequently (Broen, 1972).

The general conclusion drawn from the Stage I studies of mothers' speech was that the speech addressed to children of language learning age was well adapted to the children's own linguistic level. In view of the nature of this speech, it could also be concluded that the innate component to language ability might be considerably smaller than proposed by Chomsky (1965), McNeill (1966) or Lenneberg (1967), and that it need not contain a great deal of specific linguistic structure. Information about linguistic structure was available from the input; the innate component need only ensure that children attended to linguistic input, distinguished it from irrelevant input, and expected it to be structured.

Two additional bits of information which became available at about the same time as the results of the early mothers' speech studies supported this conclusion. First, it was found that not only mothers, but also all adults and even children aged four to five, produced simplified, redundant speech when addressing 16- to 36-month-olds (Andersen and Johnson, 1973; Sachs and Devin, 1976; Shatz and Gelman, 1973). This finding meant that such speech could be assumed to be universally available to language learning children; not just children growing up in middle-class North America and cared for by their mothers, but also children living in extended families and cared for by older siblings or cousins have access to a modified speech register. Second, it was found that children can play an active role in selecting which sentences they hear. Adult sentences which were far more complex than the child's own utterances, and those begun with an unfamiliar word, were less likely to be attended to than simple sentences begun with familiar words (Shipley *et al.*, 1969; Snow, 1972b). This finding helped explain why children did not become confused and misled by the complex utterances overheard from adult–adult conversation or from radio and television. Not only was most of the speech available to young children adapted to their linguistic level, but speech not adapted to their level could simply be filtered out.

The findings of the first set of mothers' speech studies were purely descriptive. No one had undertaken to sort out what it was about talking to children that caused speakers to speak simply, grammatically and redundantly – whether their age, their inability to speak correctly, their low status, their size, their cuteness, or their unwillingness to do as they were told was the relevant variable. An indication that feedback from the child played some role in influencing the mother to talk simply and redundantly came from a study in which mothers were asked to make tapes which would later be played to their children (Snow, 1972a). Although the mothers in this situation did speak more slowly, simply and redundantly than they would have to an adult, they did not speak as simply or redundantly as when the child was present with them. This finding suggested that the characteristics of maternal speech could be explained primarily as adjustments made in response to cues from the child. If maternal speech was too complex, the children would tend to become inattentive and would fail to comply with requests or respond to questions. These cues would cause the mother to simplify her speech until it reached a level of complexity at which the child was optimally compliant and attentive. An implication of this suggestion was that mothers' speech would be quite well adapted to the child's linguistic level. The characteristics of maternal speech would thus be expected to change abruptly in the direction of simplicity, well-formedness and redundancy at 12 to 14 months, when the child first showed signs of understanding, and then gradually over the next three to four years to reapproach the normal adult values.

Oversimplification 1: mothers' language lessons

One possible interpretation of the findings discussed above is that the mothers were providing their children with ideal 'language lessons' – a carefully graded curriculum of information about the structure of their mother tongue (Levelt, 1975). Such an interpretation is, of course, an unwarranted extrapolation from the findings. Although mothers do often teach their children about language, about the meanings of words, about how to form plurals, past tenses, etc., what mothers are doing most of the time is simply trying to communicate with their children. A side effect of their attempts to communicate is the set of modifications described. These modifications are not the result of attempts by the mothers to teach their children to talk: rather, they are the result of attempts to communicate effectively with them.

Oversimplification 2: no innate component

Another misinterpretation of these early findings was the conclusion that there was no innate component to language ability. It is, of course, absurd to argue that any complex behaviour is entirely innate or entirely learned. Innate and environmental factors always interact in the development of complex abilities, and both are of crucial importance. It is not, however, absurd to ask what proportion of the developmental variation in some complex ability like language is attributable to innate as opposed to environmental factors, for it is certainly the case that environmental factors can be relatively more important in determining an individual's achievements for one type of ability (e.g., solving arithmetic problems) than for another type (e.g., singing on key). Chomsky's position regarding language was that it was more like singing on key than like arithmetic; anyone with an innately good ear can learn to sing on key, with only minimal practice and exposure to music, and any human being (i.e., any possessor of the species-specific innate linguistic structure) can learn language on the basis of minimal exposure to even complex and ill-formed utterances. The correct conclusion to be drawn from the Stage I studies was that Chomsky's position regarding the unimportance of the linguistic input was unproven, since all children, in addition to possessing an innate linguistic ability, also receive a simplified, well-formed, and redundant corpus. Thus, the relative importance of the innate and the social factors could not be determined. The prediction was made that children without access to such a simplified, redundant corpus would be unsuccessful or retarded in learning language. If such could be proven to be the case, then it could indeed be concluded that an innate, species-specific, linguistic component was relatively less important than Chomsky had hypothesized. But the conclusion could be drawn that the innate component was of no importance only if the provision of a simplified, well-formed and redundant corpus enabled nonhumans with human-like cognitive capacities, e.g., young chimpanzees, as well as human children, to learn language.

It has been suggested that the results of the mothers' speech studies actually support Chomsky's position, by demonstrating that the speech addressed to children is really syntactically quite complex (Newport, 1976; Newport *et al.*, 1977). The basis for saying that such speech is complex, despite the short utterance length and absence of complex sentences, is that questions and imperatives are used very frequently in addition to declaratives. [. . .] Why do English-speaking children not start using verb-first orders in their declarative sentences, since imperatives and questions, which show a verb-first order, are more frequent than subject-first declaratives? One reason is certainly that the three sentence types are well distinguished in English by intonation contour. Imperatives and questions addressed to children have a final rise in intonation, whereas declaratives show a falling intonation. There is evidence that mothers use, and even very young children interpret, sentences which end in a rise as signals that some response is required (Ryan, 1978). Thus, children do have a salient acoustic basis for separating out declaratives, imperatives and questions, rather than treating them as one class of utterances. But then why do they choose the less frequent declarative rather than the more frequent question to model their word order on? Perhaps they don't in the beginning, since in fact both declaratives and almost all questions show the same order of subject and main verb. It is the auxiliary which is preposed in questions in English. If no auxiliary is present, one is introduced by the rule of *do*-support. There are various sources of evidence suggesting that children may not attend to such auxiliaries, since they are unstressed (Van der Geest, 1975) and unfamiliar (Shipley *et al.*, 1969). Thus, the child presented with the questions:

Is daddy going?
What's the doggie doing?
Who is eating the cookie?

may in fact be hearing:

Daddy going + rising intonation;
What doggie doing + rising intonation;
Who eating cookie + rising intonation.

In every case, the subject-verb order is maintained. [. . .]

The general conclusion from the available evidence must be that the basic order of elements is modelled for children more frequently than the distribution of utterances across sentence types might suggest.

2   Stage II: the here and the now

The Stage I descriptions of speech addressed to children showed a curious oversight: no description was given of what the mothers were talking about. This oversight becomes more comprehensible if one realizes that the Stage I studies were done in the late 1960s, at a time when analyses of child speech were primarily concerned with children's acquisition of syntactic knowledge. It seemed, thus, most relevant to analyse maternal speech so as to determine how it could provide information about syntactic structure. The child's task was seen as one of testing many different innately supplied hypotheses about the syntax of the language being acquired against the patterns observed in the input, and thus eventually eliminating the incorrect hypotheses. Under this view, the acquisition of semantics was seen as a separate task facing the child.

In 1972, Macnamara argued that this view of language acquisition was incorrect, that the acquisition of syntax could be explained only if it is recognized that children collect information about the relationship between syntactic forms and semantic structures. (Similar views were expressed by Schlesinger, 1971.) In other words, children figure out the rules underlying syntactic structure by using the cues provided by the meaning of an adult's utterance. This implies that children must be able to determine what an utterance means on the basis of nonsyntactic information – since the syntax is precisely what must be learned. Macnamara suggested that knowledge of the meaning of the important lexical items plus knowledge of what is likely to be said about those entities or actions given the situation must enable the child to guess correctly what the utterance means. This implies, of course, not only that the child must be a good guesser, but also that the adult must say the kinds of things the child expects to hear, that adult and child share a way of looking at the world. Greenfield and Smith (1976) have argued that such a shared view of the world does exist, and that this is what enables adults to interpret children's early, presyntactic utterances. Macnamara's argument goes the other way around – that adult utterances have no syntactic structure as far as young children are concerned, and that children in the early stages of language acquisition must, therefore, interpret adult utterances in the same way as adults interpret children's utterances, by relating the words used to aspects of the situation being described. After many thousands of chances to observe that the word referring to the agent precedes the word referring to the action in adult sentences, the child can start to induce a rule about the order of those semantic elements. Much later, after the child starts to hear sentences in which words which obviously do not refer to the agent stand in the first position (e.g., passives like *The cake got eaten*) he will be forced to abandon this simple semantic rule for a syntactic rule incorporating the notion of sentence subject.

This model of how language acquisition proceeds rests on the presumption of *semantic* limitations on adult utterances – that they describe those aspects of the situation at hand which are most obvious to the child, and that the adult utterances are limited to those topics about which the child has extralinguistic information.

If one reanalyses maternal speech keeping this model of semantic matching in mind, then it becomes clear that the semantic content of speech addressed to young children is indeed severely restricted. Mothers limit their utterances to the present tense, to concrete nouns, to comments on what the child is doing and on what is happening around the child (Phillips, 1973; Snow *et al.*, 1976). Mothers make statements and ask questions about what things are called, what noises they make, what colour they are, what actions they are engaging in, who they belong to, where they are located, and very little else (Snow, 1977b). This is a very restricted set of semantic contents, when one considers that older children and adults also discuss past and future events, necessity, possibility, probability, consequence, implication, comparison and many other semantic subtleties. This limitation on the semantic content of maternal speech can to a large extent explain the syntactic simplicity commented on above. Propositions of name, place, state and action can be expressed in short utterances without subordination or other syntactic complexities. The syntactic simplicity can thus to a large extent be seen as an artefact of semantic simplicity.

The conclusion drawn from the Stage I studies was that because of the constant 'steering' function of the child's attention and signs of comprehension, the syntactic complexity of the maternal speech would be quite well matched to the child's linguistic level. It has since been demonstrated that no high correlation exists between the child's linguistic level and most measures of the syntactic complexity of maternal input (Cross, 1977; Newport, 1976; Newport *et al.*, 1977). It is of course true that mothers speak more simply to two-year-olds than to four-year-olds or to eight-year-olds, but there is no strong evidence that there are precise gradations of complexity in maternal speech, i.e., that mothers adjust their speech complexity one notch upwards every time their children learn one new construction or expand their mean length of utterance by one morpheme. This is, of course, unsurprising, since speakers possess no mechanism for very precisely adjusting the syntactic complexity of their speech. Speakers do, however, have semantic complexity under control – their choice of lexical items (cf., Brown, 1958), of topics to discuss and of comments on those topics. So it is not surprising that the syntactic complexity of maternal speech only grows by fairly large jumps as children get older. One would expect, however, that semantic complexity would be more finely tuned to the child's linguistic level – that the topics discussed and the sorts of comments made would indeed grow slowly with the child's comprehension and production abilities. Although no one has ever performed quite the correct analysis, there is indirect evidence that such is the case. Mothers limit the kinds of semantic relations used in their own speech to those used by their children (Snow, 1977b). Furthermore, mothers start using semantic categories frequently in their speech to children only after the children have introduced these categories in their own speech (Van der Geest, 1977). Children may also introduce empty forms (cf., Van der Geest's example of his son's use of the passive with active meaning: *I am being jumped off it* for *I am jumping off it*), or unifunctional forms, thus leading their mothers to think that they control these forms fully and that they can be used in speech addressed to the child. Children almost always introduce a semantic category with no explicit marking (e.g., *Go circus* referring to a past event; *Mama do it* meaning 'Mama will do it'). After such a category is introduced by the child, the mother starts to use it frequently, thereby providing information about how these new semantic notions should be realized. Thus, although a mother's speech is morphologically and syntactically much more complex than her child's speech, semantically it is less in advance.

3 Stage III: talking to one another

Assuming that the semantic component of maternal speech is finely adjusted to the child's linguistic ability, how does this happen? By what mechanism do mothers keep their speech content pitched at the right level?

The answer to this question is quite simple, as soon as one attains the seemingly obvious (but for researchers in this field, long awaited) insight that mothers do not talk at children, but with them. A large proportion of maternal utterances are responses to child utterances, and almost all maternal utterances are directly preceded and followed by child utterances. In other words, mothers and children carry on conversations with one another. These are, in fact, very special kinds of conversations, in that the partners are very unequal. The mother can speak the language much better, but the child nonetheless can dominate the conversation, because the mother follows the child's lead in deciding what to talk about. A very common pattern is for the child to introduce a topic, and for the mother to make a comment on that topic, or for the child to introduce a topic and make a comment, and for the mother to then expand that comment. Thus, at a semantic level, the mother's speech is very much shaped by the child's linguistic abilities, his cognitive abilities, his ideas and interests.

Interestingly, the above description of child-directed discourse accounts for the occurrence of expansions, the characteristic of maternal speech which was first commented upon by Brown and Bellugi (1964). Expansions are full, correct expressions of the meanings encapsulated in children's telegraphic utterances. They are, thus, the ultimate example of a maternal utterance which is semantically related to the preceding child utterance. It was hypothesized that provision of expansions might greatly aid the acquisition of syntax, since the expansion gives information about the full, correct realization of the child's intended meaning at the time the child wishes to communicate that meaning. Evidence for positive effect of expansions has been found (Nelson *et al.*, 1973), though provision of extra conversation with the child even without including expansions seems to have an equally beneficial effect (Cazden, 1965; Nelson *et al.*, 1973). It may well be that expansions can provide crucial bits of information about syntax or morphology, but that this information if not available from expansions will be picked up from other sources. Greenfield and Smith (1976), for example note a number of cases in which early two-word utterances were modelled on sequences in the immediately preceding dialogue.

Too few conversationally based analyses of maternal speech have been performed to say anything about how general the description of maternal speech as adding comments to conversational topics introduced by the child is. Various researchers have described mother–child interaction in ways which correspond to the above model. Shugar (1978), for example, refers to mothers and children interacting dyadically to 'create text'. She has described how mothers produce utterances which create context within which very simple child utterances become meaningful parts of the rather complex whole. For example, if the mother says: 'Who's just coming in?' and the child answers, 'Dada,' then the child utterance can be interpreted semantically as referring to an agent of a presently occurring action, whereas the same utterance without the linguistic context might be uninterpretable. Cross (1978) has found that the percentage of maternal utterances which are semantically related to preceding child utterances is the best predictor of the child's linguistic ability. This implies that children who learn to talk quickly and well have constant access to such semantically related maternal utterances. Bates (1976) has suggested that second children, twins and institutionalized children may learn language more slowly than children whose input comes mainly from adults because egocentric peers do not provide enough interpretable, semantically re-levant messages. But Lieven (1978a and b) has described one mother –child pair where well-constructed dyadic texts were extremely rare. A high proportion of child utterances were not responded to by the mother at all, and the responses which did occur were very often semantically unrelated to the child utterance. They were very likely to be comments like 'Oh, really?' Despite receiving very little semantically relevant speech from her mother, the child in question did eventually learn to talk normally, though her speech at the time Lieven was studying her was highly repetitive, uninformative and difficult to interpret. Thus, though it seems clear that the provision of much semantically relevant speech is advantageous for language acquisition, it has not been proven that access to such speech is crucial to normal language acquisition. Although the amount of semantically relevant and interpretable speech available to children may vary greatly, as suggested by Lieven's findings, it seems unlikely that any but the most socially deprived children have no access at all to such speech.

Mothers are able to provide semantically relevant and interpretable speech because they follow up on topics introduced by the child. It seems clear that some mothers will be better at doing this than others but also that some children will be better at eliciting semantically relevant and interpretable speech than others. Children with poor articulation, for example, will produce fewer interpretable utterances for the mother to expand upon. Children whose speech is highly repetitive, such as the little girl studied by Lieven (1978a), are less interesting to converse with than children who frequently introduce new topics. It is also possible for mother and child to be focused on different aspects of the world, in which case the kinds of comments made by the mother do not match the child's intentions or interests. In such cases, the child's language acquisition can be slowed down (Nelson, 1973).

Interestingly, the kind of semantically relevant and interpretable speech described above begins long before the children themselves begin to talk. This indicates that it is not produced purely in response to utterances from the child. Mothers talking to babies as young as three months show many of the same characteristics of 'mothers' speech style' as are present in speech to two year-olds. Some of the characteristics, such as questions, occur with even greater frequency in speech to younger children. The most striking similarity between speech to very young babies and speech to children aged 18 to 35 months is the extent to which the mother's speech is directed by the child's activities. Infant behaviours such as reaching for something, changing gaze direction, laughing, smiling, vocalizing, even burping, coughing and sneezing, can always evoke specific relevant responses from the mother. At three months of age, the majority of maternal utterances refer only to the child. By the time the baby is six to eight months of age, and is showing many clear signs of interest in objects and activities about him, the maternal utterances also refer to those objects and activities (Snow, 1977a). Thus, the semantic steering of maternal speech by the child begins very early, and may be the basis for the child's discovery of some predictable relationship between utterances and events.

Another aspect of early mother–baby interaction which may contribute to the child's acquisition of language is the opportunity provided to the baby to communicate effectively by using some minimal signal. An example of this, described by Bruner (1975), comes in the course of bouncing games like 'Ride a cock horse'. The mother bounces the baby with a regular rhythm while reciting the first lines of the verse, but gives a 'big bounce' on the last line. After a number of repetitions, the mother often pauses before the 'big bounce' until the baby jiggles expectantly. The mother interprets the jiggle as a message to go on. This interpretation probably has two effects: (a) the mother receives the satisfaction of feeling that her baby is communicating with her, and (b) the baby learns that his own behaviours function as communicative signals. Mothers' use of questions to small babies creates a very similar situation: in response to a question like 'Have you had enough to eat?', almost any behaviour, from fussing to remaining perfectly still, can be interpreted as either, 'yes' or 'no'. By posing the question, the mother creates the possibility of interpreting her baby's behaviour. It seems very likely that much experience during the prelinguistic period with interactions within which the baby can communicate effectively, despite his limited communicative skills, contribute to the acquisition of language.

4 Conclusion

Two basic questions have motivated research into the nature of the speech addressed to children:

1 Why do people use a special speech style when addressing children?
2 Does the special speech style used with children have any effect on the course of language acquisition?

It has been hypothesized that people talk as they do to children because they are trying to teach them to talk, because they are trying to get them to understand, because they are tying to hold their attention and because they are trying to carry on conversations with them. No doubt each of these motives plays some role in producing the modifications of speech style described above. The most important factor seems to be the desire to communicate with children – to respond to their utterances and to elicit responses from them. The desire to communicate implies talking so as to hold their attention and be understood. It may also involve some explicit teaching of language, especially of vocabulary. Aside from fulfilling the communicative function, some aspects of the modified speech style used with small children undoubtedly serve an affective function. Soft tones of voice, diminutives and special baby talk words may be used with babies just because they seem appropriate for cute and cuddly addressees (Brown, 1977; Garnica, 1977). Finally, many of the features of speech addressed to children, such as the high frequency of questions, the provision of syntactic and semantic expansions on child utterances, result from the process of carrying on conversations with immature conversational partners.

Does the use of special speech styles with children facilitate language acquisition and, if so, which features of the modified speech style have an effect? All the evidence suggests that every child growing up in any culture has access to simplified, redundant, well-formed and semantically concrete speech, so it is impossible to say whether children without such input acquire language normally. There is only a small amount of evidence relevant to the question whether language acquisition can be facilitated by access to certain features of modified speech style. This evidence suggests that semantic interpretability and relevance are the crucial features in facilitating language acquisition. It seems likely that the speech must also observe certain limits on syntactic complexity and ill-formedness, but that these limitations are introduced automatically as a result of the semantic simplicity. If one were asked right now to advise an anxious mother how to teach her child to talk, the best answer would be 'Watch what he's doing, listen to what he's saying, and then respond.'

References

ANDERSEN, E. S. and JOHNSON, C. E. (1973) 'Modifications in the speech of an eight-year-old to younger children.' *Stanford Occasional Papers in Linguistics*, **3**, 149–60.

BATES, E. (1976) *Language and Context: the acquisition of pragmatics*. New York: Academic Press.

BLOUNT, B. G. and PADGUG, E. J. (1977) 'Prosodic, paralinguistic, and interactional features in parent-child speech: English and Spanish.' *Journal of Child Language*, **4**, 67–86.

BROEN, P. A. (1972) *The Verbal Environment of the Language-learning Child*. Monograph of American Speech and Hearing Association 17, December.

BROWN, R. (1958) 'How shall a thing be called?' *Psychological Review*, **65**, 14–21.

BROWN, R. (1977) 'Introduction', in SNOW, C. E. and FERGUSON, C. A. (eds) *Talking to Children: language input and acquisition*. Cambridge: Cambridge University Press.

BROWN, R. and BELLUGI, U. (1964) 'Three processes in the child's acquisition of syntax.' *Harvard Educational Review, Language and Learning*, **34**, 133–51.

BRUNER, J. S. (1975) 'The ontogenesis of speech acts.' *Journal of Child Language*, **2**, 1–19.

CAZDEN, C. (1965) 'Environmental assistance to the child's acquisition of grammar.' Doctoral dissertation, Harvard University.

CHOMSKY, N. (1965) *Aspects of the Theory of Syntax*. Cambridge, MA: MIT Press.

CROSS, T. G. (1977) 'Mothers' speech adjustment: the contribution of selected child listener variables', in SNOW, C. E. and FERGUSON, C. A. (eds) *Talking to Children: language input and acquisition*. Cambridge: Cambridge University Press.

CROSS, T. G. (1978) 'Motherese: its association with rate of syntactic acquisition in young children', in WATERSON, N. and SNOW, C. E. (eds) *The Development of Communication*. Chichester: Wiley.

DRACH, K. (1969) 'The language of the parent: a pilot study.' Working paper 14, University of California, Berkeley.

FERGUSON, C. A. (1977) 'Baby talk as a simplified register', in SNOW, C. E. and FERGUSON, C. A. (eds) *Talking to Children: language input and acquisition*. Cambridge: Cambridge University Press.

FODOR, J. A. (1966) 'How to learn to talk: some simple ways', in SMITH, F. and MILLER, G. A. (eds) *The Genesis of Language*. Cambridge, MA: MIT Press.

GARNICA, O. (1977) 'Some prosodic and paralinguistic features of speech to young children', in SNOW, C. E. and FERGUSON, C. A. (eds) *Talking to Children: language input and acquisition*. Cambridge: Cambridge University Press.

GREENFIELD, P. and SMITH, J. H. (1976) *The Structure of Communication in Early Language Development*. New York: Academic Press.

KOBASHIGAWA, B. (1969) 'Repetitions in a mother's speech to her child.' Working paper 14, University of California, Berkeley.

LENNEBERG, E. H. (1967) *Biological Foundations of Language*. New York: Wiley.

LEVELT, W. J. M. (1975) 'What became of the LAD?', in *Ut Videam: contributions to an understanding of linguistics, for Pieter Verburg on the occasion of his 70th birthday.* Lisse: Peter de Ridder Press.

LIEVEN, E. (1978a) 'Conversations between mothers and young children: individual differences and their possible implications for the study of language learning', in WATERSON, N. and SNOW, C. E. (eds) *The Development of Communication.* Chichester: Wiley.

LIEVEN, E. (1978b) 'Turn-taking and pragmatics: two issues in early child language', in CAMPBELL, R. N. and SMITH, P. (eds) *Recent Advances in the Psychology of Language: language development and mother-child interaction.* New York and London: Plenum.

MCNEILL, D. A. (1966) 'The creation of language by children', in LYONS, J. and WALES, R. J. (eds) *Psycholinguistics Papers.* Edinburgh: Edinburgh University Press.

MACNAMARA, J. (1972) 'Cognitive basis of language learning in infants.' *Psychological Review,* **79,** 1–13.

MILLER, G. and CHOMSKY, N. (1963) 'Finitary models of language users', in BUSH, R., GALANTER, E. and LUCE, R. (eds) *Handbook of Mathematical Psychology, Vol II.* New York: Wiley.

NELSON, K. (1973) *Structure and Strategy in Learning to Talk.* Society for Research in Child Development Monographs 38, 1–2.

NELSON, K. E., CARSKADDON, G. and BONVILLIAN, J. D. (1973) 'Syntax acquisitions: impact of experimental variation in adult verbal interaction with the child.' *Child Development,* **44,** 497–504.

NEWPORT, E. (1976) 'Motherese: the speech of mothers to young children', in CASTELLAN, N., PISONI, D. and POTTS, G. (eds) *Cognitive Theory, Vol II.* Hillsdale, NJ: Erlbaum.

NEWPORT, E., GLEITMAN, L. and GLEITMAN, H. (1977) 'Mother, I'd rather do it myself: some effects and noneffects of maternal speech style', in SNOW, C. E. and FERGUSON C. A. (eds) *Talking to Children: language input and acquisition.* Cambridge: Cambridge University Press.

PHILLIPS, J. (1973) 'Syntax and vocabulary of mothers' speech to young children: age and sex comparisons.' *Child Development,* **44,** 182–5.

REMICK, H. (1976) 'Maternal speech to children during language acquisition', in ENGEL, W. von RAFFLER and LEBRUN, Y. (eds) *Baby Talk and Infant Speech.* Lisse, Netherlands: Peter de Ridder Press.

RYAN, M. L. (1978) 'Contour in context', in CAMPBELL, R. N. and SMITH, P. T. (eds) *Recent Advances in the Psychology of Language: language development and mother-child interaction.* New York and London: Plenum.

SACHS, J. and DEVIN, J. (1976) 'Young children's use of age-appropriate speech styles in social interaction and role-playing.' *Journal of Child Language,* **3,** 81–98.

SACHS, J., BROWN, R. and SALERNO, R. (1976) 'Adults' speech to children', in ENGEL, W. von RAFFLER and LEBRUN, Y. (eds) *Baby Talk and Infant Speech.* Lisse, Netherlands: Peter de Ridder Press.

SCHLESINGER, I. M. (1971) 'Learning grammar: from pivot to realisation rule', in HUXLEY, R. and INGRAM, E. (eds) *Language Acquisition: models and methods.* London: Academic Press.

SHATZ, M. and GELMAN, R. (1973) *The Development of Communication Skills: modifications in the speech of young children as a function of listener.* Society for Research in Child Development Monographs **38,** 5.

SHIPLEY, E. GLEITMAN, L. and SMITH, C. (1969) 'A study in the acquisition of language: free responses to commands.' *Language*, **45**, 332–42.

SHUGAR, G. W. (1978) 'Text analysis as an approach to the study of early linguistic operations', in WATERSON, N. and SNOW, C. E. (eds) *The Development of Communication*. Chichester: Wiley.

SNOW, C. E. (1972a) 'Mothers' speech to children learning language.' *Child Development*, **43**, 549–65.

SNOW, C. E. (1972b) 'Young children's responses to adult sentences of varying complexity.' Paper presented at Fourth International Congress of Applied Linguistics, Copenhagen.

SNOW C. E. (1977a) 'The development of conversation between mothers and babies.' *Journal of Child Language*, **4**, 1–22.

SNOW, C. E. (1977b) 'Mothers' speech research: from input to interaction', in SNOW, C. E. and FERGUSON, C. A. (eds) *Talking to Children: language input and acquisition*. Cambridge: Cambridge University Press.

SNOW, C. E., ARLMAN-RUPP, A., HASSING, Y., JOBSE, J., JOOSTEN, J. and VORSTER, J. (1976) 'Mothers' speech in three social classes.' *Journal of Psycholinguistic Research*, **5**, 1–20.

VAN der GEEST, T. (1975) *Some Aspects of Communicative Competence and their Implications for Language Acquisition*. Assen, Amsterdam: Royal van Gorcum.

VAN der GEEST, T. (1977) 'Some interactional aspects of language acquisition', in SNOW, C. E. and FERGUSON, C. A. (eds) *Talking to Children: language input and acquisition*. Cambridge: Cambridge University Press.

2.7   Into print: reading and language growth

Jessie F. Reid

There are two fairly direct ways of seeing how reading theory and practice
have changed over the last twenty years. One way is to look at lists of
publications and see how dramatically the number has increased.
Another way – and a striking one – is to examine the indexes of some
standard books on the psychology and teaching of reading. If we compare
the indexes of two books from the forties and fifties, say Gates (1947) and
Anderson and Dearborn (1952), with those of three from the sixties and
seventies, say Goodman (1968), Clay (1972) and Gibson and Levin
(1975), the most arresting contrast is to be found in the amount of space
allotted to items like language, speech, syntax, sentence patterns, prediction, context, and concepts of print. While all of these topics figure
prominently in the indexes to more recent works, some of them do not
occur at all in the earlier ones. By contrast, references to visual perception,
discrimination, eye movements, association, *Gestalt* theory, and word
shape, which were common in earlier discussions, have diminished. In
other words, research on and thinking about reading has altered, not just
in volume but also in content and focus.

The change is often described as consisting in a shift of thought towards
classifying reading and writing as new kinds of language learning, rather
than new kinds of perceptual and motor skill. But to put it in this way does
not fully express the crucial nature of the change. Reading has always
been thought of as connected in one way or another with speech. What has
altered, and what has caused our view of reading to alter, is our understanding of the nature of language itself and of language acquisition. This
change has in its turn affected the ways in which we view the development
of literacy in children, and its relationship to the oral language learning
which has preceded it.

To illustrate the change, I want to use the case of a girl whom I shall call
Clare. When she was about seven and a half years old and already a good
reader, Clare came to me with a commercially-produced version of the
story of *The Sleeping Beauty*, declaring that she could not read it. She was
obviously surprised and somewhat upset, for the book had the large
colourful pictures and bold clear print that are standard in books for
'young readers'. When I asked her to tell me what was wrong, she
answered: 'I can read the words, but I don't know what they mean.'
Further questioning revealed that one of the sentences which had defeated
her ran thus: 'The princess's father and mother invited her fairy god-

---

Source: DONALDSON, M., GRIEVE, R. and PRATT, C. (eds) (1983) *Early Childhood Development and education*. Oxford: Blackwell.

mothers, seven in all, to come to her christening.' It became clear, when I asked Clare to read the sentence aloud, that she could indeed 'read the words', and that she knew the meaning of 'invited' and 'christening'; her puzzlement came entirely from three of the simplest words in the sentence – the words 'seven in all.' Indeed, the obstacle presented by this phrase was so great that she had to be encouraged to read past it, and her voice showed that it caused her totally to lose hold of the sense.

Traditional views of the nature of reading acquisition would most likely have classified Clare's problem as a failure in 'comprehension'; which in one sense it was. But in so doing, they would have implied that it was not really a basic *reading* problem at all. For these traditional views were based on the notion that the central activity in learning to read consists in 'word-recognition'. The recognition could be of overall shape (whatever that is) or of letter patterns. But the process of extracting meaning from written sentences was seen as a process of identifying written words, whose meanings (learned by 'association' from speech) were then strung together in a simple additive manner. Failure to 'comprehend' was thus a failure to grasp, or attend to, word meaning. A look at a well-known textbook on the psychology of reading, such as Anderson and Dearborn (1952) will confirm the prevalence of this view – a view which we now know to be seriously mistaken. The comprehension of language does not work that way. And to some degree Clare, aged seven, sensed this. She was concerned not with word meaning but with *sentence* meaning – with what the words collectively meant – even though her ability to talk about sentence meaning was too limited to express this adequately.

The belief that 'word recognition' lay at the heart of learning to read meant that the efforts of those who composed early materials went mainly into making this one task easier. But even during the first half of the present century, one or two notable exceptions to the prevailing orthodoxy on word recognition appeared. There were several exponents of the 'sentence method' (e.g., Jagger, 1929), and even earlier, there was the remarkable E. B. Huey (1908) who attacked the 'insidious thought of reading as word-pronouncing' (page 350). Both these writers had views on reading which were much in advance of their time, views which are only now finding adequate theoretical foundations in the accounts of language and language acquisition which have emerged over the last twenty-five years. These accounts have enabled us to look in quite new ways at the process of acquiring written language. We see, as we did not see before, the nature of the extensions of language learning which literacy entails.

In looking for a phrase which might distil the essence of what follows, I was reminded of a saying attributed to Professor Simon Lawrie. He was the first holder of the Chair of Education in the University of Edinburgh, and is recorded as having once said that the prime task of the teacher is 'to put herself into the attitude of ignorance of the learner'. A conscious attempt of this kind to adopt the mental stance of someone else is what

Piaget would call an act of decentration. It is often not an easy thing to do, but I believe Lawrie's view – that teachers (and researchers) are called upon to try – is profoundly true.

In the late fifties and mid-sixties I undertook a number of studies in which I – in an effort to improve my own decentration – interviewed five-year-olds about learning to read and write (Reid, 1958; 1966). I wanted to find out how the experience appeared to them and how they could talk about it. For the purposes of this discussion I shall first discuss the 1966 study, which provided the insights which I now want to examine.

As I listened to the children's spontaneous comments and their answers to my questions, I began to see how much I had not previously understood. I realized for the first time that there were children who did not know what reading consisted in—who had no concept of marks which stood for speech. I found for instance a child who thought she was 'past reading'. 'We finished it yesterday,' she assured me very firmly. Questioned further, she said 'Yes, we read all the pages.' When I asked her what was in the book that she had finished yesterday, she replied, 'If that one was the same and that one was not the same.' She had been working through exercises in 'visual discrimination' which did not involve any written words at all.

I also found children apparently totally ignorant of the simplest functions of writing – of names on buses, or addresses on letters. In other words, the 'attitude of ignorance' of these children was one where they needed to be helped to discover what a writing system was – indeed that such a thing existed – and that it served useful, even essential, purposes in everyday communication. That was where these children had to begin.

The work I did then was replicated and expanded, first by John Downing (1970) and later by others, with similar results. As well as finding puzzlement and ignorance about the existence and functions of written language, I and others found some very marked gaps and confusions in children's vocabulary for talking about print, even though they were actually trying to cope with a reading primer. They called letters 'numbers' or 'words'; they called words 'names' or 'the writing'; they called sentences 'stories'. They referred to individual letters as (say) 'h for horse'; some thought that 'big' letters (i.e., capitals) were 'for big animals', or that they made 'a different sort of word'. Some children called sounding 'spelling' or *vice versa*. Some said things like 'I'll write a house' and 'I'll draw my name', and indeed showed, when they tried to write, that they did not realize one of the distinctive features of written symbols – namely, that orientation mattered. It was clear that these children lacked the necessary conceptual grasp of the nature of our written language system and also the vocabulary to talk about it, either to themselves or to anyone else.

There are of course children who come to school with a good understanding of these matters (Clark, 1976). But there are many who do not, and I am now quite sure that for them the activity of reading can remain totally mysterious. It is not, after all, an activity like riding a bicycle or baking a cake, where the onlooker sees what the cyclist or the baker is doing, and where the intentions and purposes are clear. Before the actual learning of the code begins, the child must see something of the nature and aims of the task.

Work of a kind which paralleled and complemented the foregoing studies was done by Marie Clay. In 1972 she produced a test of concepts of print called 'Sand' (this being the title of the story which ran through the test material). The concepts covered by the test were in many respects the same as those with which Downing and I had been concerned. In a previous study of early reading behaviour, Clay (1969) made several observations which related closely to our interest in the child's conception of 'a word'. In particular, she noted the importance for a child of 'pointing' while reading aloud. Many teachers frown on the practice, but Clay pointed out that the child was using movement to help him make a correct word-for-word match between the words he uttered and the print on the page. This establishing of the 'print-speech match' is an important process, because as Clay showed it can lead to self-correction by children as they read, and to important discoveries about word-boundaries, which are not marked in speech. (For an extended discussion of this topic, see Downing, 1979.)

All these ideas have given a new dimension to the notion of reading readiness. They have led to the conviction, now more and more widely held, that the most relevant preparation for reading alphabetic writing consists not in practising visual discrimination with pictures and diagrams but in being helped to see what written alphabetic language looks like, to learn the conventions by which it is set out, and to discover how it is used. We are also coming to see that, in step with their growing understanding of print, children must become more aware of how their spoken language sounds and how it works.

Several publications since 1970 have embodied these notions of preparation. The principles underlying *Breakthrough to Literacy** give them a prominent place. They are the basis of much of the early work in *Link-up* (Reid and Low, 1972), and in Kit 1 of *Letter Links* (Reid and Donaldson, 1978). Downing and Thackray's book on reading readiness (Downing and Thackray, 1971) acknowledges their importance, pointing out that readiness is now more than ever to be seen as something we can induce and not just wait for. And important confirming evidence comes from a longitudinal study of early reading progress by Gordon Wells and Bridie Raban (Wells and Raban, 1978). They found the best predictor of attainment in reading at age seven to be the child's understanding of concepts of written language on entry to school. While it is true that a correlation does not by

* Originally part of the Programme in Linguistics and English Teaching funded by Nuffield and the Schools Council, the *Breakthrough to Literacy* materials are published by Longman (1972 onwards).

itself show a direct causal link, early understanding of concepts of print appears to contribute powerfully to progress in learning to read and write. This conclusion is supported by much evidence from the individual studies already described (Clark, 1976; Downing, 1970; Reid, 1966).

How can this important conceptual basis for learning the written code be further developed when the teaching of reading is begun? In terms of widespread classroom practice, it was probably the 'language-experience' approach to literacy which began the move away from emphasis on mere code-learning. In this approach, the teacher takes off from children's own utterances – things they want to communicate – and puts these into writing which the children can then 'read back'. While Huey refers to it (1908, page 339), its origins are a little obscure. It was in fairly wide use in the United States during the sixties (Spitzer, 1967), and became familiar to many people in Britain through the writings of Sylvia Ashton Warner (1966). However, the fact that it is not listed in the index to Hunter Diack's excellent survey *In Spite of the Alphabet* (Diack, 1965) suggests that its use in Britain was not yet widespread by that date.

The language-experience approach represents an advance which even its early users may not have fully realized. Firstly, it begins where the child is, and shows the transformation of speech into writing actually taking place. It therefore provides an opportunity for teacher and child to talk about this process, and for the teacher to point out those important features of written language (such as separate words, letters, lines, arrangement of text on a page, left-to-right conventions) with which the child must come to feel at home.

But the language-experience approach does something more. It places written language in meaningful situations, and shows it expressing information which the children have decided they want to convey. In the first years of the 'new wave' of studies of oral language acquisition, the primacy of meaning for children learning to comprehend and use oral language was initially neglected, because of a preoccupation with syntax and grammar (see below). It was not until the early seventies that a turning point was reached, a point marked by a paper by Macnamara (1972). His contention – that children first learn about meaning, as embodied in events, situations and sensed purposes, and then learn to fit language to these meanings – shed further light on the strange nature of written language for the novice. Written language is language in a new code – 'language by eye' instead of 'language by ear'. But it is also, as met in books, a language without situation, without a speaker, without an immediate purpose. It is what Margaret Donaldson (1978) has called 'disembedded'. It is language pared down to the words alone, with no support from intonation, gesture, or facial expression. Robert Louis Stevenson (1879) called it 'the silent, inexpressive type'. Children must, he says, 'confront the silent, inexpressive type alone, like pioneers.' This acute piece of observation, buried in one of his *Essays of Travel*, shows a rare insight into the nature of learning to read.

There is a fashion today to describe the act of reading a book as 'having a dialogue with the text.' Now whatever reading a book may be, it is not a dialogue. Rather, it is listening with the mind to a monologue, delivered by an absent and most probably unknown author. The print is fixed and unchanging. It does not add one word in answer to a question or a comment. This is not to say that reading is a passive activity. But it does mean that the child learning to read has to learn a new way of reacting to a verbal message.

A language-experience approach, however, can greatly ease the transition the child has to make. It builds on the child's intention and wish to communicate, and so provides an important bridge between the immediacy and vividness of conversation and the static remoteness of print. I have already referred to *Breakthrough to Literacy*, which can be seen as a development and a formalization of language-experience techniques. Observation of children working with the materials (Reid, 1975) showed that they came to understand the communicative function of written language very well. It was clear that the teacher's role in reading and responding to what the children had composed was a powerful element in this learning process.

Three other bridges exist, all easily accessible. One is found in the use by the teacher of written communication in the classroom – not labels on objects like tables or doors, but real messages – notices, notes to other teachers, sentences under children's paintings. Another is the reading aloud of stories, making it clear that the print on the paper, and not the pictures, is the key to the words that are uttered. The third is the use of public print – perhaps the most 'embedded' of all written language which children can encounter, apart from the writing they themselves have been involved in generating. Children can, with help, become easily aware of such things as street signs or advertisements and can understand their purposes very well. Public print can also be successfully integrated into many classroom activities and into early reading material (cf., Reid and Low, 1972).

There is yet a third outcome of the language-experience approach which recent thinking has justified. When sentences are dictated by children, it follows that they contain not only vocabulary the children know, but sentence structures which conform to the children's speech patterns. Concern with the sentence patterns that appear in the texts which young children are given to read has developed along with a changing view of language acquisition. As long as language growth was seen as mainly consisting in the acquisition of vocabulary, then early books were judged acceptable if the vocabulary reflected the words children 'knew'. The meaning was thought of as the sum of the word meanings. We now realize that much more is involved. Clare's problem, we must remember, was not with vocabulary. It was to discover how certain words were *related* to one another – how they were to be combined to produce meaning. These structural relations among words in a phrase or sentence are what we call *syntax*, and it is to the role of syntax in reading that I now want to turn.

The recognition that young children beginning to read are dealing not just with words but with the syntax and grammar of written texts – and hence with phrase and sentence meaning – was another major change in our thinking about how they should be helped. It opened new avenues in reading research and teaching methods, it altered the construction of early reading materials, and it added yet another dimension to the concept of 'readiness'. It also clarified greatly the notion of 'readability'. The new studies of language acquisition made it clear that children learning to speak acquired general rules from the language they heard adults speaking. They gradually acquired a grasp of the way words must be ordered, combined and inflected to convey meaning. The children arrived at this knowledge without any direct teaching and they made many mistakes on the way. But some of these very mistakes (like saying 'bringed' instead of 'brought') were seen as evidence that 'rule-forming' was at work. Certain features of language structure – for example, the correct word order in questions – were sometimes relatively late in being learned. A child of around four might well say, 'What they are doing?' (Menyuk, 1969). Yet by the age of five, children were seen as having an extensive grasp of basic sentence structure. They were therefore coming to the task of reading with powerful equipment to which reading theory and practice had paid little or no attention. We now begin to realize that they must be given a chance to put it to use.

How was this to be done? The answer seemed to be that the early texts which they were given to read should be of a kind which allowed them to make use of their syntactic knowledge as well as their knowledge of vocabulary and their general understanding of their world. As we have seen, text constructed in the course of language-experience activities achieves this end (unless of course the teacher alters it as she writes it down). But what about reading schemes or other early books, to which children must fairly quickly move?

The unnatural and stilted nature of sentences in primers based on word methods or on early 'phonic' methods had been noticed a long time before. They ranked high among the faults mentioned by Huey (1908). However, a general change in the style of basal reading texts was slow to come.

It is often the case that evidence appears before there is a theory to explain it. When this happens, the evidence may have to wait for years to find recognition, even from the person who discovered it. In 1958 I published a study of a group of five-year-olds in their first year of learning to read, in which I interviewed them and also gave them some experimental reading tasks. The results (Reid, 1958) opened my eyes to many things. Unlike the children in the study described above, who were from less privileged homes, this group of middle-class children were more able to give accounts of how they set about trying to read something. Some of them were remarkably articulate about certain sources of confusion and

difficulty. When questioned more closely about these, the children attributed almost all of the difficulty to 'more difficult words' or 'harder
words'. Pressed for examples, they spoke of 'long words you can't spell and
you just have to remember them' (like 'except'), of letters that 'don't say
anything' (as in 'right'), of 'words not good for sounding' or 'not sounded
that way' or where 'you'd expect it to be something else' (like 'one'). The
difficulties at the surface of their consciousness, about which they could
speak when questioned, were all to do with words, with rules for 'sounding' which did not apply, with expectations not fulfilled.

The preoccupation with words and sounds which this group showed
seems to mirror very well the preoccupation noted earlier as running
through writings on reading method up to the 1950s. This is not surprising. The teacher who concentrates on words and sounds is implicitly
telling the children that these are what 'reading' is about. But one of the
reading experiments which I conducted with these same children suggested that although individual words were the main focus of conscious
attention and effort, they were not the sole determiners of what the
children actually did when they were reading a sentence. I gave them two
sets of four sentences, with a large common vocabulary, but so constructed
that the second set was more advanced than the first in syntax and
concepts. An example from the first set was: 'Can you give me more words
to read?'; an example from the second set was: 'We must not give up when
work is hard.' In another pair, 'I can see his face in the darkness' was
contrasted with 'Darkness was upon the face of the deep.' The children all
read the eight sentences in the same order, because I wanted to find out
what happened when they met, in a more puzzling context, words they
had read correctly, or had been helped to read, in the easier one.

I found that the best readers could read both versions. Some of the
average readers however, could read the first set but not the second.
Moreover they refused, or misread, words which they had read correctly a
few moments earlier. When asked why these were difficult, they said
things like, 'Hard words you've never seen before.' Words described in
this way included 'his', 'to', 'deep', 'face', 'more', 'not' and 'darkness'.
Quite apart from the fact that these were words already identified, they
were almost all likely to be part of the sight vocabulary of middle-class
children near the end of their first year at school, as these children were. It
was obvious then, that 'word recognition' could not be the whole basis of
their success or failure. Something which at the time I called simply
'difficult context' was influencing their recognition of apparently very
'easy' words. The children, however, showed no awareness of this at all.
At the time this study was done, a great wave of interest in the role of
syntax in early reading was building up in North America; but I did not
yet know about it. So I did not fully realize how my findings demonstrated
one of the crucial links – and one of the crucial divisions – between spoken
and written language.

Four years later Ruth Strickland (1962) published a monograph on the

relationship of children's oral language to the language in basal readers. It
is interesting to reflect that a gap of over fifty years separates it from the
publication by E. B. Huey of *The Psychology and Pedagogy of Reading* (Huey,
1908). Her study was a major influence in bringing reading theory into
line with thinking on language acquisition. In it, she made a comparison,
in terms of the sentence structures used, between a large body of tran-
scripts of the speech of kindergarten children and sentences sampled from
four widely-used basal readers. Her analysis laid bare the great poverty
and rigidity of the language in these books when viewed alongside the
flexibility and variety of the sentences in children's speech. She raised the
question whether the books from which children learn should perhaps
contain language which resembles much more closely, in sentence
structure, the ways the children speak.

A close look at her data showed that there were actually two kinds of
mismatch between the books and the speech samples. The early reading
books were indeed rigid and bare in comparison with children's speech;
but in addition they contained quite a number of sentence patterns which
the children's speech samples did not contain, sometimes because they
were things that one writes but does not say. I therefore decided to use her
speech data as the basis for an analysis of four schemes in wide use in
Britain (Reid, 1970), looking particularly at this second kind of 'mismatch'. The results served to specify very clearly the main ways in which
the language of these early reading books was, in the words of E. B. Huey
'. . . totally unlike anything a child would naturally say . . .' (Huey, 1908).
And the matter at issue was not vocabulary: it was *syntax* – the ways
in which words are ordered and related to one another to convey
meaning.

To begin with, much of the language of the primers did not reflect the
ways in which 'function' or 'grammatical' words (e.g., 'to', 'but', 'so'), as
opposed to 'content' words, play their part in giving a sentence flow,
coherence, and sense. There were many instances of adverbial phrases (like
'in school' or 'by the fire') appearing in positions where children would not
put them and therefore would not expect them (e.g., a child would not say:
'By the fire sat a dog'). Many of the sentences were what Hocker (1963)
called 'hortatory' – exhortations to 'look', 'see', 'come', etc., in which it
was often unclear whether the speaker was one of the characters or the
author of the book. Two instances of the confusing nature of this kind of
writing, taken from my own records, are worth quoting at this point.

In the first instance, a child reading: 'Come here, Tip,' said: 'It says
"Come here Tip," and it says he's coming along here.'

In other words, the child interpreted the 'command' to Tip as a
statement *about* Tip. In the second instance, a child reading: 'See the
boats, John,' at the foot of a page, turned the page saying: 'Now we'll see
what John says.' But the following page merely continues to exhort John
to see the boats! This is a splendid example of a child interpreting a piece
of text as a real item of dialogue, something which would require a reply,

and anticipating that the text would conform to one of the ways she knew dialogue worked.

The arguments, then, for a radical change in the language of early readers were powerful. But many people continued to doubt whether the emphasis on sentence structures was well founded. How could we know that 'implicit knowledge' in this area was transferred to reading?

The most convincing demonstration that children's implicit knowledge of basic rules of syntax does transfer to the task of making sense of print has come from the study of early reading errors. Goodman, to whom we owe much of the impetus in this movement, called his method not the study of errors but the 'analysis of miscues' (Goodman, 1969). This choice of wording conveys the central emphasis – that many of the errors of the beginner are 'guesses' which show the child attempting to use linguistic knowledge as 'cues' to construct 'hypotheses' about meaning. Following Goodman's first study (Goodman, 1967) evidence on the errors of beginning readers came from studies by Clay (1969) and by Weber (1970). These showed that a high proportion of substitution errors fitted the preceding syntax, and that they often consisted of supplying the correct part of speech even if the sense was wrong. These high proportions could be found, moreover, in the reading of children who were not progressing very well. That is to say, children with limited word-identification skills were drawing on some of the deep implicit knowledge which guided their comprehension and production of speech.

There is now a school of thought, represented by Goodman and by Smith (1978), which looks on the construction of meaning and the use of syntactic knowledge as the principal components in reading from the very start, and proposes a radical change in how beginners are taught. It is argued that learning to read should proceed merely 'by reading'. Children should learn on 'real books' with a good story line and reasonably varied vocabulary and sentence forms. They should, according to this view, begin by having the story read to them, and then, on successive re-readings of it, supply more and more of the text themselves. Even if their first 'readings' bear little relation, at a word level, to the text, these are to be accepted. Two accounts of this method at work can be found in McKenzie (1977), and in Meek (1982).

In some places, Goodman and Smith appear to argue that any attention to the details of the code is misplaced and unnecessary (Goodman, 1981; Smith, 1978). Smith argues this on largely theoretical grounds, while Goodman (who like Smith plays down the importance of word identification) holds this view in the face of the massive body of evidence he has himself collected about 'miscues'. Yet these miscues are, in the last analysis, wrong hypotheses not corrected by checking the words on the page.

Both writers are at pains not just to stress the primacy of meaning, but to argue that reading need not be different in its nature from listening to speech. But it is inescapably different, in many ways. Some of these have already been examined in this paper. And it is these differences which argue for, rather than against, some deliberate attention to the code – though not for attention to the code in isolation from other kinds of cue. Rather they argue for modes of teaching and learning which will strengthen children's ability to switch rapidly from one kind of cue to another and to integrate them to good effect.

This very process of integration was charted by Biemiller (1970) in a longitudinal study of the reading of first-grade children. Some of the children were seen to move fairly quickly from an early reliance on prediction, producing many 'response errors', to a stage of 'non-response errors' – a stage where they fell silent when puzzled and tried to draw on their phonic knowledge. It was these children who made the best progress, eventually reaching a third stage where they made use of cues of both kinds while making many fewer errors overall. These are important findings. No one would want to deny that a skilled reader 'predicts' meaning – in some sense of that term – and economizes on cues in scanning print. But there is a world of difference between this smooth and efficient processing and the tentative 'guesses' of the beginner. In between the two states there lies a long learning period – a period in which many things have to happen. One of these things is that 'word recognition' has to become assured, quick, and in many cases context-free.

Children between the ages of seven and eleven move in their reading into fiction and 'content area' texts which contain varying blends of narrative and information. (Consider, for instance, geography as opposed to history.) In making this move they leave behind the simple syntax and supportive illustrations of their early books and encounter some of the richness and variety of written registers – the different forms which written language takes to fit differing purposes. But with this richness and variety come new kinds of difficulty, stemming not just from vocabulary but from syntax, organization, style, and – let us not forget – from new and *unexpected* content. For while it is true that expectations support our reading, it is equally true that unless a book can surprise us or tell us things we did not previously know, there is little point in our reading it.

To cope with new ideas and new language forms, good word recognition may well not be enough (as we saw in the case of Clare), but it is most assuredly necessary. If Clare had not been able to recognize all of the words in her puzzling sentence, she would probably have attributed her problem (as did the boys in my first study) to 'difficult words', and she might thus not have realized that it was a problem about meaning. Furthermore, she would have been less ready to be taught about the syntactic forms that were unfamiliar to her. Greater attention can be paid to syntactic pattern when word recognition skills are well developed.

How does efficient word recognition develop? The literature on this question is vast, and I have already touched on the theoretical accounts that were orthodox until quite recently. How should we now view this aspect of reading growth and its place in the whole complex process?

Let us look at the way we now see the task from the children's point of view. What they have to do is to build up a picture (or, if you like, a model) of the way the words in their language are written down – that is, of the orthography. They must do this not just so as to be able to write words, but also to be able to read them with increasing certainty. It is, as we have seen, not enough to entertain hypotheses about what the text says: these hypotheses must also be confirmed or disconfirmed. And this decision-making, which modern writers such as Goodman and Smith stress so much, can only come from confident knowledge of the ways in which letter patterns can – or cannot – function. To build up their internal model, children need to be given correct information about the ways in which, in the case of English, twenty-six letters are used to represent around forty-four phonemes. Teachers have for a long time referred to this area of learning as 'phonics', and have seen it as a confused and confusing mass of 'rules' and 'exceptions' which they have tried, in varying ways, to structure and simplify. The trouble is that simplifying may distort to the point where the true picture is totally obscured.

I want to suggest a somewhat different approach. I believe that as children begin to learn the details of the written code, they urgently need to learn two important general facts about the system. One is that letters sometimes function singly, and sometimes in groups (e.g., 't' and 'h' function singly, but also as the digraph 'th'). The other is that both single letters and letter groups can have more than one sound value (e.g., 'a' sounds differently in 'cat', 'was', 'make', and 'any').

It is vital that children realize these two facts at an early stage, and that the teacher acknowledges them. Otherwise, children will assuredly begin to build their picture of the system on a 'one-letter-one-sound' model, while constantly meeting words which do not fit into it. A five-year-old child in one of my studies talked of words that were 'funny – not the same letters as you say them in'. Questioned further, he gave as an instance 'me', which he thought should have 'two e's', or be written 'mE'. Another said confidently, trying to read 'how': 'I'll sound it and then I'll get it – huh/o/wuh/.' When this did not work, his resources were at an end. Children are perfectly capable, at the age of five, of dealing with choices – with the idea that if one solution does not make sense, they can try something else; all they need is correct information about what the choices are. Complicated rules, with lists of exceptions, can be put aside.

For the early reader, then, the decision as to whether a word has been correctly identified must be based on some fusion of judgments about sense and judgments about letter pattern. Later, however, word recognition has to become more confident and self-contained, because it in turn becomes the basis on which other problems – about syntax and about sentence meaning – have to be dealt with.

In an illuminating discussion of the growth of confident word recognition in reading, Ehri (1978) makes use of the notion that each word in our mental word-store has for us a 'linguistic identity'. This identity is compounded of how the word sounds, how we pronounce it, how it is constructed (e.g., whether it has a suffix), how it functions syntactically, and what it can mean. She suggests that when we learn to recognize the word in print, we add its 'graphic identity' to this complex interwoven image (as distinct, that is, from merely attaching it to the sound). She points out that growth in word recognition can therefore best take place through meeting printed words in meaningful contexts, since these allow the learner to build round each new written form a rich aggregate of knowledge about its linguistic properties.

Finally, a stage is reached where the word is instantly recognizable without contextual support of any kind. But while it makes good sense to think of form, syntax and meaning as all helping to establish word recognition, the other side of the interaction is equally important. What of the situation where syntax and meaning are the source of difficulty? For the early reader, as we have seen, the effect can be to block word identification. Later, as in the case of Clare, this does not necessarily happen. Clare 'could read the words'. But how prevalent are difficulties of the kind she found?

It is not difficult to show experimentally some of the areas where problems other than those of word recognition can exist for children beyond the beginning reader stage. In 1972 I conducted an experiment with reading tasks at different levels of syntactic difficulty (Reid, 1972). The children had to read sentences and answer a literal question on each one. For instance, one group read: 'Tom walked in front of Dick and carried a flag.' The other group read: 'Tom walked in front of Dick. Tom carried a flag.' Both groups were then asked: '*Who carried the flag?*' While the question was easy for the second group, 36 per cent of the first group thought the flag was carried by Dick. Many other items in the test gave similar results. (See also the work of Chomsky, 1969.) If syntactic features of even this simple kind can be so misleading, we must conclude that they should be discussed and taught. But if children are to learn to understand these structures, then they must read and identify the words on the page. The order and identity of the word string must be clear. Guessing and paraphrasing will only serve to blur the distinctions they must learn to make (Donaldson and Reid, 1982).

Looking at language structures in this close way involves children in becoming more aware of language form (as distinct from the total meaning) than they have formerly been in their use of speech. This kind of awareness has come to be known either as 'metalinguistic' or as 'linguistic' awareness – signifying that it is directed at the language *as a system*. Its relevance for reading progress is now a topic of lively interest and concern (see for instance Downing, 1979).

In the field of spoken language, linguistic awareness and the ability to talk about it have now taken their place alongside the many other linguistic capacities to be studied. It is clear, however, that 'linguistic awareness' can be defined in more than one way. Indeed if we stretch the meaning of 'awareness' far enough it can be viewed as a developing continuum, starting soon after birth. But what we are concerned with here is the state where in Courtney Cazden's words (Cazden, 1974), 'language becomes opaque', becomes something you contemplate, think about, talk about, instead of just seeing through it to what it means. Such awareness can be directed to the speech of others or to the language of a story heard or read – that is, to speech received; it can be directed to one's own speech or one's own writing – to language produced; and it can be directed to different features of the language – to the phonology of speech or the orthography of writing, to grammar and syntax, to vocabulary, to intonation. Children engaged in verse-speaking or drama, or playing any language game which requires them to attend to the sound or the form of what they say or hear, are having their linguistic awareness fostered in one of these ways.

Here, we are chiefly concerned with awareness of specific features of syntax and grammar – with the kind of knowledge of sentence structure and its meaning which was not available to those children in my experiment (Reid, 1972) who thought that Dick was carrying the flag. The particular syntactic pattern, described as a 'deletion' (in this case of the subject of the verb 'carried'), was something they had not learned to handle. But even more may be involved than surface syntax. Compare the two sentences in the further example (see Donaldson and Reid, 1982).

Tom followed Dick carrying a flag.
Tom saw Dick carrying a flag.

In the first, the flag-carrier is Tom; in the second it is Dick. Here however, the surface syntactic forms are identical. What the children must come to know this time is that 'perception verbs' ('saw', 'watched', 'heard', etc.) follow different syntactic rules from other verbs when the subject of a subsequent verb is not named. An interesting study of the way children learn to handle these rules can be found in Goodluck and Roeper (1978). It is worth noting that while the second sentence in the above example is something children would readily say, the first is not. It is a more literary form than the second.

The case for planned teaching about language structures found in books is therefore very strong. 'English' schemes aim their language work largely at vocabulary and at writing skills, while the 'comprehension' tasks they contain, though making demands on reading skills, do not actually serve to extend children's knowledge so much as to test them on what they already know.

Progress in reading can be seen, then, as having a fourfold nature. It involves the development of new concepts, and the learning of new terms, relating to the nature and purpose of written language. It involves the acquisition of a visual code for speech and of principles and strategies needed to understand and use it. It involves the transfer of implicit knowledge about syntax to this new medium, followed by a great expansion of syntactic understanding to cope with the language of books. And it involves developing new attitudes to language whereby conscious attention to structure takes its place alongside attention to total meaning, and the text is seen as a self-contained source of communication.

In contrast to the limited, code-oriented views which it is superseding, such a view offers much more scope for coherent and thoughtful teaching, in which the achievement of literacy is treated as a many-sided extension of linguistic and mental growth.

References

ANDERSON, I. H. and DEARBORN, W. E. (1952) *The Psychology of Teaching Reading*. New York: Ronald Press.

BIEMILLER, A. (1970) 'The development of the use of graphic and contextual information as children learn to read.' *Reading Research Quarterly*, **6**, 76–96.

CAZDEN, C. (1974) 'Play with language and metalinguistic awareness: one dimension of language experience.' *The Urban Review*, **7**, 28–39.

CHOMSKY, C. S. (1969) *The Acquisition of Syntax in Children from 5 to 10*. Cambridge, MA: MIT Press.

CLARK, M. M. (1976) *Young Fluent Readers*. London: Heinemann.

CLAY, M. M. (1969) 'Reading errors and self-correction behaviour.' *British Journal of Educational Psychology*, **39**, 47–56.

CLAY, M. M. (1972) *The Early Detection of Reading Difficulties: a diagnostic survey*. Auckland, NZ: Heinemann.

DIACK, J. H. (1965) *In Spite of the Alphabet*. London: Chatto and Windus.

DONALDSON, M. (1978) *Children's Minds*. London: Fontana.

DONALDSON, M. and REID, J. F. (1982) 'Language skills and reading: a developmental perspective', in HENDRY, A. (ed.) *Teaching Reading: the key issues*. London: Heinemann.

DOWNING, J. (1970) 'Children's concepts of language in learning to read.' *Educational Research*, **12**, 106–12.

DOWNING, J. (1979) *Reading and Reasoning*. Edinburgh: Chambers.

DOWNING, J. and THACKRAY, D. (1971) *Reading Readiness*. London: University of London Press Ltd.

EHRI, L. C. (1978) 'Beginning reading from a psycholinguistic perspective: amalgamation of word identities', in MURRAY, F. B. (ed.) *The Recognition of Words*. Newark, DE: International Reading Association.

GATES, A. L. (1947) *The Improvement of Reading* (3rd edn). New York: Macmillan.

GIBSON, E. J. and LEVIN, H. (1975) *The Psychology of Reading*. Cambridge, MA: MIT Press.

GOODLUCK, H. and ROEPER, T. (1978) 'The acquisition of perception verb complements', in GOODLUCK, H. and SOLON, L. (eds) *Papers in the Structure and Development of Child Language*. University of Massachusetts Occasional Papers in Linguistics, Vol. 4.

GOODMAN, K. S. (1967) 'Reading, a psycholinguistic guessing game', in SINGER, H. and RUDDELL, R. (eds) *Theoretical Models and Processes of Reading*. Newark, DE: International Reading Association.

GOODMAN, K. S. (ed.) (1968) *The Psycholinguistic Nature of the Reading Process*. Detroit, MI: Wayne State University Press.

GOODMAN, K. S. (1969) 'Analysis of oral reading miscues: applied psycholinguistics.' *Reading Research Quarterly*, **5**, 9–30.

GOODMAN, K. S. (1981) 'Letter to the editor.' *Reading Research Quarterly*, **16**, 477–8.

HOCKER, M. E. (1963) 'Reading materials for children based on their language patterns of syntax, vocabulary and interests.' Unpublished master's thesis, University of Arizona.

HUEY, E. N. (1908) *The Psychology and Pedagogy of Reading*. New York: Macmillan.

JAGGER, J. H. (1929) *The Sentence Method of Teaching Reading*. London: Grant.

MCKENZIE, M. (1977) 'The beginnings of literacy.' *Theory into Practice*, **16**, 315–24.

MACNAMARA, J. (1972) 'Cognitive basis of language learning in infants.' *Psychological Review*, **79**, 1–13.

MEEK, M. (1982) *Learning to Read*. London: Bodley Head.

MENYUK, P. (1969) *Sentences Children Use*. Research Monograph 52. Cambridge, MA: MIT Press.

REID, J. F. (1958) 'A study of thirteen beginners in reading.' *Acta Psychologica*, **14**, 294–313.

REID, J. F. (1966) 'Learning to think about reading.' *Educational Research*, **9**, 56–62.

REID, J. F. (1970) 'Sentence structure in reading primers.' *Research in Education*, **3**, 23–37.

REID, J. F. (1972) 'Children's comprehension of syntactic structures found in some extension readers', in REID, J. F. (ed.) *Reading Problems and Practices*. London: Ward Lock Educational.

REID, J. F. (1975) *Breakthrough in Action: An Evaluation of Breakthrough to Literacy*. London: Longman.

REID, J. F. and DONALDSON, M. (1978) *Letter Links*. Edinburgh: Holmes McDougall.

REID, J. F. and LOW, J. (1972) *Link-Up*. Edinburgh: Holmes McDougall.

SMITH, F. (1978) *Reading*. Cambridge: Cambridge University Press.

SPITZER, L. K. (1967) 'Selected materials on the language experience approach to reading instruction.' IRA Annotated Bibliography, 13. Newark, DE: International Reading Association.

STEVENSON, R. L. (1879) *Essays of Travel*. Republished by Chatto and Windus, London (1920).

STRICKLAND, R. (1962) 'The language of elementary schoolchildren: its relation to the language of reading textbooks and the quality of reading of selected children.' *Bulletin of the School of Education*, University of Indiana, **38**, 2.

WARNER, S. A. (1966) *Teacher*. Harmondsworth: Penguin.

WEBER, R. M. (1970) 'A linguistic analysis of first-grade reading errors.' *Reading Research Quarterly*, **5**, 427–51.

WELLS, G. and RABAN, B. (1978) *Children Learning to Read*. SSRC Final Report, HR 3797/1. School of Education, University of Bristol.

Section Three

Personality and self

The readings in this section fall into two parts: those dealing with important areas of contemporary concern in the study of human personality and those dealing with the specific question of how to treat disruptive and maladjusted children.

We recognize that our behaviour varies according to the situation we are in but at the same time we regard ourselves as the same person in each situation. The question which Lawrence Pervin addresses in the first article is, 'Can we usefully speak of factors inside the person that affect behaviour or should we focus our attention on situational characteristics external to the person?' This has been a perennial debate in psychology and here Pervin shows how the pendulum has swung back and forth this century. He proposes a middle way, favouring an interactional perspective which emphasizes an understanding of the interdependence between person and situation or between internal and external determinants of behaviour.

Pervin acknowledges that we can observe and reflect upon our own behaviour and it is this same phenomenon – the reflexive quality of human nature – which Sarah Hampson investigates in the second article in this section. Using a symbolic interactionist approach she surveys some of the research evidence, concluding that, in part, we perceive ourselves as we think others see us. We augment this knowledge with the private information about ourselves to which only we have access (although at times this information may be either unavailable or misleading); and on occasion we turn to self-observations of our behaviour. The disparities between these different perspectives is, Hampson suggests, one of the reasons why we continue to be fascinated and tantalized by the study of ourselves.

One aspect of the self that Hampson considers is our attempts to explain our own preferences and behaviours. How we come to attribute causes to our behaviour and, in turn, what influences these attributions has been the subject of a considerable amount of research effort in social psychology in recent years. The article by Daniel Bar-Tal is a review of some of this work as it relates to questions of educational concern, specifically the influence of teachers on pupils' causal perception of success and failure. The interrelationship between a student's personal disposition and the external information encountered in his or her situation are seen to be important and Attribution Theory's concern with personal and environmental causes of human behaviour links back to the first article in this section.

Bar-Tal is at pains to emphasize the applications of this research to education and it is with practical needs that the final two articles in this section are concerned. In a classical paper Jack Tizard appraises the effectiveness of the Child Guidance Clinics, which grew in influence following the Second World War, as a means of diagnosing and treating children with behavioural and emotional problems. Having reviewed the available research he finds them ineffective in treatment and insensitive to the needs of the community they are meant to serve. Their clinical orientation inclines them to overlook the school, the teacher and the classroom as major socializing agencies of the child and it is in such a context that Tizard suggests that there is potential for prevention and progress.

The change of approach to which Tizard's paper was an important contribution was characterized by a number of different ways of dealing with children who are disruptive. Some of the more important ones are described by Daines in his account of withdrawal units where he takes the line that problem behaviour in school is best understood in terms of school characteristics rather than in terms of personal and social inadequacies.

The pendulum keeps on swinging.

Victor Lee

3.1 Am I me or am I the situation? Personal dispositions, situationism, and interactionism in personality

Lawrence A. Pervin

If we observe and reflect upon our own behavior and our experience of ourselves behaving, we are struck by two conclusions. First, our behavior varies according to the situation we are in. Not only do we behave differently in the classroom than at a party, but we notice differences according to whether we are at a party with strangers or with friends, whether the party is formal or informal, whether we are only with members of our own sex or whether we are in mixed company. Second, at the same time that we are behaving differently in these situations we regard ourselves as the same person. The fact that I dress one way in school and another way while gardening, that I behave somewhat differently at a large cocktail party than at a small gathering of friends, that I talk more as a teacher and listen more as a therapist, that I am quick-tempered in some situations and patient in other situations – these variations in my behavior do not interfere with the sense that there is one person, me, involved in all of them. There is, then, the observation of both change and stability, of behaving differently and yet being the same person. Were my behavior to be the same in all situations, it would be perfectly predictable, but I and others would wonder about why I was so rigid and why I behaved so inappropriately in some situations. On the other hand, if no consistency or pattern could be observed in my behavior, then I might wonder whether I wasn't being a 'phoney' much of the time or I would be bothered by feelings of depersonalization – so much change would leave me without a feeling of knowing who I am or, perhaps, without a feeling of being a person at all. Indeed, most of us have struggled with such questions from time to time, particularly in adolescence when we focus our attention on forming an identity or when we behave in a way that is 'out of character' for us and try to reconcile this behavior with what we otherwise know and believe about ourselves. [. . .]

The same conclusions apply to our observations of others. If I ask you to describe someone you know well, you would come up with a list of characteristics that you feel captured the personality of this individual. Yet, if you really know this person well you could undoubtedly describe situations in which their behavior was not in accord with the characteristics you listed. Thus, in both the perception of our own behavior and in the perception of the behavior of others we see pattern and regularity in

Source: PERVIN, L. A. (1978) *Current Controversies and Issues in Personality* (pp. 4–27). New York: Wiley.

the face of diversity and variability, and we draw conclusions about 'personality characteristics' while recognizing the importance of 'situational' differences. Indeed, observations of our behavior over diverse situations might also apply to our behavior over a period of time. Our behavior certainly is different in childhood, adolescence, and adulthood, and yet generally there is at least some sense of continuity and stability as a person [. . .].

Let me illustrate these points with an example. Mr Krim served as an editor from 1961 to 1965 and tells us that during this period he generally was cool, rational, reassuring, and smiled compassionately at the temperament of his writers. In his own terms, he disciplined his own needs for approval because they were irrelevant. However, there was 'another self that lived a separate life' that came out when Mr Krim himself became an author. Then Mr Krim became aggressive and anxious about the acceptance of his writing, found it hard to relax, was blunt and demanding rather than diplomatic, and was less able than previously to be objective or to take an impersonal view. His confusion and insight were expressed as follows:

'What does it all mean?' I often ask myself with some wonder as if I were a stranger to myself. I am the same man, I smoke the same foolish cigarettes, wear approximately the same clothes, respond to the same music and movies. It means, I'm afraid, that situation is more crucial than personality; at least that is so, or seems to be so, in my case. *The situation you're in determines who you are* . . . And yet, I tell you frankly that in my heart I'm exactly the same man who used to be reasonable, detached, smilingly helpful to those many egos so aggravated by their unfulfilled position in life and so much less fortunate than myself.

S. Krim, New York Times, 18 November 1974

Mr Krim's confusion is similar to that of many, if not most, psychologists studying personality and probably has the same basis. He recognizes both stability and change in his behavior in relation to situations and recognizes the possible importance of both his personality and the situation in determining his behavior. Yet, he seeks to account for his behavior in terms of himself *or* the situation. Thus, he concludes, with some hesitance, that the situation determines who you are. Although he feels that he is the same man regardless of the idiosyncratic nature of the situation, such feelings do not match the governing characteristics of the situation. [. . .] The battle and confusion within himself concerning which is more important, the person or the situation, is not unlike the battle and confusion between psychologists who emphasize the importance of person characteristics (e.g., traits, needs, and motives) and psychologists who emphasize the importance of situation characteristics (e.g., stimuli, cues, rewards, and punishments) in regulating behavior. His conclusion that the situation is more important than the personality, though he may feel the same person regardless of the situation, is not unlike the position of psychologists who argue that behavior is situationally determined and that it is only we as observers who attribute behavior to personality characteristics and dispositions (Jones and Nisbett, 1971; Mischel, 1968). Thus, the first issue we are faced with is how do we assess and account for stability and change in behavior? Are the determinants of behavior in the person, in the situation, or where? Can we usefully speak of *factors inside the person* that affect behavior or should we focus our attention on *situational characteristics external to the person* and regard personality characteristics as virtual figments of our imagination – perhaps useful to us in going about our daily living but of limited scientific value?

The dichotomy between internal and external determinants of behavior

The issue of whether to focus attention on the person or on the situation can be viewed as an aspect of a broader issue – the relative significance of internal and external determinants of behavior. In some ways there is reason to believe that the emphasis on internal or external determinants of behavior involves broad philosophical commitments in addition to rational decisions based on scientific evidence. Historically there have been cultures that have viewed behavior as caused by forces inside the individual and other cultures that have viewed behavior as caused by forces external to the individual. [. . .]

What about psychology in general and personality theory in particular? Allport (1955) found this issue, above all others, to divide psychologists. He attributed the differences to commitment to either a Leibnitzian tradition or a Lockean tradition. In the former tradition it is the organism that is important and causes are seen as internal to the organism whereas in the latter tradition the organism is seen as reactive to events external to it. European schools of psychology (e.g., Gestalt psychology and Freud's psychoanalysis) have tended to follow the Leibnitzian tradition whereas British and American schools of psychology (e.g., associationism and behaviorism) have tended to follow the Lockean tradition. While virtually all psychologists would emphasize the importance of internal and external determinants of behavior, of organism and environment, clear differences in emphasis and interpretation emerge as one considers the history of psychology, different fields within psychology, and different theorists within a field. Obviously there is both individual and environment, person and situation, nature and nurture; yet, the tendency has remained to emphasize one or another set of variables. [. . .]

Periodically there is a shift in emphasis from internal to external or vice versa, and occasionally a call for the study of organism-environment interactions. [. . .] The balance has generally tended to be weighted in the direction of internal or external factors. Recognizing such a tendency, the personologist Henry Murray, in his *Explorations in Personality* (1938), drew a distinction between two types of psychologist – centralists and peripheralists. The centralist sees human beings as active and influenced by internal energies in virtually all spheres of activity. Activity occurs in the absence of external stimulation. While interested in overt behavior, the centralist is prepared to study, and at times infer, such intangibles as wishes, needs, impulses, desires, and intentions. Thus, although not disregarding the study of overt behavior, the centralist craves to know the internal life of the subject. Finally, there is an interest in individual differences and in the complex unity of a personality system in which each part is dynamically related to other parts and to the whole. In contrast to the centralist, the peripheralist defines personality according to behavior and focuses attention on the external stimulus or perception of it as the origin of psychological phenomena. Attention is directed to what is observable and can be reliably measured. Man is seen as inert, passive, and responsive to outer stimulation. The interest is in similarities among people and in characteristics that are true of all people.

As Murray pointed out, not every psychologist can be classified as a centralist or a peripheralist. Indeed, Murray himself tried to relate the two points of view in his own emphasis on individual-environment interaction. However, he did wish to draw attention to a fundamental difference in point of view among psychologists. As we have seen, these alternative views can have ramifications in terms of what is looked at, how it is studied, and how personality is conceptualized. [. . .] The dilemma of Mr Krim, and the debate among personality psychologists concerning the importance of person and situation determinants, can be seen as part of a broader question that runs throughout much of psychology and is fundamental to questions concerning the nature of people. [. . .]

The person-situation issue

During the 1940s and 1950s the field of personality tended to be dominated by internal, centralist theories. Freudian psychoanalysis exercised a strong influence on the issues that received attention, the kinds of assessment devices that were used, the research that was conducted, and the kind of training clinical psychologists received. There was intense interest in the mechanisms of defense and in the effects of early experience on later behavior. The Rorschach and the Thematic Apperception Test [TAT], projective techniques associated with the psychodynamic approach, were considered a necessary part of the training of clinical psychologists and a necessary component in the practitioner's bag of tools. [. . .] There was intense interest in the study of personality types – the anal character, the creative personality, the authoritarian personality. The study of the authoritarian personality was seen as a classic example of how a personality type could be defined and systematically studied in terms of the dynamics of functioning and the early determinants of character formation. The focus upon questions such as fascism, antisemitism, and authoritarianism was clearly a response to issues of concern to people during the Second World War. However, the formulation of an 'authoritarian personality' was a response to the psychoanalytic influence. In fact, several investigators associated with this classic study had either been psychoanalyzed or had received training in psychoanalysis. [. . .]

Partly out of frustration with the results of psychoanalytically based research and practice, and partly because of social-cultural changes there began to grow an interest in an alternative way of looking at the phenomena of interest. Then, in 1968 Walter Mischel came out with a book, *Personality and Assessment*, which focused attention on issues that were brewing in the field and that needed both articulation and the presentation of relevant data. Basically Mischel was critical of traditional personality theories (i.e., trait theory and psychodynamic theory) and of the assessment procedures associated with these theories. A major part of Mischel's criticism concerned the emphasis given by trait and dynamic personality theories to internal properties of the organism: 'Traditional personality theories assume an internal structural-dynamic hierarchy in which various hypothesized aspects of the person stand in superordinate or subordinate relations to each other . . . The implication in all hierarchical personality models is that some internal entities underlie others, and that their dynamic interrelations determine or produce the behavior that the person displays' (Mischel, 1968, p. 4).

The issue was being framed. Trait theory was criticized for its assumption that personality is made up of stable and enduring predispositions that exert fairly generalized effects on behavior. [. . .] Similarly, psychodynamic theory was criticized for its emphasis on internal entities and its associated emphasis on longitudinal and cross-situational stability: 'Psychodynamic theory, like trait theory, assumes that the underlying personality is more or less stable regardless of the situation. According to the psychodynamic view, the individual develops during childhood a basic personality core that does not change much in its essentials' (Mischel, 1968, p. 6).

If hierarchically arranged internal entities and stable patterns of behaving over time and across situations were to be rejected, what was to be emphasized? Instead of emphasizing broad dispositions that manifest themselves stably and independently of stimulus conditions, Mischel suggested that changes in stimulus (external) conditions modify how people behave and therefore behavior is relatively situation-specific: 'The principles that emerge from studies of the variables that control behavior in turn become the bases for developing theory, not about global traits and states, but about the manner in which behavior develops and changes in response to environmental stimulus changes' (Mischel, 1968, p. 10). Since behavior depends on stimuli, regularities in behavior are to be explained in terms of regularities in external events rather than in terms of internal characteristics. Personality consistency is dependent on stable environmental supports rather than upon stable response predispositions in people. [. . .]

Mischel's critique of traditional personality theory and assessment can be summarized as follows:

1 With the possible exception of cognitive and intellectual ability functions, there is little evidence of longitudinal stability and cross-situational consistency in behavior.

2 Since behaviors that are often construed as stable personality trait indicators are actually dependent upon evoking and maintaining conditions in the environment, traditional dispositional theories may be called into question.

3 Since assessment devices based upon dispositional theories (e.g., projectives such as the Rorschach and TAT, and personality trait questionnaires such as the Cattell Sixteen Personality Factor Inventory) are of limited utility in predicting behavior in a situation, the use of such assessment devices may also be called into question.

4 Trait terms are common in personality theory and in our everyday descriptions of others, but they must represent something other than stable predispositions. The suggestion is made that traits represent verbal terms used to describe behavior that do not mirror behavior – traits represent descriptive categories that some researchers, and people generally, use to organize their world, but they do not reflect actual behavioral regularities or internal structures. We see such modes of making judgments about people, in an extreme form, in stereotypes. Here we assume that because someone has one characteristic they also have a set of other characteristics. Another example would be the 'halo effect' where the general impression we have of someone influences our judgments about the person on a much broader range of characteristics. Finally, there is evidence that we generally assume certain linkages among personality characteristics. Thus, for example, if a person is seen as extroverted we also tend to see them as spirited, exuberant, outgoing, lively, and perhaps venturesome whereas if a person is seen as introverted we also tend to see them as quiet, timid, shy, and perhaps studious (Cantor and Mischel, 1977). When people are rated on personality traits, the ratings may reflect the rater's conceptual scheme rather than the subject's actual behavior. Responses to interpersonal checklists, personality inventories, and questionnaire interviews reflect how people (including trait psychologists) view behaviors as related to one another but they do not reflect actual behavioral relationships (Schweder, 1975).

[. . .]

Some considerations of the issues and evidence: consistency, prediction, and the attribution of causes to internal and external determinants

Let us consider now the evidence relevant to the issues raised by Mischel. We shall consider three questions here: (1) Are people consistent over time and across situations? (2) Is a trait model or a psychodynamic model of the person a useful one for predictive purposes? (3) Do concepts of internal determinants, such as traits and needs, represent accurate observations of behavior or do they represent cognitive constructions of the average person about which personality characteristics go together (i.e., stereotypes based on language, cultural images, and the unique life experiences of the individual)? We shall consider each in turn though it should be clear that the first question, concerning the consistency or situational specificity of behavior, is basic to the other two. If there is evidence of consistency, then *some* concept of person variables makes sense according to the predictions and actual observations of qualities residing in people. On the other hand, if evidence of consistency cannot be found, then one must at least give serious consideration to the possibility that person attributes are not useful for predictive purposes and perhaps largely represent constructions of observers.

Consistency versus situational specificity of behavior

The basic argument made by Mischel was that except for cognitive and intellectual functions, the evidence indicates considerable specificity. Behaviors that are often construed as stable personality trait indicators actually are highly specific and depend on the characteristics of the evoking situation. The classic study referred to in this area is that done by Hartshorne and May (1928) on honesty in children. As part of the Character Education Inquiry, children were put in situations where they were tempted to violate standards and where detection appeared to be impossible. Subjects were allowed to play with boxes containing money and were then asked to return the boxes. They did not know that the boxes had been marked and many kept some of the money. Observations were also made of cheating on tests, honesty in work done at home, honesty in reporting scores, and other behavior associated with the traits of truthfulness and honesty. As it turned out, the measures used to assess honesty and truthfulness in children did not correlate highly with one another. This lack of correlation suggested that children are not consistently honest or dishonest but rather that honest behavior is relatively specific to each situation.

Another example of research supporting the view of situational specificity comes from the efforts of psychologists serving with the Office of Strategic Services. Their job was to select individuals who would operate as spies overseas during the Second World War (OSS Assessment Staff, 1948). The task of the assessment staff [. . .] was to predict the effectiveness of candidates in dealing with stressful situations they would encounter in enemy territory. To the credit of these investigators they included in their assessment battery miniature, lifelike situation tests as well as interviews and projective tests. The situation tests covered areas such as intelligence, social adjustment, and energy and initiative. An analysis of

performance in these tests suggested sufficient situational specificity to
question a strict trait view. [. . .]

Such studies and results are representative of the body of evidence that
leads Mischel and others to question the consistency of behavior and
thereby the utility of trait and psychodynamic conceptions of the person.
What then of the counter-argument? One of the best responses to the
Mischel position has been formulated by Jack Block (1977). The counter-
argument has a number of components to it. First, some of the results do
not argue quite as strongly for situational specificity, as has been suggested by the situationists. For example, in the Hartshorne and May
study, it can be argued that the children were too young to have developed
'characterological honesty' and therefore consistency in moral behavior.
Supporting this argument is the fact that the research found that moral
consistency increased with age. Also, there were individual differences
in the consistency with which children were honest. Many children
were consistently honest and some consistently dishonest. Finally, a
later reanalysis of the data suggested that the tests were not sufficiently
reliable to allow for the demonstration of a more general personality
characteristic.

This last point related to a second argument made by Block: Many
studies in the field are poorly done – 'methodologically inadequate,
without conceptual implication, and even foolish.' Block argues that
many studies use concepts loosely, employ inadequate measures, and do
not appropriately analyze the data. He reasons that if personality research
is poorly executed then personality will appear inconsistent but, in fact,
little can be concluded from the erratic nature of the findings. [. . .]

Are there then any competently performed studies that demonstrate
consistency [. . .]? Block points to his own study of *Lives Through Time*
(Block, 1971) as illustrative of the kinds of results found when research is
done in a careful way. The study involved the independent gathering of a
great deal of information about individuals at three points in their lives –
when they were in junior high school, when they were in high school, and
when they were in their mid-thirties. In other words, the study covered
roughly a 20-year time span. The material at each age was evaluated by
psychologists who systematically presented their formulations of the
personalities of each subject. Although there was some overlap in the
psychologists doing the evaluations at the three time periods, no psychologist evaluated the same subject at more than one age. This means that
care was taken to obtain independent personality descriptions of the
subjects at each of the three time periods.

Block found that for the time period between junior high school and
high school over half of the personality ratings were found to be related at
a statistically significant level. For the senior high school to mid-thirties
time period, an interval averaging close to 20 years, about 30 per cent of
the ratings were found to be in agreement to a statistically significant
degree. Some of the personality items on which there was considerable

evidence of stability were the following: Is a genuinely dependable and responsible person; Tends toward undercontrol of needs and impulses, unable to delay gratification; Basically submissive; Emphasizes being with others, gregarious; Tends to be rebellious and nonconforming.

Block's arguments suggest that the evidence concerning consistency versus specificity of behavior is not clear-cut and that the issue is quite complex. At least part of the complexity of the issue resides in the concept of consistency itself. What does consistency mean and what type of data are necessary to justify a conclusion of consistency or one of situational specificity? The results found differ according to the type of study conducted. Studies using ratings by observers or self-observations tend to result in evidence of consistency. On the other hand, studies using more or less artificial tests or laboratory situations tend to result in evidence of situational specificity. The situationists argue that ratings by independent observers or by the self have built-in biases and do not constitute adequate, objective sources of evidence. Personality theorists who emphasize internal variables argue that laboratory data are often meaningless because they are unrelated to what occurs naturally and they excessively emphasize the role of situational considerations. In the real world people are at least partly free to create their situations or structure them whereas in the laboratory their role is to respond to a situation imposed upon them by the scientist or investigator.

Not only are there differences in consistency according to the data used but also differences in what constitutes consistency. For some psychologists, in particular situationists, the same behavior in different situations or variation in behavior independent of the situation constitutes the necessary evidence for consistency. For others, in particular psychologists who emphasize personal dispositions, the same underlying characteristic can be expressed in many different ways [. . .]. Block notes how Bandura interprets the finding that delinquent boys are nonaggressive with their harshly punishing parents but aggressive with school peers as evidence for situational specificity. However, Block suggests that such behavior can be viewed by trait and psychodynamic psychologists as consistent with the sado-masochistic or dominant-submissive character structure. Furthermore, as we shall see, trait theory does not suggest that a person will behave the same way in every situation or that he or she will maintain the same position relative to others across all situations. Consistency means pattern and regularity, not sameness.

Finally, there is the question of individual differences in consistency. There is evidence of differences among individuals in how variable they are, with some studies suggesting that great intra-individual variability is a sign of lack of personality integration (Campus, 1974; Fiske and Rice, 1955). We know that some people are more sensitive to internal cues while others are more sensitive to external cues. Perhaps the conclusion that makes most sense is that most people are consistent in their behavior some of the time and variable in their behavior the rest of the time (Bem and

Allen, 1974). In other words, each person can be expected to be consistent in ways that are salient or meaningful for him or her. The areas of consistency differ with different individuals. Thus, for example, for some individuals it may be important to be always honest while for others it may be important to be always dominant. Each individual may have many or few such areas in which there exists cross-situational consistency. Sampling of a large group of individuals on any one characteristic might suggest little cross-situational consistency since it is unlikely that more than a small proportion of the total sample will be consistent in that particular area. The consistency of a subgroup in the population can be masked by the situational specificity of the larger group: this is true for every personality characteristic that is assessed. The conclusion might then be that behavior is situationally specific rather than that behavior is stable in some ways for some individuals and in other ways for other individuals. What appears to be needed is a more differentiated picture of consistency and of the relationship between person and situational determinants.

Person versus situational prediction of behavior

The argument made by Mischel, on the basis of his conclusion that behavior is specific to the situation, was that prediction of behavior from a trait or psychodynamic model is not possible. In particular, prediction from trait personality questionnaires to actual behavior and from responses to projective tests to actual behavior is extremely hazardous. [. . .]

One can hardly question Mischel's summary of the data concerning the predictive utility of trait and psychodynamic models and in particular the utility of the assessment methods associated with such approaches. The fact is that prediction of human behavior in a complex situation remains an extremely difficult task. Even in the area of intellectual functioning, with tests that have received years of intensive study and virtually unlimited funds for development, the predictive utility of tests remains unimpressive. What are the implications of such problems in the prediction of behavior in complex situations for the trait and psychodynamic models?

The argument in this section is not so much with Mischel's conclusions from the data as with the implications drawn from these conclusions. First, we must consider whether trait theory and psychodynamic theory suggest the possibility of predicting the behavior of an individual in a specific situation when information about only the personality is given. Second, we must consider the kinds of predictions that are possible with a situationist emphasis. Finally, we want to consider whether accurate prediction is a necessary criterion for the validity of a concept.

In relation to the first question, just what do trait theory and psychodynamic theory have to say about consistency and prediction? Two leading trait theorists are G. W. Allport and R. B. Cattell. While there are differences in their theoretical positions, they both are representative proponents of traditional trait theory. Both are impressed with the evidence of *relative* stability of behavior over time and across situations. Traits, then, refer to the underlying structures that are assumed to account for this relative stability and consistency. Traits refer to behavioral patterns that are frequent, intense, and expressed over a range of situations. However, neither Allport nor Cattell suggests that this means that behavior is independent of the situation or that a person possessing a trait behaves the same way in all situations. What a person does in a situation is the result of, among other things, the individual's enduring personality characteristics and his perception of the situation and its relevant demands. Both person and situation influence behavior. What, then, is the relationship between them? 'We are forced, therefore, to the conclusion that while the situation may modify behavior greatly, it can do so only within the limits of the potential provided by the personality. At the same time, we are forced to concede that traits of personality must not be regarded as fixed and stable, operating mechanically to the same degree on all occasions. Rather we should think of traits as *ranges of possible behavior*, to be activated at varying points within the range according to the demands of the situation' (Allport, 1961, pp. 180–181). A trait expresses what a person does in the long run over many situations, not what he will do in any one situation. The trait concept refers to an aggregate of behaviors. It is a summary concept held to be useful in explaining the consistency that is found in behavior. On the other hand, recognition of the importance of the situation was necessary to explain the inconsistency or variability of behavior.

In sum, both Allport and Cattell accept that behavior is rarely entirely consistent and that prediction of behavior in any single situation cannot be done on the basis of personality alone. Behavior is relatively consistent because it is derived from internal structures. On the other hand, behavior varies because we mask our private natures, because we hold contradictory attitudes, because we respond realistically to situational demands, and because any one act generally represents the product of many interacting traits. In other words, a careful reading of these trait theorists suggests that their position in relation to person and situation factors in determining behavior is, in fact, more complex than is often assumed to be the case. It is true that relatively little attention is given to delineating relevant situational variables, to measuring them, or to specifying their relationship to the operation of trait variables. However, it is not accurate to suggest that no attention is given to the role of situation factors or that complete consistency is expected.

In many ways the psychoanalytic position in relation to the person versus situation issue is even more complex than that of the trait position. The psychoanalytic position is indeed a subtle one and, unfortunately, often much of the subtlety has been lost in the controversy surrounding the issue. Psychoanalytic theory does suggest a stability over time and across situations, but it is a stability of underlying personality or basic personality rather than one of specific overt behaviors. The main emphasis within psychoanalytic theory clearly concerns internal structures, internal processes, and the subjective world of experience. For the most part concepts such as id, ego, superego, anxiety, and the mechanisms of defense relate to characteristics internal to the organism. These internal structures and processes give a certain character, style, or consistency to the functioning of the organism. What is the relationship of internal structures to behavior and what kind of consistency can be found? First, a distinction is made between phenotype and genotype – a phenotype referring to the outer behavioral manifestation of the personality organization and the genotype referring to the underlying, internal structures. While behaviors change between infancy and later ages, there is a continuity of behavioral style and pattern of adaptation. In other words, phenotypically different behaviors may express the same style and thereby the same underlying personality organization. Similarly, an impulse can be expressed directly or, when blocked by a mechanism of defense, in a variety of other forms, including its opposite. For example, an excessively controlled, inhibited person may under certain circumstances 'explode' and allow his or her feelings to come pouring out. We have all seen people do something that seemed 'out of character' for them and that could not be attributed to the situation. Such seeming inconsistencies are, in fact, often expressive of an underlying conflict in which different parts of the conflict, involving differences in strength between impulse and defense, are expressed at different times. While the phenotypic behavior may be very different under such circumstances, it is the underlying personality organization (i.e., genotype) that remains constant throughout.

A second consideration giving complexity to the relationship between internal structure and overt behavior is that the role of internal structures will not be equally apparent in all behaviors or in all situations. Just as most laboratory experiments emphasize situation factors and specific acts, the psychoanalytic situation lends itself to an emphasis on person factors and the internal organization of experience. While the underlying personality organization may be expressed in all behaviors and in all situations, it will be particularly apparent in unstructured situations and in areas associated with conflict for the individual. Behavior in any single situation is seen as multidetermined by many internal forces and at least partly under the control of situational events. Therefore, the prediction of specific behavior or outcomes from an understanding of internal structures is extremely hazardous. [. . .]

To return to the conclusions drawn by Mischel, we may ask under what circumstances can the situationist predict the behavior of an individual in a situation? There appears to be as much evidence that individuals interpret the same situation differently, leading to behavioral differences, as there is that different situations have different behavioral consequences for the same person. Interestingly, both Mischel (1973) and Bandura

(1973), after taking a strong situationist stand, have concluded that in understanding human behavior one must also take into consideration processes inside the individual – how the person perceives and even overcomes the situation as well as how he is coerced by it.

Finally, it may be that we are too concerned with prediction, or at least certain kinds of predictions, as a criterion of truth. All too often we ask the personality theorist or clinician to predict behavior in absolute terms rather than asking them to specify the alternative possible behaviors and the predictive probabilities associated with each alternative. Perhaps we should be making predictions more like those of meteorologists, who certainly understand the phenomena they are attempting to predict to a greater extent than we do; that is, just as weather forecasters can predict the probabilities of various events and record their accuracy over the long haul, perhaps we should focus more on probabilistic statements, the accuracy of which are examined in the light of many occurrences. Just as frequent problems in weather forecasting do not mean that we know little about the causes of changing patterns in the weather, frequent problems in predicting behavior in complex situations may not mean that all our principles of person functioning are without foundation.

Cognitive attributions of the causes of behavior

In developing constructs about the functioning of others, psychologists are faced with the peculiar dilemma of seeking to understand processes in others while being influenced by these processes ourselves. In attempting to understand the causes of behavior in others, we are perhaps being influenced by our own interpretations about the causes of behavior and which characteristics are related to one another. When a person acts as an observer, whether of his or her own behavior or of the behavior of others, to what extent is he free to observe what actually occurs as opposed to being bound by his assumptions about what generally occurs? In a sense, this is the question that Mischel addressed when he suggested that the information obtained from trait ratings and personality questionnaires often reflects rater constructs rather than underlying traits. In other words, personality dimensions derived from trait ratings may come from the meanings trait words have for people, and which words tend to mean similar things, rather than from internal characteristics of persons.

We know that as we live our daily lives each of us makes judgments about the personality characteristics of others and about the causes of events. To do otherwise would be to live in a totally chaotic world. We seek to give meaning to events, to attribute causes to phenomena, and to see pattern and regularity in the world about us. What do we know about such processes and to what extent do they lead to errors in judgment? First, we know that in the course of development people develop theories of behavior, theories of 'what goes with what,' or implicit personality theories. Such theories are built up out of cultural traditions and idiosyncratic personal experience. There exists considerable evidence to suggest that in observing the behavior of others we often make judgments based on our beliefs concerning 'what goes with what' despite contradictory observational evidence. [. . .]

Thus, the suggestion has been made that the data we obtain from personality inventories and questionnaire interviews reflect the cognitive judgments of people concerning what things are similar rather than descriptions of actual behavioral co-occurrences. There appears to be considerable evidence that this is true. The suggestion has also been made, however, that the actual behavior observed makes little difference in the judgments we make and that our implicit theories create an illusion of underlying individual behavioral consistency that does not exist in actual behavior. It is one thing to suggest that our cognitive constructions influence what we perceive and at times serve to distort our judgments or bias ratings made on personality inventories and questionnaires. For this suggestion the data seem convincing. It is quite another matter, however, to suggest that actual behavior makes little difference in such judgments or, on the basis of these data, to throw out the conceptualization of personality as consisting of stable internal factors that make behavior relatively consistent from one time to another. Our notions about 'what goes with what' must have some accuracy and utility or we all would have given them up some time ago. We all make mistakes in our predictions concerning the behavior of others, and often are surprised that people do not act the way they 'usually' or 'characteristically' do. However, this does not mean that our assumptions concerning internal structures and behavioral consistency are completely erroneous. It does suggest that we need to check observations based on ratings and questionnaires against actual behavior. It does not mean that we should dismiss the possibility that individuals demonstrate consistent differences in their patterns of behavior across a wide range of situations.

A second question relating to our cognitive constructions of events concerns a tendency to attribute causes of events to factors inside the individual or to factors in the surrounding environment. To a certain extent, there are individual differences in this regard. Thus, some individuals tend to see events as following their actions while other individuals tend to see events as the result of luck, chance, fate, or the forces surrounding them [. . .]. There also exist more general tendencies to attribute causes to internal factors and not to external factors. Thus, for example, we tend to attribute the cause of accomplishments as coming from within the person (e.g., Jack succeeded because he was able), while we tend to attribute the cause of emotions as coming from outside the person (e.g., Carol cried because the movie was sad) (MacArthur, 1972). According to several studies, when we observe our own behavior we emphasize the role of environmental conditions at the moment of action while when we observe the behavior of others we emphasize the role of stable, dispositional characteristics of the person (Jones and Nisbett,

1971). When asked why they chose a major field of study, college students tend to emphasize qualities of the major field – external or stimulus attributions of cause. On the other hand, when asked about why their best friend chose a particular major, college students tended to emphasize qualities of their friend that influenced the choice – internal or person attributions of cause (Nisbett and Caputo, 1973). In other words, as actors it is the environment around us that becomes salient or important while as observers of others it is the person that becomes salient.

Such findings have led some psychologists to conclude that in reality behavior is situationally determined and that it is only we as observers who attribute stability in behavior to the person. [. . .] Since we see most other people in but a few situations, their behavior appears to be consistent and we attribute this consistency to person dispositions or traits. However, when we observe our own behavior and its variability across situations we recognize the actual limitations of personal consistency and the considerable import of situations. However, is the conclusion that stability in behavior or person dispositions are 'just' causal attributions warranted? The argument here is similar to that made above in relation to traits as cognitive constructions of behavioral co-occurrences. Such cognitive representations and causal attributions are constructions of individuals that match reality to a limited, imperfect degree. However, there are also significant individual differences in the constructs or traits used to describe people and in the extent to which causes are attributed to internal or external factors. The conclusion that causes lie in the evoking and maintaining conditions of the situation may express the ideology or attribution theory of some psychologists as much as the conclusion that causes lie in internal structures for other psychologists. The evidence is hardly convincing for either point of view and in fact, as we shall see, there is evidence to support at least parts of both. Furthermore, while some situationists suggest that we naively attribute the causes of behavior to internal structures because person factors are salient when we observe others, Skinner suggests that we attribute the causes of behavior to internal states (i.e., feelings) because they are salient. In other words, both positions are argued in support of a situationist view, the one (i.e., Skinner's) discrediting the actor's view and the other emphasizing it!

An interactional perspective

It would not be surprising if by now one is left wondering just about what the controversy is since it seems clear that people are stable in some ways and variable in others, and that behavior must inevitably express both person and situation. Perhaps the questions have been poorly posed, needlessly expressing a dichotomy between person and situation. Rather than asking whether behavior is caused by the person or by the situation, perhaps we should be asking the following question: As a function of which personal and situational characteristics does the individual remain stable and vary? [. . .]

Such an interactional view is gaining popularity in the personality field. [. . .] One of the earliest and best studies of the interaction between persons and situations involved the observation of six preadolescent boys in six different settings (e.g., eating, games, and unstructured group activities). The boys all had problems in being excessively aggressive, and there was particular interest in the extent to which the aggressive behavior was consistent across settings and in how different settings affected different children – the interaction between child and setting. The researchers found that both differences in settings and differences in children generally affected the type of behavior that occurred. With the development of maturity and controls in these hyperaggressive boys their aggressive behavior became more limited to specific situations as opposed to being relatively consistent across all situations. However, at all times it was the interaction between specific settings and individual differences that influenced the aggressive behavior. The effect of the interaction did not involve a mere summation of setting effects and person effects. Rather, the effect of the setting changed according to which child was studied, and the effect of the person changed according to which setting was studied. The kind of behavior the setting evoked was related to the personality of the particular child and the kind of behavior the child produced was to a considerable extent related to the characteristics of the particular situation that were salient for him. Do the data argue for a 'psychology of traits' or for a 'psychology of situations'? The researchers answered this question as follows: 'Our own position is that neither one of these points of view is complete. We would view traits not as a once-and-for-all-time exclusive property of the organism irrespective of the environment but as directional potentialities under certain environmental circumstances; similarly, situations would be viewed as having arousal potential for certain traits . . . There are some situations where the potential range of individual variation is highly restricted and others where individual variations are maximized. Personality factors may be similarly differentiated – for example, cognitive functions are, it is likely, somewhat less subject to situational variations than are affective aspects of personality' (Raush, Dittmann, and Taylor, 1959, p. 373).

The study of hyperaggressive boys suggested that the question of whether individual personality or situation was more important was a meaningless one – neither could be separated from the other. Yet, for some time the two tended to be considered independently by psychologists. Then an important series of studies by Endler and Hunt (Endler and Hunt, 1966; 1968) again called attention to person-situation interaction effects. In these studies subjects were presented with questionnaires in which a variety of anxiety-arousing or hostility-arousing situations were described. For each situation subjects rated the likelihood of their responding in one of several different ways. For example, to the description of the situation 'You are just starting off on a long automobile trip,' subjects would rate the extent to which their hearts beat faster, they had an uneasy feeling, they would perspire, etc. The responses showed that behavioral variation could not be primarily attributed to individual differences or to situation differences in anxiety and hostility – the interaction between person and situation was of far greater significance than the effects of persons alone or of situations alone. The dispute over whether the main source of variation in behavior is in the situations or in the persons was declared a pseudo-issue. What is important in personality description is the kinds of responses individuals make in various kinds of situations.

[. . .]

The interactional view suggests that all behavior reflects both person and situation. Within this context some behaviors may be more person determined for some people and other behaviors more situation determined for other people. Instead of deciding whether behavior generally is more person determined or more situation determined, the task of research becomes understanding the person and situation forces that account for the *pattern* of stability and change in behavior. Within such a perspective, several points can be made. First, it is not enough to say that one is an interactionist. One must be clear about what this term means. [. . .] For some psychologists it means being able to demonstrate statistical interaction effects. In other words, it has to do with statistical approaches rather than with conceptual issues. For some psychologists interactional psychology means studying people interacting with one another. In other words, it has to do with the description of interpersonal processes rather than with a mode of analysis of such processes. Thus, we are in danger because the popularity of interactional psychology may be in the room it leaves for it to mean all things to all people. The real import of the interactional approach, however, is in the conceptual emphasis it places on understanding the interdependence between person and situation or between internal and external determinants of behavior. One cannot exist without the other. [. . .]

A second implication of the interactionist position is the need for a broader temporal context than the single act. Much of our research to date has involved a freezing of behavior rather than a witnessing of how it unfolds. Observations of the flow or stream of behavior give evidence to both the stability and the plasticity of behavior. In attempting to adapt to the environment, the organism expresses both efforts to preserve its structure and to respond to environmental contingencies. The behaving organism is constantly striving to preserve order in the face of changes in the quality and quantity of internal and external stimuli. Processes such as regulation, adaptation, and exchange seem to be at the core of organismic behavior, and an understanding of such processes of individual-environment interaction may require a longer time perspective than is often given in personality research today.

Finally, the interactionist position requires the study of the behavior of organisms as it occurs in the natural environment. Such an orientation does not preclude laboratory experimentation. However, it does suggest that what is observed in the laboratory must be checked against behavior in the natural environment where person and situational factors are in constant interplay with one another.

The interactionist position suggests that our task is to define units of the person and of the situation – the critical variables internal to the organism and those external to it – and then study the processes through which the effects of one are tied to the operations of the other. The question is not person versus situation, or even how much person versus how much situation. Rather the question is *how* person and situation interact with one another. The trait, psychodynamic, and situationist positions all recognized the importance of this question but, unfortunately, never made it the center of investigation.

[. . .]

In their extreme forms, the 'person' and 'situation' positions cannot be reconciled, and neither can do a very good job in accounting for what occurs. Were it not for the fact that the dichotomy between internal and external determinants is so common, one would wonder about how the issue developed this way in the first place. Studies such as those of the hyperaggressive boys in different settings, of varied responses to diverse anxiety-arousing and hostility-arousing situations, and of the ways in which people express patterns of stability and change in their daily lives suggest that the question of which is more important, person or situation, is a meaningless one and a pseudo-issue. The real question is *how* do characteristics of the person interact with characteristics of the situation. This is the question asked by the interactionist who sees person and situation, internal determinants and external determinants, as inter-dependent – neither exists in the absence of the other and behavior always expresses both. The question no longer becomes one of understanding which is more important but one of understanding behavior as a constant process of interplay or exchange between the two. Mr Krim is not the person or the situation, he is the interplay between the two. He is always himself and his personality is his characteristic pattern of stability and change in relation to the situations he encounters in his daily life.

References

ALLPORT, G. W. (1955) *Becoming: Basic Considerations for a Psychology of Personality.* New Haven, CT: Yale University Press.

ALLPORT, G. W. (1961) *Pattern and Growth in Personality.* New York: Holt, Rinehart and Winston.

BANDURA, A. (1973) *Aggression: A Social Learning Analysis.* Englewood Cliffs, NJ: Prentice-Hall.

BEM, D. J. and ALLEN, A. (1974) 'On predicting some of the people some of the time: the search for cross-situational consistencies in behavior.' *Psychological Review*, **81**, 506–20.

BLOCK, J. (1971) *Lives Through Time*. Berkeley, CA: Bancroft.

BLOCK, J. (1977) 'Advancing the psychology of personality: paradigmatic shift or improving the quality of research', in MAGNUSSON, D. and ENDLER, N. S. (eds) *Personality at the Crossroads: Current Issues in Interactional Psychology*. Hillsdale, NJ: Erlbaum (pp. 37–63).

CAMPUS, N. (1974) 'Transituational consistency as a dimension of personality.' *Journal of Personality and Social Psychology*, **29**, 593–600.

CANTOR, N. and MISCHEL, W. (1977) 'Traits as prototypes: effects on recognition memory.' *Journal of Personality and Social Psychology*, **35**, 38–48.

ENDLER, N. S. and HUNT, J. MCV. (1966) 'Sources of behavioral variance as measured by the S-R Inventory of Anxiousness.' *Psychological Bulletin*, **65**, 336–46.

ENDLER, N. S. and HUNT, J. MCV. (1968) 'S-R inventories of hostility and comparisons of the proportions of variance from persons, responses, and situations for hostility and anxiousness.' *Journal of Personality and Social Psychology*, **9**, 309–15.

FISKE, D. W. and RICE, L. (1955) 'Intra-individual response variability.' *Psychological Bulletin*, **52**, 217–50.

HARTSHORNE, H. and MAY, M. A. (1928) *Studies in the Nature of Character: Studies in Deceit*. New York: Macmillan.

JONES, E. E. and NISBETT, R. E. (1971) *The Actor and the Observer: Divergent Perceptions of the Causes of Behavior*. Morristown, NJ: General Learning Press.

MCARTHUR, L. A. (1972) 'The how and what of why: some determinants and consequences of causal attribution.' *Journal of Personality and Social Psychology*, **22**, 171–93.

MISCHEL, W. (1968) *Personality and Assessment*. New York: Wiley.

MISCHEL, W. (1973) 'Toward a cognitive social learning reconceptualization of personality.' *Psychological Review*, **80**, 252–83.

MURRAY, H. A. (1938) *Explorations in Personality*. New York: Oxford University Press.

NISBETT, R. E., CAPUTO, C., LEGANT, P. and MARECEK, J. (1973) 'Behavior as seen by the actor and as seen by the observer.' *Journal of Personality and Social Psychology*, **27**, 154–64.

OSS ASSESSMENT STAFF (1948) *Assessment of Men*. New York: Rinehart.

RAUSH, H. L., DITTMAN, A. T. and TAYLOR, T. J. (1959) 'Person, setting and change in social interaction.' *Human Relations*, **12**, 361–78.

SCHWEDER, R. A. (1975) 'How relevant is an individual differences theory of personality?' *Journal of Personality*, **43**, 455–84.

3.2 Sources of information about the self

Sarah E. Hampson

We possess the ability to stand back and observe ourselves even though we may not always be truthful about what we see. This reflexive quality of human nature has long been a source of fascination for both philosophers and psychologists. For some, it is this capacity to be aware of ourselves and regard ourselves as objects to ourselves that distinguishes man from the other animals.

Our self-observations can take several forms: we may attempt to perceive ourselves as we think others see us; we may attempt to observe our private thoughts and feelings and thus find out things about ourselves that would not be available to others unless we chose to tell them; and we may simply observe our own behaviour in the same way that we observe another person's behaviour and make inferences about the sort of person we are from these self-observations. The first form of self-observation, perceiving ourselves as we think others see us, assumes that other people constitute a major source of information about the self. In order to obtain self-knowledge, we find out how we appear to others. Such is the view of a school of thought known as symbolic interactionism.

Other people

Symbolic interactionism is primarily associated with the names of Charles H. Cooley and George H. Mead. The 'symbolic' part of the term refers to the assumption that the environment should be regarded as consisting of objects whose significance lies in their social meaning. We are surrounded by a world of symbols, not a world of objects. 'Interactionism' refers to the fact that, via symbols, we are able to communicate with one another and to do this requires the ability to regard the world from another's perspective. The unit of analysis for symbolic interactionism is not an isolated individual but the interaction between two people: the self and the other. One of the results of interacting with another and taking the other's perspective is that the self is confronted with itself. It is in this way, argue the symbolic interactionists, that we are made aware of ourselves.

It was Cooley (1902) who aptly described the self-awareness derived from taking the other's perspective as the 'looking-glass' self. However, Mead is probably the best-known member of this tradition. Unlike most academics today who, unfortunately for their students, believe in the

Source: HAMPSON, SARAH E. (1982) *The Construction of Personality* (pp. 177–92). London: Routledge and Kegan Paul.

maxim 'publish or perish', Mead succeeded in becoming a highly acclaimed academic without writing a single book. He did, however, write several papers and it is through these and the books published after his death based on students' notes and previously unpublished manuscripts that it is possible for us today to learn about his conceptualisation of the self. Although he was a philosopher, he taught a course on social psychology and it was through giving these lectures that he developed his ideas on the self.

Mead believed that the essential quality of the self is that it is reflexive: the self can be an object to itself (Mead, 1934). We experience ourselves in the same way that we experience other people and objects in our environment. However, Mead argued, this experience can only come about through interacting with other people via the medium of language. It is by this process that we acquire a picture of ourselves referred to by Mead as the 'generalized other' which is the 'me' that 'I' am aware of. The generalized other is composed of other people's attitudes towards us. It is the product of socialisation: without interacting with others we would have no looking-glass in which to see ourselves. The self is therefore both social and socialized. By being made aware of ourselves through the attitudes of others we are aware of the effect our behaviour has on other people.

The self is composed of two parts, or phases, as Mead called them: the 'me' (the generalized other) and the 'I', and the 'I' reacts to the 'me'. The 'I' is the part of the self that decides how the 'me' will behave next. Once we begin to carry out the actions decided by the 'I', they immediately become part of our history, part of the 'me', so the 'I' can never be captured, it has always become part of the 'me' by the time we are aware of it.

The major contribution of Mead's theory of the self is his insistence on its social origins. Interaction with other people is essential for the development of the self. 'Selves can only exist in definite relationships with other selves' (Mead, 1934, page 164). This means that if a baby was abandoned on a desert island and miraculously survived to adulthood in the absence of human beings this person would have no self and would not be aware of itself. The sense of self, which feels so fundamental, is regarded by Mead not as an inherent property of human nature, but as the product of experience. Of course, we cannot test Mead's theory by depositing a baby on a desert island, but we may be able to draw some conclusions from those rare cases of children who appear to have been reared in the total absence of human beings. This strange occurrence has occasionally been documented.

One of the most detailed reports comes from India and concerns two girls who were believed to have been reared by wolves (Maclean, 1979). They were aged three and six years when they were first discovered. They were described as behaving in every way like their foster-parents the wolves. They ran on all fours, ate raw meat and howled. During the day they slept curled up together in a dark corner and at nightfall they would become restless and alert. They were fearful of human beings and ignored other children.

The Indian minister who found them tried to teach them language. Unfortunately, the younger girl died not long after they had been found and taken into his care, but the older girl did acquire a few words and learned to walk upright. Perhaps, as she began to interact with her new caretakers and learned to perceive her surroundings as possessing symbolic meaning, she began for the first time to experience the dawning of a sense of human selfhood. Tragically, she too fell ill and died before it would have been possible to discover whether this was indeed what had begun to happen.

[. . .]

Symbolic interactionism regards the self as the product of language which, as a proposition about the nature of the self, is impossible to refute since we cannot interrogate an organism which does not have a language to find out whether it has a self. It also assumes that the self is an all-or-none concept: an organism is either linguistically sophisticated and self-aware or it is not self-aware. This restricted view does not permit the possibility that an organism could be self-aware in so far as it is capable of distinguishing between its physical self and its environment even though it may not be fully self-aware in the sense that it is capable of thinking about itself. Evidence for partial self-awareness is available for chimpanzees and preverbal human infants. This evidence is derived from studies in which the subject is shown its reflection in a mirror (it is confronted with its looking-glass self in the literal sense). There are two sorts of responses to mirror reflections: one is to treat the reflection as though it were another organism which is usually evidenced by the subject attempting some form of social behaviour with the reflection; the other is for the subject to recognize the correspondence between the reflection and the self. This recognition is evidenced by self-directed behaviour such as, in the case of the chimpanzee, grooming parts of the body which would otherwise be invisible.

In a study using two chimpanzees Gallup (1970) demonstrated that after prolonged exposure to mirrors (approximately 80 hours) the chimps would stop responding socially to the image and behave as though they recognized the correspondence between the reflection and themselves. To confirm this, Gallup anaesthetized the two animals and, while they were unconscious, he painted their eyebrow ridges and the tops of their ears with red dye. On regaining consciousness, the animals were observed for the frequency with which they spontaneously touched these parts of their bodies when no mirror was present. This base rate was then compared with the amount of touching that occurred in the presence of the mirror and it was found that there was a dramatic increase in touching of the dyed areas when the animals viewed themselves in the mirror. This finding confirmed that the chimpanzees were capable of self-recognition since they did not attempt to reach out and touch the strange red patches on the chimpanzee in the mirror but instead they touched the appropriate parts of their own bodies.

A similar investigation conducted on human infants is reported by Lewis and Brooks (1975). Instead of dye, the mothers dabbed rouge on their baby's face when pretending to wipe it. The rouge was applied to the nose and then the baby was placed in front of a mirror and observed to see if it would touch its nose. The babies ranged in age from nine to 24 months and only the older babies (15–18 months and 21–24 months) showed evidence of self-recognition. Both these studies go against the symbolic interactionist position by demonstrating that organisms without language are capable of a partial form of self-awareness. However, it should be noted that Gallup was unable to observe any evidence of self-recognition in a lower species of primates (stump-tailed macaques and rhesus monkeys). Consequently, if it is conclusively established that chimpanzees are capable of acquiring language, then the symbolic interactionist position may be seen as being supported since it could be argued that physical self-recognition only occurs in animals capable of the more complete self-awareness involving language.

Symbolic interactionism proposes that other people are a major source of information about the self and this proposition is open to empirical investigation. If it is the case that our self-perceptions are based on the way we perceive others to perceive us, then a number of predictions may be made. First, there should be a high correlation between people's self-perceptions and their perceptions of the way other people see them. Second, there should be a high correlation between people's self-perceptions and other's actual perceptions of them. Third, there should be a high correlation between people's perceptions of how other people perceive them and how other people actually perceive them. Studies investigating these three predictions have been reviewed by Shrauger and Schoeneman (1979) who concluded that only the first prediction had received substantial empirical support: people's self-perceptions do correlate with their perceptions of how other people see them. There was no substantial support for a correspondence between people's self-perceptions and the way others actually see them, or for a correspondence between people's perceptions of the way others see them and the way others actually see them. Shrauger and Schoeneman point out that even if all three predictions had been supported, it still would not constitute conclusive support for the symbolic interactionist position since the direction of causal relations would remain unknown. Is it the way others see us and the way we think that others see us that causes us to hold certain self-perceptions? Or, conversely, does holding certain self-perceptions cause the way we are perceived by others and our perceptions of the way we are perceived by others?

The only way to determine the direction of causality is to study changes in self-perception, perception of others' perceptions and others' actual perceptions over time taking repeated measures of each of these view-points; unfortunately, this type of study has not been carried out. An approximation to it is to study the effects on self-perceptions of feedback about the self from others. Studies in the laboratory have been able to manipulate the content of feedback and observe its effects on self-perceptions. The general finding is that self-perceptions are changed by feedback but, as Shrauger and Schoeneman caution, the significance of these findings is in doubt because the demand effects in self-perception are such that subjects may feel obliged to report changes in self-perceptions which may not have actually occurred.

The symbolic interactionist position claims that other people are a major source of our self-knowledge and studies have shown that it is only our perceptions of other people's perceptions of us that tally with our self-perceptions. There is a disparity between these perceptions and others' actual perceptions of ourselves. It seems that we as self-perceivers, seeking information about ourselves from other people, have a tendency to distort the facts. This distortion could be due to the privileged access to past and present experience which is granted to the self-perceiver. This additional information may affect the self-perceiver's perceptions of the self and also of others' perceptions of the self resulting in the disparity between the self-perspective and the perspective of others. Other people are not in possession of all the information when they observe another and this inaccessible information could form a large component of self-knowledge.

Privileged information

When we think about ourselves one of the questions we frequently end up asking is 'Why did we do so and so?' Why did we choose that job? Why did we quarrel with that friend? Why did we like that book and not the other? These are also the sorts of questions other people ask us in daily conversation. We may sometimes have difficulty in answering them, but usually we are able to explain our preferences and behaviours in a way that is satisfactory to ourselves and others, e.g. we chose the job because it paid well, we stopped seeing the friend because of a political disagreement, we preferred one book to another because it was better written. It is generally assumed that we arrive at these explanations by going over in our minds the factors which affected our decision and the way we thought about them.

The assumption that we have access to the cognitive processes which determine our thoughts and actions has recently been challenged by Nisbett and Wilson (1977). They have gathered together an impressive array of evidence from cognitive and social psychology which suggests that we do not have access to our higher cognitive processes. According to Nisbett and Wilson, we explain our behaviour by reporting our beliefs or theories about it rather than by analysing what actually occurs. Their evidence against introspective awareness is drawn from a range of previous literature as well as some experiments of their own. Much of the evidence comes from experimental social psychology, where the findings suggest that people are often unaware of the cognitive processes the experimenter has demonstrated to be responsible for a behaviour change. For example, in reattribution studies, attempts are made to change behaviour by causing subjects to change their attributions with respect to that behaviour (Storms and Nisbett, 1970; Valins and Ray, 1967; Zimbardo, Cohen, Weisenberg, Dworkin and Firestone, 1969). However, while the experimenters assume that the behaviour change is accompanied by a conscious appraisal of the reattribution process, post-experimental questioning of the subjects typically reveals that they are unaware of the stimuli controlling their behaviour and regard the experimenters' explanations as interesting theories but inaccurate for them.

This type of study is well illustrated by Storms and Nisbett's (1970) reattribution study with insomniacs. The distinguishing features of insomnia are physical symptoms such as rapid heart rate, breathing difficulties, feeling too warm, and mental alertness and activity. Storms and Nisbett hypothesized that if they could persuade their insomniac patients to reattribute these symptoms to some cause other than to the stresses and strains in their daily lives which they believed produced the insomnia, then they would be able to ignore the symptoms and get to sleep. In other words, by changing the subjects' cognitions about their symptoms, a behavioural change would follow.

To test this hypothesis, Storms and Nisbett studied three groups of insomniacs using estimated time to get to sleep as the dependent variable. Subjects in all three groups first reported the time it took them to get to sleep on two consecutive nights in the absence of experimental manipulations. Then, for the next two nights the three groups received different treatments. The arousal group was given a placebo pill to take just before going to bed and was told that the pill would produce rapid heart beat, breathing difficulties, body heat and mental alertness – all the symptoms of insomnia. The relaxation group were told that the pill would have the effect of reducing all these symptoms; and a control group was given the pill but not informed about its possible effects.

Storms and Nisbett predicted that the arousal group would get to sleep faster with the pill than without it, whereas the relaxation group would take longer to get to sleep when given the pill. Their argument was that the arousal group would reattribute their symptoms to the pill's effects rather than to the difficulties they had experienced during the day. The relaxation group, on the other hand, would believe that their insomnia must be particularly bad if they were still experiencing all the symptoms in full even though they had taken a pill designed to reduce them. The results were in line with this argument: the arousal group got to sleep 28 per cent quicker on the pill nights whereas the relaxation group took 42 per cent longer. The control subjects reported no differences.

When the experimenters asked the experimental subjects why they had slept better or worse on the two pill nights, they did not explain the change in the same terms as the experimenters. The arousal subjects attributed their improvement to positive events in their daily lives such as having taken an exam that had been worrying them or having made up with their girl friend. The relaxation subjects would attribute their increased insomnia to equivalent negative events in their lives. When the connection between the pill and the changes in sleep patterns was pointed out, subjects were insistent that they had not associated the pills with their insomnia and doubted if any of the other subjects would have explained the effects along the lines proposed by the experimenters.

The studies of helping behaviour provide another illustration of this phenomenon. It is a reliable finding (Latané and Darley, 1970) that a person is much more likely to go to the aid of someone in distress if the person is the only bystander; the more people present who could help, the less likely it is that any one of those people actually will help. However, when subjects were asked whether they thought their helping was influenced by the number of other bystanders, they strongly denied any such influence. Of course, they may be aware of the effect of other people and find it socially undesirable to admit to it.

On the basis of these and other studies, Nisbett and Wilson argued that we probably never have direct access to our cognitive processes. Having discredited the powers of introspection, they still had to give an account of why it is that people are capable of producing explanations for their behaviour and descriptions of their thought processes, even though these explanations and descriptions are often, though not always, inaccurate. Nisbett and Wilson suggest that the origin of such explanations and descriptions lies in *a priori* causal theories. These are theories about stimulus-response relations which are widely shared within a culture and may be derived from explicit rules, e.g. 'I was driving slowly because it was a built-up area'; or beliefs about our own and other people's behaviour, e.g. 'I am feeling happy today because the sun is shining'.

In some instances there may be no *a priori* theory in existence to provide an account of a particular situation. In this case, a person will cast around for the most plausible explanation and this search process will be open to the biases of human thinking uncovered by Tversky and Kahneman (1973, 1974; Kahneman and Tversky, 1973). For example, the representative heuristic results in people assuming the similarity between a stimulus and a response implies the two are causally related. *A priori* causal theories will not necessarily be wrong, but when they are right it cannot be concluded that introspection has been accurate but rather that by lucky accident the *a priori* theory coincided with the actual state of affairs.

Nisbett and Wilson's argument is disturbing: it suggests that we have areas of apparent self-knowledge about which we feel entirely confident and others find reasonable, but which are not the product of self-examination and are frequently grossly inaccurate. Such an anti-introspectionist view is extreme. Not only does it challenge the validity of the use of introspection in cognitive studies such as reports on problem-solving processes (e.g. Newell and Simon, 1972) or mental rotation (e.g. Shepard, 1975), but also it challenges the current trends in social psychology where more attention is being paid to people's own explanations of their behaviour (Harré and Secord, 1972) and current theorising in the area of therapeutic behaviour change where changes in abnormal behaviour are seen as the product of a change in the patient's cognitions (e.g. Bandura, 1977).

In presenting such an extreme view, Nisbett and Wilson have provoked strong reactions (e.g. Smith and Miller, 1978; Rich, 1979; White, 1980). Their most cogent critics have been Smith and Miller who, in addition to making methodological comments on Nisbett and Wilson's own studies, have put forward three major criticisms of their position. The first criticism is that Nisbett and Wilson have presented a position which is not open to refutation: it has been argued that people's self-reports on their mental processes are not usually correct but that even when they are, this is due to the lucky coincidence of the *a priori* theory with the actual state of affairs and is not due to accurate introspection. Stated in this way, the theory is unverifiable and Smith and Miller argue that the issue should be presented in a different and verifiable manner. Instead of claiming that people's introspections are never correct, the issue should be under what conditions, if any, are people's introspections valid.

The second major criticism made by Smith and Miller is that Nisbett and Wilson have not paid attention to the distinction between what subjects may regard as the cause of their behaviour, given their ignorance of experimental manipulations, and what the experimenter, who is fully cognisant of all the variables, regards as causing the subject's behaviour. This is particularly important where a between-subjects design has been used, as in the Storms and Nisbett study of insomniacs. Individual subjects did not know about the differential effects on the arousal, relaxation and control groups as did the experimenters and, in the absence of this knowledge and in the light of their own personal history of insomnia, it was not inaccurate of the subjects to relate the cause of the change in their sleep patterns to events in their daily lives rather than to taking the pills.

The third major criticism was directed towards Nisbett and Wilson's inadequate distinction between mental processes and mental content. They argued that while we have access to mental content, we do not have access to mental processes. However, it is hard to maintain such a distinction. Take, for example, Shepard's work on mental rotation where subjects are asked to imagine rotating a shape presented visually through, say 180 degrees (Shepard, 1975). Subjects can be stopped in mid rotation and asked to describe the appearance of the shape at that point. Will their introspections be concerned with content or process?

Despite the doubts about the viability of their extreme position, Nisbett and Wilson have demonstrated that subjects in certain social and cognitive experiments were unaware of the stimuli determining their behaviour and were unaware of their unawareness, although this ignorance seems less remarkable in the light of Smith and Miller's comments. However, Nisbett and Wilson do not deny that we do have access to mental contents such as memories of our past experiences and there must be situations in which our rich self-knowledge results in a better understanding of ourselves than is possible for an outside observer; for example, the idiosyncratic emotional reactions to places or people of special significance which are inexplicable to the observer, ignorant of this private information.

Nisbett and Wilson are not the only psychologists to have adopted an extreme position about the limitations of self-perception. While they claim we do not have access to our mental processes, Bem (1972) has claimed that, regardless of whether we have access to this information, we do not use it as a basis for our self-knowledge. Instead, we make use of the same information which is available to an observer in understanding ourselves.

Self-observations of behaviour

Bem's theory of self-perception is strongly influenced by Skinnerian behaviourism from which it derives an underlying assumption which at first seems to stand the world on its head. Skinner argued that we do not know about our internal states until we have learned to discriminate between them and label them. Statements such as 'I have a headache' or 'I feel depressed' appear, on the face of it, to refer to internal stimuli available exclusively to the speaker: the speaker knows that he or she feels depressed or in pain and makes a statement to that effect. But how do we know that what we are feeling, which is a private event, corresponds to what other people call depression or a headache? Skinner argued that statements referring to private events are learned in the same way that names for objects in the environment are learned: by pointing and naming. The child falls over and bumps his head and the mother comforts him saying 'There, there, you've got a headache now from bumping your head.' The radical assumption in such an analysis is that the problem for psychologists to explain is not why we are unaware of some internal states, but how it is that we are ever aware of any internal states at all.

Bem has developed Skinner's discussion of the acquisition of language for describing internal states to the whole area of self-perception. He argues that we do not rely on the private information available only to ourselves but we use the same external information available to everyone when we make inferences about ourselves. For example, to decide whether we are enjoying a comedy show on television, we observe how much we are laughing and how little our attention is wandering away from the programme. Similarly, if a market researcher stops us in the street and asks us which we prefer: tea bags or loose tea, we remember we always buy tea bags and conclude we must prefer them. In both these instances, an observer would have been able to assess our internal state as accurately as we could since the inferences were based on overt behaviours. Bem does not deny that the self-perceiver has access to private information, nor that this information plays a role in self-perception, but he does argue that it is used far less than we have assumed.

The first experiments to test self-perception theory involved the self-perception of humour (Bem, 1965). Bem hoped to show how a person's attitude towards cartoons could be changed by manipulating external cues. In the first part of the experiment, the subjects answered questions about themselves into a tape recorder. They were instructed to answer truthfully if an amber light was illuminated on the recorder and to lie if the green light went on. Thus the subjects learned to believe themselves in the presence of the amber light and to disbelieve themselves in the presence of the green light. To control for the possible effect of light colour, half the subjects received the reverse training. In the second part of the experiment, the subjects were shown a series of cartoons which they had previously rated as being 'neutral' (neither funny nor unfunny) and were told to say into the tape recorder either 'This cartoon is very funny' or 'This cartoon is very unfunny' depending on the experimenter's instructions. While they were speaking, either the amber or the green light would be on. Finally, the subjects rated the humorousness of the cartoons again. The results showed that the external cues, the coloured lights, had affected the subjects' subsequent ratings. They changed their attitudes significantly more for the cartoons where they had made the statement in the presence of the 'truth' light than in the presence of the 'lie' light. Bem concluded that the subjects had learned to believe what they said in the presence of the truth light and to disbelieve what they said in the presence of the lie light. When asked afterwards, subjects reported being unaware of the effects of the lights.

When it first appeared, self-perception theory was regarded as an alternative to cognitive dissonance theory and there were several studies attempting to compare the explanatory powers of these two accounts (e.g. Bem, 1967). [. . .] The aspect of self-perception which concerns us here is the account of the self-perception of personality dispositions. According to Bem's theory, we decide what sort of person we are in the same way as an observer decides, that is by observing our behaviour and making inferences from it. For example, ask yourself 'Am I a generous person?' If you have any hesitations in saying 'yes' or 'no' then you may find yourself remembering how you have behaved in previous situations where you could have exhibited generosity: did you buy a round of drinks at the pub the other day, or give some money to the person collecting for a charity?

On the basis of your past behaviour, you assess whether or not you deserve the label of 'generous'.

It is a common reaction to feel uneasy about Bem's theory. After all, it is undeniable that from the standpoint of the self, we have a different perspective on ourselves from that of the observer; we are in possession of information of which the observer is ignorant. Since this is the case, how can Bem assert that we come to know ourselves in the same way that another person knows us: through behavioural observation? Bem's position becomes somewhat more acceptable if it is stressed that it was always intended as an explanation for self-perception under conditions of uncertainty; it is a theory about how we come to know ourselves when the 'internal cues are weak, ambiguous or uninterpretable' (Bem, 1972, page 2). In other words, when the information about ourselves to which we have privileged access fails us, it is then that we, like other people, can only understand ourselves by examining how we behave. There is a sense in which Bem's position is similar to that of the symbolic interactionists, who argue that our self-concept is the result of our perceptions of how other people see us. When we refer to our behaviour to decide what we are like, we make the same inferences on the basis of that behaviour as another person would (e.g. people who give to charity are generous) and hence arrive at an opinion of ourselves that would, presumably, match the opinion of us that we would expect another to hold. The findings reviewed by Shrauger and Schoeneman (1979) on the correspondence between self-perceptions and our perceptions of how others see us lends indirect support to Bem's theory.

Having considered the three sources of information about the self that have received considerable theoretical and empirical attention, it is reasonable to conclude that self-perceptions make use of them all. In part, we perceive ourselves as we think others see us, even though this view may not always correspond to how others actually see us; we augment this knowledge with the private information about ourselves to which only we have access, although there are times when this information is either unavailable or misleading; when these two sources are inadequate, we turn to self-observations of our behaviour to arrive at self-understanding. The most noteworthy point to emerge from this discussion is the disparity between self-perceptions and others' actual perceptions of us. Perhaps in this disparity there lies an explanation for our fascination with obtaining other people's perceptions of ourselves, be they our friends, psychologists, psychoanalysts or astrologists. Since we can never truly be an object to ourselves and see ourselves as others see us, our perceptions of ourselves and others are inescapably seen through our own eyes. Occasionally our attention is drawn to the disparity between our self-perceptions and another's perceptions of us, giving us a tantalizing glimpse of how we appear from another perspective. No wonder we are fascinated and desire the impossible: to step outside ourselves and take a longer look.

References

BANDURA, A. (1977) 'Self-efficacy: towards a unifying theory of behavioural change.' *Psychological Review*, **84**, 191–215.

BEM, D. J. (1965) 'An experimental analysis of self-persuasion.' *Journal of Experimental Social Psychology*, **1**, 199–218.

BEM, D. J. (1967) 'Self-perception: an alternative interpretation of cognitive dissonance phenomena.' *Psychological Review*, **74**, 183–200.

BEM, D. J. (1972) 'Self-perception theory', in BERKOWITZ, L. (ed.). *Advances in Experimental Social Psychology*, Vol. 6 (pp. 1–62). New York: Academic Press.

COOLEY, C. H. (1902) *Human Nature and the Social Order*. New York: Scribner.

GALLUP, G. G. (1970) 'Chimpanzees: self-recognition.' *Science*, **167**, 86–7.

HARRE, R. and SECORD, P. F. (1972) *The Explanation of Social Behaviour*. Oxford: Blackwell.

KAHNEMAN, D. and TVERSKY, A. (1973) 'On the psychology of prediction.' *Psychological Review*, **80**, 237–51.

LATANE, B. and DARLEY, J. M. (1970) *The Unresponsive Bystander: Why doesn't he help?* New York: Appleton-Century Crofts.

LEWIS, M. and BROOKS, J. (1975) 'Infants' social perception: a constructivist view', in COHEN, L. B. and SALAPATEK, P. (eds) *Infant Perception: From Sensation to Cognition. Vol. II, Perception of Space, Speech and Sound*. New York: Academic Press.

MACLEAN, C. (1979) *The Wolf Children*. Harmondsworth: Penguin Books.

MEAD, G. H. (1934) *Mind, Self and Society*. Chicago, IL: University of Chicago Press.

NEWELL, A. and SIMON, H. A. (1972) *Human Problem Solving*. Englewood Cliffs, NJ: Prentice-Hall.

NISBETT, R. E. and WILSON, T. D. (1977) 'Telling more than we can know: verbal reports on mental processes.' *Psychological Review*, **84**, 231–59.

RICH, M. C. (1979) 'Verbal reports on mental processes: issues of accuracy and awareness.' *Journal for the Theory of Social Behaviour*, **9**, 29–37.

SHEPARD, R. N. (1975) 'Form, formation, and transformation of internal representations', in SOLSO, R. L. (ed.) *Information Processing and Cognition*. Hillsdale, NJ: Erlbaum.

SHRAUGER, J. S. and SCHOENEMAN, T. J. (1979) 'Symbolic interactionist view of self-concept: through the looking glass darkly.' *Psychological Bulletin*, **86**, 549–73.

SMITH, E. R. and MILLER, F. D. (1978) 'Limits on perception of cognitive processes: a reply to Nisbett and Wilson.' *Psychological Review*, **85**, 355–62.

STORMS, M. D. and NISBETT, R. E. (1970) 'Insomnia and the attribution process.' *Journal of Personality and Social Psychology*, **2**, 319–28.

TVERSKY, A. and KAHNEMAN, D. (1973) 'Availability: a heuristic for judging frequency and probability.' *Cognitive Psychology*, **5**, 207–32.

TVERSKY, A. and KAHNEMAN, D. (1974) 'Judgement under uncertainty: heuristics and biases.' *Science*, **184**, 1124–31.

VALINS, S. and RAY, A. A. (1967) 'Effects of cognitive desensitization on avoidance behaviour.' *Journal of Personality and Social Psychology*, **1**, 345–50.

WHITE, P. (1980) 'Limitations on verbal reports of internal events: a refutation of Nisbett and Wilson and of Bem.' *Psychological Review*, **87**, 105–12.

ZIMBARDO, P. G., COHEN, A., WEISENBERG, M., DWORKIN, L., and FIRESTONE, I. (1969) 'The control of experimental pain', in ZIMBARDO, P. G. (ed.) *The Cognitive Control of Motivation*. Glenview, IL: Scott Foresman.

3.3 The effects of teachers' behaviour on pupils' attributions: a review

Daniel Bar-Tal

Introduction

In recent years, with the growing interest in attribution theory and with the increasing demand for a relevant and applied social psychology, the study of attribution processes has been applied to different social problems (see, for example, Frieze *et al.*, 1979). One attributional model which has been applied specifically to educational problems is Weiner's attributional model of achievement-related behaviour (Weiner *et al.*, 1971; Weiner, 1974).

[Here I] will review Weiner's model, present its application to the analysis of pupils' and teachers' perceptions and behaviours in the classroom, discuss the antecedents of pupils' attributions and, specifically, focus on the influence of teachers on pupils' causal perception of success and failure. Finally, I will discuss several educational applications.

Weiner's attributional model of achievement-related behaviour

Weiner presented his model as an attributional analysis of an individual's achievement-related behaviour, suggesting that individuals' causal perception of success and failure may be of major importance in understanding such behaviour. According to Weiner, causal perceptions of success and failure mediate between the antecedent conditions and achievement-related behaviour (Weiner, 1974; Weiner *et al.*, 1971).

Specifically, in the most recent formulation, Weiner (Weiner, 1977, 1979; Weiner *et al.*, 1978) has suggested that individuals use a variety of causes to explain their success or failure on achievement tasks. These causes can be classified in three dimensions. One dimension, locus of causality, differentiates the causes in terms of their internality/externality. While some causes, such as ability, effort, personality, mood or health might be considered internal, because they might be believed to originate within the person, other causes such as luck, others' interference, home conditions or task difficulty might be considered external, because they might be believed to originate outside the person. The second dimension differentiates causes in terms of their stability over time. While

Source: ANTAKI, CHARLES and BREWIN, CHRIS (eds) (1982) *Attributions and Psychological Change* (pp. 177–94). London: Academic Press.

some causes, such as mood, effort or luck, may be considered unstable, because they may be believed to fluctuate over time, other causes, such as ability, task difficulty or home conditions may be considered as stable, since they may be believed not to change over time. The third dimension differentiates the causes in terms of their controllability. While some causes, such as effort, attention, or others' help, may be believed to be under the volitional control of the person, other causes, such as mood, luck, health or ability, may be believed not to be under the volitional control of the person.

The above described dimensions have important consequences. They are related to individuals' cognitive reactions (such as their expectations regarding future outcomes), to their affective reactions (such as self-esteem changes), and to their behavioural reactions (such as achievement-related behaviour). Weiner (1974, 1979) postulated that expectancy for future success is determined by stability of the causes. Ascription of an outcome to unstable causes produces greater shifts in expectancy of achievement to the desired outcome than does ascription to stable causes (see McMahan, 1973; Valle and Frieze, 1976; Weiner *et al.*, 1976 for empirical support). Failure at an achievement task attributed to unstable causes may result in expectations for eventual success, since unstable causes might change. Failure due to stable causes is expected to continue, since these causes are believed to remain. Similarly, if success was attributed to stable causes, continued success would be expected.

The locus of causality dimension is an important determinant of affective reactions (Weiner *et al.*, 1978). Individuals who attribute their success to internal causes experience affects of pride, competence, confidence, and satisfaction, while individuals who attribute failure to internal causes experience feelings of guilt and resignation.

Of special interest for the present paper is the link between causal perception of success or failure and achievement-related behaviour. There is a substantial amount of evidence indicating that causal perception of success and failure influences the individual's persistence, intensity and choice behaviour of achievement tasks (e.g. Butkowsky and Willows, 1980; Diener and Dweck, 1978; Dweck, 1975; Fyans and Maehr, 1979; Kukla, 1972; Weiner *et al.*, 1972). Individuals who tend to attribute their failure to unstable-controllable causes, such as effort, tend to persist for a long time even in failure situations. This attribution of failure enables them to believe that there is a possibility of modifying the outcome in the future. Conversely, attribution of a failure to stable-uncontrollable causes does not leave the possibility of changing the outcome in the future and, therefore, there is no reason to persist. The belief in unstable-controllable causes such as effort causes the person to assume that the outcome depends on will. Therefore, these individuals perform with great intensity on achievement tasks. On the other hand, the belief in stable or uncontrollable causes, such as ability or mood, does not motivate the person to perform with intensity, since there is no belief in having control over the

causes of success or failure. Finally, it was found that pupils tend to prefer
to perform tasks that are compatible with their causal perception. For
example, pupils who generally attribute their achievement outcome to
ability are likely to choose tasks in which competence is requisite to
outcome. Conversely, pupils who tend to attribute their success to luck
prefer tasks which depend on chance and avoid tasks requiring competence. In view of these findings, which demonstrate the importance of
causal perception for achievement behaviour, it is not surprising that
Weiner's model has been applied to education for the analysis of pupils'
behaviour.

Antecedents of pupils' attributions

The first, important question is how pupils decide what causes are
responsible for their success or failure. On the basis of Weiner's model
(Weiner, 1974), it is suggested that two general categories of antecedents
influence pupils' causal perception: their own personal dispositions and
the external information available to them. The personal dispositions
category consists of three subcategories: (a) personality tendencies; (b)
demographic status; and (c) causal schemata. The available information
consists of five subcategories: (a) own performance; (b) others' performance; (c) constraints and nature of the achievement task; (d) parents' or
others' influence; and (e) teachers' influence. The list of antecedents and
their effects are depicted in Figure 1.

Differences in pupils' personal dispositions

Personal dispositions consist of the motivational biases of pupils to form
and hold attributions that serve their needs and desires. The personal
dispositions to ascribe specific patterns of causality derive from personality characteristics, demographic status and causal schemata.

Several studies contended that certain personality characteristics are
related to differential attributional tendencies. Thus, for example, a series
of empirical studies (e.g. Bar-Tal and Frieze, 1977; Kukla, 1972; Murray
and Mednick, 1975) has demonstrated that need for achievement influences causal ascription. While persons high in achievement needs tend
to attribute success to ability and effort, persons low in achievement needs
do not display clear attributional preferences for success. In cases of
failure, while persons high in achievement needs tend to attribute failure
to lack of effort, persons low in need for achievement tend to attribute it to
lack of ability. Differential attributions were also found with regard to
different self-esteem tendencies (e.g. Ames and Felker, 1979; Fitch, 1970)
and different locus of control dispositions (e.g. Davis and Davis, 1977;
Krovetz, 1974). Regarding self-esteem the results showed that low self-
esteem persons tend to take more personal responsibility for failure than

Antecedents

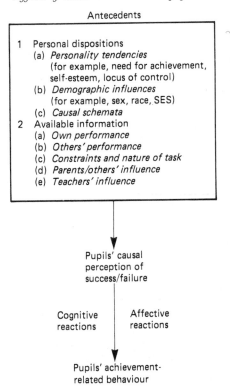

1 Personal dispositions
   (a) *Personality tendencies*
       (for example, need for achievement,
       self-esteem, locus of control)
   (b) *Demographic influences*
       (for example, sex, race, SES)
   (c) *Causal schemata*
2 Available information
   (a) *Own performance*
   (b) *Others' performance*
   (c) *Constraints and nature of task*
   (d) *Parents/others' influence*
   (e) *Teachers' influence*

Pupils' causal
perception of
success/failure

Cognitive   Affective
reactions   reactions

Pupils' achievement-
related behaviour

Figure 1   Antecedents of causal perception mediating achievement-related
behaviour

do high self-esteem persons. Differences regarding locus of control indicate that internal individuals tend to use more internal causes to explain
their achievement outcome, especially in the case of failure, than do
external individuals.

There is evidence that demographic characteristics are associated with
attributional patterns. For example, sex differences indicate that females
tend to be more external and to employ more luck attributions than do
males and that females, in general, rate their ability less highly than do
males (e.g. Bar-Tal and Frieze, 1977; Dweck *et al.*, 1978; Murray and
Mednick, 1975; Nichols, 1975). Attributional differences were also found
with regard to race and socio-economic status (SES) variables. Friend and
Neale (1972) found that white children considered internal causes (ability
and effort) to have more influence on the outcome than external causes
(luck and task difficulty), especially in failure situations. Black children,
on the contrary, considered external causes to have more influence than
internal ones. Raviv *et al.* (1980) found that low SES pupils tended to
attribute their failure more to stable than to unstable causes, while high

SES pupils tended to attribute their failure more to internal than to external causes, especially unstable ones. In this vein, Falbo (1975) found that middle-class children tended to choose effort as causal ascription more often than did lower-class children.

Causal schemata, defined as personal conceptions as to which causes produce specific effects, and formed on the basis of past experience (Kelley, 1972), also determine individuals' attributional patterns. Bar-Tal (1974), for example, identified groups of students who employ similar causal schemata in explaining their achievement outcomes. Kun and Weiner (1973) and Kun (1977) demonstrated how students use different causal schemata in achievement situations.

Differences in the information available to pupils

The information on which pupils base their attributions comes from many sources. The most salient information is one's own performance. It has been shown that information regarding one's own outcome, past outcome history, or past outcome history on similar tasks may indicate to pupils why they succeeded or failed. Thus, for example, outcomes evaluated as successes tended to be ascribed to internal causes, while outcomes evaluated as failures to external ones (e.g. Bar-Tal and Frieze, 1976; Luginbuhl *et al.*, 1975). A comparison of the achievement with past outcomes indicates the stability of the causes involved. That is, on the basis of this comparison, the pupil can know whether the outcome was accidental and unusual due to unstable-uncontrollable causes, such as luck or others' help; planned, due to unstable-controllable causes, such as effort; or usual, due to stable causes such as ability.

The results show that the consistency of the achieved outcome with past results on the same task increases the attribution to stable causes, such as ability and task difficulty, while an inconsistent outcome increases attribution to unstable causes, such as effort and luck (e.g. Ames *et al.*, 1976; Frieze and Weiner, 1971; Frieze and Bar-Tal, 1980; Meyer, 1980).

Knowledge about others' performance may also be important information for attribution. When one's outcome is different from others', one can learn a great deal about oneself. The inconsistent outcome provides information about one's ability and exerted effort. Consistent outcome provides information, mainly about the difficulty of the achievement task. Frieze and Weiner (1971), Frieze and Bar-Tal (1980) and Meyer (1980) found, for example, that students tend to ascribe outcomes inconsistent with others' results mainly to internal causes (such as ability and effort), but also to luck, and consistent outcomes to external causes (mainly to task difficulty).

The nature of the task and the constraints regarding the performance can be another source of information about the causes of the outcome. On the basis of such information, pupils can decide how the nature of the task influenced their achievement outcome. Moreover, it provides insights regarding other causes, such as ability, luck, or effort. For example, Frieze and Weiner (1971) found that the amount of time a person spends on a task affects the causal ascription. When a person spends a short time at the task, failure tends to be attributed to lack of effort and success to good luck and ease of task. However, when a person spends a long time at the task, failure is ascribed to bad luck and task difficulty, while success is attributed to the presence of effort.

Pupils do not only infer causes of their successes or failures on the basis of the available information about their own performance, others' performance or the nature of the task, but are also provided directly, often explicitly, with information about the causes from significant individuals in their lives. It seems obvious that parents react to their children's achievement outcomes and either explicitly or implicitly supply causes as to why such outcomes were achieved. Empirical evidence indicates that parents ascribe causes to the successes or failures of their children (e.g. Bar-Tal and Guttmann, 1981; Beckman, 1976). In addition, it has been demonstrated that parents communicate their attributions to their children (e.g. Bar-Tal and Goldberg, 1980). It can be assumed, therefore, that parents, being important agents of socialization, influence their children's attributions. Such information can also be provided by other significant figures in the social environment of the pupil, such as other members of the family, friends, or teachers.

Of special interest for the present paper is the influence of teachers on pupils' causal perception of success or failure. Teachers have been found to have powerful influence over pupils' perceptions and attitudes regarding achievement situations (Cooper, 1979; Hargreaves, 1972). In the case of attribution, Bar-Tal and Guttmann (1981) found that pupils' causal perceptions of success or failure were more similar to that of their teachers than that of their parents. These results were interpreted as indicating that teachers have more influence on pupils' attributions than do parents. This raises the possibility that, where little can be done on such things as pupils' demographic status and personal characteristics, it might be possible to affect children's attributions by guiding and training their teachers. The remainder of the paper will explore this possibility by analysing in greater detail teachers' influence on pupils' attributions.

An attribution model of pupils' and teachers' behaviour

Bar-Tal (1979) extended the Weiner model and applied it specifically to the classroom situation, where it is used to analyse the perceptions and behaviours of pupils and teachers in interaction. The model suggests that many classroom situations involve evaluation of pupils' achievements as success or failure. In these situations, both pupils and teachers tend to ascribe causes to explain the pupils' success or failure on achievement tasks (e.g. Bar-Tal and Darom, 1979; Bar-Tal *et al.*, 1980; Cooper and Burger, 1980; Darom and Bar-Tal, 1981; Frieze and Snyder, 1980). The teachers' causal perceptions, which may not correspond to those of their pupils, are important determinants of teachers' behaviour towards their pupils. The relationship between teachers' causal perception and their behaviour towards pupils can be explained through the mediating process of teachers' expectations regarding pupils' future outcomes. It is suggested that teachers decide whether the same outcome will be repeated in the future on the basis of the classification of the causes on the dimensions of stability and controllability. If the teachers believe that the success or failure of their pupils is caused by stable causes, they might expect the same outcome to be repeated, since people believe that stable causes do not change over time. If the success or failure is attributed to unstable, but controllable, causes, the teachers might believe that the pupils will experience success in the future, on the assumption that pupils want to succeed. However, if the success or failure is attributed to unstable and uncontrollable causes, the teachers cannot predict the future achievement outcome of the pupils. In turn, it is proposed that teachers' expectations regarding pupils' future achievement affect their behaviour towards the pupils. This proposal has been supported by numerous studies which have shown that teachers' differential behaviour towards pupils is determined by their expectations regarding future outcomes (see reviews by Braun, 1976; Dusek, 1975; Cooper, 1979; and Rogers, 1982).

Finally, the model suggests that pupils' achievement behaviour influences teachers' causal perception of pupils' success or failure and that teachers' behaviour towards pupils determines pupils' causal perception of their success or failure. The former link is supported by evidence reviewed by West and Anderson (1976) which indicates that teachers' expectations seem to be formed on the basis of observed pupils' behaviour and not on the basis of irrelevant cues. The latter link will be extensively discussed in the final sections of this paper, before which, however, the effect of teacher's behaviour on pupils' attributions will be described.

The effect of teachers' behaviour on pupils' attributions

In classroom situations, teachers dominate the interactions with the pupils, pupils' attention is directed towards the teachers, whose verbal and non-verbal behaviour provides much information regarding not only academic content, but also regarding events occurring in the classroom, the pupils themselves, etc. To a large extent, this information determines pupils' reactions, such as attitudes, self-perception, or causal perception of success and failure. With regard to pupils' causal perception, it seems that teachers sometimes communicate the causes directly and sometimes pupils infer them on the basis of teachers' behaviour (Blumenfeld *et al.*,

1977). It is suggested that teachers' behaviours which influence pupils' causal perception, can be classified into five categories: (a) verbal appeals; (b) instructions; (c) reinforcements; (d) verbal feedback; and (e) direct references to causality.

Verbal appeals

Verbal appeals are defined as teachers' addresses to pupils with reference to their behaviour (achievement or non-achievement), without relation to a specific performance outcome on an achievement test. Studies by Dweck and her associates (Dweck and Bush, 1978; Dweck *et al.*, 1978) showed how verbal appeals and direct reference to causality influence pupils' attributions. In a study by Dweck *et al.* (1978), teachers' reactions towards pupils were observed and coded. The observations revealed that: (a) teachers more often approach boys than girls with negative appeals regarding non-intellectual aspects of their work; (b) teachers more often approach boys than girls with positive appeals regarding intellectual quality of their work; (c) teachers provide girls more often than boys with positive appeals regarding non-intellectual aspects of their work; (d) teachers provide girls more often than boys with negative appeals regarding intellectual quality of their work; and (e) teachers refer directly to lack of motivation of boys more often than that of girls in cases of failure. These differential reactions were found to determine differences in boys' and girls' causal perceptions of success and failure: girls place less emphasis than do boys on effort as a cause of failure and are more likely than boys to attribute failure to a lack of ability. The negative appeal of teachers towards intellectually irrelevant aspects of boys' behaviour is attributed by pupils to teachers' attitude toward them, but is not perceived as an objective evaluation of their academic ability. However, the teachers' positive appeal towards boys, which was focused mainly on intellectual performance, provides a good indicator of boys' academic ability. In addition, teachers' use of effort attribution, in the case of boys' failure, indicates to boys that their failure is due to lack of effort exertion. Girls were not taught to use effort attribution, because teachers do not tend to use this cause in making attributions for girls' failure. Teachers' appeals increase girls' tendency to attribute failure to lack of ability. The diffuse use of positive appeals is attributed by girls to teachers' attitude towards them, and not as a reflection of their academic ability. On the other hand, a highly specific negative appeal regarding the intellectual quality of girls' work in the case of failure indicates to girls that they failed as a result of low ability.

Cooper (1977) confirmed Dweck's findings. In his study, pupils who were criticized, often for reasons external to their personal effort, were found not to perceive that effort covaried with outcome on achievement tasks.

Instructions

Instructions are teachers' explanations of a task given prior to its performance. Instructions can refer to such elements as task difficulty, constraints,
skills required, and motivation required. Several studies demonstrated
how instructions may affect pupils' causal perception of success and
failure and their achievement behaviour. These studies compared two
groups of subjects who differed in their needs for achievement. As
described previously, individuals low in achievement needs do not recognize the importance of effort in performance needs in general, and
specifically tend to attribute their failure to lack of ability. Conversely,
individuals high in achievement needs emphasize the importance of effort
for success or failure.

In an experiment carried out by Kukla (1972), one group of subjects
was instructed to perform a task and was told that successful performance
on it depended only on ability. Another group was instructed to perform
the same task, but was told that successful performance on it depended on
ability and effort as well. Both groups consisted of students high and low in
achievement needs. The results of this study showed that although there
was no difference in achievement performance between students with high
and low needs for achievement in the situation that emphasized the
importance of ability, students with a high need for achievement performed significantly better than did students with a low need for achievement when the instructions emphasized ability and effort. These results
indicate that the instructions probably affected students' causal perceptions. Students with a high need for achievement, who recognized the
importance of effort, tried harder to succeed when they heard that the
outcome depended also on exerted effort. They believed that effort would
be one of the determinants of the achievement. In contrast, for students
with a low need for achievement, effort was not perceived as a determinant
of successful outcome, therefore they were not influenced by the instructions that also emphasized effort. These students, receiving the information that ability would determine the outcome, did not try hard, since
ability either existed or did not. Similar reactions were recorded in the
case of students high in achievement needs who were instructed that the
outcome of the task would depend on their ability only. In another
experiment by Weiner and Sierad (1975), two groups of subjects, consisting of students high and low in achievement needs, were instructed to
perform an achievement task, each under different instructions. Subjects
in one group were given a placebo pill and were told that it would interfere
with their performance on an achievement task, while the second group
did not receive a placebo and no reference was made to possible causes of
their success or failure. The results showed that, while students high in
achievement needs displayed greater achievements on the task having
taken the pill than they did in the no-pill condition, an opposite direction
of achievement was displayed by students low in achievement needs.

Thus, students low in achievement needs could use the pill as a cause for failure, and thereby reduce their anxiety caused by attributing failure to lack of ability. Therefore, they performed with great intensity on hearing the instructions in reference to possible pill interference with performance. Students high in achievement needs, who usually recognize the importance of effort attributions, accepted the instructions about the interference of the pill and shifted their usual beliefs to the placebo. In this case, students believed that the detrimental effects of the placebo could not be changed, and, therefore, did not try as hard as they normally did.

Reinforcements

Reinforcements refer to teachers' use of tangible rewards or punishments in relation to a performance on an achievement task. Ames *et al.* (1977) demonstrated that the form of reward contingencies used by the teachers in the classroom might be an important factor determining pupils' causal perception of success or failure following achievement tasks. In this study, pupils were rewarded either under competitive reward contingencies or under non-competitive reward contingencies for their performance on an achievement task. Whereas under the former reward contingency only one person (the winner) of two people could receive a reward, under the latter reward contingency both pupils could get their reward irrespective of their outcome. After the task, the pupils were asked to ascribe causes for their success or failure to ability, effort, task difficulty and luck. The results showed that under a competitive reward contingency pupils tended greatly to use luck attribution. Moreover, pupils failing under a competitive reward contingency rated their own ability lower than did those failing under a non-competitive reward contingency. Thus, competitive reward structures may lead to self-derogatory attribution. The consequences of such attribution could be negative. As Ames *et al.* noted:

Repeated experiences of this nature could conceivably contribute to a low-achievement-motive syndrome or to "learned-helplessness". Students may begin to expect failure since a low-ability attribution is a relatively stable dispositional property, and to associate negative affect with achievement setting. The consequences of failure are obviously negative, but the impact of failure in competitive conditions seems to be rather devastating to a child's self-perceptions (p. 7).

The competitive situation probably accentuates social comparison, and failure under this condition exposes one's own ability, thus enhancing the possibility of attributing failure to lack of ability.

Verbal feedback

In a series of experiments Meyer *et al.* (1979) investigated the effect of verbal feedback (praise or criticism) on perceptions of ability following performance. Most (5 out of 6) of the experiments they reported were studies of subjects' perception of the abilities of other people (always hypothetical). Subjects were adults, university students, high school students and grade school pupils. The experiments showed that hearing that someone had been praised after success on an easy task, or had received only a neutral reaction after failure, led subjects to conclude that the person's ability was low. If they heard however that the person had received only a neutral reaction after success on a difficult task, or had been criticized after failing on an easy task, then subjects concluded that the person must have had a high ability. One way of explaining the findings is to suppose the subjects expected those with low ability needed to be praised comparatively extravagantly while those who really could do the work did not, and could take negative criticism. Although these findings come from paper and pencil tests they do seem plausible accounts of what people think of the meaning of praise and blame feedback. One experiment (experiment 5) provided data on how people assessed such feedback information when they heard it applied to themselves. Subjects were asked to imagine themselves in the place of a student who received positive neutral or negative feedback after failing or succeeding at an easy or difficult task. The university students in this experiment responded in a way consistent with the general finding reported above.

Direct reference to causality

Dweck (1975) demonstrated that direct reference to causality by teachers may influence pupils' causal perception and also their achievement behaviour. In her study, subjects identified as helpless – those who do not take personal responsibility for their outcomes and did not perceive a covariation between outcome and the effort exerted – were given an achievement task on which there were programmed failures. Following each failure, the teacher said that the pupil had failed and added, 'That means that you should have tried harder' (page 679), implying that the effort was the cause of failure. Following a training session, these pupils showed a significantly greater tendency to emphasize the role of effort in determining failure. Moreover, these subjects started to show one adaptive pattern of reaction in the face of failure – persistence.

Similar results were obtained by Chapin and Dyck (1976). They also provided their pupils with a direct reference to causality following a failure. The teacher said, 'No, you didn't get that. That means you should have tried harder' (1976, p. 512). Lack of effort was explained as a cause of failure. Pupils who heard this reference began to persist in their achievement performance.

Finally, Andrews and Debus (1978) also demonstrated that direct reference to causality by teachers influenced pupils' causal perception and achievement behaviour. Subjects who did not recognize the importance of effort for achievement outcomes were given a task, following which they were asked to ascribe causes for the outcome. When they did not use effort attribution, the teacher directed them to use this cause and even explicitly stated, following failure, that pupils usually fail because they do not try hard enough. If the pupils used this cause to explain their outcome, they were reinforced. The results showed that following this training pupils increased their effort attributions and improved their achievement performance.

Educational applications

Three major conclusions can be derived from the material reviewed in the present paper: (a) pupils ascribe causes for their failures or successes on achievement tasks; (b) causal perceptions of pupils mediate between the antecedent factors and achievement-related behaviour, which means that pupils' attributions determine their achievement behaviour; and (c) teachers greatly influence pupils' use of causes to explain their successes or failures.

If we accept the evidence indicating that certain attributional patterns are more adaptive and, therefore, more desirable for educational achievement, then the influence of teachers has special meaning for applying the theoretical considerations and empirical findings to educational practices. The analysed attributional model indicates that pupils who tend to attribute success to internal, mainly stable or controllable, causes, and who attribute failure to internal-unstable-controllable causes, tend to exhibit adaptive, mastery-oriented achievement behaviour. That is, they tend to approach rather than avoid achievement tasks, tend to persist in the face of failure, and tend to perform achievement tasks with greater intensity. Pupils who tend to attribute success to external causes and failure to internal-stable-uncontrollable causes show a very different pattern. These pupils tend to exhibit maladaptive, helpless achievement behaviour. That is, they tend to avoid achievement tasks, tend to give up in the face of failure and do not perform achievement tasks with great intensity.

In view of the evidence regarding the behavioural consequences of pupils' attributional patterns, one educational objective should be to encourage pupils to use the adaptive pattern of causal perception of their success and failure. Within the framework of such an objective, teachers could play a major role. Their behaviour is one of the determinants of pupils' causal perception. Therefore, they can direct pupils to adaptive attributions. The primary objective should be to convince pupils that effort, as an unstable-controllable factor, is an important cause of achievement outcome. Hard trying might cause success, while lack of trying might cause failure. Pupils should be convinced that effort, which can take the form of preparation at home, paying attention during lectures, or trying hard during tests, can be changed by their will. Teachers should also direct pupils to attribute their successes to internal causes. Such a

212   *Daniel Bar-Tal*

tendency increases satisfaction and feelings of competence and enhances the possibility of approaching achievement tasks. Teachers should also prevent attribution of failure to stable-uncontrollable causes, such as lack of ability, because this pattern facilitates the development of helplessness. It should be pointed out that teachers should not encourage in pupils an unrealistic perception which could imply that achievement depends only on effort. Pupils should be encouraged to establish realistic self-perceptions of ability. But, within the realistic perception, the importance of effort for achievement should be emphasized.

Several behavioural practices can be recommended to teachers, in order to facilitate the use of adaptive attributional patterns. Teachers should directly refer to effort attribution in the case of pupils' success or failure. In either case, pupils should be told that effort is the cause of their outcome. Such information should not be provided only as feedback, but also it should already be emphasized in the instructions that success on achievement tasks will depend on exerted effort. In addition, praise and criticism following pupils' performance should not be applied indiscriminately. Pupils should be especially praised after success on a difficult task, which implies that they tried hard and have ability. They should be criticized following failure when they did not try hard enough. Special precautions should be taken by teachers not to diffuse their negative and positive appeals, but to focus as much as possible on achievement behaviour. Frequent use of negative and positive appeals by teachers with regard to social, management and achievement problems discounts the appeals. Pupils interpret them as reflecting teachers' general attitudes toward pupils and not as feedback regarding their ability or exerted effort. Finally, it is suggested that competitive reward contingencies should not be used, since they facilitate self-derogatory attributions.

In order to affect teachers' behaviour in the described direction, there is the need to inform them of the importance of pupils' causal perception of success and failure, and to indicate to them their own influence on such perceptions. This might affect their behaviour. A stronger effect could be achieved by in-training procedures in which teachers would be able to learn how to interact with their pupils in order to facilitate the use of adaptive attributional patterns. In in-training sessions teachers can be exposed to attribution theory and its application to classroom situations. Moreover, they can learn the behavioural practices described above. It is important to recognize that although teachers may not be able to dramatically change everything about their pupils, their actions might be a significant determinant of pupils' achievement-related behaviour.

References

AMES, C. and FELKER, D. W. (1979) 'Effects of self-concept on children's causal attributions and self-reinforcement.' *Journal of Educational Psychology,* **71,** 613–19.

AMES, C., AMES, R. and FELKER, D. W. (1976) 'Informational and dispositional determinants of children's achievement attributions.' *Journal of Educational Psychology*, **68**, 63–9.

AMES, C., AMES, R. and FELKER, D. (1977) 'Effects of competitive reward structure and valence of outcome on children's achievement attributions.' *Journal of Educational Psychology*, **69**, 1–8.

ANDREWS, G. R. and DEBUS, R. L. (1978) 'Persistence and the causal perception of failure: modifying cognitive attributions.' *Journal of Educational Psychology*, **70**, 154–66.

BAR-TAL, D. (1974) *Causal schemata as a determinant of attributions of achievement-related behavior.* Unpublished doctoral dissertation, University of Pittsburgh.

BAR-TAL, D. (1979) 'Interactions of teachers and pupils', in FRIEZE, I. H., BAR-TAL, D. and CARROLL, J. S. (eds), *New Approaches to Social Problems* (pp. 337–58). San Francisco, CA: Jossey-Bass.

BAR-TAL, D. and DAROM, E. (1979) 'Pupils' attributions of success and failure.' *Child Development*, **50**, 264–7.

BAR-TAL, D. and FRIEZE, I. H. (1976) 'Attributions of success and failure for actors and observers.' *Journal of Research in Personality*, **10**, 256–65.

BAR-TAL, D. and FRIEZE, I. (1977) 'Achievement motivation for males and females as a determinant of attributions for success and failure.' *Journal of Sex Roles*, **3**, 301–13.

BAR-TAL, D. and GOLDBERG, M. (1980) *How pupils form their causal perceptions of success and failure.* Unpublished manuscript, Tel-Aviv University.

BAR-TAL, D. and GUTTMANN, J. (1981) 'A comparison of pupils', teachers' and parents' attributions regarding pupils' achievement.' *British Journal of Educational Psychology*, **51**, 301–11.

BAR-TAL, D., GOLDBERG, M. and KNAANI, A. (1980) *Causes of success and failure and their dimensions as a function of SES and gender: Phenomenological analysis.* Unpublished manuscript, Tel-Aviv University.

BECKMAN, L. J. (1976) 'Causal attributions of teachers and parents regarding children's performance.' *Psychology in the Schools*, **13**, 212–18.

BLUMENFELD, P. C., HAMILTON, L., WESSELS, K. and FALKNER, D. (1977) '"You can", "You should", and "You'd better": teachers' attributions regarding achievement and social behaviors.' Paper presented in KUN, A. (Chair) *Success and failure attributions and student behavior in the classroom.* Symposium presented at the meeting of the American Psychological Association, San Francisco, 1977.

BRAUN, C. (1976) 'Teachers' expectation: sociopsychological dynamics.' *Review of Educational Research*, **46**, 185–214.

BROPHY, J. E. and GOOD, T. L. (1974) *Teacher-student Relationships: Causes and Consequences.* New York: Holt.

BUTKOWSKY, I. S. and WILLOWS, D. M. (1980) 'Cognitive-motivational characteristics of children varying in reading ability: evidence for learned helplessness in poor readers.' *Journal of Educational Psychology*, **72**, 408–22.

CHAPIN, M. and DYCK, D. G. (1976) 'Persistence of children's reading behavior as a function of N length and attribution retraining.' *Journal of Abnormal Psychology*, **85**, 511–15.

COOPER, H. M. (1977) 'Controlling personal rewards: professional teachers' differential use of feedback and the effects of feedback on students' motivation to perform.' *Journal of Educational Psychology*, **69**, 419–27.

COOPER, H. M. (1979) 'Pygmalion grows up: a model for teacher expectation communication and performance influence.' *Review of Educational Research*, **49**, 389–410.

COOPER, H. M. and BURGER, J. M. (1980) 'How teachers explain students' academic performance: a categorization of free response academic attributions.' *American Educational Research Journal*, **17**, 95–109.

DAROM, E. and BAR-TAL, D. (1981) 'Causal perceptions of pupils' success or failure by teachers and pupils: a comparison.' *Journal of Educational Research*, **74**, 233–9.

DAVIS, W. L. and DAVIS, D. E. (1977) 'Internal-external control and attribution of responsibility for success and failure.' *Journal of Personality*, **40**, 123–36.

DIENER, C. I. and DWECK, C. S. (1978) 'An analysis of learned helplessness: continuous changes in performance, strategy, and achievement cognitions following failure.' *Journal of Personality and Social Psychology*, **36**, 451–62.

DUSEK, J. B. (1975) 'Do teachers bias children's learning?' *Review of Educational Research*, **45**, 661–84.

DWECK, C. S. (1975) 'The role of expectations and attributions in the alleviation of learned helplessness.' *Journal of Personality and Social Psychology*, **31**, 674–85.

DWECK, C. S. and BUSH, E. S. (1978) 'Sex differences in learned helplessness: (I) Differential debilitation with peer and adult evaluators.' *Developmental Psychology*, **12**, 147–56.

DWECK, C. S., DAVIDSON, W., NELSON, S. and ENNA, B. (1978) 'Sex differences in learned helplessness: (II) The contingencies of evaluative feedback in the classroom and (III) An experimental analysis.' *Developmental Psychology*, **14**, 268–76.

FALBO, T. (1975) 'The achievement motivations of kindergarteners.' *Developmental Psychology*, **11**, 529–30.

FITCH, G. (1970) 'Effects of self-esteem, perceived performance, and choice on causal attributions.' *Journal of Personality and Social Psychology*, **16**, 311–15.

FRIEND, R. M. and NEALE, J. M. (1972) 'Children's perceptions of success and failure. An attributional analysis of the effects of race and social class.' *Developmental Psychology*, **7**, 124–8.

FRIEZE, I. H. and BAR-TAL, D. (1980) 'Developmental trends in cue utilization for attributional judgments.' *Journal of Applied Developmental Psychology*, **1**, 83–93.

FRIEZE, I. and SNYDER, H. N. (1980) 'Children's beliefs about the causes of success and failure in school settings.' *Journal of Educational Psychology*, **72**, 186–96.

FRIEZE, I. and WEINER, B. (1971) 'Cue utilization and attributional judgments for success and failure.' *Journal of Personality*, **39**, 591–606.

FRIEZE, I. H., BAR-TAL, D. and CARROLL, J. S. (eds) (1979) *New Approaches to Social Problems*. San Francisco, CA: Jossey-Bass.

FYANS, L. J. and MAEHR, M. L. (1979) 'Attributional style, task selection, and achievement.' *Journal of Educational Psychology*, **71**, 499–507.

HARGREAVES, D. (1972) *Interpersonal Relations and Education*. London: Routledge.

KELLEY, H. H. (1972) *Causal Schemata and the Attribution Process*. Morristown, NJ: General Learning Press.

KROVETZ, M. L. (1974) 'Explaining success or failure as a function of one's locus of control.' *Journal of Personality*, **42**, 175–89.

KUKLA, A. (1972) 'Attributional determinants of achievement-related behavior.' *Journal of Personality and Social Psychology*, **21**, 166–74.

KUN, A. (1977) 'Development of the magnitude-covariation and compensation schemata in ability and effort attributions of performance.' *Child Development*, **48**, 862–73.

KUN, A. and WEINER, B. (1973) 'Necessary versus sufficient causal schemata for success and failure.' *Journal of Research in Personality*, **7**, 197–207.

LUGINBUHL, J. E. R., CROWE, D. H. and KAHAN, J. P. (1975) 'Causal attributions for success and failure.' *Journal of Personality and Social Psychology*, **31**, 86–93.

MCMAHAN, I. D. (1973) 'Relationships between causal attributions and expectancy of success.' *Journal of Personality and Social Psychology*, **28**, 108–14.

MEYER, J. P. (1980) 'Causal attribution for success and failure: a multivariate investigation of dimensionality, formation and consequences.' *Journal of Personality and Social Psychology*, **38**, 704–18.

MEYER, W. U., BACHMANN, M., BIERMANN, U., HEMPELMANN, M., PLOEGER, F. O. and SPILLER, H. (1979) 'The information value of evaluative behavior: influences of praise and blame on perceptions of ability.' *Journal of Educational Psychology*, **71**, 259–68.

MURRAY, S. R. and MEDNICK, T. S. (1975) 'Perceiving the causes of success and failure in achievement. Sex, race, and motivational comparisons.' *Journal of Consulting and Clinical Psychology*, **43**, 881–5.

NICHOLS, J. G. (1975) 'Causal attributions and other achievement-related cognitions: effect of task outcomes, attainment value, and sex.' *Journal of Personality and Social Psychology*, **31**, 379–89.

RAVIV, A., BAR-TAL, D., RAVIV, A. and BAR-TAL, Y. (1980) 'Causal perceptions of success and failure by advantaged, integrated, and disadvantaged pupils.' *British Journal of Educational Psychology*, **50**, 137–46.

ROGERS, C. G. (1982) 'The contribution of attribution theory to educational research', in ANTAKI, C. and BREWIN, C. (eds) *Attributions and Psychological Change*. London: Academic Press.

VALLE, V. A. and FRIEZE, I. (1976) 'Stability of causal attributions as a mediator in changing expectations for success.' *Journal of Personality and Social Psychology*, **33**, 579–87.

WEINER, B. (1974) *Achievement Motivation and Attribution Theory*. Morristown, NJ: General Learning Press.

WEINER, B. (1977) 'An attributional approach for educational psychology,' in SHULMAN, L. (ed.) *Review of Research in Education*. Ithaca, IL: F. E. Peacock.

WEINER, B. (1979) 'A theory of motivation for some classroom experiences.' *Journal of Educational Psychology*, **71**, 3–25.

WEINER, B. and SIERAD, J. (1975) 'Misattribution for failure and enhancement of achievement strivings.' *Journal of Personality and Social Psychology*, **31**, 415–521.

WEINER, B., FRIEZE, I., KUKLA, A., REED, L., REST, S. and ROSENBAUM, R. M. (1971) 'Perceiving the causes of success and failure,' in JONES, E. E. *et al.* (eds) *Attribution: Perceiving the Causes of Behaviour*. Morristown, NJ: General Learning Press.

WEINER, B., HECKHAUSEN, H., MEYER, W. and COOK, R. E. (1972) 'Causal ascriptions and achievement behavior: the conceptual analysis of effort.' *Journal of Personality and Social Psychology*, **21**, 239–248.

WEINER, B., NIERENBERG, R. and GOLDSTEIN, M. (1976) 'Social learning (locus of control) versus attributional (causal stability) interpretations of expectancy of success.' *Journal of Personality and Social Psychology*, **44**, 52–68.

WEINER, B., RUSSELL, D. and LERMAN, D. (1978) 'Affective consequences of causal ascriptions,' in HARVEY, J. H, ICKES, W. J. and KIDD, R. F. (eds) *New Directions in Attribution Research, Vol. 2*. Hillsdale, NJ: Erlbaum.

WEST, C. H. and ANDERSON, T. H. (1976) 'The question of preponderant causation in teacher expectancy research.' *Review of Educational Research*, **46**, 613–30.

3.4 Maladjusted children and the child guidance service

Jack Tizard

The paper is concerned only with child guidance services for children of school age. It does not discuss the needs of preschool children, nor the services provided by special classes and special schools for maladjusted pupils. Nor does it consider the role of the police, the juvenile courts or the approved schools (community homes) services.

The background

All children are 'difficult' at times, but some are more difficult – and more often difficult – than others. It is these children to whom the term 'maladjusted' is applied in the education service.

By and large the problems which children who are deemed maladjusted present to parents and to teachers can be divided into two broad groups or classes: problems of antisocial and deviant behaviour, and problems of nervousness, insecurity, or neurosis. Some children are both aggressive and antisocial, and also fearful and neurotic. And small numbers of children suffer from more severe clinically definable neurological or psychiatric disorder (Rutter, 1965). Though much is written about such children, and though their problems are of great interest and importance, neurologically impaired, hyperkinetic, psychotic and grossly psychopathic children are fortunately few.

The development of the child guidance service

'Special educational treatment' is a deliberately vague term, first introduced officially in the 1944 Education Act, which laid down that every child is to be educated in accordance with his age, ability and aptitude. The Act recognized that some children require educational treatment either in ordinary or in special schools because they suffer from disabilities of body or mind, including emotional or psychological troubles. It imposed the obligation to define in regulations the categories of pupils requiring special educational treatment. Up to 1944 only five categories of handicapped pupils had been recognized, corresponding to the present categories of educationally subnormal, physically handicapped, blind, deaf and epileptic. Among the six added by the Handicapped Pupils and

Source: *London Educational Review* (1973), **2**, 2, 22–37.

School Service regulations, 1945, was the category of maladjusted pupils (Ministry of Education, 1955).

The most recent, and indeed the only full-scale review 'to inquire into and report upon the medical, educational and social problems relating to maladjusted children, with reference to their treatment within the educational system' was carried out by the Underwood Committee (1950–5). The Committee discussed the causes and treatment of maladjustment and the role of different services – the school psychological service, the school health service, the child guidance clinic, day special schools and classes, residential treatment, after-care, and the juvenile courts – which play a part in remediation and treatment. The 'principal means of attacking the problem' was, in the Committee's view, the child guidance service 'involving a school psychological service, the school health service and child guidance clinic(s), all of which should work in close co-operation'. To be effective, they said, child guidance arrangements should be designed not only to treat maladjusted children but also to prevent maladjustment arising.

It was thought that psychologists in the school psychological service could, by treating a number of learning and other difficulties on the spot, and by helping to improve the ability of parents and teachers themselves to handle the minor problems of children and prevent them 'developing into maladjustment', in the course of time reduce the number of children referred for investigation by the whole child guidance team. Likewise, the school health service could do much to lessen the number of children who have to be referred to child guidance clinics, by devoting more attention to emotional and behaviour difficulties. However, it was argued, it was the child guidance clinic that should bear the main responsibility for dealing with anything more than minor problems. The psychologist (and the school doctor) needed to know the limitations of what he could do unaided and the contribution which each of the other members of the child guidance team could make. The most adequate arrangements could be made in a clinic 'staffed by the usual three-fold team of psychiatrist, educational psychologist and psychiatric social worker, working under the clinical direction of the psychiatrist'.

It was envisaged that the psychiatrist would normally spend only part of his time in the child guidance clinic and the remainder in the hospital service or in private practice, and that he would be the main link between the clinic and the hospital and general practitioner services in the area. The educational psychologist would be the clinic's main link with the schools and the teacher, and wherever possible would work part-time in the clinic and part-time in the school psychological service. The psychiatric social worker would deal, as necessary, with the parents both of the children being treated in the clinic, under the direction of the psychiatrist, and of those receiving special help in the schools on the advice of the psychologist.

These arrangements were confirmed by Ministry of Education Circular

347 published in 1959 and endorsed by the Ministry of Health. As Warren (1971) points out, this laid down the 'important principle that the child psychiatrist was the medical director of the child guidance clinic, so emphasizing that the service was medical rather than educational: a point that is still not everywhere agreed, as some educational psychologists have remained well entrenched and so have continued to direct a proportion of child guidance clinics up and down the country'.

How the clinics function

Information about how child guidance clinics function, where their patients come from, how they diagnose them and treat them, and what the outcomes are, is not easy to come by. Of the 260 or so articles published in the first thirteen volumes of the *Journal of Child Psychology and Psychiatry*, the official organ of the Association most directly concerned with clinical and interdisciplinary problems of child development and pathology, there is only one, and that by an American (Hunt, 1961) concerned with the intake of patients (by age, sex and service patterns) to a large community child guidance clinic in St Louis. The results are, of course, not very relevant to English practice; none the less some of the findings are intriguing. Thus, there were two boys referred to every one girl; 88 per cent of the children were between five and 14 years of age; and most intriguing of all, only 7 per cent 'received full treatment'. In 24 per cent of the total number of cases the 'family quit during the intake period'; 39 per cent of cases were referred by the clinic to other agencies; in 11 per cent the family refused treatment offered by the clinic; and in 19 per cent the family 'entered treatment; and quit against medical advice'. Of those who received full treatment, only 57 per cent were rated as showing definite improvement.

The findings of a survey undertaken by the Department of Education and Science and published in *The Health of the School Child* (1964–5) give what is, in the absence of more detailed British information, the most comprehensive account of 'current ideas, attitudes and approaches in the work of the clinics with disturbed children . . . and the organization and varying strengths, particularly in staffing, of the child guidance clinics'. In the majority of clinics the clinical director was a psychiatrist (as recommended in Circular 347), but in some clinics the director was a psychologist, and in others the psychologist was administratively responsible. Most clinics housed the school psychological service, but in only approximately a fifth were there facilities for remedial teaching. The average waiting time was approximately six months, but the range was from two weeks to eighteen months. The children attending presented varying degrees of emotional and educational difficulties, approximately 4 per cent being school refusals, generally not more than 1 per cent 'psychotic', with a small number of 'brain-damaged' children. The proportion of delinquent children rarely exceeded 6 per cent. No less than 90 per cent of children referred were in the age-group eight–11 years. Few children of under five attended, while the number of children of secondary school age referred 'remained small unless there was a particular local interest in this group and unless special provision was made'.

It may be surprising that the average waiting time was as long as six months, but the reason for this becomes clear when we are told that with a full working team the number of children seen averages about one new case per session of attendance of a psychiatrist (who, it will be remembered, usually works only part time at the clinic).

Is this a valuable service? The DES Report asks the question, but makes only a half-hearted attempt to answer it. As would be expected, it says, all workers respond to this question with a strong affirmative, but at the same time they are convinced that it is difficult to produce clear evidence clinically or statistically. Some clinics have attempted follow-up studies. Usually these are small-scale investigations and the results are tentative. 'The most convincing evidence of the value of the service is the increasing demand from those who have made use of it.'

But is it really a valuable service?

The brief DES report on the working of the child guidance clinic service raises a number of misgivings. The numbers of new cases seen is very small (perhaps only four to six a week in most clinics – and as few as one a month in some), and the waiting times for assessment are inordinately long. The intake of cases is pretty well confined to older children of junior school age, and whether or not younger children or adolescents are seen is allowed to depend on the interests of the staff rather than more clinically or socially relevant factors. Little research is done, despite the short working hours during which children and parents are seen. And the traditional pattern of assessment – an initial visit by a social worker, an examination by a psychologist and an interview with the psychiatrist, followed often by a full case conference – is certainly not economical in time and may not be the most effective way of working. We know also that some clinics make little contact with schools, and that many see their primary responsibility as being to provide the best possible treatment for small numbers of children, rather than the best possible service for the community whose needs they serve. One might well ask whether doubling, tripling or quadrupling the numbers of child guidance clinics would do much to solve the problems that beset children, parents, teachers and schools, while clinics are organized as they are and while they adhere to the philosophy which in the main they subscribe to.

If these criticisms of the *service* are valid, is there a remedy? We cannot, I think, make any strong claims that new forms of child guidance service will 'work' in that they will largely solve the psychological problems of children, parents and teachers. What we can do is first restate the problems which still require preventive and remedial action. And then, if we can do this, we may be able to reformulate the objectives of the child guidance service in realistic terms. If, in addition, we can devise criteria by which to measure how far objectives are being met, we can in principle at least both design better services and examine their working in order to improve them.

The main issues

Knowing the size of the problem

Neither the Underwood Committee nor its Scottish counterpart (Scottish Education Department, 1964) was prepared to risk an estimate of the prevalence of maladjustment, chiefly because they both shied off operational definition of the kinds of problems they were dealing with. As Professor Wall has indicated, however, later investigators have been more successful in delineating these problems. They have laid down standards by which to assess children, and criteria by which to rate the severity of 'maladjustment'. Screening procedures of known reliability and validity have been developed. Properly constituted samples of total populations have been examined. And as a result of a modest amount of carefully directed effort the epidemiology of psychiatric disorder in specified populations has been worked out. The findings, incidentally, gained through team research using recently developed methods, do not differ greatly from those obtained by Sir Cyril Burt (1935) in his London surveys carried out during and after the First World War.

To illustrate the value of an epidemiological approach to the provision of services, Table 1 presents the findings of the prevalence of four major types of handicap studied in the Isle of Wight survey of 2,200 children, who constituted the total population of children aged nine to 11 years whose homes were on the island. The figures in the bottom row of the table give the age specific rates per 100 children for each type of handicap, while those in the body of the table give the percentages of children with each type of handicap who had additional handicaps. There were 5.4 per cent of the children who were diagnosed as having a significant psychiatric handicap of moderate or severe degree; in all but one case the duration of the disorder was more than one year, and in the great majority of cases the duration was more than three years. Of these children 63.6 per cent had no significant additional handicap, but 26.3 per cent had one additional handicap, 5.9 per cent had two additional handicaps and 4.2 per cent had three additional handicaps.

Several implications follow from this table and from other Isle of Wight findings. First, even in a relatively prosperous part of Britain, in which the problems of inner-city disorganization do not occur, about 1 child in 20 presents fairly serious behavioural or emotional problems, which continue to trouble him (and usually his family and school) for at least a year, and

Table 1   Percentage of children with intellectual, educational, psychiatric or physical handicaps who have additional handicaps

	Intel-lectual	Educa-tional	Psychi-atric	Physical	% with different nos of handicaps
One handicap only	10.3	56.6	63.6	71.1	75.0
Two handicaps					18.8
Intellectual+	—	15.6	0.8	1.7	
Educational+	46.6	—	18.7	5.8	
Psychiatric+	1.7	12.7	—	6.6	
Physical+	3.4	4.0	6.8	—	
Three handicaps					4.8
Intellectual + educational + psychiatric	6.9	2.3	3.4	—	
Intellectual + educational + physical	17.2	5.8	—	8.3	
Intellectual + psychiatric + physical	5.2	—	2.5	2.4	
Educational + psychiatric + physical	—	—	—	—	
Four handicaps					1.4
Intellectual + educational + psychiatric + physical	8.6	2.9	4.2	4.1	
Total number of cases	58	173	118	121	354
% of total population having each handicap	2.6	7.9	5.4	5.5	16.14

in most cases for several years. Secondly, children with one handicap are especially likely to have others. Thus, while only 5.4 per cent of the total child population were diagnosed as having a psychiatric disorder, more than a fifth of those with an intellectual handicap (1.7 + 6.9 + 5.2 + 8.6 = 22.4) were also diagnosed as having a psychiatric disorder, and of those with an educational handicap 23.7 per cent also had a psychiatric one. Of those with a chronic physical handicap 13.1 per cent also had a chronic psychiatric disorder. Children with other handicaps thus constitute groups who are specially prone to have difficulties in adjustment. One would therefore expect the child guidance service to be vigilant in seeking out such children – after all they have a lot to bear. (At present, however, the child guidance service often sees rather few children with other handicaps – many expressly exclude the severely subnormal altogether, regarding them apparently as non-persons.)

A third set of findings which emerges fairly consistently from epidemiological inquiries concerns the sex ratios of boys to girls with different types of problem. In the Isle of Wight Survey, for example, there were nearly twice as many boys as girls who were finally diagnosed as having a psychiatric disorder, but the proportions in the different diagnostic categories were quite different. Thus there were only 17 girls, but 26 boys, with a neurotic disorder; however, 56 boys compared with only 14 girls had a conduct disorder or mixed disorder in which conduct problems were prominent. Neurotic children were not on the whole educationally backward, but the majority of children with conduct disorders were failing in their school work. A number of other studies have shown (Robins, 1966) that whereas neurotic disorders tend to remit, conduct disorders are likely to persist into adult life.

The Isle of Wight Survey, which, incidentally, covered the age-range of children who at present make up 90 per cent of all children referred to child guidance clinics, left many questions unanswered: the efficacy of treatment, the role of the school and the family exacerbating or mitigating problems, the definition of successful and unsuccessful patterns of management – and the prevalence of maladjustment in other age-groups. However, it gave an estimate of the numbers of children who were maladjusted, an indication of sex differences and of the duration of the problems up to the time of the survey, information about vulnerable groups of children, and the relation between educational failure and psychiatric disorder, and a wealth of other data about families and children. It thus provided baseline information showing the size of the problem and the nature of children's difficulties; and in doing so it highlighted the inadequacy of the child guidance service and other services in meeting the children's needs.

Assessment, remediation and treatment

The numbers of children with chronic disabilities of behaviour who presumably need help set the stage for the work of the child guidance service. But as Table 1 shows, the total numbers of 'handicapped' children who require special services are very much greater than the one child in 20 who is diagnosable as 'maladjusted'. There are, in addition, the intellectually backward, the educationally retarded and the physically handicapped; and, in large areas of London and in other towns and cities, there are also numbers of socially disadvantaged children who face difficulties in school adjustment as well as other problems of everyday living. Excluding the socially disadvantaged, the prevalence rates for other chronic handicapping conditions of educational concern was, in the Isle of Wight Survey, 16.14 per cent – one child in six. In parts of London, using the same criteria, this proportion might be doubled – one child in three. This is, indeed, a formidable number for the school psychological service and the school health service to deal with.

As to how these services, working with the child psychiatrist, the paediatrician and with social workers of the social services department should plan to use their time, this will depend upon what they think they can accomplish. Opinions differ about the value of assessment and success of treatment. My own views, which for reasons of space must be set out dogmatically (though they are in fact held tentatively) are as follows:

ASSESSMENT

1   Much of the present assessment on which a very large amount of time is spent is irrelevant or useless. Even the *educational* value of routine intelligence testing is dubious – it may do as much harm (in denying a child opportunities for remedial education, for example) as good (in suggesting that a different educational regimen is required for a child who is failing in school). Personality testing, projective tests and so on are without any value – at best a waste of time and often positively misleading (Mischel, 1968). The testing of educational attainments is useful, and is, indeed, often a necessary part of assessment.

2   Many of the data obtained from the present *routine medical screening* of children are so unreliable as to be a waste of time. This is recognized by the school health service, which is in favour of more rigorously conducted neuro-developmental examinations of selected children (DES, 1969–70).

3   Data collected from parents at interview are likely to be unreliable; this applies to almost all information about events in the child's past, and to much of what is said about family relations. More important, the information so collected is largely unusable: it doesn't make any difference to treatment, though it may give the clinician a feeling (possibly misleading) that he understands the family better.

4   What we need to know – and rarely get – is a detailed account of how the key informants see the child's behaviour problems today, and how they react to them. This provides the basis for attempts to change the regimen.

In short, as Kirk and McCarthy (1961) have argued, psychological diagnosis which has no remedial implications usually tells us nothing that is of importance. This maxim is a good guide to practice. If it were rigorously applied, the time spent on assessment could be drastically reduced and there would be a great saving in clerical time and in paper.

TREATMENT OF INDIVIDUAL CHILDREN

This is the nub of the problem, but perhaps opinions on the value of treatment differ less sharply today than twenty years ago. The following conclusions seem to me justified.

1   'Except in some fairly straightforward instances such as vocational counselling, the effects so far isolated [of psychotherapy and counselling] are still often small and inconsistent, indicating that expert diagnosis and treatment may not, as one would have expected, have much more to offer than naive methods. Particularly important . . . is the lack of any demonstrated superiority for deep-rooted methods' (Vernon, 1964, p. 136). Put into a service context, this implies that long-term psychotherapy is not

helpful and should be discontinued, and that naive counselling is often as useful as other forms of therapy.

2   'There is some modest evidence that short-term psychotherapy, drug treatment, and conditioning techniques can, within limits, be effective forms of treatment for child psychiatric disorders if correctly employed for the right type of patient. Whether or not all clinics are making the best use of the existing limited knowledge on treatment is another matter. Furthermore, it may be that for some types of problem behaviour different approaches, such as manipulation of the classroom situation, may be more effective than the traditional psychiatric methods. This may be particularly so for aggressive and antisocial children, a group with a poor prognosis, and one for which counselling and psychotherapeutic methods have been generally unsuccessful' (Rutter and Graham, 1970; references in the original omitted).

3   'Drugs have only limited usefulness in child psychiatry. The main indications for their use are in the control of epilepsy, and in the treatment of the hyperkinetic syndrome, some behaviour disorders associated with brain damage, certain depressed children and possibly some of the more severe anxiety states' (Barker, 1971).

4   Remedial education, though often it is still disappointingly unsuccessful in its outcome, offers a direct approach to the child's *scholastic* difficulties, and at the same time gives opportunities to establish a closer relation with a skilled and sympathetic adult. This service needs greatly expanding (DES, 1972.).

5   Behaviour modification techniques offer promise in eliminating *specific* behavioural problems. If the child's difficulties are indeed specific, the elimination of the 'symptoms' cures the problem. (There is little evidence for 'symptom substitution' – the replacement of one set of symptoms by another if the 'basic' problems are not removed.) But irrespective of whether or not the child is cured, the modification of irritating or other dysfunctional behaviour patterns is in any case almost always desirable, since it enables the child to cope better with his environment, and inevitably changes in positive fashion the behaviour of others towards him. Thus it makes him more acceptable and boosts morale all round.

These important exceptions apart, my own view of the success of individual treatment of maladjusted children is a pessimistic one. Psychotherapy, play therapy, and other forms of individual therapy based on dynamic beliefs have not proved successful in practice. Changes in children's behaviour are consequences either of growth (as every wise general practitioner and teacher knows) or, more immediately they occur as responses on the part of the child to changes in his environment. Where there is no growth, and no environmental changes occur, the counsellor is unable to cure.

What he can do, instead, is however very important. He can listen, comfort, explain – and give advice that seems appropriate. By listening, explaining and giving comfort to parents and children (especially older ones) he can alleviate their suffering or help them put up with it. By giving sympathetic and practical advice about management he may help them further, whether or not they take the advice. As for the minority of children who have much more serious psychiatric problems, specialized treatment is certainly needed whether or not this is likely to be 'successful'. The point is that the child whose behaviour is grossly disordered or bizarre falls outside the realm of experience of all but a few specialists. Upon them, therefore, falls the task not only of prescribing and carrying out treatment, but, more important, of making the child's behaviour intelligible and acceptable to parents and others.

The specialist has another duty which is unfortunately often overlooked, namely to advise class-teachers. Ten years ago Miss Johnson (1962–3, pp. 57–9) reported on a survey that showed that teachers of children with severe hearing losses who were being educated in ordinary classes 'too often had little or no knowledge of the handicaps imposed by impaired hearing and their consequent effects upon speech and language development and upon communication and social growth. Very few of them had received any guidance or help in the handling of deaf children . . . the lack of exchange of information was quite surprising.' Elizabeth Anderson (1973) reports similar problems encountered by some teachers of physically handicapped children. They had never even met the school doctor, and in consequence had little idea of what the child should be allowed or encouraged to do. Teachers of backward and of maladjusted children who have been seen by specialists sometimes make the same, fully justifiable complaints – no one puts them in the picture. When this happens the assessment of children is, to the teacher, merely a frustrating waste of time.

Prevention

The evidence in favour of the attractive proposition that prompt remedial treatment in infancy or early childhood will prevent later psychiatric breakdown is, unfortunately, slight. The *prima facie* case in favour owes its plausibility to the fact that children who have a hard time in infancy are likely to continue to suffer in an environment which continues to be harsh. Where there is a marked change in environmental circumstances children tend to respond to it (Clarke, 1968). Similarly when circumstances deteriorate, behavioural development also suffers.

This does not mean that the happiness and well-being of young children are unimportant, or that the effects of good services provided for young children can only 'really' be known when the children are adolescent. Nor does it mean that unless children have a happy infancy they are destined to become psychopaths. Social, cultural, educational and medical services are required for people of all ages, not in order to preserve their integrity at later ages, but to enhance their well-being at the time they are using the services. Anything more than this is a bonus. Services for preschool children are important because the well-being of young children is important.

Implications for the organization of a service

Views about the value of assessment and treatment determine in large part the kind of service one plans. Current child guidance practice, as we have seen, is medically based. The theory is that the child has a *disorder*, which requires *diagnosis* before *treatment* is carried out. Of course, everyone recognizes that treatment of a child cannot be carried out in isolation from the family. Therefore 'family psychiatry' rather than 'child psychiatry' is practised in some clinics.

If you think this way, you are dubious of the value of superficial treatments, pernickety in the selection of cases for treatment, and sceptical of the possibility of providing an effective service for more than a small number of patients – though as a public gesture you may see two or three new cases a month for supportive therapy. If, on the other hand, you think as I do that the individual treatment of children (except in the limited context described above) offers a poor return for time and effort, you will wish to spend most of your time on other things. My own prejudices would lead me to look carefully at schools as social institutions, possibly influencing the incidence and duration of maladjusted behaviour patterns, at the routines of particular schools which may provide a more or less benign environment for the pupils, at the classroom as a place where children spend long periods of time in a more or less congenial, more or less stressful environment, and at individual, vulnerable or problem children in a naturalistic rather than in a clinic setting. If we can, through doing such things, get clues as to factors which seem harmful to children, we may be able to modify them or at least mitigate their effects. This is the basis both for preventive work and for treatment.

Schools as social institutions

Psychologists and sociologists have been incurious about the influence of the school in affecting behaviour. On the whole they have tended to accept the views of Burt and Wiseman that variations among schools are not associated with variations in the prevalence of maladjusted behaviour. To anyone who has boarded a bus about four o'clock on a weekday this belief contradicts the evidence of the senses. Moreover, in respect of one type of antisocial behaviour at least there is unambiguous evidence that the school *does* make a difference to incidence rates. In a most carefully controlled epidemiological study Power (1972) and his colleagues have shown that, in the London borough of Tower Hamlets not only is area of residence a strong determining factor in affecting conviction rates for juvenile delinquency, but also that particular schools differ markedly in the numbers of boys from them who are convicted in the juvenile courts. In twenty secondary modern schools in the Borough the average annual delinquency rates for boys over a five-year period range from six per 1,000 in one school to 77 per 1,000 in another; and two schools, matched closely for 'external characteristics' (of the sort believed by Wiseman, 1967, to be the factors most responsible for the small differences in educational attainment that he found between schools in his factor-analytic study) had average annual first court appearance rates of 14 and 59 over a ten-year period. One would expect this study to be followed by more intensive inquiries to elucidate the factors responsible for the differences – but the authors have, alas, not been allowed by the education authority to proceed with such studies (Morris and Power, 1972). One would also expect that comparative studies of the prevalence of maladjustment in different schools would be informative in elucidating the part that schools might play in reducing the incidence of maladjustment generally.

School organization and children's behaviour

Very many children dislike school, are bored with school or are unhappy there. It is, however, rare for anyone to make a systematic study of why ordinary children find difficulties in adjusting to school – and it is perhaps even less common for schools to act on the findings of such studies.

A study by Terence Moore (1966) of problems faced by the ordinary child in coping with everyday school life examines primary schooling 'from the consumer's point of view'. Most children, it was found, experienced difficulties in the infant school, of which nearly one half were of moderate or marked severity. The number decreased slightly in the junior school, but a substantial number of children still showed more than mild disturbances. Moore lists a number of 'difficulties' and discusses reasons for them. Some could be easily remedied with different organization, better parent–teacher communication, more volunteers (parents) in the school, or a little money spent on furniture or fittings (locks on lavatory doors and toilet paper, for example). Playground supervision may be inadequate, school dinners an unpleasant and noisy occasion, physical education and rough play rather frightening to a timid child, a teacher rather unsympathetic, or school work a cause for anxiety. How many causes of unhappiness could be removed if we set about trying to do so systematically, calling upon teachers and community resources for co-operation, no one really knows. It would be worth trying to reduce avoidable difficulties which make children unhappy – but someone must give a lead. This is not perhaps something for the child guidance service to do. But to initiate interest in such matters, to draw the attention of head-teachers and class-teachers to problems they may be only half aware of, and to make constructive suggestions about how such problems might be tackled – these are things the child guidance service might well spend more time on.

Child guidance in the classroom

Educational psychologists today spend rather little time in classrooms. Thus in 1965 only one educational psychologist in five spent more than half a day a week of his time 'discussing individual children with teachers', and practically no one spent as much as a whole day a week doing this. Likewise, fewer than one psychologist in 14 spent half a day a week 'treating children in schools or children's homes' (DES, 1968). This suggests that, at least seven years ago, contact with schools was not great (and at that time the average psychologist spent more time writing reports than talking to teachers). The average teacher, indeed, doesn't get much direct help from any of the special services: contact with the school doctor is often fleeting or non-existent, remedial teachers often take children out of the class rather than help teachers in the class, educational advisers may visit only infrequently, and the psychiatrist and social worker not at all. In consequence the average teacher lacks advice; and equally often he lacks the skills to deal with particular problems.

In the United States increasing interest is being shown by educational psychologists in the application of techniques of behaviour modification to the control of children's behaviour in the classroom. Much of the current literature is superficial, and this may lead teachers in Britain to dismiss the whole approach. It would be a pity if this were to happen, because operant technology offers directly usable approaches to how to control a class (or a difficult child) successfully. Operant theory, writes Hilgard (1970) (himself no operant man), emphasizes 'a few simple theoretical ideas: that behaviour starts at an operant level, is furthered by reinforcement, weakened by extinction and not controlled very well by punishment. While these principles are simply stated, they are very powerful. An enormous amount of laboratory work stands behind them; hence teachers know the theoretical basis of what they are doing. Because these principles can be simply stated, they are communicable to teachers. These are large gains, gains that cannot be attributed to the placebo effect of the novelty of the method and the enthusiasm of the users. . . . The technology enables us to control some complex behaviour. Furthermore, it works across diagnostic categories, and across age-groups, and across types of disturbed behaviour. Hence behaviour modification contains some solid techniques and theory that should be held on to. It gives some useful approaches to baffling problems.'

To the educational psychologist an operant approach offers other useful leads. It draws attention to the fact that the starting-point for assessment and treatment is not the child in the clinic, but the child in the classroom – or at home if that is where it all starts. To the classroom or home, then, the educational psychologist should go – and there he can usefully spend much of his time. I have little doubt that the work of the educational psychologist would be more effective if he spent more time with his clients and less with his colleagues. They can always be contacted by 'phone if necessary.

The treatment of individual children

Even if most assessment and most remedial treatment for behavioural dysfunction went on in the ordinary school, there would still be children who required something more. Children are often victims of family circumstances, and it may be the families rather than the children who need help in some instances. To cope with families is the job of social services departments – though a psychologist if he is consulted about a child may also want to see the parents on occasion, and in such instances he would no doubt consult his social work colleagues first where possible. That social services departments today still fail lamentably in their efforts to provide needy and distressed families with the help they require is not a good reason why other services should attempt to give this. It is not as though they could handle their own problems very effectively. To take on additional burdens doesn't help at all: it merely delays the development of a responsible and effective *social* service. So whereas in the child guidance service the experts customarily discuss their findings face to face and communicate by post to the school, it might make more sense and save time if the face to face contact was with the school and if the experts informed each other by letter, or preferably by 'phone.

How many children should be referred to a clinic, and who should see them there, needs some rethinking. The child psychiatrist, whose training equips him to diagnose and treat children with gross pathology, is the proper person to take the leading role in the hospital-based clinics to which such children are normally referred. For children with milder handicaps I doubt if he has anything very special to offer: too often in child guidance he functions as an unqualified psychologist. There is no great harm in this – but it is a misuse, and to the National Health Service an expensive misuse, of psychiatric man-power which is, and is likely to remain, in short supply. Psychiatrists are, in my view, a bit of a luxury in the child guidance service outside hospital-based units. Rather than train more child psychiatrists to make good the present shortfall in staffing ratios it would be better to devote additional psychiatric man-power to the field which needs it most – psychogeriatrics.

To advocate fewer psychiatrists, fewer case conferences, less teamwork, shorter reports, less clinic-based practice, less therapy, and, on the other hand, more responsibility for more psychologists, much closer links with schools, more emphasis on remedial work, and more use of the telephone as a means of communication sounds decidedly old-fashioned, anti-medical and partisan. And to pin the responsibility for family casework on social services departments may seem irresponsible – though in law this is their job. The truth as I see it is, however, that none of our social and health services today are working very well, yet all are trying to take over the duties of other departments. More clear-cut lines of responsibility, more autonomy, different orientations, better staff training and better staff deployment would do much to change this situation. A continuation of the present system doesn't, I think, offer so much for the future.

References

ANDERSON, E. M. (1973) *The Disabled School Child: A Study of Integration in Primary Schools*. London: Methuen.

BARKER, P. (1971) *Basic Child Psychiatry*. London: Staples Press.

BURT, CYRIL (1935) *The Subnormal Mind*. Oxford: Oxford University Press.

CLARKE, A. D. B. (1968) 'Learning and human development. The 42nd Maudsley Lecture.' *British Journal of Psychiatry*, **114**, part 2, 1061–75.

DEPARTMENT OF EDUCATION AND SCIENCE *The Health of the School Child* (1962–3), (1964–5), (1966–8), (1969–70). London: HM Stationery Office.

DEPARTMENT OF EDUCATION AND SCIENCE (1968) *Psychologists in Education Services* (The Summerfield Report). London: HM Stationery Office.

DEPARTMENT OF EDUCATION AND SCIENCE (1972) *Children with Specific Reading Difficulties*. Report of the Advisory Committee on Handicapped Children. London: HM Stationery Office.

HILGARD, E. R. (1970) Foreword to FARGO, G. A., BEHREN, C. and NOLEN, P. *Behavior Modification in the Classroom*. Belmont, CA: Wadsworth Publishing.

HUNT, R. G. (1961) 'Age, sex and service patterns in a child guidance clinic.' *Journal of Child Psychology and Psychiatry*, **2**, 3, 185–92.

JOHNSON, M. (1962–3), in DES *The Health of the School Child* (above).

KIRK, S. A. and MCCARTHY, J. J. (1961) 'The Illinois test of psycholinguistic abilities – an approach to differential diagnosis.' *American Journal of Mental Deficiency*, **66**, 399–412.

MINISTRY OF EDUCATION (1955) *Report of the Committee on Maladjusted Children* (The Underwood Report). London: HM Stationery Office.

MINISTRY OF EDUCATION (1959) *Child Guidance*. Circular 347. London: HM Stationery Office.

MISCHEL, W. (1968) *Personality and Assessment*. New York: Wiley.

MOORE, T. (1966) 'Difficulties of the ordinary child in adjusting to primary school.' *Journal of Child Psychology and Psychiatry*, **7**, 1, 17–38.

MORRIS, J. N. and POWER, M. J. (1972) Letter in *The Times*, 25 May.

POWER, M. J., BENN, R. T. and MORRIS, J. N. (1972) 'Neighbourhood school and juveniles before the courts.' *British Journal of Criminology*, April, 111–32.

ROBINS, L. N. (1966) *Deviant Children Grown Up*. Baltimore, MD: Williams and Wilkins.

RUTTER, M. (1965) 'Classification and categorization in child psychiatry.' *Journal of Child Psychology and Psychiatry*, **6**, 2, 71–83.

RUTTER, M. and GRAHAM, P. (1970) 'The treatment of children with psychiatric disorder', in RUTTER, M., TIZARD, J. and WHITMORE, K. *Education, Health and Behaviour*. Harlow: Longman.

SCOTTISH EDUCATION DEPARTMENT (1964) *Ascertainment of Maladjusted Chil-*

dren. Report of the Working Party appointed by the Secretary of State for Scotland. Edinburgh and London: HM Stationery Office.

VERNON, P. E. (1964) *Personality Assessment: A Critical Survey*. London: Methuen.

WARREN, W. (1971) ' "You can never plan the future by the past." The development of the child and adolescent psychiatry in England and Wales.' *Journal of Child Psychology and Psychiatry*, **11**, 4, 241–58.

WISEMAN, S. (1967) 'The Manchester Survey.' Appendix 9 to DES *Children and their Primary Schools* (The Plowden Report), *Vol. 2*. London: HM Stationery Office.

3.5 Withdrawal units and the psychology of problem behaviour

Robert Daines

The development of 'withdrawal units' has been idiosyncratic and piecemeal: they did not form a coherent national development but were established to meet the perceived local needs of a school or education authority. By 1976, and as a consequence of their considerable growth in the early seventies, such units began to attract some attention. Topping and Quelch produced a small survey in that year and Her Majesty's Inspectorate (HMI) and the Schools Council initiated studies that were published in 1978 (HMI, 1978a and b). The national picture drawn by these surveys is a highly varied one but despite this, some important general principles and implications emerge.

Units demonstrate every conceivable variation in finance and organization. They may be located on a school campus or housed in separate premises. They may serve one school or several. The HMI survey (1978b) found that the latter case applies in two-thirds of the units which draw from between two and 10 schools. They noted that one, two and three-teacher units each account for approximately a third of the total. The number of pupils varies considerably, a pattern further complicated by the part-time nature of some attendance. The typical unit has two teachers for between 12 and 16 pupils. The Schools Council Project team observe that larger units, with two or three teachers, were on the whole 'more successful' than one-teacher units. They add that the ideal group size is between eight and 12. Above and below this range they detect problems of 'group cohesion'. Both major surveys agree on the high qualifications and wide experience of unit staff. The HMI survey reports the average length of service as 11½ years.

For whom are units intended? One unit may be designed to provide for 'non-attenders'; others for 'school phobics', 'disrupts', 'aggressive and violent pupils' or those who are 'emotionally disturbed'. Even units which have a special remit to consider all children with 'behaviour problems' find these categories relevant. However, a 'school phobic' is also a 'non-attender'; an emotionally withdrawn pupil may be a 'school refuser'; a 'disrupt' may also absent himself from school; he may or may not be 'aggressive and violent'. Clearly, instead of taking these categories at face value, a survey must ask questions to establish which classifications most generally apply. HMI observe that most pupils are in units because of disruptive behaviour in the classroom and that for a quarter of them this

---

Source: GILLHAM, B. (ed.) (1981) *Problem Behaviour in the Secondary School* (pp. 101–12). London: Croom Helm.

had led to suspension from school. They also find that many have long histories of non-attendance; that over half of them are in their fourth and fifth years; and that the majority can be described as 'low achievers' or 'remedial pupils'. A very similar picture is drawn by the Schools Council Project team.

All that the survey data so far tells us, besides indicating certain years and ability bands, is that units contain pupils who have adopted certain roles in relation to the school-system. In general terms it is difficult to proceed beyond this point in characterizing the children in withdrawal units. The Schools Council report refers to 'emotionally disturbed' and 'conduct disordered' pupils but fails to clarify or define these terms. HMI comment that the problems that had resulted in particular pupils being referred to units were 'extremely complex'. They distinguish between two groups: those experiencing acute difficulties arising out of transient crises, and those with chronic problems of adjustment and/or serious social and family breakdown. In both surveys, and with no examination, inadequacies in homes, neighbourhoods or children are used to explain pupils' behaviour in school. These observations stand uncomfortably alongside the data which show that children in units can most easily be characterised in terms of their school life – i.e. as fourth or fifth years or as 'academically poor'. There is little direct research evidence that helps to fill out the picture. Lane (1976) looked in detail at the 'most' disruptive and unmanageable boys drawn from a school population of 10,000. He confirmed that 'poor achievers' were disproportionally represented: 20 per cent were 'non-readers', while a further 40 per cent were still in the process of mastering basic written English. At a more interpretive level, Lane also found, using Eysenck's (1952) personality dimensions, that there were personality differences between his selected group and 'normal' students. The former tended to be more 'toughminded' and 'extravert'. Lane relates these observations to difficulties in getting such pupils to accept rules and constraints, to their hostility to adults and their concern with immediate reward.

How the behaviour of unit pupils is understood and interpreted is reflected in the philosophies and practices of the units. This brings us to the further question of their function. HMI note that a few are seen as punitive institutions. Pupils work hard on tasks which are not primarily selected for their curricular relevance, and are closely supervised during every part of their school day. The operating principle of these units is that placement is undesirable and that in order to avoid this outcome pupils will be motivated to control their behaviour. Unit staff are forced to play an unpleasant and unrewarding role if this *modus operandi* is to be effective. Such units are almost exclusively 'on site' and serve only one school. In the vast majority of cases a more positive approach is taken, however. The reasons for the pupils' behaviour are explored, or projected, and the work of the unit then organized in these terms. According to the Schools Council team, 90 per cent of the teachers see their main purpose as helping pupils with social and emotional problems. This aim has its practical expression in social skills training, education for personal relationships and various types of counselling. HMI comment on the wide range of aims and philosophies to be found in units. These observations tie in with the conventional picture of pupils' problems that presuppose causal inadequacies in families, neighbourhoods and the children themselves.

With regard to the nature of the educational provision itself the pattern is more uniform. HMI remark that, whatever the emphasis, teachers overwhelmingly stress the need for pupils to develop systematic patterns of working. They find that 46 per cent of units place a major emphasis on remedial work and add – not surprisingly – 'this seemed to reflect the belief that low achievement can lead to disruptive behaviour'. Similarly the Schools Council team find that more than half the units include educational progress as part of their main purpose. They stress that the 'most successful' ones have carefully planned programmes to develop good working habits and intensive remedial help to ensure competence in the basic skills. The singular nature of unit educational programmes appears to be a better guide to their 'undoubted success' than the diversity of their other aims and practices.

Observed changes in pupil behaviour, between school and unit, are used as the criteria for success by both surveys. They are impressed by the 'good working atmosphere' generally found and the absence of the type of incident that marks the disrupt's behaviour in school. HMI report 83 per cent as the average attendance figure, which indicates a much improved situation. This is confirmed by the Schools Council team. However, one major theme in the role and function of units is set to confound this satisfactory picture.

Given their budgets, staffing and facilities, withdrawal units cannot be expected to provide their pupils with a complete educational programme. They differ from the special schools in being planned on the basis of part-time and/or short-term attendance. Both surveys note that most units have as their principal aim *the return of the pupils to normal schooling*. Despite this, periods of stay were said to vary from two terms to seven years! In the case of off-site units serving several schools, a form of alternative education has often developed by default. This is particularly true for the large number of disaffected 14- to 16-year-olds. In view of their age and the technical difficulties of fitting into the complex curricular patterns at this stage, few of these pupils are likely to see school again, so teachers are faced with the difficult choice of either looking ahead to the world of further education and uncertain prospects for employment, or directing their efforts towards returning pupils to school.

But there are important differences between regarding units as alternative education for fourth- and fifth-year pupils and viewing them as rehabilitation centres for secondary pupils regardless of age. The criteria for success clearly change. Successful adjustment to the unit only applies where it is recognized as a 'no return' alternative form of schooling. If the aim is to return the pupil to ordinary school then successful adjustment there, following re-integration, is the appropriate criterion.

There is a third possible model. This involves 'supporting' a pupil while he continues to attend school, a role already played by some part-time units. In the 'sanctuary' or 'home base', the pupil spends a certain amount of time each week in the close company of a sympathetic teacher; hopefully, he comes to like and respect him. As well as being in a position to communicate school values, the teacher can begin to make his interest conditional on the pupil's good behaviour and provide an incentive for regular attendance. In order to work effectively this model is necessarily restricted to single-school, on-site units. The unit must be bound up with the values and events of a particular school's life and be suitably placed to monitor the pupil's behaviour. The model also presumes that the child can sustain a personal response. In spite of its current popularity the rationale of the rehabilitation model is decidedly weak. Short-term placements only make sense if the problem behaviour is related to either temporary social circumstances or easily remediable characteristics of the child. Examples of the former would include stress caused by the break-up of a family or the onset of a handicapping condition. For the latter, we have to consider the 'treatment' programmes of the units. There are three main emphases (and mixtures of them).

By carefully manipulating a pupil's circumstances, particularly in terms of what he finds rewarding, old habits and behaviours can be broken down and new ones built up. The techniques involved travel under the label of behaviour modification. But the circumstances of the pupil's problem behaviour are a school, not a unit, phenomenon. Successful adjustment to the unit, in as much as it results from employing these techniques, cannot ensure re-adjustment to school. There is every likelihood that a return to former situations will lead to a return to former behaviour. It may be possible to transfer some of the 'new circumstances' along with the pupil; apart from being of limited scope, however, this transfer depends on the unit having a powerful voice within the school's pastoral-care system.

Another approach uses the influence gained through developing a personal relationship with a pupil. By making his expectations clear, a teacher can alter the student's behaviour, and the longer the time he spends with a particular teacher, as in the home-based model, the wider the teacher's influence. Return to school is a return to different, and various, teachers with varying expectations of him. The third approach is a development of the second. The pupil's relationship with the teacher facilitates conversation about attitudes and experiences. Counselling techniques are based on this model. They depend on the existence of numerous subtle connections between thought and behaviour. Though the likely success of such techniques is theoretically very difficult to evaluate, some relevant empirical evidence has been collected. Wolff (1976), in reviewing the literature on anti-social behaviour, has found that there is little evidence that it can be modified using such means. Lane observed that his 'disruptive' group responded to utilitarian rewards rather than counselling and linked this, plausibly, with his earlier observations on their personalities.

Unit educational programmes stand up better to close examination. They tackle problems that are central to school life and are thus working towards the successful re-integration of the pupil. The educational deficits of academically poor and remedial students can easily lead to frustration and failure. Under the regime of the subject timetable they can find themselves pursuing low priority tasks of impossible accomplishment – e.g. learning French when they can barely read and write English, or studying physics when simple multiplication still presents problems. They are more likely to discover that they cannot carry out assignments or that rote copying is the only way to complete them.

The pupil's behaviour in school must be related to his experiences of school life. Despite its comparatively poor resources a unit has distinct advantages over a school as an educational placement. Given its small pupil/teacher ratio and its flexible organisation, it can offer an individually tailored curriculum and a great deal more pupil-directed teaching. The absence of the frustrations and failures of school may well be a factor in the numerous examples of successful adjustment to units. For some pupils, return to school, with improved literacy and numeracy skills, may change their experiences of school life to the extent that the problem behaviour fails to reappear. Although in this form the notion of the unit as a 'rehabilitation centre' has some substance, the role is appropriate for only some of the children referred.

Does the problem behaviour disappear in units because their circumstances are different from those of the school? This possibility has been raised in a number of contexts. Units can offer specific techniques for managing pupils' behaviour, influential personal relations, to the same end, and relevant and sensitive teaching. Other advantageous changes include the absence of organizational demands, such as finding correct rooms for particular lessons, and removal from the inappropriate expectations of teachers and peer group. These differences between schools and units mean that the latter are in a better position to ensure that pupils pursue educational activities under the guidance of experienced and able staff.

That unit teachers are of a high calibre is confirmed by both the major surveys. The Schools Council team observe that the general principles of 'treatment' in successful units were the caring attitudes of teachers, control through explicit rules and consistent expectations, allied to the judicious use of approval and success. They note that academic work was often very structured and add that 'this reflected the view that pupils in the unit work better and feel more secure within a tightly structured programme'. HMI suggest that a factor contributing to the good attendance record was the small size of the units which 'enabled close personal relationships between teachers and pupils'. Flexibility of organization and working patterns and less-complex academic demands were also held to be beneficial influences. In summary, both surveys found that 'circumstantial' factors were of paramount importance in securing the successful adjustment of the pupil. This point is generally recognized by the staff of referring schools. How often have they been heard to say 'he needs more individual attention and supervision'?

Testimony also comes from the children's own behaviour. HMI comment that though pupils often become good attenders in part-time units, their attendance at school remains poor. If pupils' adjustment is relative only to their changed circumstances then the notion of units as rehabilitation centres fails to have any substance. Despite this, both surveys found that a large majority of units aim to return pupils to school, re-integration being considered appropriate *when a child's behaviour ceases to present problems to unit staff*. HMI note that regular assessment and constant observation are the usual means of assessing the possibility of a return to normal schooling.

But when a pupil is returned to school, not only does he lose his close relationship with a teacher, but also a compact familiar environment and standards of a particular order, for the school and unit invariably have different ones. He also loses a certain consistency in treatment – i.e. two teachers can be more consistent than sixty-two – and an educational programme far more individually tailored than anything the school can offer. Therefore, to any positive statement on a unit report – e.g. 'he has learned how to control his temper, relate to his peers, organize his own work, or relate and respond to teachers' – must be added the qualification '*in the unit*'. However able and well intentioned the staff, there remains an inconsistency between the knowledge that they can work with a certain pupil and the confidence that as a consequence he will be able to adapt to school life again.

In an informal survey by the author carried out in two northern counties, it was found that problem behaviour re-appeared in over 60 per cent of re-integrated pupils. The classic pattern seemed to be that its re-appearance followed an initial six- or seven-week period of successful adjustment. This is consistent with the view that a return to the original circumstances will eventually lead to the re-emergence of the original problem behaviour. Even the policy of gradually re-integrating pupils over a period of weeks fails to tackle the issue. Both major surveys bypass the question of re-integration. HMI states that 'the percentage of pupils who returned to school was difficult to calculate'. They make no attempt to evaluate the success of the policy. The only problems they project are those created by the reputations of the pupil and unit, leading to negative expectations; and those concerned with the technicalities of curriculum adjustment.

Successful integrations do occur. We have already discussed the possibility that the notion of rehabilitation may have some substance for academically poor children who are given intensive remedial teaching. The criteria by which they are deemed ready for school have little to do with their social behaviour in the unit. By developing literacy and numeracy skills, unit staff hope to remove the frustrations and failures of school life. If the intervention aims at changing problem behaviour by approaching it through an educational programme, then the role of the unit is akin to that of a conventional remedial department. Even those changed circumstances that lead to better management of the pupil in the unit have usually been features of remedial departments – i.e. small groups, a close relationship with a teacher, and so on. The only difference is that units make a more conscious adaptation to the problem of managing the pupil. For example, they are more likely to use specific behaviour-modification techniques, and when pupils attend part time, their withdrawal from lessons is often linked to the requirement to contain their behaviour. If the problems are related to the child's educational competence then the criteria for re-integration has to be in these terms, and a judgment made to the effect that the pupil can now 'cope' in school: in essence that he can now manage a subject timetable. This criterion is identical to that used by the remedial department. However, if the pupil is re-integrated, on the basis of his behaviour in the unit, into an unchanged school setting, there is a greatly increased chance that the problem behaviour will re-appear. The fact that a pupil 'settles down' in a unit, attends regularly and engages in the required educational activities may be, in itself, largely irrelevant to the question of whether he should be re-integrated. None the less this is the general form of criteria employed for return to school.

Unit pupils can most easily be characterized in terms of their school life, and the success of withdrawal units can best be understood by viewing them as educational placements. If the problem exhibited in schools later prove to be largely manageable in educational terms, then can we be confident that schools are meeting their obligations to pupils? What, if anything, does the success of units tell us about the failure of schools? Though units are in a better position than schools to educate certain pupils, cannot mainstream schools emulate their circumstances? Does every big comprehensive have a group of pupils that necessarily require the services of a unit? Does every school need a 'sanctuary', 'remedial' and fourth- and fifth-year unit? No school has all three types and many have none. To what extent are units picking up problems that are the schools' responsibility?

What clearly emerges from studying the operation of withdrawal units is that problem behaviour in school is best understood in terms of school characteristics. However actually or apparently justified, there are dangers in construing it in terms of personal and social inadequacies. Such a view overlooks the fact that the behaviour occurs in school and usually exclusively in school. As we have seen, the circumstances surrounding the behaviour are a factor in determining it – and changing it. Failure to appreciate this can mean that units adopt complex programmes and interventions that are difficult to evaluate, i.e. education for personal relationships, social skills training and counselling. The point is not that these are ill conceived or unnecessary, but that they are secondary. The work of a unit needs to be primarily organized in terms of the factors in the immediate situation in which the behaviour occurs. There is considerable evidence that these 'primary' interventions are successful in eliminating the problem behaviour whether it be disruption or non-attendance. If units are succeeding in manipulating the 'primary' school factors then it is vital that we scrutinize these same variables within schools to see if the behaviour problems referred to units can be tackled at source.

A first question is: how do schools view problem behaviour? In examining this we meet the same distinction between social and personal definitions and school ones. Where the main emphasis is placed seems to be related to the dynamism or lethargy of the 'construing' school's system. To the extent that a school is reluctant to change and adapt in response to the needs of its intake, it will be inclined, in order to defend itself, to locate problems in external causes. Thus pupils' behaviour is seen to spring eternal from social and personal factors. Along with the one surveying units, Her Majesty's Inspectors prepared a separate report that discussed truancy and behavioural problems in schools (HMI, 1978a). They found that where schools successfully manage disruption and non-attendance, difficult behaviour is defined in terms of school factors. Their central point is that 'schools should accept the fullest responsibility for coping with *their* problems'. HMI note that discipline depends on mutual respect between pupils and staff and that the desire to maintain good relationships with the teachers is a powerful incentive for many pupils to behave acceptably. They stress 'the need to offer relevance and success to students as a means of avoiding behaviour and attendance problems', and observe that '*if you want something to happen in a large organization you must structure it to happen*'.

In pursuing the question of the school's responsibility for problem behaviour it is useful to distinguish between those children who lack basic educational skills and those who have little aptitude for a conventional skill curriculum. The former can be defined as those whose level of literacy and numeracy are such that they find it difficult to cope with a subject timetable. For them the educational activities are both of a low priority and difficult to execute. Remedial pupils can more easily encounter frustration, failure, mechanical tasks and inappropriate and uninteresting activities. It is common to underestimate what a history of failure to gain a reasonable literacy-level means to pupils. There is nothing more true generally of schools than the requirement to read, write and spell, and nothing more likely to lead to widespread rejection than failure to learn them. Usually 'remedial' pupils are only withdrawn from certain lessons.

It may well be that the large percentage of such pupils in units indicates that the referring schools are failing to give them appropriate and relevant education. In the informal study, previously mentioned, eight out of ten pupils were judged by their unit teachers to be 'unable to cope with subject teaching and to be in need of full-time literacy education'. *None* had been receiving this in their referring schools.

There are a large number of children referred to units who, although basically literate and numerate, find much of the school curriculum inappropriate, irrelevant and uninteresting. Raven (1979) has recently completed a major study into the attitudes of secondary school pupils and their teachers. He has found that roughly a third of pupils sometimes or always hate going to school. More than half of them consider that over 50 per cent of their school subjects are 'boring and useless'. Raven comments that 'so great is the disenchantment that it is difficult to see how teachers can achieve any goal effectively'. He notes that there is a reciprocal attitude on the part of the teachers. The majority defined less academic pupils as 'lazy, disruptive, uninterested, incapable of learning and no good at anything'. From Hargreaves (1967) and Power *et al.* (1967) we know what a significant factor, in fostering anti-social behaviour, teachers' expectations are.

In their study of attendance and behaviour in secondary schools, HMI note (HMI, 1978b) that 'absence rates support the view that much of the provision for the less academic student is missing its mark'. They suggest that some truancy may be attributable to poor and unimaginative teaching which fails to recognize the changed interests and attitudes of adolescents. Ravens' most significant finding is that pupil disenchant-ment is strongly related to expectations of their future social destination, i.e. job, career interests, etc. He comments that 'if pupils don't like schools it is because they cannot see the relevance of what they are doing there'. In this event we should expect the level of 'disenchantment' to increase markedly as pupils progress through the school with concomitant effects on attendance and disruptive behaviour. HMI noted, in their survey of units (HMI, 1978b), that over half the pupils are fourth and fifth years; Galloway (1976) found that fourth-year absence rates were nearly double those of the third year and that this doubling process was repeated again in the fifth year. In their other study of attendance and behaviour in secondary schools, HMI observe that all schools reported a recognizable and steady increase in unauthorized absence from the third year onwards. They add that 'in some areas truancy in the fifth year presented almost intractable problems', and provide a direct link with 'pupil disenchant-ment' when they comment that 'for some pupils motivation diminishes rapidly from the third year onwards, particularly for those with a poor level of achievement and low aspirations'.

Given the current picture of much secondary schooling, and the nature of unit success, it seems that the provision of a unit can easily become an alternative to tackling serious problems within the school. Before a unit is created, the scale and nature of the problem behaviours at issue need to be carefully examined. In this process a first step is to define the problems in terms of school variables. In the past this has frequently not been the case. The HMI survey (1978a) found that many units were housed in very poor conditions with low budgets. They appeared to be a 'scratch' provision following on from the need to withdraw pupils rather than the projection of a constructive educational environment.

Topping and Quelch, in their 1976 survey, obtained information from twenty local authorities. They found that only a small number had made any attempt to assess the incidence of the problem before setting up units. There were nearly as many different aims reported as authorities replying; these were often ill defined and confused aims. Few stated concrete aims in such a way as to make it possible to determine whether or not they had been achieved. Very few authorities had clear-cut criteria for admission and there was little agreement about the technique needed to change behaviour. The procedures for discharge were even less clear than the vague criteria for admission. These points, taken in conjunction with observations on the high quality of unit staff (confirmed by HMI and the Schools Council team) led Topping and Quelch to conclude that dedicated staff are left to wrestle with the problems of running units that are ill conceived and inadequately provided for. Experienced teachers have been attracted to units by the prospect of being able to put into effect practices and philosophies that are difficult to develop in the ordinary school. In saying this our picture of the 'ordinary school' must be informed by our earlier discussion.

Would tackling problem behaviour at source eliminate the need for withdrawal units? We have already noted the fundamental differences between units and schools. Their cohesiveness and small size, their good pupil/teacher ratio, and their ability to isolate a pupil from the behaviour-maintaining expectations of others, are difficult to emulate in the large comprehensive. It could be that some pupils may only be manageable by maximizing the circumstances that units can offer. If the pupils' background problems are temporary ones then the notion of units as short-term placements is appropriate; if their problems relate to a need for remedial teaching, then the same consideration applies. Where the background problems are long term – and this may be due to the long-term failure of the school – then units either function as alternative provision or provide a 'home base' for the child throughout his school life.

In attempting to answer the question whether or not schools can manage problem behaviour without devising units, we can do no better than quote the HMI truancy report (1978a). They cite the example of four schools in 'poor' areas with 'difficult' intakes, who have succeeded in managing their problems. All placed the major emphasis on setting consistent, attainable and appropriate educational objectives for their pupils. Of these schools, one established a unit but closed it after eighteen months; a second closed theirs after only three weeks; the staff of a third didn't feel that there was a need for a unit, of any type, and a fourth had a unit but this functioned as an integral part of the remedial department.

References

EYSENCK, H. J. (1952) 'The effects of psychotherapy: an evaluation.' *Journal of Consulting Psychology*, **16**, 319–24.

GALLOWAY, D. M. (1976) 'Size of school, socio-economic hardship, suspension rates and persistent unjustified absence from school.' *British Journal of Educational Psychology*, **46**, 40–7.

HARGREAVES, D. H. (1967) *Social Relationships in a Secondary School*. London: Routledge and Kegan Paul.

HER MAJESTY'S INSPECTORATE (1978a) *Truancy and Behaviour Problems in some Urban Schools*. London: Department of Education and Science.

HER MAJESTY'S INSPECTORATE (1978b) *Behavioural Units: A Survey of Special Units for Pupils with Behavioural Problems*. London: Department of Education and Science.

LANE, D. (1976) 'Limitations on counselling.' *Remedial Education*, **11**, 3, 120.

POWER, M. J. *et al.* (1967) 'Delinquent schools?' *New Society*, 19 October.

RAVEN, J. (1979) 'School rejection and its amelioration.' *Educational Research*, **20**, 1.

TOPPING, K. and QUELCH, T. (1976) *Special Units and Classes for Children with Behaviour Problems*. Calderdale Education Department.

WOLFF, S. (1976) 'Non-delinquent disturbance of conduct', in RUTTER, M. and HERSOV, L. (eds) *Child Psychiatry*. Oxford: Blackwell.

Section Four

Psychology in practice

The first article in this Reader began:

> Psychology ought certainly to give the teacher radical help . . . And yet . . . not a few of you may experience some disappointment at the net results (James, 1899).

Close to a century later, we can look again at the successes and failures of psychology to provide help to educators, both in suggesting specific recommendations for teaching and in providing general laws or explanations of human development and behaviour. The seven readings in this section only touch on a number of 'interfaces' between psychology and education. They do not attempt to cover all the areas in which psychology has or might have contributed to classroom concerns; that would be an impossible task. Rather, articles have been chosen which review and evaluate various standpoints about the role of psychology in practice.

The opening article by Ann Clarke presents a useful overview of psychology and education (4.1). Many of the topics raised here are developed further in the articles that follow: in particular, the influence of psychologists such as Burt and Thomson (4.2); the explanations that psychologists have offered for children's development (4.3 and 4.4, focusing particularly on biological explanations); and the attempts deliberately to modify development through curriculum policies based on psychological theories (4.6 and 4.7). As well as serving as a useful introduction to the section, Clarke also looks at some of the ideas stimulated by educational psychologists. Here she points to some 'net results' of psychological enquiry, particularly enquiries which have begun with educational concerns like: 'How can we improve retention of material?' 'How do teachers and pupils interact?' Such questions point to a more general question about the effectiveness of schools, an issue explored in 4.5.

In tracing the background to educational psychology, Clarke refers to two models: the model presented by Burt to educational psychologists 'which assumed their function to be the diagnosis of defects which were predominantly to be found in the child . . .' and the American psychometric model which was concerned with the prediction of success. These roles for the educational psychologist as predictor and as diagnostician are explored further in 4.2 and 4.3.

An obvious example of the psychologist as predictor is found in the development of intelligence tests. When used in 11 plus examinations or recruitment tests the psychological test is, in effect, helping to decide what kind of education or position a person should have. Such psychological decisions do not develop in a social vacuum; rather they develop alongside political decisions about the educational system. It becomes very difficult to determine the extent to which psychology influences political decisions and the extent to which psychology is merely invoked when it suits a political decision. For example, was the decision to separate primary from secondary education at age 11 based on some psychological theory about the nature of development, or was it based on political-pragmatic grounds, such as the amount of space available, with some psychological evidence brought in as and when appropriate? Deborah Thom's article looks at the spread of intelligence tests during the 1940s, a period assumed to be one where radical changes in education occurred, and evaluates the relationships between psychology and social policy.

The psychologist has a role not only as a tester for selection purposes but also as a diagnostician and a provider of prescriptions. An example looked at here of such a role is of the psychologist called in with his or her black bag to identify and help cure the 'learning disabled' child. Inverted commas are used here for, as Gerald Coles' article points out, it is not at all evident that learning disabilities can be defined or identified. Coles subjects the currently available measures of disability to severe scrutiny and finds them wanting in many respects. While some of the remedies offered appear effective, it is not clear why they are effective or whether their effectiveness confirms the existence of learning disabilities. Perhaps the remedies merely instance 'good' teaching which would help everyone? Coles' critical evaluation leads him to conclude that 'the entire field of learning disabilities has an empirical foundation too frail for the ponderous structure that has been erected upon it'.

Tests of intelligence and tests of learning disability have usually rested on biological explanations of educational success and failure. Underlying the intelligence test is the concept of a fixed intelligence, an innate endowment susceptible to environmental influence but, in the final analysis, biologically rather than culturally determined. Learning Disability tests, similarly, usually assume biological causes, such as neurological impairment, whenever the child's 'potential' does not match the 'actual'. Biological explanations are, according to John Archer, commonly used to 'equate *what is* with *what ought to be*'. In his article, Archer examines the use of biological explanations in one particular area of psychological study: the study of differences between men and women. Biological explanations, he argues, tend to be well-supported because they support the norm or the status quo; they are easy to understand (an interactionist viewpoint being much more complex); and, thirdly, they call on physical sciences such as biology and chemistry which seem to provide status for such theories. His examples of biological theories for existing sex-roles demonstrate the need (as do the previous two readings) to recognize the influences of the social context on psychological theories.

The last three articles in this section, although different from each other, share a similar focus: the ways in which schools and teaching practices can be made more effective. David Reynolds' article starts with the question which has to be raised first: that is, are schools effective and does it make a difference which school you go to? The search for effective schools (also the title of 4.5) on both sides of the Atlantic has produced many contradictory and disputed conclusions. Recent studies seem to agree that schools can be more, or less, effective in reaching their educational objectives though what accounts for effectiveness is far from clear. It seems to rest on something called the 'culture' of the school, involving factors like 'ethos' and 'staff-pupil relationships', rather than the 'structure' of the school.

While Reynolds concentrates on the possible effects at the level of school organization, others have explored differences in effectiveness resulting from particular curriculum practices. Educationists are always hungry for new ideas to improve their teaching and to enable those marked for failure to achieve educational success. A theory or model developed in psychology can be quickly assimilated into educational thinking often before that theory has been fully evaluated.

Charles Brainerd looks at a translation from theory to practice that has occurred with respect to Piaget's developmental theory. In his article (a continuation of the one begun in Section 1, pages 39–54), he asks how 'a theory whose predictions about the relationship between learning and development fare so poorly should prove influential in education'. One does not want to be overcritical of educators who adopt and adapt psychological thinking even when that thinking was not designed with education in mind – the 'film of the book' can be very stimulating – but caution is needed when policies seem to rest on psychological 'facts' which are far from being hard truths. Another quote from William James seems appropriate:

I say, moreover, that you make a great, a very great mistake, if you think that psychology, being the science of mind's laws, is something from which you can deduce definite programmes of instruction for immediate classroom use. Psychology is a science, and teaching is an art; and sciences never generate arts directly out of themselves. An intermediary inventive mind must take the application, by using its originality (James, 1899, p. 8).

The final short article echoes some of the questions raised in the other readings, opening up the Pandora's box of ideology, psychological theories and educational policies. A. H. Halsey illustrates how tentative research findings can be used to bolster policy decisions at a national level, and raises questions about the possible uses and abuses of psychology.

While one would not wish to deny or belittle the many advances made in psychology and the potential of many such advances to help inform some educational practices and policies, psychology is open to misuse if taken directly into classrooms or merely invoked when it is politically convenient. As John Head said, in relation to science education:

The biggest danger is that protagonists in debates about science education will seize on fragments of psychological evidence, or worse still, unsupported opinion, and removing them from their context use them as testimony in favour of their particular viewpoint (Head, 1982).

This danger seems applicable to all areas of education.

Pam Czerniewska

References

HEAD, J. (1982) 'What can psychology contribute to science education?' *Social Science Reports*, June.

JAMES, W. (1899; 1918) 'Psychology and the teaching art', in *Talks to Teachers on Psychology: and to students on some of life's ideals* (Chapter 1). London: Longmans, Green. Reprinted in this Reader on pages 1–4.

4.1   Psychology and education

Ann M. Clarke

[. . .] Psychology in the English-speaking world is firmly rooted in a tradition of empirical science with a positivist orientation. Perhaps its most important contribution to educational theory has been through the use of certain agreed procedures many of which we share with clinical medicine. It is no accident that some of the more important contributions to the methodology of human science are to be found in the two *Handbooks of Research on Teaching* and are reflected in the style of many articles published in journals which incorporate educational psychology in their title. This is not to imply a necessary superiority of this approach to all problems, but to suggest that it is an essential way of specifying relevant questions and designing research which should yield both some coherent answers and also indicate further questions to be tackled.

The selection of topics for discussion here reflects both the author's commitment to this orientation in psychology, and also something of the range of educational problems which have been researched within a developing conceptual context. Education is an area in which appropriately a number of different philosophical positions may be adopted; it is also one in which may be found dogmatic advocates of child rearing and teaching methods which range from the cranky to the antediluvian. Obviously it is important that both values and methods should be freely debated. However, if opinions are not subject to critical scrutiny and proper evaluation, then not only may one opinion appear as good as any other, but we risk falling prey either to anarchy or to mindless fashion. It is important that a wide range of approaches to educational practice should be attempted, but it is equally necessary that the sophisticated methods of evaluation research should be routinely used.

The background

Thirty years ago educational psychology in this country [Britain] was dominated by Sir Cyril Burt, although he was in the process of retiring from the Chair of Psychology at University College, London, held since 1931 when he moved from what is at present known as the London Institute of Education. Godfrey Thomson in Scotland also enjoyed high prestige, and their combined influence significantly affected both research and practice in this area. Human ability was to be explored by means of factor analytic studies, and applied psychologists were encouraged to

Source: *British Journal of Educational Studies* (1982), XXX, 1, 43–56.

construct and use standardized tests of intelligence and attainment to assess individual differences which were assumed to be largely constitutional in origin and relatively unchanging in rate of individual development. Although Burt understood and wrote extensively about the effects of social disadvantage on children, he gave to practising educational psychologists a model which assumed their function to be the diagnosis of defects which were predominantly to be found in the child rather than as a consequence of an ongoing transactional process between biological endowments and the social environment, including the school.

Across the Atlantic a somewhat similar tradition developed from the work of Goddard who had first introduced the Binet test there, and others such as Yerkes and Terman who were concerned with the prediction of achievement in the armed forces, industry and education. The mental testing movement gathered momentum, attracting many able scientists and also shrewd business men.

However, there was in addition a different and very powerful force achieving rapid development in America, namely experimental psychology. The experimenter, instead of measuring the average mind and its variance, attempted to measure the effect of some specified environmental change; in the endeavour to emulate the vigour of the physical sciences he resorted to the controlled conditions of the laboratory, using as subjects animals who could (unlike humans) be bred and reared in a predetermined manner. Learning theories were almost exclusively American and for a long time were largely the product of theoretical models based on elegant experimental work in the area of conditioning. For these psychologists a deliberate manipulation of the environment resulted in demonstrable and often important changes in the organism's behaviour; small wonder, then that J. B. Watson in 1930 chanced his arm with the statement: 'Give me a dozen healthy infants, well-formed, and my own specified world to bring them up in and I'll guarantee to take any one at random and train him to become any type of specialist I might select – doctor, lawyer, artist, merchant-chief and, yes, even beggarman and thief, regardless of his talents, penchants, tendencies, abilities, vocations, and race of his ancestors.'

Much later Skinner declared 'Don't test – teach!' and set about developing an educational technology based on the use of Thorndike's Law of Effect which he referred to as the law of *positive* reinforcement (i.e. stimulus-response sequences which were satisfying in their consequences were thereby strengthened). In his book *The Technology of Teaching*[1] he argued that there was too much about schools that was negative, leading to passive compliance among pupils, rather than active learning, and, further, that teachers often unwittingly reinforced unruly and maladaptive behaviour by drawing attention to it. Moreover, it appeared that by appropriate use of positive reinforcement and 'time-out' procedures every kind of desirable behaviour from problem-solving to creative activities could be elicited and encouraged, while sloth, aggression and deceit would be reduced in a brave new world.

With these traditions pervading university departments of psychology, it is not surprising that in the main educational psychologists in the USA looked to the social context as the most important factor in pupil learning, many of them dismissing, often absurdly, cognitive and emotional factors as contributors. Furthermore, the experimental analysis of behaviour became a major focus of endeavour among researchers in human as well as animal laboratories, resulting in a shift of emphasis from factorial studies of interrelationships to controlled experiments which demanded different research strategies and statistical design.

The Genevan school

Meanwhile in Geneva another theoretical approach had been developed which was to be espoused by many psychologists who shared an equal distaste for both psychometrics and behaviourism. Piaget's theory presented for the first time a process model of development concerned to account for cognitive changes from infancy to adult life; it was destined to have a profound influence on educational thinking in many parts of the world. As is well known, Piaget's genetic epistemology was based in the conceptual framework of a zoologist concerned with the manner in which organisms adapt to their environment, a process which he considered as occurring through an active interaction between biological structures and environment by means of assimilation and accommodation. He explicitly disassociated himself from behaviourism, arguing that the concept of association, which the various forms of associationism from Hume to Pavlov and Hull had used and abused, had been obtained only by artificially isolating one part of the general process defined by the equilibrium between assimilation and accommodation (Piaget, 1970).[2] He was equally critical of those environmentalists who sought to accelerate children through the stages, cautioning against a false optimism which some educational psychologists had encouraged in teachers. Genuine optimism, in Piaget's opinion, would consist in believing in the child's capacities for invention.

Nature and nurture

To many psychologists and educators a developmental theory which assumes an interaction between biological and social factors, while at the same time describing the maturational process in terms of clearly delineated stages, had considerable appeal. By contrast, others whose training was in psychometrics were attracted to a different methodological approach, namely a statistical estimation of the relative importance of genetic and environmental factors in accounting for differences in ability. Barbara Burks (1928)[3] was probably among the first to place a value of 80% as the genetic contribution to IQ differences, an estimate based on the results of a large scale and carefully planned adoption study. Others were to follow her lead, but not always with as much care, and unfortunately rather little attention was paid to the *nature* of environmental factors which might influence the developing child, or indeed, apart from Piaget's rather speculative conjectures, *how* these interacted with developing biological structures. The environment (together with errors of measurement) was accorded the *remainder* after the heritability percentage had been estimated. There was, however, an important exception to the neglect of environmental factors, mentioned by Freeman, Holzinger and Mitchell (1928)[4] and vigorously elaborated by the Iowa school in the 1930s, namely the allegedly critical significance for later development of environmental events in the first few years of life. This theory became, with the publication in 1949 of D. O. Hebb's *Organization of Behaviour*,[5] and in 1951 of Bowlby's influential monograph *Maternal Care and Mental Health*,[6] the focus of considerable empirical study, mostly, but not exclusively, using animals.

The methodological problems inherent in most of the researches investigating child development, and many using animals, were overlooked when social policies relating to young children were formulated, the most famous being the Headstart programme in America which aimed to give children from disadvantaged domestic environments enriched opportunities prior to school entry at the age of six. The assumption was that if children were to be shielded from later educational failure, preschool intervention was certainly necessary if not sufficient. When careful evaluation of the outcome of these programmes indicated no advantage accruing to the children after three years in primary school, now known as the 'washout' effect, one professor felt able in 1969 to write from the Department of Education at Berkeley, 'Compensatory education has been tried and it apparently has failed' (Jensen, 1969).[7]

Jensen then proceeded to account for the substantial disparities in educational attainment across social classes and ethnic groups in terms of genetically determined differences in IQ, and concluded that for the vast majority of children in American schools it would not be possible substantially to boost the IQ and scholastic achievement. He did, however, concede that differences in attainment are more affected by social influences than are intelligence test scores. The article in the *Harvard Educational Review* resulted in a furious response in many quarters, particularly from those concerned with the education of disadvantaged children. 'Jensenism' became a term of abuse, and some researchers started to look very critically at the quality of the empirical evidence on which the conclusions were based. In this connection the extensively cited researches by the late Sir Cyril Burt were (belatedly) pronounced fraudulent to an extent not as yet fully established (Kamin, 1974;[8] Gillie, 1976;[9]

Hearnshaw, 1979;[10] Clarke and Clarke, 1980[11]). The scientific credentials of Britain's most prominent educational psychologist were at least diminished if not demolished, and his supporters on both sides of the Atlantic suffered a considerable blow.

However, sophisticated researchers, including Jensen, had gained from this unhappy affair, and they proceeded carefully to collect and evaluate evidence, much of it published in the last decade, which points to the following conclusions with respect to IQ scores:

1 biological relatives show significantly greater resemblance than do adopted relatives reared in the same social milieu;
2 social factors unrelated to biological differences have as yet not been shown to contribute, except relatively trivially, to variations in intelligence in families representing a wide spectrum of environments, excluding, however, the socially deprived;
3 the environment can be shown to have deleterious effects where circumstances are exceptionally disadvantageous;
4 removal of children from disadvantaged environments to favourable circumstances results in improvement in cognitive functioning;
5 as yet no early period in development has been identified which can be considered critical in the sense that the demonstrated effects of social disadvantage are irreversible, provided there is total ecological change.

Intelligence can justifiably be seen as a product of biological and social factors in interaction. In environments which are above a certain undefined threshold, almost certainly the vast majority in an advanced society, genetic factors are most readily inferred as major causes of intellectual differences, while below the threshold the environment may, to an unknown extent, be inferred as suppressing potential development. The nature of the transactions which serve to accelerate or retard development during the first fifteen years of life and thereafter are, however, as yet quite inadequately understood, but several large scale longitudinal studies have already been initiated with a view to clarifying some of the issues. The analysis offered here is based upon a consideration of a very large number of research reports which as yet have not been satisfactorily summarized in a single review. Each point is separately supported by several careful and recent studies too numerous to list.

Cognitive views of learning

As already mentioned, during the middle part of this century, behaviourism became the major theoretical model for American researchers interested in learning, with important applications in the form of programmed instruction and educational technology. However, the rise of behaviourism was accompanied by a considerable neglect of cognitive psychology across the Atlantic, although in Britain F. C. Bartlett had initiated important research at Cambridge into factors influencing the reception and retention of meaningful discourse, and had inspired a generation of students many of whom are today, in parallel with colleagues abroad, developing sophisticated models of human information-processing.

To this reviewer, one of the more exciting areas in educational psychology is the study of factors which influence the reception and retention of meaningful prose material, an activity which occupies perhaps more time in classrooms than any other. The radical initiator of this movement was David Ausubel whose first paper on the use of advance organizers was published in 1960 and who in the introduction to his lengthy text *Educational Psychology: A cognitive view* (1968)[12] stated that he was not prepared to consider topics such as child development, adjustment, personality and group dynamics except in so far as they bear on and are *directly* relevant to classroom learning. Further, since educational psychology is an immensely complex subject, there would be no attempt to simplify and water down the material to be presented; Ausubel maintained that his aim was to furnish the prospective teacher with the basic psychological sophistication needed for classroom teaching. He proposed 'assimilation theory', which has many elements in common with Bartlett's position with respect to 'schemata', and in essence proposes that learning involves relating new, potentially meaningful material to an assimilative context of existing knowledge. Thus the conditions of meaningful assimilative learning are that the new material must be received; the learner must possess, prior to learning, a meaningful context for integrating the new material; and he must actively use this context to integrate the new information with old.

Ausubel introduced the concept of advance organizers to provide a conceptual bridge between existing knowledge and new material, by presenting the novel ideas at a high level of generality and abstraction. Early experimental work suggested that the effects of advance organizers were greatest for those of relatively low ability or poor background knowledge and the differences obtained between groups with and without the use of organizers were chiefly due to students of this kind.

Latterly, however, as so often is the case with new strategies for promoting learning, a somewhat confused and confusing situation has arisen with a sufficient number of experimenters finding no difference between 'treated' and 'untreated' groups for Barnes and Clawson (1975)[13] to conclude that 'advance organizers as presently constructed, generally do not facilitate learning'. The fact that two recent reviewers (Mayer, 1979[14] and Luiten *et al.*, 1980[15]) disagree with the former assessment does little to mitigate the unsatisfactory nature of many of the researches and their reporting. In addition, the majority of those participating in these brief learning experiments have been college students. Perhaps, as with compensatory education, advance organizers have not failed, but have as yet not been systematically tried in contexts where they might be effective.

A somewhat similar situation is to be found in the literature on so-called mathemagenic behaviours introduced by Rothkopf (1965).[16] The most often researched of these activities, designed to promote learning, are note-taking and the effect of inserted questions in prose passages. Insufficient effort has been devoted to analysing the relative efficacy of different kinds of question in relation to various types of subject matter and the level of question in relation to various types of subject matter and the level of conceptual knowledge of the students. Furthermore, although as is the case with advance organizers small positive effects have been demonstrated in most experiments, learning *time* has usually not been controlled, leaving open an alternative interpretation of the results. Nevertheless, despite the inadequacies, a start has been made, and it must be hoped that more sophisticated experiments will in future yield insights into cognitive processes during learning activities which are urgently needed to improve strategies available to classroom teachers, particularly in connection with children of average ability. The evidence for biological factors interacting with the social environment during development to create the conditions for attainment at any point in time suggests that there is likely to be an interaction between the state of maturation and the most effective methods of enabling children to advance, a point of view corroborated in researchers reviewed by Cronbach and Snow (1977).[17]

Often it seems that a failure to comprehend the complexity of the ongoing processes is at the root of the apparently conflicting results of attempts to observe or measure some brief intervention of the 'main effect' variety. Furthermore, the emphasis on recall of large amounts of factual material (sometimes verbatim) has often seemed at variance with an important educational objective, namely the acquisition of new concepts or principles. A major contribution to an advance of this kind was presented in a recent symposium on learning processes and strategies in the *British Journal of Educational Psychology*. Two of the contributors, Marton and Säljö,[18,19] argued that a description of *what is learned* is more important than a summary of *how much is learned*. They presented students with substantial passages of prose and obtained information both on their comprehension of the discourse and also on the strategies used in processing. The authors were able to categorize the answers into those showing evidence of attention to learning the text itself, a reproductive strategy, or surface-level processing, and those which were concerned with comprehension of principles, deep-level processing. Attempts were made to modify processing strategies by means of inserted questions, and the conclusion reached was that the demand characteristics of assessment procedures have a considerable impact on how students proceed: learning can be technified and runs the risk of being reduced to a search for the type of knowledge expected on the test. There is a clear implication here that thinking and proper understanding can be encouraged or discouraged according to how the pupil expects the material to be assessed. Watts and Anderson (1971)[20] had shown that deeper processing was encouraged by questions requiring the application of a text example to an unfamiliar situation, and distinguished between questions which measure true comprehension and those merely requiring textual repetition. Anderson (1972)[21] found that the vast majority of questions used in learning experiments failed to assess comprehension, and further that in those experiments in which depth of processing was manipulated by the insertion of questions demanding deep processing, retention and delayed recall were significantly increased. It appears to be much easier to produce questions demanding factual answers than problems requiring some deeper level of understanding for their solution, but it also seems likely that it would pay teachers to devote time and reflection to their routine methods of assessing their pupils' learning. A theoretical framework for studies in this area is provided by Craik and Lockhart (1972)[22] and Craik and Tulving (1975)[23] whose elegant experiments on depth of processing provide important insights into factors affecting learning and memory.

Learning time

As already noted, some of the experiments reporting superior learning as a function of changes in the structuring of material failed to control for time. A vast literature suggests that, of many factors available for teacher manipulation, this may be the single most significant factor in pupil learning, provided a clear distinction is made between available time and time-on-task, as Bloom (1980)[24] has put it. It seems likely that many children are not enabled effectively to utilize the time they are by law compelled to spend in school, resulting in serious waste of potential both to themselves and to the community. Investigations using a variety of procedures to determine the amount of time a student spends overtly or covertly engaged in learning suggest that the percentage of engaged time is highly related to subsequent measures of achievement. In turn, time-on-task is largely determined jointly by the quality of instruction, teacher-pupil relationships and the extent to which pupils have the cognitive prerequisites to accomplish tasks. Bennett (1976)[25] identified time spent on work-related activities as an important difference between formal and informal classrooms, a conclusion reiterated by Bell *et al.* (1976)[26] who believed that primary school children in an informal classroom wasted much of their time in aimless wandering, watching movements of other classes and interacting without useful purpose with their own classmates. Rutter *et al.* (1979)[27] from their study of senior high schools found that attainment and adjustment were related to classroom management strategies and that 'one of the hallmarks of successful class management is keeping pupils actively engaged in productive activities rather than waiting for something to happen', a statement greatly amplified by some of the painstaking researches on the successful use of behaviour modification in schools collated by O'Leary and O'Leary (1972),[28] Thoresen (1973)[29] and Merrett (1981).[30]

Teacher-pupil interactions

No review of the contribution of psychologists to education would be complete without consideration of the important, if diverse, researches on *teacher-student relationships*, to use the title of Brophy and Good's book (1974),[31] although space precludes the detailed discussion which the topic deserves.

In recent years a major stimulus to the extensive study of attitudinal and motivational factors in the social ecology of the classroom appears to have arisen from Rosenthal and Jacobson's *Pygmalion in the Classroom* (1968),[32] although this particular investigation into the effects of teacher expectation on pupil performance had too many methodological defects to be acceptable as valid evidence for the effect. A summary of the major criticisms has been compiled by Elashoff and Snow (1971).[33] In this country Pidgeon (1970)[34] reviewed a wide range of research into factors bearing on pupil motivation, including several studies of his own, arguing, among other things, that the general atmosphere of schools, or what Rutter would call their ethos, may differentially affect pupils' motivation and therefore their collective achievements.

Examination of the question of the extent to which individual teachers' attitudes hinder or help pupils of different ability levels or social background has been fraught with the usual difficulties surrounding experimental research in social psychology – particularly the problem of deceiving teachers so that they were unaware of the purpose of the research, which in some studies appears to have been ineffective and may have a bearing on the frequent failures to demonstrate the effect. The studies reported by Schrank (1968 and 1970)[35,36] and by Seaver (1973)[37] are among those which avoided the difficulty, and in each case showed a *small* effect of expectation on performance with US airmen and primary school children respectively. Seaver's method was ingenious in using existing school documents relating to young children whose older siblings either had or had not been taught by the same teacher who, hypothetically, in the former case might have formed an expectation based on knowledge of the achievement of an older sibling. He also raised the possibility that expectation effects might be as much pupil- as teacher-generated, and very recently the effect of student expectation on teachers has been explored (see, for example, Feldman and Prohaska, 1979).[38]

The better designed studies in the area of teacher-pupil interactions have been particularly useful in distinguishing between outcome and process variables, although it must be confessed that very few researchers have managed to provide evidence on both measures within the same study. It is increasingly apparent that many of the differences in teacher-pupil interactions in mixed ability classrooms are generated by the pupils (see, for example, Brophy and Good, 1970),[39] thus providing important evidence on how children differentially contribute to their own learning environments. Dusek (1975)[40] in an important review article has made the distinction between *teacher expectation* which is a natural and often beneficial phenomenon and *teacher bias* in which children whose potential for learning does not apparently differ are accelerated or retarded by virtue of social or racial prejudice.

Home and school

The question of the relative importance of school and home effects on attainment and social adjustment continues to provoke controversy. Recently a group of psychologists have called attention to an important variation among homes which can, at least to some extent, be harnessed as an educational resource: parental teaching. J. Hewison and the late Jack Tizard (1980[41], 1982[42]) have reported a project which is outstanding in its methodological sophistication, provocative in the evaluation of results, and heartening as an object lesson in productive partnership between administrators, schools and research workers. Starting with the solidly based correlations between tests of academic attainment and various demographic characteristics associated with parental social status, they aimed to discover whether differences in reading achievement *within* a working-class population could be related to differences in children's home backgrounds. The usual modest correlations were obtained between reading attainment and various measures which included aspects of mothers' language and their attitudes to education. One factor, however, unexpectedly was found to be by far the most powerful predictor, namely whether mothers regularly heard their children read, in other words effectively coached them. The difference between pupils with and without this advantage amounted to almost one standard deviation, and could not be accounted for merely as a correlate of other influential factors including IQ, although the coached children were substantially brighter than those who were not. Two further important points emerged: first, that the total amount of help children received over several years was relevant, and second, that nearly half of the samples of working-class parents spent time helping their children with the mechanics of reading although none had been encouraged by the schools.

The next important question was, of course, whether an advantage accruing to some pupils by virtue of their parents' initiative could be reproduced in families where this had not occurred naturally. With the co-operation of the Heads and teachers in six primary and junior schools in the London borough of Haringey two types of intervention were employed for a two-year period. In one experimental condition teachers invited parents to hear their children read, books were supplied· and regular checks made; in another condition an additional teacher was employed in the school to accelerate reading skills. Allocation to experimental or carefully designated control conditions was on a random basis, and the scoring of the standardized reading tests was done by experienced teachers unconnected with the intervention.

The results indicated that in this disadvantaged area of London, which included an immigrant population, inviting parents to coach their children produced a very significant effect in one school although not in another, while in neither school receiving additional teacher help was there any gain in reading accruing to the experimental pupils.

These findings are consistent with the results of intervention research which suggest that unless parents become involved with an on-going process, gains for children are likely to be both limited and ephemeral.

In conclusion

Inevitably some topics to which educational psychologists have contributed have been omitted from this essay, including the area of backwardness and mental retardation which remain a focal point of interest and concern to this author. Had I indulged all my personal predilections a section on delinquency and maladjustment would have been included, together with a consideration of the school's potential role in helping troubled children from disadvantaged backgrounds. Unfortunately several important research reports have had to be excluded, and with them the names of respected colleagues and friends. My endeavour has been to sketch a broad outline of psychologists' contributions to mainstream education, and to suggest that there is a gradually changing outlook which should serve us well in the future.

Among the more important changes in orientation are a better recognition of the complex interrelations of biological and many social factors which underlie various developmental trajectories, and strongly influence attainment and adjustment during the school years and later. Developmental psychology is increasingly perceived as life-span psychology in which there is always some potential for change in a majority of the population, sometimes in an upward and sometimes in a downward direction.

There is an awareness of the limitations of laboratory studies for defining accurately events in the field, leading to a greater sophistication in the design of experiments in classrooms, youth clubs, leisure centres and elsewhere, together with the use of quasi-experimental designs which make use of naturally occurring events. There is an increasing preoccupation with the investigation of *processes* as well as *outcomes* in the investigation of both cognitive and social-emotional characteristics. The fact that as yet research has not advanced very far in producing a proper understanding of the former in relation to the latter should not diminish the importance of investigating across both time and space.

It seems increasingly evident that children react differently to the same social or educational context, in many cases contributing directly to the nature of the environmental events which will in turn affect sequential transactions, in which the child may unwittingly affect his or her own development.

Perhaps it should not be assumed that each of the factors which can separately be shown to accelerate learning would, if added together, make a *vast* difference to most pupils' competence, although there is substantial reason to suppose they are important. Many of them are procedures naturally adopted by competent teachers, who modify their techniques according to the cognitive level of their pupils and the subject matter which is being taught. Thus they are probably correlated characteristics of inspired educators who will, in addition, form flexible judgments concerning their pupils, avoiding rigid expectancy effects and creating classroom climates in which children will have a maximal opportunity to develop. In discussing the apparent unpredictability of human development, the playwright Bertolt Brecht neatly makes the point that this is not because there are no determinants of personal characteristics, but rather that there are too many. This complexity is a challenge to both teachers and researchers.

References

1 SKINNER, B. F. (1968) *The Technology of Teaching*. New York: Appleton-Century Crofts.
2 PIAGET, JEAN (1970) 'Piaget's theory', in MUSSEN, P. H. (ed.) *Manual of Child Psychology* (Chapter 9). New York: Wiley.
3 BURKS, BARBARA (1928) 'The relative influence of nature and nurture upon mental development: a comparative study of foster parent–foster child resemblance and true parent–true child resemblance', in *Yearbook of the National Society for the Study of Education, Part 1*, **27**, 219–316.
4 FREEMAN, F. N., HOLZINGER, K. J. and MITCHELL, B. C. (1928) 'The influence of environment on the intelligence, school achievement, and conduct of foster children', in *Yearbook of the National Society for the Study of Education, Part 1*, **27**, 103–217.
5 HEBB, D. O. (1949) *Organization of Behaviour*. New York: Wiley.
6 BOWLBY, J. (1951) *Maternal Care and Mental Health*. Geneva: World Health Organization.
7 JENSEN, A. R. (1969) 'How much can we boost IQ and scholastic achievement?' *Harvard Educational Review*, **39**, 1–123.
8 KAMIN, L. J. (1974) *The Science and Politics of IQ*. New York: Erlbaum.
9 GILLIE, OLIVER (1976) 'Crucial data faked by eminent psychologist.' *The Sunday Times*, 24 October.

10 HEARNSHAW, L. S. (1979) *Cyril Burt: Psychologist.* London: Hodder and Stoughton.

11 CLARKE, ANN M. and CLARKE, A. D. B. (1980) 'Comments on Professor Hearnshaw's "Balance sheet on Burt".' *A Balance Sheet on Burt*: Supplement to the *Bulletin* of the British Psychological Society, 33, 17–19.

12 (a) AUSUBEL, DAVID P. (1960) 'The use of advance organizers in the learning and retention of meaningful verbal material.' *Journal of Educational Psychology*, **51**, 145–70.
(b) AUSUBEL, DAVID P. (1968) *Educational Psychology: A Cognitive View.* New York: Holt, Rinehart and Winston.

13 BARNES, B. R. and CLAWSON, E. V. (1975) 'Do advance organizers facilitate learning? Recommendations for further research based on an analysis of thirty-two studies.' *Review of Educational Research*, **45**, 637–59.

14 MAYER, R. E. (1979) 'Twenty years of research on advance organizers: assimilation theory is still the best predictor of results.' *Instructional Science*, **8**, 133–67.

15 LUITEN, J., AMES, W. and ACKERSON, G. (1980) 'A meta-analysis of the effects of advance organizers on learning and retention.' *American Educational Research Journal*, **17**, 2, 211–18.

16 ROTHKOPF, E. Z. (1965) 'Some theoretical and experimental approaches to problems in written instruction', in KRUMBOLTZ, J. D. (ed). *Learning and the Educational Process* (pp. 193–221). Chicago, IL: Rand McNally.

17 CRONBACH, L. J. and SNOW, R. E. (1977) *Aptitudes and Instructional Methods: A Handbook for Research on Interactions.* New York: Irvington.

18 MARTON, F. and SÄLJÖ, R. (1976) 'On qualitative differences in learning – I: Outcome and process.' *British Journal of Educational Psychology*, **46**, 1, 4–11.

19 MARTON, F. and SÄLJÖ, R. (1976) 'On qualitative differences in learning – II: Outcome as a function of the learner's conception of the task.' *British Journal of Educational Psychology*, 46, **2**, 115–27.

20 WATTS, G. H. and ANDERSON, R. C. (1971) 'Effects of three types of inserted questions on learning from prose.' *Journal of Educational Psychology*, **62**, 5, 378–94.

21 ANDERSON, R. C. (1972) 'How to construct achievement tests to assess comprehension.' *Review of Educational Research*, **42**, 2, 145–70.

22 CRAIK, F. I. M. and LOCKHART, R. S. (1972) 'Levels of processing: a framework for memory research.' *Journal of Verbal Learning and Verbal Behaviour*, **11**, 671–84.

23 CRAIK, F. I. M. and TULVING, E. (1975) 'Depth of processing and the retention of words in episodic memory.' *Journal of Experimental Psychology: General*, **104**, 3, 268–94.

24 BLOOM, B. S. (1980) *Better Learning in Schools: A Primer for Parents, Teachers and Other Educators.* New York: McGraw Hill.

25 BENNETT, N. (1976) *Teaching Styles and Pupil Progress.* London: Open Books.

26 BELL, A. E., ZIPURSKY, M. A., and SWITZER, F. (1976) 'Informal or open-area education in relation to achievement and personality.' *British Journal of Educational Psychology*, **46**, 3, 235–43.

27 RUTTER, M., MAUGHAN, B., MORTIMORE, P. and OUSTON, J. (1979) *Fifteen Thousand Hours: Secondary Schools and their Effects on Children.* London: Open Books.

28 O'LEARY, K. D. and O'LEARY, S. G. (1972) *Classroom Management: The Successful Use of Behavior Modification.* New York: Pergamon.

29 THORESEN, C. E. (1973) *Behaviour Modification in Education. The 72nd Yearbook of the National Society for the Study of Education.* Chicago, IL: University of Chicago Press.

30 MERRETT, F. E. (1981) 'Studies in behaviour modification in British educational settings.' *Educational Psychology*, **1**, 13–38.

31 BROPHY, J. and GOOD, T. L. (1974) *Teacher-Student Relationships: Causes and Consequences.* New York: Holt, Rinehart and Winston.

32 ROSENTHAL, R. and JACOBSON, L. (1968) *Pygmalion in the Classroom.* New York: Holt, Rinehart and Winston.

33 ELASHOFF, J. D. and SNOW, R. (1971) *Pygmalion Reconsidered.* Worthington, OH: Charles A. Jones.

34 PIDGEON, D. A. (1970) *Expectation and Pupil Performance.* Slough: NFER.

35 SCHRANK, W. R. (1968) 'The labeling effect of ability grouping.' *Journal of Educational Research*, **62**, 2, 51–2.

36 SCHRANK, W. R. (1970) 'A further study of the labeling effect of ability grouping.' *Journal of Educational Research*, **63**, 8, 358–60.

37 SEAVER, W. B. (1973) 'Effects of naturally induced teacher expectancies.' *Journal of Personality and Social Psychology*, **28**, 3, 333–42.

38 FELDMAN, R. S. and PROHASKA, T. (1979) 'The student as Pygmalion: effect of student expectation on the teacher.' *Journal of Educational Psychology*, **71**, 485–93.

39 BROPHY, J. and GOOD, T. L. (1970) 'Teachers' communication of differential expectations for classroom performance.' *Journal of Educational Psychology*, **61**, 365–74.

40 DUSEK, J. B. (1975) 'Do teachers bias children's learning?' *Review of Educational Research*, **45**, 4, 661–84.

41 HEWISON, J. and TIZARD, J. (1980) 'Parental involvement and reading attainment.' *British Journal of Educational Psychology*, **50**, 209–15.

42 TIZARD, J., SCHOFIELD, W. N. and HEWISON, J. (1982) 'Collaboration between teachers in assisting children's reading.' *British Journal of Educational Psychology*, **52**, 1–15.

4.2 Intelligence tests and educational reform in England and Wales in the 1940s

Deborah Thom

Intelligence testing during the 1930s had been used increasingly in the educational selection process for secondary education, but its use was still seen as experimental. By the 1940s, however, intelligence testing was used in practically all English schools. It has often been argued that this transition into the commonplace reflected the changes in education brought about by the 1944 Education Act. I want to assess the relative influence of local and central government, educational psychologists and political theorists on these developments. I hope to demonstrate that there was in fact little change involved and that it is the change in social policy represented by the notion of equality of opportunity that is most responsible for making intelligence tests an issue of public debate and their use acceptable in practice. The argument is in many ways a general one about the relationship between science and society – and intelligence testing in particular demonstrates how the two cannot be properly understood unless they are seen in relation to one another.

1918–1938[1]

By 1938 two crucial principles of educational provision after 1944 were already accepted in theory and widely adopted in practice. These were that the age of 11 marked the end of the first phase of children's lives and that, after that age, they should go into differentiated schools. The Education Act of 1902 had given County Councils powers to create and maintain secondary schools. As these schools expanded, the practical advantage of a uniform age of entry and one which gave even those who left at the earliest possible age (14) a school life of reasonable length became plain; and already by 1920 a number of authorities had adopted 11 as this age. A Departmental Committee of the Board of Education (which ran state education until it became a Ministry in 1944) reported in 1921, 'it has been put to us that the age of eleven does mark a definite stage in the development of most children'. When, in 1926, the psychologist Cyril Burt made the same point he was providing useful substantiation for existing administrative practices, not creating them.

In 1926 the second principle was added to the first. Both were articulated in the Board of Education's Consultative Committee's report *The Education of the Adolescent* (usually known as the Hadow Report, after its

Source: specially written for this volume.

chairman, Sir Henry Hadow). At the end of their primary school careers, i.e. at 11, children were to be classified by aptitude, some to proceed to 'secondary grammar' schools, others to 'secondary modern' schools and others to remain in senior classes attached to the primary (elementary) schools. The report summed up: 'all go forward, though along different paths. Selection by differentiation takes the place of selection by elimination.' By 1938 the Spens Committee, which had been sitting since 1933, refined the system further by a report suggesting that senior classes should be abolished so that at 11 all children could be differentiated into grammar, modern and technical schools.[2]

The Reports also recommended an examination as the mechanism for selection by differentiation. An examination was already being used to select children for free or special (means-tested) places in secondary schools – the special places examination in which children demonstrated 'ability to profit' from secondary education. Hadow, Spens and His Majesty's Inspectors of Schools offered clear guidance on the best type of examination: papers in English and Arithmetic and a properly standardized group intelligence test. Local Education Authorities (LEAs) were responsible for the examination in their area and many still clung to methods which owed more to patronage than to notions of equity.

The adoption of measures of intelligence as part of selection procedure was piecemeal and very dependent on local conditions. Many LEAs were already clients of the Edinburgh-based Moray House testing service under the direction of Professor Godfrey Thomson. Some authorities used an intelligence test as an independent arbiter over their own tests of attainment and then moved to a package of standardized tests produced and marked at Moray House. The justification was usually on the grounds that this was the best way to demonstrate 'ability to profit' since the intelligence test added an element in the selection procedure which compensated for difference in environment – both home and school – by providing a measure of innate ability, thus showing differences in heredity. Such a justification was loosely translated to mean that intelligence was 'fixed', though psychologists differed in their views about this.

Equality of opportunity

The notion of equality of opportunity as the desirable basis of improvement in English education took two forms. The first was that of the Labour Party, most sociologists and the members of the Conservative Party associated with reform organizations like PEP (Political and Economic Planning). In part, this was a simple idea of social justice but it was also highly meritocratic. The demand to alter the class-based access to secondary education and its economic rewards was based on the assumption that many intelligent working class children were excluded from secondary schools by poverty. R. H. Tawney formulated this idea of equality of opportunity clearly in 1938:

Unless a society is to utilise only a fraction of the intelligence at its disposal it must obviously in one way or another make sufficient provision for vertical mobility to ensure that capacity passes, unimpeded by vulgar irrelevancies of class or income to the type of education fitted to develop it.

He spoke of the great waste of 'exceptional talent, which is sterilized for want of educational opportunities'.[3] This sense of wastage, of intelligence going unused, prompted many to demand improvements in the education system.

Grace Leybourne and Kenneth White surveyed London school children and published the results in *Education and the Birth-Rate* in 1940.[4] They showed that the majority of children with high scores in intelligence tests who were not getting a secondary education were those from the working class. These findings condemned both the existing secondary education provision and plans for reform that ignored this wastage of talent. Merit should be the measure of educability at secondary level, not income – and merit was seen as equivalent to ability shown by intelligence tests.

Eugenics

Pressure from eugenists provided the other major impetus towards acceptance of the notion of equality of opportunity. Eugenics had provided the theoretical rationale for a fixed endowment of intelligence but it now attempted to provide a rationale for change in social policy too. In 1937 R. B. Cattell published *The Fight for our National Intelligence*, in which he correlated fertility and intelligence levels, and showed that the least intelligent children came from the largest families, the most intelligent from the smallest. He assumed a direct link between the intelligence of children and parents and predicted a decline of three points in the national level of intelligence in the space of a generation. He predicted that in fifty years those with an intelligence quotient below 70 points, the so-called mental defectives, would constitute a quarter of the population. The book was written in a florid, hyperbolic style.

In the path of progress of England and most civilised nations stands a threat, challenging to all who have the intelligence to perceive it.

For it is not a menace apparent to all eyes, as are the perils of economic collapse, or cultural or religious confusion, nor is it as easily dramatised as political reaction or war. Yet it strikes insidiously at the very roots of national life and brings all these evils and many more in train.[5]

The book was extreme but the issue it dealt with was central to the war-time debate over social reform and the development of British psychology.

Many leading psychologists were members of the Eugenics Society in the 1940s – Godfrey Thomson, Cyril Burt, R. B. Cattell, Philip Vernon and Hans Eysenck. They accepted the central idea of eugenics, that breeding was the shaping force of the individual's character. Intelligence was a central part of that character and, perhaps more importantly, measurable. Their concern led them to ask how they could maximize intelligence in society, as well as encouraging it to flourish in the individuals who possessed it. The answer in both cases was to improve the environment.

The secretary of the Eugenics Society, Dr C. P. Blacker, summarized the eugenists' conclusions in this way.

It would be eugenically more desirable, as well as socially more practicable to aim at raising the fertility of the people in *all groups* who in intelligence are above the mean for the entire population than to try to raise the collective fertility of the upper (and on the whole more intelligent) groups at the expense of those lower and less intelligent. In other words the discrimination should be within people *within each group* rather than between groups as a whole.[6]

Concern for the improvement of the intelligence level of British society, as identified by tests, led to a commitment to abolish fees and extend secondary education.

The Beveridge report of 1942, the Royal Commission on Population in 1949, and the final acceptance of Eleanor Rathbone's long fight for family allowances reflect the same concerns. Education was a crucial part of the changes regarded as necessary to improve society. Richard and Kathleen Titmuss' book, *Parents Revolt*, expressed the views of many when they pointed out that rational parents received neither reward nor support from British society for having children, and might well choose to limit their family to only one child, in order to give that child the best chance.[7]

War

Pressure to expand post-primary education had built up from these various concerns in the inter-war years. Spens had crystallized these demands and some LEAs had begun to make changes based on its recommendations, particularly in separating children at 11 and developing the 'Modern' school for children of 11–14 who did not go to secondary (grammar) school. Ten new modern schools were begun in 1938. War slowed down reform and re-organization in the short-term. The raising of the school leaving age was deferred, schools were appropriated for defence, and funding, which had begun to rise, fell back. The demand for reform could not remain unheeded, however, and in 1940, Herwald Ramsbotham, President of the Board of Education, formally asked his chief officials to prepare a programme of Reconstruction. They complied with alacrity and in many ways their intentions were to pre-empt. R. S. Wood argued:

The war is moving us more and more in the direction of Labour's ideas and 'ideals' . . . We need to be adventurous so that our advice is not discounted and the job of Reconstruction given elsewhere . . .[8]

It took four years, much public discussion and the process of legislation through Parliament, for their deliberations to produce a final result. The group of civil servants within the Board who wanted as little change as possible won their case, with the result that the new secondary education that was to be made available to all was organized on the same lines as the old with roughly the same proportion of children going on to grammar schools. Sir Maurice Holmes, Permanent Under-Secretary at the Board and later the Ministry, expressed the intention in the dominant, meritocratic terms.

I take it that it was the clear intention of Parliament (certainly it's in line with my own inclination) that the net of secondary education should be cast more widely into the lower income scales; that class-distinction should be tempered and blurred throughout the educational field, and that merit – whatever that may be – should be the test, rather than money or social background, of a person's fitness to receive an expensive secondary education. It was not the intention, of course, that all of this should come to pass at one stroke, nor is it clear that the goal is further 'democratisation' (is there a decent word for this?); whether the goal is a worthy one or not – this is of course arguable – we are bound to proceed towards it.[9]

This description of gradual change within an existing system is much more appropriate than the talk and writings of the period which refer to a revolution in the educational system. R. A. Butler claimed he hoped to make Britain 'educationally not two nations, but one'.[10] But, as A. J. P. Taylor recorded in his history of the period, in fact the reform simply refined the existing class distinction between those who had a grammar school education and those who did not.[11]

Reformers had agreed that equality of opportunity and free secondary education for all meant, if nothing else, easier access to grammar schools on intellectual not social grounds. Although no new types of school were to be built, nor even new curricula used in existing schools, the intention was that all children should be assessed and fairly allocated in the appropriate type of secondary education. Nearly all agreed on one theme, the abolition of the old special places examination. R. H. Tawney described it as an 'abomination' and as a 'barbarity'.[12] *The Times Educational Supplement* deplored them:

Some day our successors may come to marvel at the degree of assurance which leads us to think that ability to profit can be predicted thus.[13]

These comments and those from other commentators show how little even those closely concerned with education recognized that the existing special places examination already included intelligence tests in many areas. The White Paper on *Educational Reconstruction* of 1943 recommended that the examination be replaced by school records, supplemented if necessary by intelligence tests. The Act included no such recommendation, though it did use the formula 'appropriate to age, ability and aptitude'. It was left to the LEAs to decide what that meant, although it is clear from later discussions that the answer of the previous twenty years was what was envisaged – separation at 11 for age, ability as a ranking device, aptitude to allow for technical education. This suited the LEAs, who had lost some powers under the Act and it suited the government who believed that assessment of ability was possible using existing procedures.

At the same time as the 1944 Act was being drafted and discussed, both inside and outside Parliament, local authorities were making changes in their special places examinations. Between 1940 and 1944, 28 LEAs changed their examinations – most by adding an intelligence test to the tests in English and Arithmetic. More changed their procedures in the same way between 1944 and 1947, the year in which development plans for the future of education in each LEA had finally to be sent to the Ministry. From this it would seem that the Act did not initiate the increased use of intelligence tests but was merely a response to the same forces for social change. What, and who, was responsible for the shift in public opinion which made intelligence tests so much more rapidly acceptable?

Central government

Central government intervention had an effect on local authority activity, but it did not initiate it. The Board of Education was responsible for overseeing the LEAs administration of the special places scheme before 1944. War made this task more difficult and also made the procedures by which children were examined more subject to public concern and scrutiny. Evacuation exposed the differences in level of provision and in difficulty of examinations; rising incomes meant that many parents would pay fees for special places for the first time; bombing put great strain on local administration. The role of the Board's officials was consistently one which combined concern for economy with an attempt to keep local authorities moving in step.

The most influential group of civil servants as far as the promotion of selection was concerned were the Inspectorate. But their role appears to be limited. They had taken an informed interest in testing for some time but had to be reminded in a memorandum of December 1942 not to argue too strongly for tests:

These examinations are to be regarded as a domestic affair of the Local Education Authorities for the conduct of which no responsibility must rest upon Inspectors . . .

If an Inspector was consulted, the memorandum continued,

. . . on the value of intelligence tests of the reliability of certain statistical devices used in these examinations, there is no reason why he should not give his views, but he will no doubt make it clear how far the views are personal to himself.[14]

The memorandum went on to explain that it was the Inspector's duty to make representations about the conduct of the examination 'where that leaves something to be desired'.

An example of the Inspectorate's indirect influence occurred in the Isle of Ely. In 1938, the Isle of Ely's Education Committee's own Examinations Board recommended dropping dictation from the examination, but the Education Committee persisted in keeping it. By 1941 the arguments of some of the committee's own members and the increasingly acerbic comments of the Inspectorate prevailed; the committee abandoned dictation and accepted a new structure in which a minimum standard of English and Arithmetic qualified a child to go on to an intelligence test to measure capacity.[15]

Ely shows the limits of central government's power, their belief in the efficacy of standardized tests having less influence on the outcome than did the efforts of local teachers on the Examination Board. Inspectors could provide arguments but they could not coerce.

The power to adopt tests, or drop them, to use attainment tests or intelligence tests, remained firmly with the local authority and the pressures on LEAs were diverse.

Psychologists

Intelligence tests had been developed by psychologists and the techniques of factor analysis (used to justify a single dimension of ability) and test standardization were well refined by the 1940s. Did the claims of psychologists for their technique – either for its accuracy or for its freedom from social determinants – affect public reception of the use of tests in selection? Psychologists promoted their tests as a fairer means of selection, but the increase in test use lay in the desire in the 1940s for such fairness.

The relationship between what was measured by intelligence tests and secondary school performance had been assumed by those who wrote the first tests in the 1920s. Godfrey Thomson, writer on factor analysis and creator of the first production unit for mass-produced tests saw his mission in life as giving bright but disadvantaged children access to the education their abilities deserved. The clientele for his Moray House tests grew slowly through the inter-war years, and slightly faster through the early 1940s.[16] In 1939 Thomson published the *Factorial Analysis of Human Ability* which provided a lucid and accessible account of the technique on which tests were based. The Scottish Council for Research in Education, of which Thomson was a leading member, commissioned an investigation by W. McClelland into the correlation between various methods of selection and success in secondary education, published as *Selection for Secondary Education* in 1942.[17] The book showed very clearly that the best correlation with secondary school success (measured by the leaving examination) was that provided by a battery of tests, English, Arithmetic and Intelligence. The best single device was a teacher's record. The test battery provided a 'best' correlation of .8, which, as McClelland wrote, was better than if children had been placed by guesswork though not much better. As Charlotte Fleming wrote in 1949, for the National Union of Teachers survey on tests:

> Such results therefore may fairly be interpreted as indicating the uncertainty of any prediction based on the result of entrance examinations or tests, however carefully they have been conducted.[18]

These psychologists were diffident about making great claims for their techniques, only arguing that such assessments reduced unfairness or chance, not that they eliminated them.

National Foundation for Educational Research

It has been argued that the first English producer of group tests on a large scale, the National Foundation for Educational Research (NFER), stimulated the demand for tests. However the NFER was set up in 1943 and only became independent in 1947. Its foundation demonstrates the demand for tests from local authorities but does not suggest that it acted as a stimulus to testing. It was originally mainly dependent on funds from LEAs and its treasurer was W. P. Alexander, who was secretary of the Association of Education Committees, the LEAs collective voice.[19] In the 1940s the NFER began the process of assessing selection procedures before it began to produce its own tests. The tests which it did produce were modelled on those of Moray House and the test unit was advised by two of the workers from Moray House so that the first tests differed little in form from those produced by the rival testing organization.[20]

Cyril Burt

One psychologist who is generally credited with encouraging the spread of testing is Cyril Burt. However, he could not influence events directly in war-time as he no longer worked for the London County Council (LCC) and had few contacts either in the LEAs or in the Board of Education. Evans and Waites argue in *IQ and Mental Testing* that Burt was influential as a theorist. They see his 1943 article, 'Ability and income' (which is the first of his pieces generally acknowledged to be fraudulent) as his attempt to re-establish the pre-war psychometric consensus in the face of egalitarian reform.[21] I see the piece as a reflection of Burt's exclusion from the new psychometric consensus which was a factor encouraging reform. The contrast with Godfrey Thomson is illuminating. Both men were eugenists, both gave Galton Lectures on the correlation between intelligence and heredity, devised intelligence tests and shared a concern about 'declining national intelligence' (both submitted memoranda to the Royal Commission on Population on the subject). But Thomson's eugenics rested on a belief that intelligence was independent of cultural determinants, so that improved education and more equality of opportunity would give innate intelligence a chance to flourish without inhibition. Burt saw the existing inhibitions of class and income as part of the individual's innate endowment and argued for a return to an older eugenics. It was an argument he lost. The article was published in the *British Journal of Educational Psychology* and although it must have reached a wide professional audience it was little cited. Burt got very little support from the audience when he debated the piece at an educational conference in 1946 with Alexander and Professor C. W. Valentine of Birmingham.[22]

The contribution of psychologists to a popular acceptance of tests was general and diffuse. The debate about national levels of intelligence helped to create an impression of children's intelligence as a national resource. The professional press added to this the notion that any social survey of children should include a description of their intelligence. The next step was to see tests of intelligence as the best tool to achieve equality of opportunity. Eugenist social reformers and sociologists had already made this claim but it was in war-time that it appears to have been most widely accepted. The archives of the Mass Observation social survey organization demonstrate this clearly. In 1942 71% of Mass-Observers said that the reform they most wanted in education was 'equality of opportunity'. Many used the slogan 'the sons of duke and dustman should sit side by side'. Many, particularly teachers, suggested, unprompted, that intelligence tests provided the best way of overcoming class differences in access to schooling and therefore success in attainment tests. The replies also show much evidence of popular eugenics with talk of 'a noble stock' and a 'fine race'. A few suggest the 'regulation of breeding' to eliminate the unfit, but far more common is the notion of children as a natural resource going untapped.[23]

Such popular support was essential if any change was to be made in selection procedures – and it was evident in some of the local discussion about education reform. Another factor which made tests acceptable was their use in war-time forces' selection which helped to familiarize parents with testing as a comparatively benign activity.[24] A third war-time factor was the effect of measures such as rationing in creating a spirit of equality. General factors of that sort, as well as the special interests of education professionals, need to be taken into account in any explanation of why a technique which had been available for years and was already proven in use should have broken through to general acceptance.

The diversity of local change

Several local authorities, London in particular, anticipated reform. The LCC Education Officer, E. G. Savage, had been very excited by the comprehensive approach of the American High Schools. London had an experienced education committee, mostly with very long service; it had a multiplicity of very old schools and, following the blitz, of empty sites, and it had an interested and critical electorate. The London Plan assumed free secondary education and proposed a multilateral school system. In the 1930s London had used an attainment test and it adopted intelligence tests briefly in the 1940s because of the differences in schooling between evacuees, those who had been bombed and those who had lost schooling. This was a stop-gap, as the intention was to absorb intelligence testing into the back-up machinery for school records. When free secondary education for all was introduced, London was able to continue on exactly the same lines as before until 1948.[25] Middlesex, too, saw the 1944 Act as a means of extending existing improvements and introducing a common secondary school – the multi-lateral. Here intelligence tests had been in use for some time as part of a test battery and the same tests were used to 'allocate' to streams after 1944 as had been used to select for Grammar schools before.[26]

Other LEAs took major initiatives in this period. Brighton education committee wrote a novel and systematic account of the ways in which secondary education could be re-organized to provide equality of opportunity and sent it to all LEAs. They had used Moray House tests on the advice of W. P. Alexander and continued to do so in the 1940s. Their creative thought about the educational future was suppressed by their own council who argued that a sub-committee should not act independently, and little practical change ensued.[27] Anglesey were able to argue that in their case geography, population and buildings all pointed to one solution to the extension of the secondary population – the comprehensive school – and won their case, on pragmatic grounds.[28]

Much of the innovation in testing derived from the same sort of pragmatic adaptation to circumstance. Kent developed the local record card during the late 1930s and it became so sophisticated that a large booklet was written about how to maintain it and the NFER modelled their own best-selling record card on it. This arose because tests on their own were already seen as inadequate in Kent, where they had been in use for some time.[29] Hertfordshire used tests in 1942 because it 'borrowed' them from neighbouring Essex, having neither time, staff nor money to examine children in the way they had before.[30] Economy was a factor in the adoption of standardized tests since they cost 7½d per child which was usually cheaper than an examiner's fee of £100, or the employment of a member of staff with a responsibility for examining.

If economy had been the only consideration it seems likely that intelligence tests would have sufficed, but this step was neither politically expedient nor intellectually acceptable. One major interest group was, by and large, opposed to placing great reliance on tests of intelligence alone – the teachers. Some found the backwash effect of attainment tests desirable – that is secondary teachers wished to rely on the 11+ as a qualifying test, ensuring basic competence; primary teachers sometimes welcomed the disciplinary effects of the scholarship ahead, or the demonstration the results gave of their abilities as teachers. The NUT had recorded in 1942 that they were worried that intelligence tests would be used to put all the brightest children in one sort of school – a fear that in general was fully justified.[31] Teachers in the West Riding of Yorkshire were so concerned about the effects of testing that they conducted their own survey and concluded that school records, partly based on intelligence tests, should be used for allocation. The education officer of the West Riding, Alec Clegg, and the chairman of the Education Committee, Walter Hyman, doubted the Ministry of Education's belief that tests could identify technical ability at 11 so they wrote to three psychologists, Sir Fred Clarke, Charlotte Fleming and Godfrey Thomson, to enquire and received the unanimous reply that it could not. As a result they developed their own scheme for the grading of school reports to allow for differences between schools.[32]

Authority after authority took the notion of equality of opportunity to mean the chance of all 11-year-olds to take the same examination for allocation to different types of schooling as a few had taken for selection for grammar schools. The addition of an intelligence test was a refinement of an existing procedure – an addition to tests of attainment with little distinction between them. Since these tests were often supplied, marked and validated by the same body, it is not surprising that junior schools should have begun early on to teach impartially for all three. The first mention of coaching in the classroom – so far as I know – was in 1948, four years before the controversy on the subject in the educational press, and of the possibility of coaching being effective (as opposed to the certainty that it was), was in 1943. The gap between a theory of unalterable, culture-free ability and the practice of measuring it was perceived long before it became a major political issue in 1952. It is because the notion of intelligence as a single, demonstrable, hierarchical measure *was* politically acceptable between the years 1934 and 1952 that intelligence tests could be so easily added to the selection system. It was the doubts about that selection system which led to the technique that served it being called into question. And those doubts appear to have been raised by both affluence and the growth in the child population.

The issue then is a complex one. By 1938, educational reform had long been demanded and intelligence tests had been in use for some time. A combination of pressures – eugenists' conversion to social engineering, the lifting of restraint on expenditure and a widespread belief that equality of opportunity was necessary – led to increased demand for change in the secondary system. Psychologists, civil servants and some education officers could argue from experience, validated sociologically, that tests of intelligence diminished cultural effects, particularly schooling, and therefore increased equality of opportunity. War accentuated the urgency for reform, particularly as the notion grew that it was a democratic war leading to a necessary reconstruction of British society. The 1944 Education Act provided legislative backing for a change already underway, the separation of children at 11 into different types of schools. By making secondary education free, government made LEAs even more concerned to demonstrate evenhandedness, and tests were seen as providing that equity. The result was a refined selection process not a new allocation system. Intelligence tests were not used as a check on attainment tests but simply added on to them. The multiplicity of local decisions involved in test use reflects the fact that the LEAs kept control of school organization and that testing was subsidiary to secondary re-organization. The technique and the technicians did not sweep all before them. Intelligence testing remained a tool in the hands of local government. To test or not to test was in the widest sense always a political issue.

Acknowledgments and references

I would like to thank Gillian Sutherland, Ian Patterson and Kum-Kum Bhavnani for much valuable discussion on this piece. The work for this was based on the SSRC research project 'Mental Testing and Education in England and Wales, 1940–1970' based at the Department of Education, Cambridge.

1 This section is derived directly from SUTHERLAND, GILLIAN (1984) *Ability, Merit and Measurement: mental testing and English education 1880–1940*. Oxford: Oxford University Press.
   I am very grateful to Dr Sutherland for permission to abstract her detailed discussion so briefly.
2 Report of the Consultative Committee to the Board of Education (1926) *The Education of the Adolescent* (Hadow Report). London: HM Stationery Office.
   Report of the Consultative Committee to the Board of Education (1938) *Secondary Education* (Spens Report). London: HM Stationery Office.
3 TAWNEY, R. H. (1938) *Some Thoughts on the Economics of Public Education* (p. 9). Oxford: Oxford University Press.
4 LEYBOURNE, G. and WHITE, K. (1940) *Education and the Birth-rate*. London: Cape.
5 CATTELL, R. B. (1937) *The Fight for our National Intelligence* (pp. 1–2). London: P. S. King.
6 BLACKER, C. P. (1942) *Eugenics Review*, 33, April (emphasis original).
7 TITMUSS, R. and K. (1942) *Parents Revolt*. London: Secker and Warburg.
8 Cited by GOSDEN, P. H. J. H. (1976) *Education in the Second World War* (p. 248). London: Methuen.
9 ED-53, Sir Maurice Holmes, Memorandum on the Bedfordshire Direct Grant Schools, 9 June 1945.
10 BUTLER, R. A. (1971) *The Art of the Possible* (p. 96). London: Hamish Hamilton.
11 TAYLOR, A. J. P. (1965) *English History 1914–1945* (p. 568). Oxford: Oxford University Press.
12 In *Manchester Guardian*, 7 April 1943, 17 July 1943 (unsigned but attributed to Tawney by Jay Winter in his biography of R. H. Tawney).
13 16 January 1940, p. 5.
14 ED-135, NS 113. 'The special place examination', 2 December 1943.

15 ED-110, 18. The Isle of Ely.
16 Godfrey Thomson Collection, University of Edinburgh. I am very grateful to the Godfrey Thomson Unit for access to this material and for much help with other records from the testing unit.
17 MCCLELLAND, W. (1942) *Selection for Secondary Education* (Scottish Council for Research in Education Publication 19). London: University of London Press Ltd.
18 FLEMING, C. (1949) *Transfer from Primary to Secondary Schools*, Appendix III (p. 150). London: Evans.
19 YATES, A. (1971) *The First Twenty-five Years* (p. 6). Slough: NFER.
20 Interview with W. G. Emmett, May 1983.
21 BURT, C. (1943) 'Ability and income.' *British Journal of Educational Psychology*, **13**, 83–98.
   EVANS, B. and WAITES, B. (1981) *IQ and Mental Testing* (p. 101). London: Macmillan.
22 *Education*, September 1946.
23 Mass Observation archive, University of Sussex, File reports A1269. Panel reports (which are the individual replies on which the file report was made) DR44.
24 VERNON, P. E. and PARRY, J. B. (1949) *Personnel Selection in the British Forces*. London: University of London Press Ltd.
25 SIMON, B. (1974) *The Politics of Educational Reform, 1920–1940* (p. 330). London: Lawrence and Wishart.
26 There are also very full discussions of the London Plan in the educational press in 1944.
   From 1940–2 Middlesex had a nomination system because of evacuation and bombing – i.e. no examination except for disputed cases (*The Times Educational Supplement*, 27 January 1940). In 1943 a quota system was used by which schools listed candidates and their lists were ranked by the school's performance in a test (*Education*, 17 December 1943).
27 *The Times Educational Supplement*, 13 December 1941.
   Interview with Lord Alexander, 2 February 1983.
   Education, 8 January 1943.
28 SIMON, B. (1978) *Intelligence, Psychology and Education* (p. 97). London: Lawrence and Wishart.
   DAVIS, R. (1967) *The Grammar School* (p. 73). Harmondsworth: Penguin Books. The author points out that these schools did their own testing on entry for streaming.
29 Godfrey Thomson Collection, 1954, correspondence on open testing.
30 *Education*, 20 March 1947.
31 NUT Conference Report, 1942.
32 *British Journal of Educational Psychology*, November 1941, pp. 223–6. *The Times Educational Supplement*, 10 May 1941, p. 214.
   GOSDEN, P. H. J. H. and SHARP, P. R. (1978) *The Development of an Education Service* (p. 166). Oxford: Martin Robertson.

4.3 The learning-disabilities test battery: empirical and social issues

Gerald S. Coles

Efforts to solve the problems of learning disabilities have experienced a period of growth unparalleled by almost any other specialized field. [. . .] As the field has grown, however, so too has criticism of it. [. . .] One reassessment that must be made concerns the special knowledge the field claims to possess. The special knowledge of learning-disabilities specialists, and, indeed, the special knowledge on which the entire field rests, is the ability to diagnose the presence of learning disabilities in children and prescribe effective programs of treatment. Using a medical model and equipped with their own black bag of diagnostic instruments, the learning-disabilities specialists, sometimes together with other specialists, examine child patients. If they think there are learning disabilities, they write authoritative diagnoses stating that, based on the results of certain tests, it has been determined that the children have neurological problems that impede learning. Parents and teachers will be likely to accept these findings as true. Because the children have been given a set of seemingly scientific and valid tests, the conclusions must also be valid. The children, now proclaimed to be learning disabled, begin the remedial path toward cognitive competence.

Although many professionals in the field believe that they possess special knowledge, much of the current debate revolves around the basic question of whether or not the field can back up its claims to knowledge with valid empirical evidence. The answer rests in large part on the nature of the learning-disabilities test battery – the set of tests used to determine the quantity and quality of learning disabilities in children. Certainly subjective clinical experience and preclinical research on cognitive functioning are important diagnostic tools, but the test battery itself, with its objective, formally validated instruments, is the core of the learning-disabilities diagnosis. The battery provides credibility to the conclusions and recommendations of the learning-disabilities professional.

The central tests in a learning-disabilities battery evaluate perception, language, intelligence, and neurological function. Although the tests are often categorized as dealing with separate areas, they often overlap because they are all designed to fit a single model of neurological impairment based upon the accepted definition of learning disabilities first formulated by the National Advisory Committee on Handicapped Children in 1968:

Source: *Harvard Educational Review* (1978), **48**, 313–40.

Children with special learning disabilities exhibit a disorder in one or more of the basic psychological processes involved in understanding or using spoken or written languages. These may be manifested in disorders of listening, thinking, talking, reading, writing, spelling, or arithmetic. They include conditions which have been referred to as perceptual handicaps, brain injury, minimal brain dysfunction, dyslexia, developmental aphasia, etc. They do not include learning problems which are due primarily to visual, hearing, or motor handicaps, to mental retardation, emotional disturbance, or to environmental disadvantage (page 4).

It is apparent that this definition has its limitations. What a learning disability is remains extraordinarily vague; it is primarily a definition by exclusion. The specific conditions mentioned, such as dyslexia, are no more precisely defined than the encompassing term 'learning disabilities', and by excluding environmental disadvantage, it limits attention to middle- and upper-class children. Nonetheless, what remains essential to the definition, and to this discussion as well, is that a learning disability is defined in terms of an organic and neurological dysfunction of the cerebral processes. The purpose of a learning-disabilities test battery is to determine whether or not a minimal neurological dysfunction is impeding the child's ability to learn under otherwise normal conditions.

Although a standard learning-disabilities battery does not exist, the guidelines in handbooks and texts for setting up a battery are all similar, and the inclusion of certain tests is fairly standard. An individual learning-disabilities battery will, of course, vary according to the problems a child is suspected of having, an examiner's preference for particular tests, and the resources of an agency. Nonetheless, it is possible to describe a representative battery.

[EDITOR'S NOTE
The most common components of the learning disabilities battery in the USA are a range of perceptual tests, the intelligence tests, a neurological examination, and an electroencephalogram (EEG). In the full version of Cole's paper, he examines in detail the evidence of all of these and concludes that there are serious problems in the way of accepting them as valid means for identifying children with learning disabilities. Here we include his analysis of two of the commonest perceptual tests, the use of intelligence tests, and neurological examinations.]

The learning-disabilities battery

[. . .]
Validation studies testing the presence of learning disabilities frequently use retarded readers as a means of identifying children who are learning disabled. (In this paper, 'retarded readers' refers to normally intelligent

children reading below grade level, not to mentally retarded readers.) Using this approach investigators assume that, although retarded reading can have many causes, if environmental deprivation is excluded, a significantly large group have problems attributable to faulty neurological processing – they are learning disabled. Consequently, it is assumed that retarded readers, because they are certain to include some neurologically impaired children among them, will perform differently on learning-disabilities tests. Clearly, this assumption is not necessarily valid, but it was thought to be necessary to avoid a logical dilemma in trying to identify subjects as 'learning disabled'. The identification could be made either through an exclusionary process, that is, by excluding exogenous, sensory, and mental-retardation factors that are not regarded as causing learning disabilities, or through learning-disabilities tests. Both methods for identification are logically faulty: the exclusionary because it does not positively identify a child as learning disabled; the testing because positive classification is based on the learning-disabilities tests, which themselves are under investigation.

While most people understand that retarded readers are not necessarily learning disabled, they sometimes overlook the converse – that learning-disabled children are not necessarily retarded readers. An individual might be learning disabled and still have adequate reading skills; his problems can lie in other areas such as speaking or writing. Despite this, the overwhelming number of children identified as learning disabled in either schools or clinics are poor readers; they may or may not have other language difficulties. For this reason, most studies dealing with children who have been identified as learning disabled have used reading level as the criterion by which to distinguish the learning disabled from the non-learning-disabled.

Perceptual tests

The Illinois Test of Psycholinguistic Abilities (ITPA) (Kirk, McCarthy and Kirk, 1968) purports to measure those input, processing, and output abilities that underlie language development; it is perhaps the most frequently used learning-disabilities test. The research on the relationship between the ITPA and academic achievement has been reviewed by Newcomer and Hammill (1975). They included studies of children classified as learning disabled or as retarded readers, and they tabulated correlation coefficients for each of the twelve ITPA subtests, the composite score, and the indices of reading, spelling, and arithmetic. A .35 median coefficient was accepted as indicating significant correlation. The following results were the same whether the subjects had been categorized as retarded readers or learning disabled.

With regard to the question of which tests could predict reading success, only three subtests – Auditory Association, Grammatic Closure, and Sound Blending – and the composite score reached the minimal level of predictive significance; and of these, only Grammatic Closure retained a significant relationship with reading in studies that were controlled for intelligence, a variable closely correlated with the ITPA. For spelling, only Grammatic Closure was significantly related under general conditions, but when intelligence was controlled for, even that coefficient did not reach a practical level of significance. Similar results were obtained for arithmetic, to which neither subtests nor composite score were related when mental ability was partialed out. In short, 'nine of the twelve ITPA subtests lack predictive validity for any aspect of academic achievement studied' (page 735), and two of the three remaining subtests, as well as the composite score, dropped below practical significance when intelligence was controlled.

The Grammatic Closure subtest remained significantly correlated with reading achievement when intelligence was controlled, but its psycholinguistic value was questioned by the reviewers. Although the test is a measure of standard English morphology, 'linguistic measures of this type are highly influenced by sociological factors such as race and social class, variables which have extensive influence on school performance' (p. 736).

A second part of Newcomer and Hammill's review examined the diagnostic validity of the ITPA by determining how well the test distinguished between good and poor readers. Research results were tabulated to see which subtests distinguished between good and poor readers in at least 50 per cent of the studies. When IQ was not controlled, only Grammatic Closure and Sound Blending met this criterion; when mental ability was controlled, neither the subtests nor the composite score reached the 50 per cent level for successful discrimination of good from poor readers.

[. . .]

The Frostig Developmental Test of Visual Perception (Frostig, Lefever and Whittlesey, 1964) is said to provide a perceptual quotient that indicates each child's level of visual-perception development. Research on the Frostig has not, however, supported the use of the test as a predictor of reading success. Only in studies of first-grade children can strong support for the test be found (Bryan, 1964; Frostig *et al.*, 1964; Gamsky and Lloyd, 1971). Although some studies give evidence of correlations between some of the subtests and academic achievement (Olson, 1966; Olson and Johnson, 1970), by and large, research has shown that beyond the first-grade level the Frostig rapidly decreases in usefulness and is not an accurate predictor of reading achievement (Ashlock, 1963; Black, 1976; Colarusso, Martin and Hartung, 1975; Frostig *et al.*, 1964; Liebert and Sherk, 1970; Nielsen and Ringe, 1969; Olson, 1966; Robinson and Schwartz, 1973; Rosen, 1966). The entire assumption of the test has been challenged by some researchers who now conclude that the Frostig measures intelligence and not different perceptual functions (Corah and Powell, 1963; Gamsky and Lloyd, 1971).

Another approach to assessing the Frostig test is through the Frostig Visual Perception Training Program used to remedy 'perceptual' problems diagnosed with the test. Comparisons of children trained with this program and other children working solely with regular reading materials show that the Frostig-trained children usually score higher on the Frostig perceptual test, but their scores are not significantly different from those of other children on standardized reading tests (Buckland and Balow, 1973; Cohn, 1966; Jacobs, 1968).

[. . .]

Intelligence tests

The very question of the relationship between intelligence and learning disabilities involves a contradiction. On the one hand, a child classified as learning-disabled is by definition of near-average, average, or above-average general intelligence and therefore does not have intelligence problems. A child with educational problems and lower-than-average intelligence is considered to be retarded rather than neurologically impaired. The IQ test is only included in a learning-disabilities battery to confirm that the child does not have general intelligence problems and therefore might be learning disabled.

On the other hand, there is evidence that while the IQ scores of children classified by schools as learning disabled are often not low enough to categorize them as retarded, the majority are below the mean of the general population (Hallahan and Kauffman, 1977). In a survey of over 3,000 learning-disabled children, Kirk and Elkins (1975) found that their median IQ was 93 and that 35 per cent of them had IQs below 90. In practice, many children appear to be diagnosed as learning disabled for reasons other than those in accord with the strict learning-disabilities definition.

In addition, the argument has been advanced that an IQ test can help to diagnose learning disabilities through evaluation of subtest scores and disparities. For example, in research on the Wechsler Intelligence Scale for Children (WISC) (Wechsler, 1949), a discrepancy of 15 points between verbal and performance scales was said to be indicative of minimal brain dysfunction (Black, 1974; Holroyd and Wright, 1965). The relevance of this conclusion to learning disabilities is not apparent. In Black's study, for example, even though the children with a discrepancy of 15 points or greater did show a greater incidence of neurological abnormalities, no significant differences in reading, spelling, or arithmetic achievement were discerned between these children and those without a discrepancy. In a later study Black (1976) found that the percentage of children with minimal brain dysfunction having a 15-point verbal-performance discrepancy was consistent with normal probabilities for the chronological age of the subjects. Other studies have also found no significant differences in verbal-performance scales between learning-disabled and normal children (Black, 1973; Kallos, Grabow and Guarino, 1961; Rudel and Denckla, 1976).

[...]

Neurological tests

When an evaluation of a child suspected of being learning disabled proceeds from the learning-disabilities specialist to the neurologist – the ultimate expert in assessing neurological dysfunction – two assessments are usually made: a neurological examination for 'soft signs' (sometimes called equivocal or borderline signs) and an electroencephalogram (EEG).

In contrast to an EEG, which may record abnormal brain-wave patterns, soft signs are physical characteristics and responses which are not clear indications of brain damage but are developmentally abnormal and are thought to constitute minimal brain dysfunction (MBD). Among these soft signs are fine and gross motor-co-ordination deficiences, mixed and confused laterality, strabismus, defective or slow speech development, short attention span, poor balance, gait disturbance, inadequate muscle tone, and general awkwardness.

Learning-disabilities studies investigating neurological dysfunction, as expressed in soft signs, have generally used two procedures: the first distinguishes between groups by the extent of their neurological dysfunction and then examines their respective differences on measures of academic achievement; the second classifies groups by academic achievement and then seeks evidence of differences in neurological impairment through a neurological assessment.

To date, research shows that neurologists are no closer than learning-disabilities specialists to establishing a relationship between minimal neurological dysfunction and learning problems. Claims of neurological deficiencies in academically retarded children have been reported, but the majority of this research has been marred by serious methodological shortcomings or by omission in the published studies.

[...]

A follow-up study (Dykman, Peters and Ackerman, 1973) of children already diagnosed as learning disabled [...] done approximately five years after the original diagnosis, found that at age 14 these children continued to have significantly lower academic achievement levels and significantly greater neurological impairment than had normal children identified in the original evaluation. One serious methodological problem in the study was that the investigators who performed the neurological examination of the children had apparently been told beforehand which of the children had been categorized as learning disabled. Other researchers have recognized this potentially biasing factor, and they have performed 'blind' examinations of subjects and controls.

Support for the relationship between neurological dysfunction and

learning disabilities was also reported by Cohn (1961). Having first distinguished between groups of children according to their academic achievement, he reported significantly more abnormal neurological signs among a group with reading and writing difficulties than among the normally achieving children. Unfortunately, the author did not indicate whether or not the neurological examinations were blindly administered.
[. . .]

A study by Boshes and Myklebust (1964) divided 85 academic under-achievers into three groups according to neurological status – negative, suspect, or positive. The neurologist who examined the children had no knowledge of the clinical history of the subjects. When the authors compared the results of the academic-achievement tests, they found no significant differences among the groups in silent or oral reading, syl-labification, auditory blending, or spelling.

Another study, also dividing groups of children according to the results of an examination for suspected neurological signs, used nine separate neurological and visual-motor status comparisons. Edwards, Alley and Snyder (1971) reported that they found no significant differences in academic achievement among the groups and concluded that the results provided 'no evidence that a diagnosis of minimal brain dysfunction based on the pediatric neurological evaluation . . . is a useful predictor of academic achievement' (page 20).

In a blind study by Myklebust (1973), in which children were first grouped according to a learning-disability formula based on intellectual and academic criteria, no differences in neurological status were found between learning-disabled and academically successful children when they were classified as either neurologically normal or abnormal by pediatric neurologists. Nor did any one of the 137 neurological signs used in the examination significantly distinguish between the groups. Only when the total number of signs was compared were the groups signifi-cantly different, with the learning-disabled group having the greater number. It is important to note, however, that a large number of soft signs were found in the control group as well: the totals were 528 and 475 respectively.
[. . .]

These studies are typical of investigations which have failed to find a significant relationship between neurological functioning and academic achievement. [. . .]

Evaluation of the learning-disabilities thesis

Taken as a whole, the tests used in a representative learning-disabilities battery fail to demonstrate that children categorized as learning disabled are neurologically impaired. Some research validating the intent of each test is available, but the predominant finding in the literature suggests that each test fails to correlate with a diagnosis of learning disabilities. The evidence from studies using formal neurological examinations of learning-disabled children is especially damaging to the neurological impairment explanation. Surely, if the neurological thesis were to find support anywhere, it would find it in the techniques and science available to neurologists. Unfortunately for those who have held this thesis, studies of borderline symptoms, soft signs, have uniformly failed to contribute to the diagnosis of academic underachievement.

One factor preventing these studies from reaching definitive conclusions is that the research contains numerous methodological deficiencies, some of which have already been noted. Because elaboration of these deficiencies would require another paper, I can mention only briefly a few serious examples, the most salient, perhaps, being the failure to identify personal characteristics essential to the definition of learning disabilities. More often than not, children with emotional problems were either not distinguished from those without, or they were distinguished only on subjective criteria, such as a teacher's assessment. Frequently children were classified as learning disabled solely because they were underachievers or were referred to clinics for sundry other reasons. Similarly, many of the investigations failed to account for, and partial out, additional variables such as intelligence, age, social class, and race.

[. . .]

Another methodological deficiency – and one which is extraordinary in view of the large number of studies that have been done – is that apparently no study examines the teaching and school environment of learning-disabled children to see how the quality of their education might have contributed to, if not actually created, the difficulties they encounter in acquiring basic skills. Despite the literature critical of teaching and its effect on children participating in learning-disabilities studies, the quality of the instruction these children receive is always assumed to be adequate – as well it must be if it is to accord with the definition of learning disabilities cited previously.

The evidence appears to point to the conclusion that the tests do not measure neurological dysfunctions in learning-disabled children, but that methodological inadequancies prevent us from drawing this conclusion with certainty. These same methodological problems do, however, provide support for the position that we do not know what these tests measure. Even if all of the tests were significantly correlated with academic achievement, we would still not have much evidence to demonstrate that the etiology of the test performance was neurological, emotional, pedagogical, developmental, or attributable to any number of other factors. Controlling for and identifying these factors is clearly a difficult undertaking, but this undertaking should be within the scope of our present investigatory skill. Unfortunately few of the studies reported here have acknowledged the complexity of their task, and fewer still have used procedures that adequately take it into account.

[. . .]

Given the lack of empirical support for these tests, whether used individually or collectively, we may well ask why these tests have been used to draw conclusions about children and to classify them. Although we have not discussed the chronological development of the research for these tests, it should be apparent by now that their validity has always been questionable. Yet, in spite of the speculative nature of these tests, learning-disabilities professionals have acted, not as if they had tests that required abundant field assessments before their value could be judged, but rather as if they had in their hands diagnostic instruments that could lay bare the cognitive processes of a child's mind. In books, manuals, and courses, these and similar tests have been presented as mature tools for a mature profession. The lack of scientific foundation for the learning-disabilities battery, in contrast to ubiquitous recommendations for its use, forces the conclusion that, by replacing science with assertion, analysis with alchemy, and modesty with hyperbole, the learning-disabilities battery appears to have sprung fully formed out of the heads of learning-disabilities professionals like Athena out of Zeus.

[. . .]

Without question, many youngsters have been diagnosed as learning disabled and have worked with clinicians and teachers who have demonstrably improved their academic abilities. But it is not evident that this improvement was the result of anything more than the proper application of the remedial techniques themselves and sympathetic treatment of the children and the specific symptoms they might have. These techniques have been and are now being used successfully with children in remedial clinics, regardless of the causes of their failure to learn. Within this process, it has yet to be demonstrated that certain remedial techniques work better for learning-disabled retarded readers than for non-learning-disabled retarded readers, or vice versa. The same may be said for published remedial materials. It might well be that the remedial techniques used for a specific academic problem actually treat a neurological dysfunction that is causing the problem and that the techniques are equally successful, whatever the cause, but this remains· a hypothesis. What is more certain is that the success of learning-disabilities specialists in remedying the problem results from their ability to use general remedial techniques and not from their special knowledge of neurological dysfunction.

Do problems of minimal neurological dysfunction exist which impede academic learning? At present, the evidence in support of the thesis is far from compelling. While it cannot be said that no evidence exists, the entire field of learning disabilities has an empirical foundation too frail for the ponderous structure that has been erected upon it. I would suggest that, while there appears to be evidence that, among some persons, a minimal neurological dysfunction does play a contributory role in impeding learning, that role is relatively minor and becomes influential only in combination with other factors. Before valid and useful diagnoses can be made we must discover what exactly constitutes a minimal neurological dysfunction. Furthermore, we have no evidence to substantiate the claim that neurological dysfunctions are a major factor in inhibiting academic achievement.

If we continue to use the term 'learning disability' at all, it should be restricted to its narrow neurological definition and not be made synonymous with educational deficiencies resulting from an entire spectrum of causes (Bannatyne, 1971).

Certainly the issue of etiology is important, for without an answer to the question of why some children fail to learn, remedial education will continue to be a bastion of liberal education ministering to generation after generation of poorly developed casualties. The evidence persists, however, that the predominant cause of educational underachievement, whether viewed historically (Cippolla, 1969), internationally (Carnoy, 1974; UNESCO, 1976), or nationally (Greer, 1973; Bowles and Gintis, 1976), is social class injustice, with such corollaries as racial and ethnic discrimination contributing heavily. Educators concerned with etiology might better turn their attention to these primary social factors which find expression in educational practice, family relations, and the child's sense of self, and which, if eliminated, would produce the most noticeable degree of educational improvement.

Social context of the learning-disabilities test battery

In the concluding portion of this paper I would like to make a few remarks about the learning-disabilities test battery within a broader context than we have considered thus far. [. . .]

The learning-disabilities battery has been developed partly in an attempt to provide a rational way of understanding children whose inability to learn appears otherwise inexplicable. These children do not remember words from one day to the next; they constantly reverse letters and words; after five minutes of work they are squirming and anxious to do something else. Nothing seems to help them, so they appear to many educators to have neurological problems of perception, memory, or motor control.

But these inexplicable problems and the genuinely useful remediation that learning-disabilities specialists perform still do not fully explain the emergence of the battery. Researchers as far back as Samuel Orton in the 1920s have been concerned with the issue of neurological impairment. We still have to explain why the learning-disabilities battery has been unleashed only in the past decade or so. Obviously, it was not because the field struck empirical gold.

The reason, I believe, lies to a great extent in our social system – a system now requiring vast structural changes to remedy its present state of instability. Unable to make these changes, and in an effort to make unassailable its deteriorating institutions, the system, in its own defense, has generated and nurtured the growth of such fields as learning disabilities – providing, in other words, biological explanations for problems that require social solutions.

As Allan Chase (1977) has documented, these biological explanations have been used to explain social maladies in times of social instability since the beginning of the nineteenth century. Beginning with Malthus and continuing with Galton, Spencer, Goddard, and others, biological analyses have been used to provide an ostensibly scientific explanation for social problems such as poverty and crime. But, in Chase's words, these have actually been pseudoscientific claims put forth with neither scientific knowledge to support them nor available research data to refute them. More than mere viewpoints in scientific debates, these explanations have served the ideological purpose of justifying social and economic inequities and of bolstering the malfunctioning social order. This 'biologizing' of social problems has posited organic causalities for poverty, aggression, and violence, as well as for educational underachievement (Anderson, 1972; Delgado, 1971; Jensen, 1969; Mark and Ervin, 1970; Wilson, 1975).

The ideological functions of particular biological explanations have been noted in a number of recent analyses. For example, [. . .] in an examination of IQ testing, Kamin (1974) discussed the political uses of the IQ test and concluded:

The IQ test in America, and the way in which we think about it, has been fostered by men committed to a particular social view. That view included the belief that those on the bottom are genetically inferior victims of their own immutable defects. The consequence has been that the IQ test has served as an instrument of oppression against the poor – dressed in the trappings of science, rather than politics. The message of science is heard respectfully, particularly when the tidings it carries are soothing to the public conscience. . . . The poor, the foreign-born, and racial minorities are shown to be stupid. They are shown to have been born that way. The underprivileged are today demonstrated to be ineducable, a message soothing to the public purse as to the public conscience (page 2).

[. . .]

Within this framework, we can begin to understand both the emergence and the major function of the concept of learning disabilities. By positing biological bases for learning problems, the responsibility for failure is taken from the schools, communities, and other institutions and is put squarely on the back, or rather within the head, of the child. Thus, the classification plays its political role, moving the focus away from the general educational process, away from the need to change institutions, away from the need to rectify social conditions affecting the child, and away from the need to appropriate more resources for social use toward the remedy of a purely medical problem. It is a classic instance of what Ryan (1972) has called 'blaming the victim'. That is, it is an explanation of a social problem that attributes its cause to the individual failings, shortcomings, or deficiences of the victims of the problem. Balow (1971) referred to this shifting of responsibility when, in a paper critical of giving neurological explanations for reading problems, he asked rhetorically:

If reading disability is at root a medical problem, why is it that the vast preponderance of serious cases come from those geographic areas where the home, community, and school environment are most hostile to academic learning? Why are up to 60 per cent of slum area children and only two percent of suburban children severe reading disability cases? (page 517)

Coupled with this biological emphasis, several additional influences have emerged that help to nurture the claims attributed to the learning-disabilities test battery. One influence is the pharmaceutical industry which, through heavy promotional work aimed at professionals from education, psychology, and medicine, has fostered the use of cerebral stimulants as a means of treating learning-disabled children (Schrag and Divoky, 1975). Precise marketing information on these drugs is difficult to obtain, but the figures on Ritalin, the major stimulant prescribed, suggest that their distribution and sales have been, and remain, substantial. [. . .]

Another influence supporting the test-battery claims – more psycho-social than economic, although for many clinicians it has economic advantages as well – is the prestige of the biomedical professions. As Friedson (1970) has observed, the characteristics that mark a 'profession' are its claims of 'knowledge of an especially esoteric, scientific, or abstract character' and of work that is 'extraordinarily complex and nonroutine, requiring for its adequate performance extensive training, great intelligence and skill, and highly complex judgment' (pages 106, 153–4). Of all professional groups, it is the medical profession which has the clearest claim to this kind of prestige and authority, particularly in its prerogative to diagnose, treat, and direct treatment. Thus, in a professional relationship where there is the opportunity to share assumptions about the biological nature of a 'disorder', the closer a profession comes to acquiring the terminology and characteristics of the medical profession, the more that profession can increase its prestige and 'its position in the class structure and in the market place' (page 153).

It is my firm impression that educators, consciously or not, have attempted to enhance their profession, which otherwise has only moderate social status. They have sought affiliation with the medical world not only because multidisciplinary work is valued but also because it provides them with an aura of greater knowledge, authority, and importance. And who can blame them? How mundane to tell someone you teach remedial reading. How awesome to announce that you do clinical work with minimally brain dysfunctional children, more dyslexic than dyscalculic, who are benefitting from methylphenidate. [. . .] Sharing the language of the physician signifies both affiliation with those in power and acknowledgment of the disparity in power – a disparity which always contains potential antagonism. In the case of learning-disabilities specialists, tensions appear to be commensurate with the controversy that exists within the specialty as a whole. I have known a number of learning-disabilities specialists and clinical staff who give little credence to neurological interpretations of academic underachievement, but who continue to diagnose children in those terms because they believe that their superiors expect this kind of diagnosis. To do otherwise would place the diagnostician's professional competence and standing in jeopardy. Others have reluctantly diagnosed children as neurologically impaired primarily because only with this diagnosis could children be placed in a Neurologically Impaired (NI) class that had a better curriculum than they could obtain in a regular classroom. Their view of the NI classroom, was not that it was particularly good at remedying problems of neurological impairment, but that it used a method of instruction beneficial to all kinds of underachievers.

There is little question that eventually the tests reviewed here will be discarded; the evidence against them is mounting. The central question is really whether recognition of the invalidity of these tests will result in abandonment of an untenable professional dogma, or whether it will merely result in the test battery being replaced by other equally questionable instruments. I have sketched the context of the test battery because I believe the answer lies in the political and social realm and not in the worth of other less well-known instruments that are standing in the wings; these tests, in any case, do not yet exist. The future of the learning-disabilities test battery will depend upon how we answer the following questions: How catastrophic then will it be for dependent industries, institutions, and professionals to acknowledge that, so far as we can tell, Johnny's neural connections are intact? If we do not 'blame the victim', where then does the blame lie?

References

ANDERSON, C. (1972) *Society Pays: The High Costs of Minimal Brain Damage in America.* New York: Walker.

ASHLOCK, P. A. (1963) *Visual Perception, of Children in the Primary Grades and its Relation to Reading Performance.* Unpublished doctoral dissertation, University of Texas.

BALOW, B. (1971) 'Perceptual-motor activities in the treatment of severe reading disability.' *Reading Teacher,* **24**, 513–25.

BANNATYNE, A. (1971) *Language, Reading and Learning Disabilities: Psychology, Neuropsychology, Diagnosis and Remediation.* Springfield, IL: Charles C. Thomas.

BLACK, F. W. (1973) 'Neurological dysfunction and reading disorders.' *Journal of Learning Disabilities,* **6**, 313–16.

BLACK, F. W. (1974) 'WISC verbal-performance discrepancies as indicators of neurological dysfunction in paediatric patients.' *Journal of Clinical Psychology,* **30**, 165–7.

BLACK, F. W. (1976) 'Cognitive, academic, and behavioral findings in children with suspected and documented neurological dysfunction.' *Journal of Learning Disabilities*, **9**, 182–7.

BOSHES, B. and MYKLEBUST, H. R. (1964) 'A neurological and behavioral study of children with learning disorders.' *Neurology*, **14**, 7–12.

BOWLES, S. and GINTIS, H. (1976) *Schooling in Capitalist America*. New York: Basic Books.

BRYAN, Q. R. (1964) 'Relative importance of intelligence and visual perception in predicting reading achievement.' *California Journal of Educational Research*, **15**, 44–8.

BUCKLAND, P. and BALOW, B. (1973) 'Effect of visual perception training on reading achievement.' *Exceptional Children*, **39**, 299–304.

CARNOY, M. (1974) *Education as Cultural Imperialism*. New York: McKay.

CHASE, A. (1977) *The Legacy of Malthus: The Social Costs of the New Scientific Racism*. New York: Knopf.

CIPPOLLA, C. M. (1969) *Literacy and Development in the West*. Baltimore, MD: Penguin Books.

COHN, R. (1961) 'Delayed acquisition of reading and writing abilities in children.' *Archives of Neurology*, **4**, 153–64.

COHN, R. I. (1966) 'Remedial training of first grade children with visual perception retardation.' *Educational Horizons*, **45**, 60–3.

COLARUSSO, R., MARTIN, H. and HARTUNG, J. (1975) 'Specific visual-perceptual skills as long-term predictors of academic success.' *Journal of Learning Disabilities*, **8**, 651–5.

CORAH, N. L. and POWELL, B. J. (1963) 'A factor analytic study of the Frostig developmental test of visual perception.' *Perceptual and Motor Skills*, **16**, 59–63.

DELGADO, J. M. W. (1971) *Physical Control of the Mind: Toward a Psychocivilized Society*. New York: Harper and Row.

DYKMAN, R. A., PETERS, J. E. and ACKERMAN, P. T. (1973) 'Experimental approaches to the study of minimal brain dysfunction: A follow-up study.' *Annals of the New York Academy of Science*, **205**, 93–108.

EDWARDS, R. P., ALLEY, G. R. and SNYDER, W. (1971) 'Academic achievement and minimal brain dysfunction.' *Journal of Learning Disabilities*, **4**, 134–8.

FRIEDSON, E. (1970) *Professional Dominance: The Social Structure of Medical Care*. New York: Atherton.

FROSTIG, M., LEFEVER, W. and WHITTLESEY, J. (1964) *Developmental Test of Visual Perception*. Palo Alto, CA: Consulting Psychologist Press.

GAMSKY, N. R. and LLOYD, F. W. (1971) 'A longitudinal study of visual perceptual training and reading achievement.' *Journal of Educational Research*, **64**, 451–4.

GREER, C. (1973) *The Great School Legend*. New York: Viking Press.

HALLAHAN, D. P. and KAUFFMAN, J. M. (1977) 'Labels, categories, behaviors: ED, LD, EMR reconsidered.' *Journal of Special Education*, **11**, 139–49.

HOLROYD, J. and WRIGHT, F. (1965) 'Neurological implications of WISC and Bender Gestalt test in predicting arithmetic and reading achievement for white and non-white children.' *Journal of Consulting Psychology*, **29**, 206–12.

JACOBS, J. N. (1968) 'An evaluation of the Frostig visual perception training programme.' *Educational Leadership*, **25**, 332–40.

JENSEN, A. R. (1969) 'How much can we boost IQ and scholastic achievement?' *Harvard Educational Review*, **39**, 1–123.

KALLOS, G. L., GRABOW, J. M. and GUARINO, E. A. (1961) 'The WISC profile of disabled readers.' *Personnel and Guidance Journal*, **39**, 476–8.

KAMIN, L. J. (1974) *The Science and Politics of IQ*. New York: Wiley.

KIRK, S. A. and ELKINS, J. (1975) 'Characteristics of children enrolled in the child service demonstrations centers.' *Journal of Learning Disabilities*, **8**, 630–7.

KIRK, S. A., MCCARTHY, J. J. and KIRK, W. D. (1968) *Illinois Test of Psycholinguistic Abilities*. Urbana, IL: University of Illinois Press.

LIEBERT, R. and SHERK, J. (1970) 'Three Frostig visual perception subtests and specific reading tasks for kindergarten, first and second grade children.' *Reading Teacher*, **24**, 130–7.

MARK, V. H. and ERVIN, F. R. (1970) *Violence and the Brain*. New York: Harper and Row.

MYKLEBUST, H. F. (1973) 'Identification and diagnosis of children with learning disabilities: An interdisciplinary study of criteria.' *Seminars in Psychiatry*, **5**, 55–77.

NATIONAL ADVISORY COMMITTEE ON HANDICAPPED CHILDREN (1968) *Special Education for Handicapped Children* (First Annual Report). Washington, DC: US Department of Health, Education, and Welfare.

NEWCOMER, P. L. and HAMMILL, D. D. (1975) 'ITPA and academic achievement: A survey.' *Reading Teacher*, **28**, 731–41.

NIELSEN, H. J. and RINGE, K. (1969) 'Visuo-perceptive and visuo-motor performance of children with reading disabilities.' *Scandinavian Journal of Psychology*, **10**, 225–31.

OLSON, A. V. (1966) 'School achievement, reading ability and specific perception skills in the third grade.' *Reading Teacher*, **19**, 490–2.

OLSON, A. V. and JOHNSON, C. I. (1970) 'Structure and predictive validity of the Frostig developmental test of visual perception in grades one and three.'' *Journal of Special Education*, **4**, 49–52.

ROBINSON, M. E. and SCHWARTZ, L. B. (1973) 'Visuo-motor skills and reading ability: A longitudinal study.' *Developmental Medicine and Child Neurology*, **15**, 281–6.

ROSEN, C. L. (1966) 'An experimental study of visual perceptual training and reading achievement in first grade.' *Perceptual and Motor Skills*, **20**, 979–86.

RUDEL, R. G. and DENCKLA, M. B. (1976) 'Relationship of IQ and reading score to visual, spatial, and temporal matching tasks.' *Journal of Learning Disabilities*, **9**, 169–78.

RYAN, W. (1972) *Blaming the Victim*. New York: Vintage.

SCHRAG, P. and DIVOKY, D. (1975) *The Myth of the Hyperactive Child*. New York: Pantheon Books.

UNESCO (1976) *The Experimental World Literacy Programme: A Critical Assessment*. Paris: UNESCO Press.

WECHSLER, D. I. (1949) *The Wechsler Intelligence Scale for Children*. New York: Psychological Corporation.

WILSON, E. O. (1975) *Sociobiology: The New Synthesis*. Cambridge, MA: Harvard University Press.

4.4 Biological explanations of sex-role stereotypes

John Archer

General introduction: psychology and the nature-nurture issue

The question of whether individual differences can be accounted for in terms of heredity or in terms of environmental conditions forms the essence of the nature-nurture controversy. It is one which has recurred in academic debates throughout the history of psychology. Theories relying heavily on one or other source of influence have, at different times and in different places, alternated with the opposing viewpoint in being the most influential type of explanation. In many instances, the prevailing view can be linked to the social and political climate of opinion. Scientific theories, particularly those from the social sciences, have often been used to support either conservative or radical policies, and in turn the political climate can influence the type of theory which becomes accepted. For example, in Nazi Germany, a type of social Darwinism was used to support racialist doctrines, which in turn provided a political atmosphere in which theories emphasizing the importance of heredity (e.g. those of Konrad Lorenz) could develop (Crook, 1970).

At about the same time, behaviourism was dominating American psychological thought. Crook (1970) has suggested that the focus on individual enterprise within an ethnically diverse population in North America encouraged this emphasis on the environment in the study of behaviour. More recently, criticisms from a variety of sources have been levelled at the shortcomings and narrowness of the behaviourist approach to psychology. Included in these criticisms are attacks on the behaviourists' one-sided emphasis on environmental determinants of behaviour. Although this is generally a valid criticism, one unfortunate result has been the reassertion of rather crude nativist explanations in some areas of the behavioural sciences. Thus the German school of ethologists, following the earlier writings of Konrad Lorenz, have extended concepts such as 'instinct' and 'fixed action patterns' to human behaviour (Eibl-Eibesfeldt, 1970), and a number of popular but misleading works have sought to explain wide areas of complex human behaviour using simple concepts derived from observational studies of animals (e.g. Morris, 1967; Ardrey, 1967). The race and IQ debate provides another area in which simple-minded views of the application of genetics to behaviour have flourished (Richardson and Spears, 1972). Similarly, some of the theories attempting to explain psychological sex differences are of this type.

Source: CHETWYND, JANE and HARTNETT, OONAGH (eds) (1978) *The Sex Role System: Psychological and Sociological Perspectives* (pages 4–17). London: Routledge and Kegan Paul.

However, many of the current generation of ethologists and developmental psychologists have emphasized the necessity to consider the
interaction of nature and nurture in formulating an adequate explanation
of human behaviour (Blurton-Jones, 1972; Richards, 1974; Archer and
Lloyd, 1975).

Despite the existence of this interactionist approach, which is clearly
more realistic than emphasizing only environment or heredity, the question of deciding which source of influence is foremost in determining a
particular aspect of behaviour is often regarded as being of practical
importance in debates about appropriate social policy. For example, if one
takes the view that criminals are such because of their genetic make-up
(Eysenck, 1975), the implication is that money spent on improving social
conditions as a way of eradicating crime will be largely wasted. However,
if one takes the view that some identifiable environmental conditions are
the important factors, one can then suggest social remedies to prevent
crime.

In making inferences affecting social policy from nativist or environmental theories, it is therefore implied that an environmentally influenced
characteristic is readily modifiable whereas an hereditary character is
largely unchangeable. This implication is the result of some misconcep-
tions. The first of these, pointed out by Blurton-Jones (1972) and Hinde
(1974) is the artificial nature of dividing influences on development into
innate and acquired: no characteristic can be produced by *either* heredity
or the environment, since it must require both sources of influence from the
beginning of its development. The genetic material in the chromosomes
provides a flexible plan for the sequence of development, but this is by no
means a rigid blueprint: it provides the developing organism with ways of
acting on the environment, rather than specifying the outcome of these
actions (Richards, 1974). The outcome depends on the result of each
successive interaction between the organism and the environment. A
common fault of writers on the subject of 'genetic' or 'innate' influences
on behaviour is to ignore the complexities of this interaction and to
discuss genetic and environmental influences as if they had a simple
additive relationship (Archer and Lloyd, 1975). An interactionist
approach to development thus renders the nature-nurture controversy
obsolete.

Sex roles, nature and nurture

In the early part of this century, North American psychologists characteristically explained the existence of measurable sex differences in abilities
and temperament in terms of differential learning associated with the
establishment of sex-role behaviour (Kagan and Moss, 1962; Mischel,
1967). During the last ten years, as part of a general reaction against these
wholly environmental theories, there has been a reversion to attempts at

explaining psychological sex differences in terms of biological characteristics (e.g. sex hormones, brain development). These arguments have also
been extended to include evolution, with the suggestion that present-day
sex roles are adaptive features resulting from natural selection during
hominid evolution. Such ideas are often used to imply a relatively fixed
biological basis for the sex roles, claiming either that they cannot be
changed (Goldberg, 1973; Tiger, 1970) or that they cannot be changed
without risks for the 'well-being' of those concerned (Hutt, 1972a, 1972b).
To derive such inferences from the existence of a biological influence in
development is, as discussed in the first section, unwarranted. But it is this
particular aspect of biological explanations which has made them attractive to defendants of traditional sex roles at a time when they are being
challenged by the Women's Movement (e.g. Stassinopoulos, 1972). It is
this social use of biological theories of sex roles which will be next
discussed.

Social use of biological theories

If we consider the way in which biological and related arguments have
been used in other societies, it is apparent that a wide variety of such
explanations – many of which we would dismiss in terms of factual content
– have been used at one time or another to justify prevailing attitudes to
sex roles. By taking such a view, the content of the argument can be
separated from the use which is made of it.

In one of the New Guinea tribes referred to in Margaret Mead's famous
study (Mead, 1950), sex roles were described as being largely the reverse
of those found in modern western societies, with the women being the
dominant partner and manager of business. The men were described as
more dependent than, and submissive to, the women, and more responsive to the feelings of the children than were the women. What is
particularly interesting for the present discussion is that the members of
this tribe regarded these sex roles as 'biologically natural'. Many societies
have ideas of this type to justify their particular sex-role arrangements.
Whether the ideas are religious or scientific, and whether we would accept
or dismiss their factual content, they all serve the same purpose – to justify
the status quo; in other words, to equate 'what is' with 'what ought to be'
(Lloyd, 1976).

The general argument that men and women not only have clearly
defined respective roles in society, but that they are each *designed* for a
particular role, is used in almost exactly the same manner by those
arguing from religious sources and by those using evidence from biology.
For example, a Jehovah's Witness writer has attacked the ideas of
Women's Liberation on the grounds that each sex is 'designed for a role'
(*The Guardian*, 1972). A report of a scouting manual involved a more
specific argument, stating that a girl's hormones cause her to possess a

'more adaptive and subtle nature' which fits her for being the one who will make the home (*Ink*, 1972).

Since the time of Charles Darwin, the notion of an evolutionary plan has gradually come to eclipse that of a divine plan as an argument used to justify the preservation of traditional arrangements in society. In the nineteenth century, Darwin's ideas were used as a basis for arguments linking brain size with the supposedly lower intelligence of women (Burnstyn, 1971). Even Darwin himself viewed the evolution of mental and physical differences between the sexes in a way that was strongly influenced by the ideas of Victorian society. He remarked that, intellectually, men attain higher excellence in whatever they take up, whether this requires deep thought, reason, imagination or skill with the hands (Darwin, 1871). Darwin viewed the evolutionary origins of this intellectual superiority in terms of men always having had to provide for and defend their womenfolk. Modern anthropological studies of surviving hunter-gatherers (e.g. Draper, 1975) indicate that this is an unrealistic view of the economic role of women in prehistoric societies (see also Slocum, 1975).

This last example in particular illustrates the dependence of particular biological explanations of sex roles on the wider attitudes of the society from which they arose, and the preceding discussion showed how such explanations may be used to justify conservative views of sex roles, in a manner almost identical to the use of religious arguments. Crook (1970) made the general point that biological explanations may provide a substitute for the ethical code, lost when religious beliefs are no longer followed, and he suggested that this is particularly likely to be the case in a society (such as our own) where there are many conflicting standards and norms of social behaviour. It is therefore reassuring for many people to believe that their own particular norm, although perhaps considered old-fashioned by some members of society, is nevertheless the one which is consistent with the 'natural order'.

Crook (1970) also offered other reasons why biological explanations of social behaviour seem to be readily accepted. One is that they are relatively easy to understand; thus a doctrine of the instinctive nature of aggression (e.g. Lorenz, 1966) is easily understood, whereas a more realistic multifactorial analysis (Archer, 1976b) is more difficult to grasp. Archer and Lloyd (1975) made a similar point in relation to the 'interactionist' approach to sex differences: because this involves a relatively complex model of the processes involved, it may fail to produce an easily comprehensible explanation, so that even writers who begin by recognizing its value often revert to an approach based largely on either biological or environmental factors.

A third reason for the ready acceptance of biological explanations concerns the notion of 'reductionism' in science. Reductionist philosophy involves the arrangement of sciences in a hierarchical order, from 'higher level' disciplines such as sociology and anthropology, through to psychology, biology, chemistry and physics at the base, and claims that higher level sciences can be explained in terms of lower level ones (Rose and Rose, 1973). This general approach is certainly apparent in the way that much research in psychology is carried out, and one consequence is that explanations for psychological phenomena are often sought at a 'lower' (i.e. biological) level. Archer and Lloyd (1975) have also suggested that the appearance of more material reality in the variables measured by biologists may impress those working in the social sciences and cause them to be attracted by explanations involving biological terminology.

There are, therefore, at least three reasons why biological explanations of a behavioural feature such as our sex roles have proved attractive despite any intellectual faults they may have. These are, first, their use in arguments on social policy to imply the existence of simple natural order, second, their ease of understanding, and third, that they follow directly from a reductionist philosophy. Having discussed in some detail the reasons for the widespread acceptance of biological explanations, I shall now consider the stereotypes to which these biological explanations have been applied.

Psychological sex differences and sex-role stereotypes

In the previous section, I discussed how biological theories have been used to imply that traditional sex roles are the 'natural ones'. It is also apparent that widespread notions of sex-role stereotypes have influenced the theories themselves. The stereotypes entail a far wider range of attributes than those on which psychologists, have actually found sex differences (Maccoby and Jacklin, 1974). There is *some* overlap between the perceived stereotypes and the measured attributes (e.g. in aggression), but a recent survey of the psychological literature by Maccoby and Jacklin (1974) revealed that there was no evidence for differences in a number of other characteristics on which men and women were supposed to differ; e.g. there was no evidence that women are more 'social' than men or that they were more suggestible, or lacking in achievement motivation, all of which are commonly held stereotypes about masculinity and feminity in western society (e.g. Bem, 1975).

The review of psychological sex differences by Maccoby and Jacklin is very useful in that it enables us to assess those psychological abilities and attributes for which there is good evidence for the existence of sex differences. It also concentrates on the test measures themselves and does not make unwarranted generalizations. Other reviews of similar research areas, particularly by those authors offering biological explanations, tend to conclude that there is a wider range of attributes on which men and women differ, and that these can be described by a number of general psychological characteristics. These accounts are, however, inconsistent in their identification of the characteristics. Broverman *et al.* (1968)

referred to 'activation' and 'inhibition' as the important concepts for considering psychological sex differences on a variety of test measures. Garai and Scheinfeld (1968) suggested a number of differences including male 'orientation to the environment' contrasting with female 'response orientation', male interest in novelty and complexity, contrasting with female affiliative needs. Hutt (1972a, 1972b) proposed the characteristics of conformity, consistency and nurturance as female ones, and she described men as more exploratory, vigorous and group-orientated. More specific abilities and attributes have also been mentioned: these include the widely recognized differences in aggression, verbal, spatial and mathematical abilities (Maccoby and Jacklin, 1974; Buffery and Gray, 1972; Gray, 1971; Hutt, 1972a, 1972b), but also a number of others, such as clerical abilities (Garai and Scheinfeld, 1968), rote memory, and creativity or divergent thinking (Hutt, 1972a) which have not been identified in Maccoby and Jacklin's review.

There are also examples of specific test measures being related to a more generalized characteristic, thus making the sex difference appear more wide ranging than the measures justify. Hutt (1972a) generalized from measures of 'aggression' to include also sex differences in 'ambition' and 'drive'. Witkin *et al.* (1962) generalized from tests involving visual-spatial tasks to more general sex differences in 'cognitive style' or approach to the environment.

In the ways described above, the extent of psychological differences between the sexes is made to appear greater than a careful examination of the evidence would justify. Hence the supposed sex differences are often regarded as conforming more closely to widely held stereotypes than the evidence would warrant. There are two general issues raised by this wide range of, and wide variety of, names given to psychological characteristics on which men and women are supposed to differ. One is that by giving two different aspects of behaviour the same label, a relationship is implied between them. The second is that such labels are, in the behavioural sciences, seldom value-free. Thus a name can not only imply relationships to general phenomena but also a value-judgment.

Considering the first of these points, many terms used in the behavioural sciences are imprecise and therefore lend themselves to different usages. It is thus not surprising to find that words which have been used to describe psychological sex differences often refer to a heterogeneous class of characteristics whose sole justification for being placed together is convenience for the author's theoretical viewpoint. One extreme example of this is in the theory of Broverman *et al.* (1968), referred to in the next section. Speed of colour naming, clerical aptitude tests, speech and reading abilities, manual dexterity, speed of eyeblink conditioning, and sensory thresholds were all referred to as tests of 'rapid repetitive responding' and it was claimed that the same characteristic was measured in rats by tests of wheel-running activity, distance travelled in a novel arena and speed of learning a conditioned avoidance response. Similarly, Gray's

(1971) theory of sex differences in fear and aggression referred to a variety of measures not necessarily related to one another (Archer, 1971, 1975, 1976a).

The second issue is that of implied value-judgments influencing descriptive terms. When studying sex differences, it appears to be difficult for research workers not to be influenced by attitudes about sex-role stereotypes. This influence affects both description and interpretation.

Even the supposedly 'value-free' descriptions of the biological sciences may show influences of this type. Thus, in naming the steroid hormones secreted by the sex organs ('sex hormones'), what are referred to as 'male hormones' (androgens) are secreted in relatively large quantities by the testes of the male, in lesser quantities by the adrenal cortex of both sexes, and by the ovary of the female. The difference in concentrations of androgens between the sexes is, therefore, a statistical one, and not an absolute one as is implied by the name 'male hormone'. This is not merely a pedantic point, since androgens have been found to have physiological influences in women, such as facilitating growth of pubic and axilla hair (Glucksmann, 1974) and increasing sexual interest (Money and Ehrhardt, 1972).

Descriptive labels attached to findings from studies of hormones and behaviour can also be misleading. Hutt (1972a) used the term 'male brain' to describe the physiological changes produced by the administration of androgens to newborn female rats. This very general term implies a much wider ranging and clearer cut type of neural differentiation between the sexes than is the case: androgens administered at this time act on certain parts of the brain which control the adult pattern of sex hormone secretion, and also sexual and aggressive behaviour, thus the term 'male brain' is a deduction from later behavioural differences between animals treated with androgen and those not, rather than a direct description of anatomical or physiological changes in the brain during infancy. Describing these behavioural differences as resulting from a 'male brain' implies that they can be related to definite structural (and permanent) changes in the developing brain. It can also lead to some misleading ideas if the term is used in general discussions of human sex differences, since it implies that there are widespread anatomical differences in the brain between the sexes. It is then but a short step to arguments that these differences are responsible for psychological sex differences.

A third example of how the choice of terminology can reflect wider beliefs comes from the studies of Witkin and his colleagues (e.g. Witkin *et al.*, 1962; Witkin, 1967). They have carried out a series of studies involving two tests of whether a particular visual stimulus is perceived as separate from the surrounding field or as part of it (embedded figure and rod and frame tests). In many of these studies, men are found to separate the stimulus from the background to a greater extent than women (Maccoby and Jacklin, 1974). Although it appears unlikely that anything more than visual-spatial differences underlie these findings (Maccoby and Jacklin,

1974; Sherman, 1967), Witkin has interpreted the differences as indicating different 'cognitive styles' between the sexes. He described the typically male characteristics of separating the visual stimulus from its background as 'field independence' and the typically female characteristic of perceiving the stimulus as part of the background as 'field dependence'. This terminology reflects and reinforces society's stereotypes of the passive dependent female and active independent male (McGuinness, 1976). This is particularly so in view of Witkin's claim that the tests measure a general personality dimension or approach to the environment, rather than being specifically related to visual-spatial analysis. Hartnett (personal communication) suggests that renaming 'field dependence' as 'context awareness' would eliminate the negative connotations of being passive and dependent.

These three examples show the importance of choosing appropriate terminology when dealing with a research area which has controversial social and political implications.

Biological theories of psychological sex differences

In this section, I shall outline the main types of biologically based theories which, on the one hand, have been used to justify sex-role stereotypes, and on the other reflect in their formulation popular notions about sex differences. I have already discussed a number of general criticisms of this type of explanation, notably the simplification of the nature-nurture issue, and the use of general concepts to describe more restricted test measures. In this section I shall also mention a number of additional problems associated with each type of explanation.

Hormone theories

These include several suggestions that sex hormones, either early in development (Dawson, 1972) or later in life (Broverman *et al.*, 1968; Andrew, 1972) affect cognitive abilities. Detailed arguments have been presented against each of these, e.g. that Dawson misinterpreted research on sex hormones in development (Archer, 1976a), that Broverman *et al.* selected the evidence to fit their basic premise concerning the nature of the sex differences involved (Parlee, 1972; Archer, 1976a), and that Andrew's theory cannot explain the direction of sex differences in visual-spatial tests (Archer, 1976a).

Various writers have implicated the high levels of androgens in the male as an explanation for male aggression (e.g. Hutt, 1972a; Gray, 1971; Maccoby and Jacklin, 1974; Goldberg, 1973). Although this is the one behavioural characteristic for which there is some direct experimental evidence on the possible involvement of sex hormones in the human male, there are nevertheless serious flaws in these particular arguments. First, they derive nearly all their evidence from experiments on rodents. There is now increasing evidence that hormonal influences on behaviour are different in rodents and primates (e.g. Herbert, 1970; Money and Ehrhardt, 1972). Second, the recently available data from studies investigating the relationship between hormone levels and measures of aggression in adult men have produced largely negative results (e.g. Kreuz and Rose, 1972; Doering *et al.*, 1974). Inferences derived only or largely from rodent experiments are not adequate bases for deciding the relationship between androgens and aggression in humans. The eagerness of some writers (e.g. Goldberg, 1973, Gray, 1971) to find evidence for a relationship between the two measures has led to their making premature conclusions based on very limited evidence. A more thorough examination of a wider range of animals reveals a more complex picture, both in relation to sex differences and in relation to hormonal influences on aggression (Archer, 1976b).

Another point to consider in relation to research on hormones and sex differences in aggression is the extent to which our ideas about appropriate sex-role behaviour have influenced research in animal behaviour. Doty (1974) has referred to a male bias in the study of courtship and copulation in rodents. If one examines studies of aggression in rodents, it becomes apparent that a similar bias exists there. Research has concentrated on male aggression, of the type that occurs when male strangers encounter one another. Maternal aggression, aggression by females during late pregnancy and lactation, also occurs in many mammals, but has been little studied. Rather less obvious than maternal aggression are forms of female aggression which are not concerned with protection of young. This has been almost completely ignored (except in recent studies of hamsters, e.g. Payne and Swanson, 1972). It has long been claimed, for example, that female mice seldom fight, but recently two (women) research workers have examined female aggression in wild mice and found that 25 per cent would fight following a period of isolation (Ebert and Hyde, 1976).

Other theories involving hormones include that of Gray (1971) on sex differences in fear, which is again based on generalizations from experiments on rodents. I have argued (Archer, 1971, 1975) that the rodent sex differences are not as clear-cut as Gray has suggested, that his choice of tests sampled only a proportion of the measures related to fear, and that the measures involve a wide range of characteristics besides fear. Similarly, Gray's inferences from human studies also involved a wider range of characteristics than could adequately be described by the term 'fearfulness'.

Brain development

Although theories involving sex hormones are the most common form of biological theory of psychological sex differences, a different line of argument has implicated lateralization of the brain. It has been shown that the two halves of the cerebral cortex control different types of skills, the left or dominant hemisphere being concerned with verbal abilities and the right being concerned with spatial abilities. Buffery and Gray (1972) suggested that, owing to the more advanced development of the brain of the female at the time of language acquisition, verbal skills become more completely localized in the dominant hemisphere of young girls. They then suggested that male superiority in spatial skills is an indirect consequence of the greater lateralization of language ability in the female, so that spatial ability becomes localized more bilaterally in males, giving better three-dimensional representation.

McGuinness (1976) has criticized the lateralization hypothesis on the grounds that many skills on which there is no male superiority are also located in the non-dominant hemisphere (e.g. singing ability). Maccoby and Jacklin (1974) also point out that many functions controlled by the dominant hemisphere do not show female superiority.

Evolutionary theories

A third type of biological theory concerns evolutionary origins. In many ways these explanations illustrate better than any the general points made in previous sections about the social influences on, and the uses made of, biological theories. Arguments such as those of Hutt (1972a), Tiger (1970) and Gray and Buffery (1971) claim that the psychological make-up of men and women clearly reflect evolutionary adaptations for different sex roles. Their choice of characteristics on which the sexes differ include male ability to form bonds with other men, male ability to dominate political life (Tiger, 1970), and female conformity and nurturance (Hutt, 1972b); this choice is very much influenced by our present notions of stereotyped sex roles, and contains many unwarranted generalizations and assumptions (see previous sections, and Archer, 1976a). They also involve some dubious arguments from human evolution, notably their emphasis (and dependence) on the importance of male co-operative hunting as the major economic force in the lives of developing hominids (see Draper, 1975; Slocum, 1975, for arguments against this view).

Theories suggesting evolutionary adaptation for different sex roles have also been used to justify the continuation of these roles nowadays. The most extreme variant of this argument is that men and women possess psychological characteristics which have adapted them for different sex roles, men for hunting in groups (or some modern substitute) and women for a domestic and child-rearing role; consequently they are genetically programmed to pursue such activities in modern societies. I have already discussed at some length the fallacy of arguments which use the term genetic in the sense of fixed and unmodifiable. There is also a more subtle variation of the argument (e.g. Hutt, 1972a) – not that we cannot change our sex roles, but that it is not desirable to do so. This argument claims that there are disadvantages in adopting sex roles different from those for which we are assumed to have been adapted in the course of evolution. Such disadvantages might involve personal unhappiness or long-term deleterious consequences for the species as a whole. It is uncertain what sex roles evolving humans adopted, but evidence from surviving hunter-gatherer groups (Martin and Voorhies, 1975; Draper, 1975) indicates that they were probably very different from what we today regard as 'tradition-al' sex roles; thus, the assumptions made about evolutionary adaptations by Tiger, Hutt and others are very likely to be incorrect, and to portray an unjustified sedentary role for women. They are also illogical in that, on the one hand, they argue against changing the role of women, and on the other, accept that the present-day role of men is very different from their original one of hunting large game. In fact, many aspects of our contem-porary lives bear little relation to the lives and activities of evolving human beings. Thus, to start examining sex roles against a hypothetical criterion of 'naturalness', we should not only find no evidence to justify existing stereotypes but we should also have to question many other major areas of contemporary life.

Conclusions

In this article I have discussed issues relating to biological theories of sex differences in human behaviour. My main conclusion is the importance of viewing such theories in their wider social context rather than as the totally objective statements of 'experts', from which there follow certain clear implications for social policy. Social context is used in a broad sense to indicate influences within the biological and social sciences, and from the prevailing political and social climate of opinion. Some of the main influences within the academic disciplines themselves include the ready acceptance of biological explanations into the reductionist framework of psychological research, and the ready acceptance of nativist arguments as a reaction against extreme environmentalist viewpoints. Wider influences include the easily understandable nature of simple biological arguments, and their ready acceptance as justifications of the 'natural order' in place of a religious justification.

References

ANDREW, R. J. (1972) 'Recognition processes and behaviour with special reference to effects of testosterone on persistence', in LEHRMAN, D. S., HINDE, R. A. and SHAW, E. (eds) *Advances in the Study of Behaviour, Vol. 4.* New York and London: Academic Press.

ARCHER, J. (1971) 'Sex differences in emotional behaviour: a reply to Gray and Buffery.' *Acta Psychologica*, **35**, 415–29.

ARCHER, J. (1975) 'Rodent sex differences in emotional and related behaviour.' *Behavioral Biology*, **14**, 451–79.

ARCHER, J. (1976a) 'Biological explanations of psychological sex differences', in LLOYD, B. B. and ARCHER, J. (eds) *Exploring Sex Differences*. London and New York: Academic Press.

ARCHER, J. (1976b) 'The organisation of aggression and fear in vertebrates', in BATESON, P. P. S. and KLOPFER, P. (eds) *Perspectives in Ethology*. New York: Plenum.

ARCHER, J. and LLOYD, B. B. (1975) 'Sex differences: biological and social interactions', in LEWIN, R. (ed.) *Child Alive*. London: Temple Smith.

ARDREY, R. (1967) *The Territorial Imperative*. London: Collins.

BEM, S. L. (1975) 'The measurement of psychological androgyny.' *Journal of Consulting and Clinical Psychology*, **42**, 155–62.

BLURTON-JONES, N. (1972) 'Characteristics of ethological studies of human behaviour', in BLURTON-JONES, N. (ed.) *Ethological Studies of Child Behaviour*. London: Cambridge University Press.

BROVERMAN, D. M., KLAIBER, E. L., KOBAYASHI, Y. and VOGEL, W. (1968) 'Roles of activation and inhibition in sex differences in cognitive abilities.' *Psychological Review*, **75**, 25–50.

BUFFERY, A. W. H. and GRAY, J. A. (1972) 'Sex differences in the development of spatial and linguistic skills', in OUNSTED, C. and TAYLOR, D. C. (eds) *Gender Differences, their Ontogeny and Significance*. London: Churchill.

BURNSTYN, J. N. (1971) 'Brain and intellect: science applied to a social issue 1860–1875.' *XIIᵉ Congrès International d'Histoire des Sciences*, **IX**, 13–16.

CROOK, J. H. (1970) 'Introduction – social behaviour and ethology', in CROOK, J. H. (ed.) *Social Behaviour in Birds and Mammals*. London and New York: Academic Press.

DARWIN, C. (1871) *The Descent of Man, and Selection in Relation to Sex*. London: Murray (1901 edition).

DAWSON, J. L. M. (1972) 'Effects of sex hormones on cognitive style in rats and men.' *Behavior Genetics*, **2**, 21–42.

DOERING, C. H., BRODIE, H. K. H., KRAEMER, H., BECKER, H. and HAMBURG, D. A. (1974) 'Plasma testosterone levels and psychologic measures in men over a 2-month period', in FRIEDMAN, R. C., RIEHART, R. M. and VAN DE WIELE, R. L. (eds) *Sex Differences in Behaviour*. New York: Wiley.

DOTY, R. L. (1974) 'A cry for the liberation of the female rodent: courtship and copulation in *Rodentia*.' *Psychological Bulletin*, **81**, 159–72.

DRAPER, P. (1975) '!Kung women: contrasts in sexual egalitarianism in foraging and sedentary contexts', in REITER, R. (ed.) *Toward an Anthropology of Women*. New York and London: Monthly Review Press.

EBERT, P. D. and HYDE, J. S. (1976) 'Selection for agnostic behaviour in wild female *Mus musculus*.' *Behavior Genetics*, **6**, 291–304.

EIBL-EIBESFELDT, I. (1970) *Ethology: The Biology of Behaviour*. New York: Holt, Rinehart and Winston.

EYSENCK, H. J. (1975) 'Crime as destiny.' *New Behaviour*, **3**, 46–9.

GARAI, J. E. and SCHEINFELD, A. (1968) 'Sex differences in mental and behavioural traits.' *Genetic Psychology Monographs*, **77**, 169–299.

GLUCKSMANN, A. (1974) 'Sexual dimorphism in mammals.' *Biological Review*, **49**, 423–75.

GOLDBERG, S. (1973) *The Inevitability of the Patriarchy*. New York: Morrow.

GRAY, J. A. (1971) 'Sex differences in emotional behaviour in man: endocrine bases.' *Acta Psychologica*, **35**, 29–46.

GRAY, J. A. and BUFFERY, A. W. H. (1971) 'Sex differences in emotional and cognitive behaviour in mammals including man: adaptive and neural bases.' *Acta Psychologica*, **35**, 89–111.

HERBERT, J. (1970) 'Hormones and reproductive behaviour in rhesus and talapoin monkeys.' *Journal of Reproduction and Fertility, Supplement*, **11**, 119–40.

HINDE, R. A. (1974) *Biological Bases of Human Social behaviour*. New York and London: McGraw Hill.

HUTT, C. (1972a) *Males and Females*. Harmondsworth: Penguin Books.

HUTT, C. (1972b) 'Sex differences in human development.' *Human Development*, **15**, 153–70.

KAGAN, J. and MOSS, H. (1962) *Birth to Maturity*. New York: Wiley.

KREUZ, L. E. and ROSE, R. M. (1972) 'Assessment of aggressive behaviour and plasma testosterone in a young criminal population.' *Psychosomatic Medicine*, **34**, 321–32.

LLOYD, B. B. (1976) 'Social responsibility and research on sex differences', in LLOYD, B. B. and ARCHER, J. (eds) *Exploring Sex Differences*. London and New York: Academic Press.

LORENZ, K. (1966) *On Aggression*. New York: Harcourt Brace Jovanovich.

MACCOBY, E. E. and JACKLIN, C. N. (1974) *The Psychology of Sex Differences*. London: Oxford University Press.

MCGUINNESS, D. (1976) 'Sex differences in the organisation of perception and cognition', in LLOYD, B. B. and ARCHER, J. (eds) *Exploring Sex Differences*. London and New York: Academic Press.

MARTIN, M. K. and VOORHIES, B. (1975) *The Female of the Species*. New York and London: Macmillan.

MEAD, M. (1950) *Male and Female*. Harmondsworth: Penguin Books.

MISCHEL, W. (1967) 'A social learning view of sex differences in behaviour', in MACCOBY, E. E. (ed.) *The Development of Sex Differences*. London: Tavistock.

MONEY, J. and EHRHARDT, A. A. (1972) *Man and Woman, Boy and Girl*. Baltimore, MD, and London: Johns Hopkins University Press.

MORRIS, D. (1967) *The Naked Ape*. London: Cape.

PARLEE, M. B. (1972) 'Comments on "Roles of activation and inhibition in sex differences in cognitive abilities" by D. A. Broverman, E. L. Klaiber, Y. Kobayashi and W. Vogel.' *Psychological Review*, **77**, 180–4.

PAYNE, A. P. and SWANSON, H. E. (1972) 'The effect of sex hormones on the aggressive behaviour of the female golden hamster.' *Animal Behaviour*, **20**, 782–7.

RICHARDS, M. P. M. (1974) 'The biological and the social', in ARMISTEAD, N. (ed.) *Reconstructing Social Psychology*. Harmondsworth: Penguin Books.

RICHARDSON, K. and SPEARS, D. (eds) (1972) *Race, Culture and Intelligence*. Harmondsworth: Penguin Books.

ROSE, S. P. R. and ROSE, H. (1973) 'Do not adjust your mind, there is a fault in reality – ideology in neural biology.' *Cognition*, 2, 479–502.

SHERMAN, J. A. (1967) 'Problems of sex differences in space perception and aspects of intellectual functioning.' *Psychological Review*, **74**, 290–9.

SLOCUM, S. (1975) 'Woman the gatherer: male bias in anthropology', in REITER, R. (ed.) *Toward an Anthropology of Women*. New York and London: Monthly Review Press.

STASSINOPOULOS, A. (1972) *The Female Woman*. London: Davis-Poynter.

TIGER, L. (1970) 'The possible biological origins of sexual discrimination.' *Impact of Science on Society*, **20**, 29–45.

WITKIN, H. (1967) 'A cognitive-style approach to cross-cultural research.' *International Journal of Psychology*, **2**, 233–50.

WITKIN, H. A., DYKE, R. B., PATERSON, H. F., GOODENOUGH, D. R. and KARP, S. A. (1962) *Psychological Differentiation*. New York: Wiley.

4.5 The search for effective schools

David Reynolds

For the many people in our society who have had hopes of changing
society through modifying the educational system, the experiences of the
last decade must have been profoundly depressing. In Third World and in
developed countries it is clear that increasing educational expenditure
does not necessarily generate faster economic growth. Educational expansion itself is also now not seen as enough in itself to generate equality of
opportunity between advantaged and disadvantaged groups. Specific
organizational changes such as comprehensivization, curriculum modification and compensatory education have all been found to be relatively
unsuccessful in generating the sorts of changes that reformers had hoped
for.

Schools have increasingly been viewed, then, as making no difference to
anything of importance. Educational services have become, as Wilby
(1977) aptly labelled them, the Titanics of the State welfare systems.
Educational reforms of the kind pursued in the past are increasingly
regarded as equivalent to rearranging the furniture on the ship's maiden
voyage.

In this paper, I want to try to affirm again the conventional radical faith
which sees schooling as an important determinant of the nature of
adolescent and adult society, social problems and social patterns. [. . .]
We will proceed to examine critically and in detail the quality of the
evidence from which it is deduced that 'schools make no difference' to the
nature of their pupils' development. The recent body of American research and British knowledge, principally contributed by Michael Rutter
and his associates from London and by myself and my associates from
South Wales, which suggests the existence of substantial school effects will
then be presented, together with an assessment of both its limitations and
its implications. After looking at further evidence, I conclude – echoing
the old, radical faith – that the school itself may be able to combat
adolescent problems by means of processes that involve institutional
change and modification. [. . .]

Do schools make no difference?

One of the important factors that has eroded the faith in the school has
been the accumulation of evidence which suggests that differences between schools have only quite minimal effects upon their pupils and that,

---

Source: *School Organization* (1982), **2**, 3, 215–37.

therefore, the individual school is not a strong determinant of the nature of children entering the wider society. The research evidence upon which these claims are made – and we will see that this evidence is not really capable of supporting the definitive conclusions that have been widely drawn from it – is mostly American, although an increasing contribution to the debate has been made from British sources.

The American debate on this issue was begun by the much publicized Coleman Report, entitled *Equality of Educational Opportunity* which was published in 1966 (Coleman *et al.*, 1966). Data collected from over 600,000 children, from 60,000 teachers and from 4,000 schools showed when analysed by means of multiple regression analysis that there were substantial differences between the verbal ability levels of the children from various minority races and those the report called white children. Whilst the differences between these groups of children were substantially greater upon leaving school than on entering it, the report argued that these apparent effects of schools upon pupils' attainments were merely a reflection of the social composition of the pupil body in the schools that the children of different races attended at that time and were not a reflection of the quality of the schools themselves. When all things were equal, factors such as the amount of money spent on each pupil, the number of books in the school library, the quality of the schools' physical and recreational resources and even differences in the nature of the schools' curriculum seemed to make little appreciable difference to minority group or white children's levels of attainment on verbal ability tests. The data collected for the Coleman Report and other longitudinal data upon pupils, schools, school districts and communities was re-analyzed by Christopher Jencks and his colleagues and published in 1972 under the title of *Inequality* (Jencks *et al.*, 1972). In most respects, the results of this second major study parallel those of the first. As with the Coleman Report, measures of school resources are shown to be a very poor predictor of student performance – a much higher proportion of variance between individuals in their ability scores is explicable by knowledge of the socio-economic status of the individual's parents and of the intelligence quotient of that individual, rather than by the physical or social quality of the schools that the individual might attend. Jencks attempted to quantify precisely how much variation in attainment is attributable to school resources and concluded very pessimistically that: '. . . if we could equalize everyone's total environment, test score inequality would fall by 25–40 per cent. . . . Equalizing the quality of elementary schools would reduce cognitive inequality by three per cent or less. Equalizing the quality of high schools would reduce cognitive inequality by one per cent or less' (Jencks *et al.*, 1972, page 109). Further analysis suggested that if all schools were as good at facilitating student attainment as the top 20 per cent of all schools, national test scores would rise merely by something like three per cent and, in a final analysis, the impact of school quality upon rates of staying on at school, rather than simply on student test scores, is also shown to be slight. The available data suggested that measures of school resources have virtually no relationship to the number of years of schooling that students achieve. Jencks concluded that: 'Qualitative differences between high schools seem to explain about two per cent of the variations in students' educational attainment' (Jencks *et al.*, 1972, page 159).

The findings above which suggest that school characteristics have relatively little effect upon student attainment or student performance have been replicated in a veritable host of studies published in America from the late 1960s to the mid 1970s. Work by the economist Hanushek (1972), for example, shows no relationship between school resources and student performance on test scores. The small relationship he finds between test scores and the verbal ability of teachers hardly suggests, as Hurn (1979) notes, an easy strategy that would narrow the differences in achievement between students from different social origins. The review of a further twenty-one studies by authors working for the Rand Corporation (Averch *et al.*, 1971) concludes unequivocally that 'Research has not identified a variant of the existing system that is consistently related to students' educational outcomes' (page 171). A review of the literature by Stevens (1967) also suggests that, contrary to the opinion of many educationists, there is no clear evidence that any factors such as pupil/teacher ratios, different teaching styles and different curriculum patterns have a consistent relationship with differences in student ability.

The findings of the American research undertaken on the effects of schools were, then, apparently clear cut. Combined with similar results from the detailed analysis of the influence of home and school factors in the Plowden Report (Peaker, 1967) and set alongside the continuing tendency of British educational research to concentrate upon detailed analysis only of the influence of the family and community factors that might affect pupil development – as exemplified by the studies such as *From Birth to Seven* (Davie *et al.*, 1972) that have emanated from the National Children's Bureau – the combined effect of these factors was to substantially erode any belief in the effectiveness of schooling amongst the academic community undertaking educational research, amongst politicians (particularly in America) and also amongst teachers exposed to simplistic portrayals of the findings of the research by the popular media.

School may make a difference

In the decade following the erosion of liberal beliefs as to the effectiveness of schooling as a mover of social change, two major factors have combined to generate a reassessment of the pessimistic conclusions that have been summarized above. Firstly, detailed criticisms of the American studies from both American (Dyer, 1968) and British commentators considerably affected the confidence which could be placed in the great majority of the earlier studies. These used, it was argued, only a very limited number of measures of the school environment in their analyses, thereby increasing the chances that the school would have less influence than the other influences upon pupil life for which many more measures were included – the Coleman analysis used only one measure of school environment (volumes per student in the school library) for their analysis of reading ability at grades one, three and six; and at grades nine and twelve, the library measure was supplemented merely by one other measure representing the presence or absence of science laboratory facilities. Other commentators (Rutter and Madge, 1976) have suggested that the absence of school effects may merely reflect the fact that the variables chosen to measure school quality have usually been of a 'resource-based' variety and have not included detailed assessment of many aspects of within school life (for example, teacher/pupil relations, school 'ethos' and school organizational structure) that may have important effects upon the nature of pupil outputs. The tests used to measure these pupil outputs were, it was further argued, mostly of verbal or numerical ability and did not usually measure the 'social' outputs of the educational system (such as values, attendance rates, delinquency rates, self perceptions, feelings of locus of control, etc.) on which schools may have had greater effects. Lastly, the technique of analysis used in most of the early studies was multiple regression, in which a series of sets of variables are entered into the analysis in logical sequence, thereby permitting an estimate of the total variance that is due to the effect of the different sets of variables. The usual ordering for the entry of the variables into the regression equation was family variables, community variables and school variables in sequence, with such an analysis usually showing, as mentioned above, that 20 per cent or 30 per cent of the variance was explicable by the first two sets of variables, and perhaps only three to five per cent by the set of school variables. If there was a high inter-correlation between the set of family and the set of school variables, however, much of the variation that might have been due to school variables would have been exhausted after the prior entry of the family variables. This, it is argued, led to an artificially low estimate of school effects.

The second set of factors that has served to erode much of the early confidence in the studies arguing for limited school effects have been generated by further analysis of the data bases of the studies themselves. Such analysis suggests that, firstly, the schools in the Coleman Report had a quite marked effect upon children as they grew into adolescence and that, secondly, the effect of school factors at all age groups was substantial for the groups of low ability, low social class and non-white children, though not for others. Thirdly, school factors were also shown in the Coleman data to be very highly inter-correlated with certain of the 'non-cognitive' outcomes of the educational process – Mayeste's re-analysis shows a multiple correlation of .59 between sense of control (re-labelled by him 'attitude towards life') and an optimum combination of thirty-one school variables, which do not include characteristics of the student body (see Dyer, 1968, for further details).

The further erosion of earlier beliefs in the ineffectiveness of schooling as a medium of social change has also been generated by the appearance of an increasing number of the studies in both America and Britain that indicate, contrary to earlier suggestions, the existence of substantial school effects upon pupil outcomes of all kinds. [. . .]

The American studies

One of the first American studies to demonstrate substantial school effects was that of Goodman (1959), who showed that a higher per pupil expenditure, a good ratio of special staff and the existence of a more 'child-centred' classroom atmosphere were all positively associated with students' 'composite achievement' at grade seven. The well known *Project Talent* studies by Shaycroft (1967) of a cohort of over 6,000 pupils passing through high school also suggested that on all but two of the forty-two measures of student attainment used, student gains in knowledge varied significantly from school to school. Although Shaycroft claimed that students in some schools learnt more, or improved their ability more than in other schools, the sources of these differences apparently resisted easy identification.

Subsequent work by McDill and his associates (1967; 1973) built on these earlier studies by suggesting that the key factors that accounted for the differential effectiveness of American high schools were to be found in the social climates of these institutions themselves. Factor analysis of both questionnaire data and more objective information collected by the research team on school organizational characteristics eventually generated six 'constructs' or factors, each of which contained a number of characteristics that grouped together both statistically and substantively. McDill titles the factors as:

1 Academic Emulation: the degree to which academic excellence is valued by the student body.
2 Student Perception of Intellectualism-Aestheticism: the degree to which acquisition of knowledge is valued.
3 Cohesive and Egalitarian Aestheticism: the degree to which the student social system emphasises intellectual criteria for status as opposed to family background or other ascribed criteria.
4 Scientism: the degree of scientific interest in the school.
5 Humanistic Excellence: the degree of artistic and humanistic interest in the school.
6 Academically Orientated Student Status System: the degree to which intellectual and academic performance is rewarded by student peers.

Crucially, these factors appeared to affect student academic performance even when the differences in socio-economic composition between schools had been parcelled out and McDill concludes: 'More specifically, the findings lead to the tentative conclusion that in those schools where academic competition, intellectualism and subject matter competence are emphasized and rewarded by faculty and student bodies, individual students tend to conform to the scholastic norms of the majority and achieve at a higher level' (McDill *et al.*, 1973, page 199).

Although McDill and his associates were unable in these studies to determine those factors that had generated the different value climates of over-achieving and under-achieving schools, subsequent work by Weber (1971), by the New York State Office of Education (1974), by Madden *et al.* (1976) and by Brookover and Lezotte (1976) has begun to unravel the complexity of within school life and suggest the factors in this area that may have the effects upon pupil development that the above studies have noted. Weber (1971) focused upon the characteristics of four inner city schools in which the children's reading ability was clearly above national norms. All four schools had 'strong leadership' from their principals, all also had high expectations from their students. All the schools had 'an orderly, relatively quiet and pleasant atmosphere' and all had 'a strong emphasis upon pupil acquisition of reading skills and on evaluation of pupil progress'.

[. . .]

The importance of the leadership role, of staff expectations and of the general 'school ethos' in affecting pupil performance that is evident in the work of McDill, and Weber is also confirmed by the Californian work of Madden and associates (1976). Their study of twenty-one high achieving schools and twenty-one low achieving schools (matched on the basis of having similar pupil characteristics at entry) revealed the following findings:

1   In comparison to teachers at lower-achieving schools, teachers at higher-achieving schools report that their principals provide them with a significantly greater amount of support.
2   Teachers in higher-achieving schools were more task-oriented in their classroom approach and exhibited more evidence of applying appropriate principles of learning than did teachers in lower-achieving schools.
3   In comparison to classrooms in lower-achieving schools, classrooms in higher-achieving schools provided more evidence of student monitoring processes, student effort, happier children, and an atmosphere conducive to learning.
4   In comparison to teachers at lower-achieving schools, teachers at higher-achieving schools reported that they spent relatively more time on social studies, less time on mathematics and physical education/health, and about the same amount of time on reading/language development and science.

5   In contrast to teachers at lower-achieving schools, teachers at higher-achieving schools reported:
    (a) A larger number of adult volunteers in mathematics classes;
    (b) Fewer paid aides in reading; and
    (c) They were more apt to use teacher aides for non-teaching tasks, such as classroom paperwork, watching children on the playground, and maintaining classroom discipline.

6   In comparison to teachers at lower-achieving schools, teachers at higher-achieving schools reported higher levels of access to 'outside the classroom' materials.

7   In comparison to the teachers of lower-achieving schools, teachers at higher-achieving schools believed their faculty as a whole had less influence on educational decisions.

8   In comparison to teachers at lower-achieving schools, teachers at higher-achieving schools rated district administration higher on support services.

9   In comparison to grouping practices at lower-achieving schools, the higher-achieving schools divided classrooms into fewer groups for purposes of instruction.

10 In comparison to teachers in lower-achieving schools, teachers in higher-achieving schools reported being more satisfied with various aspects of their work.

The Michigan work of Brookover and Lezotte (1976) is the last American study we consider here and its importance lies in the support it gives to the major findings of the earlier studies we have noted. Analysis of the test results of all Michigan school children in grades four and seven was used to identify elementary schools characterized by 'improving' or by 'declining' pupil performance, schools which were subsequently visited by trained interviewers to assess the nature of their educational and social life. Analysis suggested that:

1   The improving schools are clearly different from the declining schools in the emphasis their staff places on the accomplishment of the basic reading and mathematics objectives. The improving schools accept and emphasize the importance of these goals and objectives while declining schools give much less emphasis to such goals and do not specify them as fundamental.

2   There is a clear contrast in the evaluations that teachers and principals make of the students in the improving and declining schools. The staffs of the improving schools tend to believe that *all* of their students can master the basic objectives; and, furthermore, the teachers perceive that the principal shares this belief. They tend to report higher and increasing levels of student ability, while the declining school teachers project the belief that students' ability levels are low and, therefore, they cannot master even these objectives.

3   The staff of the improving schools hold decidedly higher and apparently increasing levels of expectations with regard to the educational accomplishments of their students. In contrast, staff of the declining schools are much less likely to believe that their students will complete high school or college.

4   In contrast to the declining schools, the teachers and principals of the improving schools are much more likely to assume responsibility for teaching the basic reading and mathematics skills and are much more committed to doing so. The staffs of the declining schools feel there is not much that teachers can do to influence the achievement of their students. They tend to displace the responsibility for skill-learning on to the parents or the students themselves.

5   Since the teachers in the declining schools believe that there is little they can do to influence basic skill-learning, it follows they spend less time in direct reading instruction than do teachers in the improving schools. With the greater emphasis on reading and mathematical objectives in the improving schools, the staffs in these schools devote a much greater amount of time toward achieving reading and mathematical objectives.

6   There seems to be a clear difference in the principal's role in the improving and declining schools. In the improving schools, the principal is more likely to be an instructional leader, to be more assertive in his instructional leadership role, is more of a disciplinarian and, perhaps most of all, assumes responsibility for the evaluation of the achievement of basic objectives. The principals in the declining schools appear to be permissive and to emphasize informal and collegial relationships with the teachers. They put more emphasis on general public relations and less emphasis upon evaluation of the school's effectiveness in providing a basic education for the students.

7   The improving school staffs appear to evidence a greater degree of acceptance of the concept of accountability and are further along in the development of an accountability model. Certainly they accept the results of Michigan State tests as one indication of their effectiveness to a much greater degree than the declining school staffs. The latter tend to reject the relevance of the testing programme and make little use of these assessment devices as a reflection of their instruction. (Michigan was running a comprehensive Educational Assessment Program.)

8   Generally, teachers in the improving schools are less satisfied than the staffs in the declining schools. The higher levels of reported staff satisfaction and morale in the declining schools seem to reflect a pattern of complacency and satisfaction with the current levels of educational attainment. On the other hand, the improving school staffs appear more likely to experience some tension and dissatisfaction with the existing condition.

9 Differences in the level of parent involvement in the improving and declining schools are not clear cut. It seems that there is less overall parent involvement in the improving schools. However, the improving school staffs indicated that their schools have higher levels of *parent initiated* involvement.

10 In general, the improving schools are not characterized by a high emphasis upon para-professional staff, nor heavy involvement of the regular teachers in the selection of students to be placed in compensatory education programmes. The declining schools seem to have a greater number of different staff involved in reading instruction and more teacher involvement in identifying students who are to be placed in compensatory education programmes. The regular classroom teachers in the declining schools report spending more time planning for non-compensatory education reading activities. The decliners also report greater emphasis on programmed instruction.

[. . .]

The British studies

One of the most influential of the British studies that have been undertaken into the effects of schooling was the important work of Power *et al.* (1967; 1972) undertaken in the secondary schools of Tower Hamlets. In an article entitled somewhat provocatively *Delinquent Schools?* published in 1967, Power argued that the large differences between his sample of schools in their delinquency rates for boys, from 0.7 per cent to 17.0 per cent of pupils officially delinquent per annum, may well (given the relatively homogeneous nature of the communities that they served) have reflected variation in the effects of the local secondary modern schools themselves. In part because of the furore triggered off by the publication of this article, Power and his team were never able to pursue their investigations into the schools themselves. Subsequent criticisms of the methodology by which Power claimed to show the independence of the schools' delinquency rates from the delinquency rates of their catchment areas (Baldwin, 1972) and later evidence from the longitudinal Cambridge Institute of Criminology study, suggesting that high delinquency rate schools in their London sample were merely reflecting the high levels of delinquency proneness in their intakes (Farrington, 1973), combined to cast strong doubts upon the validity of Power's hypotheses of substantial school effects.

Although the publication of findings by Gath (1972) and Gath *et al.* (1977), suggesting substantial variation in the child guidance referral rates and delinquency rates of schools taking from similar catchment areas, and the publication of preliminary findings by Rutter (1973), showing a substantial variation in the behavioural deviance rates of pupils at London primary schools, hinted at the existence of school effects of a moderate size, it is probably the work in South Wales by myself and my associates and the continued work in London by Rutter and his associates that has been most influential in leading to a re-assessment of the former evidence from Britain and America that schools made little difference to the level of development of their pupils.

The work of Rutter *et al.* (1979) was undertaken in a sample of twelve London comprehensive schools and was concerned to answer two linked questions. First, whether or not the different schools had a differential effect upon their pupils and, secondly, if they did, what factors within the schools could account for these differences. Four different indicators of school output were selected – delinquency, attendance, within school behaviour and public examination results – and the substantial variation that was found between the schools in their performance on these measures remained even after differences between the schools in the quality of their pupil intake were taken into account. Furthermore, schools tended to perform consistently 'well' or consistently 'badly' on all four of the measures of school output. Detailed investigation of the internal organization, within school processes, school ethos and teacher/pupil interaction within the twelve institutions suggested that physical aspects of the schools, such as size or the age of the buildings were not important determinants of output and that further variation in the nature of the formal academic organization, formal pastoral care organization, pupil/teacher ratio and size of classes also appeared to make little difference to school outcomes.

In a recent discussion of these findings (Rutter, 1980), the important within-school influences upon school outcome were argued to be:

1   The balance of intellectually able and less able children in the school since, when a preponderance of pupils in a school were likely to be unable to meet the expectations of scholastic success, peer group cultures with an anti-academic or anti-authority emphasis may have formed.
2   The system of rewards and punishments – ample use of rewards, praise and appreciation being associated with favourable outcomes.
3   School environment – good working conditions, responsiveness to pupil needs and good care and decoration of buildings were associated with better outcomes.
4   Ample opportunities for children to take responsibility and to participate in the running of their school lives appeared conducive to favourable outcome.
5   Successful schools tended to make good use of homework, to set clear academic goals and to have an atmosphere of confidence as to their pupil capacities.
6   Outcomes were better where teachers provided good models of behaviour by means of good time keeping and willingness to deal with pupil problems.

7   Findings upon group management in the classroom suggested the importance of preparing lessons in advance, of keeping the attention of the whole class, of unobtrusive discipline, of a focus on rewarding good behaviour and of swift action to deal with disruption.

8   Outcomes were more favourable when there was a combination of firm leadership together with a decision-making process in which all teachers felt that their views were represented.

The above research has, of course, been subjected to vigorous criticism from many sources (for example, Hargreaves, 1980; Goldstein, 1980; Acton, 1980). It has been alleged that the study over-estimated the effect of the schools upon their output measures because only two measurements (pupil ability and pupil occupational group) of the quality of the school intakes were used, thereby underestimating the variance that may have been explicable by other intake factors. It is also alleged that insufficient attention was given to possible important factors such as the curriculum content and the relationships between teachers and pupils that may also have been responsible for differential school effects. Nevertheless, it seems likely that the authors' conclusion (Rutter *et al.*, 1979, page 205) that 'the results carry the strong implication that schools can do much to foster good behaviour and attainment and that even in a disadvantaged area schools can be a force for the good' is still substantially correct.

Our own work in South Wales, although undertaken in a group of secondary modern schools and in a relatively homogeneous former mining valley that is very different in its community patterns from the communities of inner London, has produced findings that in certain ways are parallel to those of Rutter and his team. Our work involved the collection of data on the pupil inputs, pupil outputs and school processes of eight secondary modern schools, each of which was taking the bottom two thirds of the ability range from a clearly delineated catchment area. We found substantial differences in the quality of the school outputs from the eight schools when we began our work in 1974, with a variation in the delinquency rate of from 3.8 per cent delinquent per annum to 10.5 per cent, in the attendance rate of from 77.2 per cent average attendance to 89.1 per cent and in the academic attainment rate of from 8.4 per cent proceeding to the local technical college to 52.7 per cent proceeding on to further education.

Our early analysis (Reynolds, 1976; Reynolds *et al.*, 1976) of our intake data showed no tendency for the schools with the higher levels of performance to be receiving more able intakes on entry. In fact, high overall school performance was associated with lower ability intakes as measured by Raven's Standard Progressive Matrices test of non-verbal ability. Although subsequent full analysis of our full range of intake data reveals a tendency for the higher performance schools to have intakes of higher verbal and numerical ability, the personality variables for these intakes (higher extraversion and higher neuroticism scores) suggest, on the contrary, a poor educational prognosis. Simply, the intake scores still seem to be unable to explain the variation between our schools.

Detailed observation of the schools from 1974 to 1977 and the collection of a large range of material upon pupils' attitudes to school, teachers' perceptions of pupils, within school organization, school resource levels, etc. (for further information see Reynolds *et al.*, in preparation) has revealed a number of factors within the school that are associated with more 'effective' regimes. These include a high proportion of pupils in authority positions (as in the Rutter study), low levels of institutional control, low rates of physical punishment, small overall size, more favourable teacher pupil ratios and more tolerant attitudes to the enforcing of certain rules regarding 'dress, manners and morals' (see Reynolds, 1975, for further information on this point). Crucially, our observation has revealed differences between the schools in the ways that they have attempted to mobilize pupils towards the acceptance of their predetermined goals.

Such differences seem to fall within the parameters of one or other of two major strategies, 'coercion' or 'incorporation'. Five of the eight schools that took part in the research appeared to be utilizing the incorporative strategy to a greater (three schools) or lesser (two schools) extent. The major components of this strategy are two fold; the incorporation of pupils into the organization of the school and the incorporation of their parents into support of the school. Pupils were incorporated within the classroom by encouraging them to take an active and participative role in lessons and by letting them intervene verbally without the teacher's explicit directions. Pupils in schools which utilized this strategy were also far more likely to be allowed and encouraged to work in groups than their counterparts in schools utilizing the coercive strategy. Outside formal lesson time, attempts were made to incorporate pupils into the life of the school by utilizing other strategies. One of these was the use of numbers of pupil prefects and monitors, from all parts of the school ability range, whose role was largely one of supervision of other pupils in the absence of staff members. Such a practice appeared to have the effect of inhibiting the growth of anti-school pupil cultures because of its effect in creating senior pupils who were generally supportive of the school. It also had the latent and symbolic function of providing pupils with a sense of having some control over their within-school lives; the removal of these symbols also gave the school a further sanction it could utilize against its deviants. Attempts to incorporate pupils were paralleled by attempts to enlist the support of their parents by the establishment of close, informal or semi-formal relations between teachers and parents, the encouraging of informal visits by parents to the school and the frequent and full provision of information to parents that concerns pupil progress and governor and staff decisions.

Another means of incorporation into the values and norms of the school was the development of *inter*personal rather than *im*personal relationships between teachers and pupils. Basically, teachers in these incorporative schools attempted to tie pupils into the value systems of the school and of the adult society by means of developing 'good' personal relationships with them. In effect, the judgement was made in these schools that internalization of teacher values was more likely to occur if pupils saw teachers as 'significant others' deserving of respect. Good relationships were consequent upon minimal use of overt institutional control (so that pupil behaviour was relatively unconstrained), low rates of physical punishment, a tolerance of a limited amount of 'acting out' (such as by smoking or gum chewing, for example), a pragmatic hesitancy to enforce rules which may have provoked rebellion and an attempt to reward good behaviour rather than punish bad behaviour. Within this school ethos, instances of pupil 'deviance' evoked therapeutic, rather than coercive, responses from within the school.

In contrast, schools which utilized the 'coercive' strategy to a greater or lesser extent (three of the eight schools) made no attempt to incorporate pupils into the authority structure of the school, an action which would have been seen by them as akin to Montgomery inviting Rommel to become one of his staff officers. Furthermore, these schools made no attempt to incorporate the support of parents, because the teachers believed that no support would be forthcoming and they exhibited high levels of institutional control, strict rule enforcement, high rates of physical punishment and very little tolerance of any 'acting out'. The idea, as in the incorporative schools, of establishing some kind of 'truce' with pupils in these schools was anathema, since the teachers perceived that the pupils would necessarily abuse such an arrangement. Pupil deviance was expeditiously punished which, within the overall social context of these schools, was entirely understandable; therapeutic concern would have had little effect because pupils would have had little or no respect for the teacher-therapist.

The most likely explanation of the choice of different strategies is to be found in the differences (in the two groups of schools) in the teacher perceptions of their intakes. In schools which have adopted a 'coercive' strategy, there is a consistent tendency to over-estimate the proportion of pupils whose background can be said to be 'socially deprived' – in one such school, teachers thought such children accounted for seventy per cent of their intake whilst in one of the incorporative schools teachers put the proportion only at ten per cent – and a consistent tendency to under-estimate their pupils' ability. In these coercive schools, teachers regard pupils as being in need of 'character training' and 'control' which stems from a deficiency in primary socialization, a deficiency which the school attempts to make good by a form of custodialism. Such perceptions are germane seeds for the creation of a school ethos of coercion.

This variance between the teaching staffs of the two different groups of schools is wide and bears, as we have seen, virtually no correspondence with the reality (insofar as we are able to define reality) of their situation.

If the crucial factor in the generation of different school strategies is, as we believe, perceptions amongst teachers, then a plausible explanation would seem to be offered by the notion that the process at work in the 'coercive schools' is one where, to use William Ryan's apt phrase, teachers 'blame their victims'. What appears to be happening is that the staffs at the coercive schools externalize their failure by identifying their pupils as of less potential and as 'under-socialized'. Once such perceptions are generated, they are passed on to incoming teachers and incoming pupils, resulting in changes of values and of behaviour for both groups.

What makes an effective school?

Although it is clear then that the search for effective schools is still in its infancy and although it is clear that much remains to be discovered, we probably know enough from the American and British studies to attempt to draw together what makes for effective schooling and, just as important, what appears to make no difference to schools' levels of effectiveness.

1   Resource levels/expenditure per pupil

It seems unlikely that this factor is of major importance in affecting effectiveness. Coleman et al. (1966), McDill (1969) and Jencks et al. (1972) amongst others suggest this, although there are some hints that expenditure on teachers' salaries may have some effect on outcome (Thomas, 1962; Bowles and Levin, 1968; and some of the studies reported in Averch et al., 1971).

2   Quality/quantity of plant/buildings

Studies suggest this is unimportant, Coleman et al. (1966) for the United States and Reynolds (1976; 1980) for Britain. Physical aspects of school buildings such as plant size or whether the school is split across several sites appear of little importance (Rutter et al., 1979), as is actual age of buildings (Rutter et al., 1979; Reynolds, 1976). In the Reynolds study, more effective schools were actually situated in older buildings and in buildings rated as less adequate educational environments by educational officials! There are hints though that the day-to-day upkeep of buildings, rather than their basic adequacy or plant 'volume' per pupil, may be associated with school outcomes, as in the Rutter study and as in the Pablant and Baxter (1975) work, where vandalism was seen to be less in schools taking trouble over building upkeep and maintenance of their grounds.

3   Class size/pupil-teacher ratio

Evidence suggests this factor to be of doubtful importance (Davie, 1972;

Rutter *et al.* 1979; Wiseman, 1964). Recent Assessment of Performance Unit data upon the closely associated variable of pupil/teacher ratio suggests language, science and mathematical development at age 11 to be higher in schools with a *higher* ratio of pupils to teachers (1981a, b and c). Only the Reynolds' study (1976) suggests a relationship between this ratio and outcome, suggesting more favourable outcomes from more favourable ratios. Whether this association merely *reflects* school performance (because of difficulty in attracting staff to less effective schools for example) is unclear.

4   School size

Evidence here is contradictory. In Britain, the evidence suggests size of institution *per se* may not be an important factor (as in Rutter, 1980; Galloway, 1976; Halsall, 1973), the exception again being the Reynolds (1976) work which showed more effective schools to be consistently smaller. [. . .] It is possible that school size may be important up to a certain 'threshold', above which further increases in size are not associated with further decline in effectiveness (Garbarino and Asp, 1982) and it is equally possible that schools large on scale may be able to generate an institutional functioning characteristic of smaller institutions if they react appropriately.

5   Academic press

Schools high on this somewhat elusive concept of 'academic press' consistently appear as effective institutions (Rutter *et al.*, 1979; Brimer *et al.*, 1978; Garbarino and Asp, 1982; Madaus *et al.*, 1980; McDill, 1969, and many more summarized in Marjoribanks, 1979a and b). 'What seems important in affecting achievement are the academic demands of the courses, the students' concern for and commitment to academic values, the amount of time spent on study and homework and, in general, a climate of high expectations on the part of students and their teachers' (Madaus *et al.*, 1979, page 225).

6   Pupil participation in school life

Both major British studies suggest strongly that encouraging children to participate in the running of their schools appears conducive to good attainment, attendance and behaviour (Rutter *et al.*, 1979; Reynolds, 1976). Such mechanisms of fracturing potentially anti-school peer group sub-cultures by means of encouraging the development of pro-social, involved pupils is also argued to be effective in boarding school institutions (Lambert, 1970) and in specialist child care settings (Millham *et al.*, 1982).

7   *Psychological environment of the classroom*

Numerous reviews of the literature confirm the importance of classroom environment as a determinant of wider school effectiveness, although the partial independence of the school variables and the classroom variables suggest a complicated interaction, possibly with further intervening variables. [. . .] Recent comparative analysis with several thousand students, several hundred classrooms and four countries by Haertel and Walberg (1981) suggests positive learning outcomes are associated with Cohesiveness, Satisfaction, Task Difficulty, Formality, Goal Direction, Democracy, and negative association with Friction, Cliqueness, Apathy, Disorganization and Favouritism.

8   *Teacher expectations*

In spite of consistent failure to replicate the teacher expectations work of Rosenthal and Jacobson's (1968) study on *Pygmalion in the Classroom* researchers operating at the school rather than the individual level and operating in real life rather than experimental situations have consistently identified teacher views of and expectations of their pupils as affecting outcome (Cuttance, 1980 a and b; Douglas, 1964; Rist, 1970; Williams, 1976). The relationship between teacher perceptions of pupils' home background and pupil outcome is shown to be important in the delinquency study of Wadsworth (1979) and in Reynolds' work (especially 1979).

9   *Institutional control*

Evidence here is contradictory. Rutter *et al.* (1979) and Millham *et al.*, (1982) suggest that organizationally 'tight' regimes that attempt high expressive control of pupils within institution lives are 'effective', whereas Reynolds (1976; 1979) argues that schools with high institutional control are more 'ineffective'. It seems likely that harsh, authoritarian or 'custodial' school regimes may have adverse effects (Finlayson and Loughran, 1976; Rafalides and Hoy, 1971) but also that disorganized or 'anomic' institutions may have the same effect of generating weakly controlled pupils (D. H. Hargreaves, 1979; 1980; 1981). Rutter's 'tight' London comprehensives and Reynolds' low-control traditional Welsh secondary modern schools may therefore both be similarly placed between 'ineffective' ends of the distribution, both 'permissive' and 'authoritarian'. Effective schools may be characterized by a form of *balanced* control.

10   *Rewards and punishments*

Schools attempting to control pupils by offering rewards rather than punishments seem to be more effective (Rutter *et al.*, 1979) as do those avoiding heavy use of physical punishment (Clegg and Megson, 1968) and of caning (Reynolds, 1976).

[. . .]

What remains to be discovered?

There are a large number of areas that our research effort needs to focus upon in the future. We need future research that is undertaken across a wide range of geographical areas to see if the 'effective' school is the same type of institution in different catchment areas. We need work on primary schools to see if the same school factors are important as within secondary schools and we need to judge if the primary school has more or less effect upon outcome than the secondary school. We need to know what creates successful or effective schools. Is it LEA policy, a headteacher hero-innovator, a community-evoked response, or the result (partly) of past school output quality? We need to know how modifiable are the processes that determine within-school interaction and we need to know which forms of modification – behaviourist technology or psychodynamic stress on relationships – are most effective. We need to know the extent to which schools may affect different categories of children differently, boys as against girls, lower stream as against upper stream, host nation children as against those from ethnic minorities. We need also to explore the person/environment 'fit' at an individual level by focusing on the individual child's experience of school, which may of course be very different from child to child. The school needs to be viewed as a network of interlocking levels from individual, class, year and house to the full collectivity itself.

All we can say with confidence from looking at the evidence at the present time is that the evidence suggests that change in the nature of the products of secondary schooling is unlikely to be attained by further attempting to aim at the modification of the formal organization, the resource levels, the teaching methods and the curriculum content that much past school reform has focused on, since it seems unlikely that these factors are important determinants of outputs from schools in Britain and America. It is much more likely that the key to successful modification of school practice is likely to lie in the phenomenological world of schooling, in the perceptions that teachers in different schools have of their pupils, in the interpersonal relations and mutual perceptions of teachers and in the mutual interpersonal perceptions that govern teacher and pupil relations. Both the American and British studies that have been reported suggest that it is the 'culture' of schools rather than their structure that needs to be the focus for our efforts at reform. Whilst structural change at a classroom or school level is likely to affect attitudes and perceptions, successful modifications of school environments may well necessitate direct forms of intervention in the social relations of school life.

320   *David Reynolds*

References

ACTON, T. A. (1980) 'Educational criteria of success.' *Educational Research*, **22**, 163–9.

ASSESSMENT OF PERFORMANCE UNIT (1981a) *Language Performance in Schools.* London: HM Stationery Office.

ASSESSMENT OF PERFORMANCE UNIT (1981b) *Mathematical Development.* London: HM Stationery Office.

ASSESSMENT OF PERFORMANCE UNIT (1981c) *Science in Schools.* London: HM Stationery Office.

AVERCH, H., CARROLL, H., DONALDSON, T., KIESLING, H. and PINCUS, J. (1971) *How Effective is Schooling?* Santa Monica, CA: Rand Corporation.

BALDWIN, J. (1972) 'Delinquent schools in Tower Hamlets: a critique.' *British Journal of Criminology*, **12**, 399–401.

BOWLES, S. and LEVIN, H. M. (1968) 'The determinants of scholastic achievement – an appraisal of some recent evidence.' *Journal of Human Resources*, **3**, 1–24.

BRIMER, A., MADAUS, G. F., CHAPMAN, B., KELLAGHAN, T. and WOOD, R. (1978) *Sources of Difference in School Achievement.* Slough: NFER.

BROOKOVER, W. B. and LEZOTTE, L. W. (1976) *Changes in School Characteristic Coincident with Changes in Student Achievement.* College of Urban Development, Michigan State University.

CLEGG, A. and MEGSON, B. (1968) *Children in Distress.* Harmondsworth: Penguin Books.

COLEMAN, J. S., CAMPBELL, E., HOBSON, C., MCPARTLAND, J., MOOD, A., VEINFELD, F. and YORK, R. (1966) *Equality of Educational Opportunity.* Washington, DC: Government Printing Office.

CUTTANCE, P. (1980a) 'Do schools consistently influence the performance of their students?' *Educational Review*, **32**, 3, 267–80.

CUTTANCE, P. (1980b) *Coleman, Plowden, Jencks and now Rutter: An Assessment of a Recent Contribution to the Debate on School Effects.* Edinburgh: Centre for Educational Sociology.

DAVIE, R. (1972) 'Where is the evidence that children suffer from being in large classes?' *Where*, **67**, 73–108.

DAVIE, R., BUTLER, N. and GOLDSTEIN, H. (1972) *From Birth to Seven.* London: Longmans.

DOUGLAS, J. W. B. (1964) *The Home and the School.* London: McGibbon and Kee.

DYER, H. S. (1968) 'School factors and equal educational opportunity.' *Harvard Educational Review*, **38**, 38–56.

FARRINGTON, D. (1973) 'Delinquency begins at home.' *New Society*, **21**, 495–7.

FINLAYSON, D. and LOUGHRAN, J. L. (1976) 'Pupils' perceptions in high and low delinquency schools.' *Educational Research*, **18**, 2, 138–45.

GALLOWAY, D. (1976) 'Size of school, socio-economic hardship, suspension rates and persistent unjustified absence from school.' *British Journal of Educational Psychology*, **46**, 40–7.

GARBARINO, J. and ASP, C. E. (1982) *Successful Schools and Competent Students.* Lexington, MA: Lexington Books.

GATH, D. (1972) 'Child guidance and delinquency in a London borough.' *Psychological Medicine*, 2, 185–91.

GATH, D. *et al.* (1977) *Child Guidance and Delinquency in a London Borough.* Oxford: Oxford University Press.

GOLDSTEIN, H. (1980) 'Fifteen thousand hours: a review of the statistical procedures.' *Journal of Child Psychology and Psychiatry*, **21**, 364–6.

GOODMAN, S. M. (1959) *The Assessment of School Quality*. Albany, NY: State University of New York, Division of Research.

HAERTEL, G. D. and WALBERG, H. J. (1981) 'Socio-psychological environments and learning.' *British Educational Research Journal*, **7**, 27–36.

HALSALL, E. (1973) *The Comprehensive School*. London: Pergamon.

HANUSHEK, E. (1972) *Education and Race*. Lexington, MA: D. C. Heath.

HARGREAVES, A. (1980) 'Review article on *Fifteen Thousand Hours*.' *British Journal of Sociology of Education*, **1**, 211–16.

HARGREAVES, D. H. (1979) 'Durkheim, deviance and education', in BARTON, L. (ed.) *Schools, Pupils and Deviance*. Driffield: Nafferton.

HARGREAVES, D. H. (1980) 'Classrooms, schools, and juvenile delinquency', in HARGREAVES, D. H. (ed.) 'Classroom studies.' *Educational Analysis*, **2**, 2.

HARGREAVES, D. H. (1981) 'Schooling for delinquency', in BARTON, L. (ed.) *Schools, Teachers and Teaching*. Lewes: Falmer Press.

HURN, C. (1979) *The Limits and Possibilities of Schooling*. New York: McGraw-Hill.

JENCKS, C., SMITH, M., ACLAND, H., JOBANE, M., COHEN, D., GINTIS, H. HEYNS, B. and MICHELSON, S. (1972) *Inequality: A Reassessment of the Effects of Family and Schooling in America*. New York: Basic Books.

LAMBERT, R. (1970) *Manual to the Sociology of the School*. London: Weidenfeld and Nicholson.

MCDILL, E. L. (1969) 'Educational climates of high schools.' *American Journal of Sociology*, **74**, 567–86.

MCDILL, E. L. and RIGSBY, L. (1967) 'Institutional effects on the academic behaviour of high school students.' *Sociology of Education*, **40**, 181–99.

MCDILL, E. L. and RIGSBY, L. (1973) *Structure and Process in Secondary Schools*. Baltimore, MD: Johns Hopkins University Press.

MADAUS, G. F., KELLAGHAN, T., RAKOW, E. A. and KING, D. (1979) 'The sensitivity of measures of school effectiveness.' *Harvard Educational Review*, **49**, 165–83.

MADAUS, G. F., AIRASIAN, P. and KELLAGHAN, T. (1980) *School Effectiveness*. New York: McGraw-Hill.

MADDEN, J. V. *et al.* (1976) *School Effectiveness Study*. State of California.

MARJORIBANKS, K. (1979a) 'Family and school related characteristics of intelligence, personality and school related affective characteristics.' *Genetic Psychology Monographs*, **99**, 165–83.

MARJORIBANKS, K. (1979b) *Families and their Learning Environments*. London: Routledge and Kegan Paul.

MILLHAM, S., BULLOCK, R. and HOSIE, K. (1982) *Issues of Control in Child Care*. London: HM Stationery Office.

NEW YORK STATE OFFICE OF EDUCATION (1974) *School Factors Influencing Reading Attainment: A Case Study of Two Inner City Schools*. New York State Office of Education.

PABLANT, P, and BAXTER, J. C. (1975) 'Environmental correlates of school vandalism.' *Journal of the American Institute of Planners*, **241**, 270–9.

PEAKER, G. F. (1967) 'The regression analysis of the National Survey,' in *Children and their Primary Schools, Vol. 2*. London: HM Stationery Office.

POWER, M. J. *et al.* (1967) 'Delinquent schools?' *New Society*, 19 October.

POWER, M. J. *et al.* (1972) 'Neighbourhood, school and juveniles before the courts.' *British Journal of Criminology*, **12**, 111–32.

RAFALIDES, M. and HOY, W. K. (1971) 'Student sense of alienation and pupil control orientation of high schools.' *The High School Journal*, **55**, 101–11.

REYNOLDS, D. (1975) 'When teachers and pupils refuse a truce', in MUNGHAM, G. (ed.) *Working Class Youth Culture*. London: Routledge and Kegan Paul.

REYNOLDS, D. (1976) 'The delinquent school', in WOODS, P. (ed.) *The Process of Schooling*. London: Routledge and Kegan Paul.

REYNOLDS, D. (1980) 'School factors and truancy', in HERSOV, L. A. and BERG, I. (eds) *Out of School*. London: Wiley.

REYNOLDS, D., JONES, D. and ST LEGER, S. (1976) 'Schools do make a difference.' *New Society*, 19 July, 223–5.

REYNOLDS, D. and SULLIVAN, M. (1979) 'Bringing schools back in', in BARTON, L. A. (ed.) *Schools, Pupils and Deviance*. Driffield: Nafferton.

REYNOLDS, D., JONES, D., ST LEGER, S. and MURGATROYD, S. (in preparation) *Bringing Schools Back In*.

RIST, R. (1970) 'Student social class and teacher expectations – a self-fulfilling prophecy in ghetto education.' *Harvard Educational Review*, **40**, 411–51.

ROSENTHAL, R. and JACOBSON, L. (1968) *Pygmalion in the Classroom*. New York: Holt, Rinehart and Winston.

RUTTER, M. (1973) 'Why are London children so disturbed?' *Proceedings of the Royal Society of Medicine*, **66**, 1221–5.

RUTTER, M. (1980) *Changing Youth in a Changing World*. London: Nuffield Provincial Hospitals Trust.

RUTTER, M. and MADGE, N. (1976) *Cycles of Disadvantage*. London: Heinemann.

RUTTER, M., MAUGHAN, B., OUSTON, J. and MORTIMORE, P. (1979) *Fifteen Thousand Hours*. London: Open Books.

SHAYCROFT, M. (1967) *The High School Years: Growth in Linguistic Skills*. Pittsburgh, PA: American Institute for Research in Education.

STEVENS, J. M. (1967) *The Process of Schooling*. New York: Wiley.

THOMAS, J. A. (1962) *Efficiency in Education: A Study of the Relationship between Selected Inputs and Mean Test Scores in a Sample of Senior High Schools*. Unpublished Ph.D. dissertation, Stanford University School of Education.

WADSWORTH, M. J. (1979) *Roots of Delinquency*. London: Martin Robertson.

WEBER, G. (1971) *Inner City Children can be Taught to Read: Four Successful Schools*. Washington, DC: Council for Basic Education.

WILBY, P. (1977) 'Education and equality.' *New Statesman*, 16 September.

WILLIAMS, T. (1976) 'Teacher prophecies and the inheritance of inequality.' *Sociology of Education*, **49**, 223–35.

WISEMAN, S. (1964) *Education and Environment*. Manchester: Manchester University Press.

4.6 Cognitive development and the preschool

Charles J. Brainerd

[NOTE: this is the second half of Charles Brainerd's article 'Modifiability of Cognitive Development'. The first half is on pages 39–54 in this volume. References to both halves are on pages 333–7.]

Cognitive development and the preschool

I turn now to the implementation of Piaget's theory in the classroom. To many readers, it may seem odd that a theory whose predictions about the relationship between learning and development fare so poorly should prove influential in education. Nevertheless, it has. The chief reason for the anomaly is that the researchers who have conducted learning experiments and the educators who have devised Piaget-based curricula have not been the same people. Hence, curriculum development has tended to proceed in isolation from basic research on children's concept learning.

During the 1970s, Piagetian theory was at the center of what has come to be known as the 'cognitive curriculum movement' in North America. A number of pilot and experimental curricula were developed during this period which sought to translate the theory into educational practice. Nearly all of these curricula were in the area of early-childhood (pre-school) education rather than elementary or secondary education. [. . .]

Global recommendations about instruction

Piaget wrote many papers on education during his life, some of them as early as the 1930s. From these articles, as well as from the theory itself, educators have isolated several recommendations that might be implemented in a variety of ways. In some cases, there has been controversy over whether or not some particular recommendation actually follows from the theory. To avoid becoming mired in ethereal disputes, I concentrate on the specific recommendations that most educators regard as uncontroversial. For convenience, they are discussed under three headings: (a) readiness recommendations; (b) recommendations about what to teach; and (c) recommendations about teaching methods.

Source: MEADOWS, S. (ed.) (1983) *Developing Thinking* (ch. 2, pp. 47–66). London: Methuen.

Readiness

We have previously seen that Piaget's view of learning is what is usually called a readiness doctrine – i.e. he believed that children cannot and should not be taught concepts until they are developmentally prepared to learn them. This leads to four specific proposals about when children should be taught target concepts. We have already encountered one of them: do not teach children things that exceed their current stage of cognitive development. With preschoolers, it is the pre-operational and concrete-operational stages that we are concerned with. The age range in most preschools is roughly 2½–5½ years. Thus, the children in the lower half of this range will be almost entirely pre-operational, whereas those in the upper half of the range will be a mixture of pre-operational and concrete-operational children. According to the first proposal, instruction should focus on pre-operational concepts (e.g. identity, topology) with the former children and blend in some concrete-operational concepts (e.g. classification, seriation) with the latter.

The second readiness proposal is concerned with the *rate* at which instruction proceeds. Because learning must await development, Piagetians tend to oppose fast-paced instruction designed to accelerate children's progress through curriculum material. To Piagetians, such programs smack of trying to speed up the 'natural' rate of cognitive development. In place of acceleration, they favor what is usually called *mastery learning*. Here, instruction follows a more leisurely pace wherein each topic or concept must be thoroughly mastered before proceeding to the next one: 'if we want learning to be permanent and solid enough to permit cognitive development throughout the child's life, we must (1) let the child go from one stage after another of being "wrong" rather than expect him to reason logically like an adult, and (2) allow for a certain slowness in the developmental progress' (Kamii, 1973a, page 225).

The next readiness proposal deals with the order in which things are taught to children. In all of Piaget's research on cognitive development, much attention was given to describing the exact sequences in which children acquire concepts in everyday life. [. . .] In line with the notion that learning should mirror spontaneous development as much as possible, the third proposal is that we should teach children concepts in exactly the same order in which they acquire them naturally. We saw earlier, for example, that most children understand number conservation before length conservation, and that they understand length conservation before quantity conservation. Thus, if we sought to teach these three concepts to children, introducing them in the order number → length → quantity would be 'developmentally correct', but any other ordering would be 'developmentally wrong'.

The last readiness proposal follows from the first three. If we seek to teach only concepts that are in accord with the current stage (first proposal), to avoid acceleration (second proposal), and to teach things in the correct sequence (third proposal), it is obvious that we shall have to know a great deal about each child's state of conceptual knowledge: implementing the first proposal requires that we have sufficient information to decide whether a given child is concrete-operational or pre-operational; implementing the second proposal requires that we know just how completely a given child has learned the material that is currently being taught; implementing the third proposal requires that we know which concepts in a sequence are already understood by a given child and which are not. All this means that Piagetian instruction is always a two-step process of *cognitive diagnosis followed by instruction*. Instruction should only proceed when extensive diagnostic information is available for a child. Of course, the diagnostic instruments are the usual Piaget tests for logical concepts, spatial concepts, arithmetical concepts, and so forth.

This last readiness proposal is not easy to carry out. The problem is that having sufficient diagnostic information available on a child means that teachers must spend large amounts of time in one-on-one testing. If the instruction of other children is not to suffer as a consequence, there must be other teachers available. In other words, the teacher-pupil ratio must be very low to put the diagnostic recommendation into practice, much lower than is typical in preschools. Because the first three proposals all hinge on being able to do detailed diagnostic work-ups for individual children, the fact that it is rarely possible to do such work-ups means that it is difficult to incorporate any of the Piagetian readiness recommendations in most preschools.

What to teach

First, we return again to the fact that most preschool classes will consist of a mixture of pre-operational and concrete-operational children, with the latter predominating. Hence, the proper content of a Piaget-based early-childhood curriculum will be whatever concepts and skills are deemed to be essential to these stages. The concepts in question fall into the general areas of logic (e.g. transitive inference), mathematics (e.g. number), science (e.g. conservation), and space (e.g. Euclidean geometry). Thus, the most general recommendation about what to teach is that the key concepts of the pre-operational stage are all fair game for children who have been diagnosed as pre-operational, and the key concepts of the concrete-operational stage are all fair game for children who have been diagnosed as concrete-operational. But some rather more explicit recommendations about curriculum content are also possible.

One of the most interesting of these is in the area of geometry. Historically, instruction in the initial elementary grades concentrated on two areas, namely, language (including reading and writing) and mathematics. With respect to the latter, the focus was chiefly on arithmetic. Geometry was usually left until high school. However, Genevan research on spatial development (Piaget and Inhelder, 1956; Piaget, Inhelder and Szeminska, 1960) suggests that concepts of topological geometry are acquired during the pre-operational stage, while concepts of Euclidean and projective geometry are acquired during the concrete-operational stage. Thus, by the time most children have reached the second or third grade, the theory says that they are developmentally prepared for instruction in most forms of geometry. For this reason, Piaget-based curricula often include some exposure to geometrical concepts.

A second proposal about curriculum content is concerned with the physical medium that teachers use to transmit knowledge to children. From the earlier discussion of self-discovery learning, it should not be surprising that Piagetians favor the use of instructional materials that consist of *concrete objects* of some sort that can easily be *manipulated* by children. With respect to concreteness, Piaget believed that children cannot understand concepts at an abstract, linguistic level until they have reached the formal-operational stage. When teaching pre-operational and concrete-operational children, therefore, instruction that relies entirely on language (e.g. teachers lecturing to children) is destined to fail. Rather than simply explaining ideas to children verbally, teachers must demonstrate them using concrete objects. Also, since learning is ostensibly an active self-discovery process, the objects should be things that children can manipulate in such a way that they can demonstrate concepts *to themselves*. [. . .]

An interesting implication of this emphasis on manipulability of materials is that not all concrete methods of demonstrating concepts are equally good. In fact, some may not be very good at all if they involve passive reception of information by children. Two obvious examples that are mainstays of most classrooms are films and textbooks. Films are very concrete, involving as they do pictures and sound, and textbooks can be made concrete with the inclusion of pictures and illustrations. But children do not *do* anything to either of these media. They merely sit and observe in both cases. Consequently, they should not be especially effective as learning aids. It is worth reiterating here that this claim does not square with the learning research considered earlier.

How to teach

Last, I consider three recommendations about 'styles' of instruction that most educators believe to be endorsed by the theory. The first is our old friend self-discovery learning: 'Good pedagogy must involve presenting the child with situations in which he himself experiments, in the broadest sense of the term – trying things out to see what happens, manipulating symbols, posing questions, and seeking his own answers, reconciling what he finds one time with what he finds at another, comparing his findings with those of other children . . .' (Duckworth, 1964, p. 2). As the available learning research does not support Genevan claims about self-discovery, I shall not belabor this point.

The second teaching strategy grows out of the previously discussed construction principle. Recall here that according to this principle, cognitive progress occurs through a disequilibrium/equilibrium process in which, broadly speaking, children attempt to reconcile their current beliefs about how the world works with discrepant information. Educators interpret this principle to mean that teaching strategies which promote this sort of disagreement between objective reality and what children currently believe should be especially effective.

This proposal has led to an interesting line of learning research by Murray and his associates (e.g. Botvin and Murray, 1975; Murray, 1968, 1972). In these experiments, a group of children is first selected that show little or no understanding of some target concept, usually conservation. These subjects are then exposed to older children who do possess the concept. The basic idea is to produce cognitive conflict ('disequilibrium') in the subjects by making them aware that their current beliefs are not the same as those of other children. The standard procedure is to form groups comprised of one child who does not understand the to-be-learned concept and two children who do understand it. Tests for the concept are then administered to the group. The children are encouraged to debate their answers and to formulate a consensual response. This method, which is called conflict training, has proved to be quite effective.

The third strategy, peer teaching, has its origins in some of Piaget's earliest work. In his first book on cognitive development, *The Language and Thought of the Child*, he concluded that a child's peers play a major role in his or her cognitive development. [. . .]

As the most natural mechanism of peer interaction among young children is play, this has led to an emphasis on play-based instruction in Piagetian curricula. In some of the most recently developed programs, attempts have been made to base the entire curriculum on activities such as constructive play or dramatic play (e.g. Forman and Hill, 1980). [. . .]

Illustrative Piagetian preschool programs

Extant Piaget-based curricula can be conveniently divided into those that were developed during an initial spate of educational enthusiasm for the theory in the late 1960s/early 1970s and those that have been developed more recently. I discuss two influential representatives from each category.

Early programs

Of the various Piagetian curricula that were piloted during the late 1960s/early 1970s, the two that had the greatest impact were the Early

Childhood Curriculum and the Open Framework Program. The former was developed by the late Celia Lavatelli (1970, 1971) at the University of Illinois, and the latter was developed by David Weikart (1973; Weikart, Rogers, Adcock and McClelland, 1971) in Ypsilanti, Michigan.

The principal distinguishing feature of Lavatelli's Early Childhood Curriculum is that it was the first program to bring systematic instruction in Piagetian concepts into the preschool. We have already seen that an important difficulty with Piaget-based curricula is the requirement of extensive diagnosis and testing of children's current states of knowledge. To deal with this problem, Lavatelli developed a battery of tests for various concrete-operational concepts that was subsequently made available to preschool teachers as a kit. The kit incorporated tests for concepts from five categories, namely, classification, measurement, number, seriation, and space. By administering the various tests in the Lavatelli kit, it is possible, at least in principle, to obtain a reasonably clear fix on children's current stage of cognitive development: children who perform poorly in all five areas would obviously be regarded as pre-operational by the theory; children who perform well in all five areas would be regarded as concrete-operational; and other children would be regarded as transitional.

When it comes to instruction, the emphasis is squarely on learning concepts by having children manipulate concrete objects. Lavatelli (1970) gave the following illustration about learning number conservation: 'Using toys and pennies, for example, a child may on a perceptual level state that there are more toys in a long row than there are pennies to buy these toys when an identical amount of pennies is placed in a pile near the row of toys. Moving the pennies one-to-one beside each toy may cause the child to reconsider; now there is one penny for each toy. . . . His thinking has been challenged by operating on real materials in an enjoyable activity' (p. 4).

Peer interaction is also stressed in the Early Childhood Curriculum. The main strategy for promoting such interactions is what might be called 'committee work'. Teachers are encouraged to organize children into small working groups of about five children each. The working groups then carry out the manipulative activities that are designed to teach concrete-operational concepts, and presumably, assist each other in learning the concepts.

A final, important feature of the Early Childhood Curriculum is that the teacher, not the children, plays the dominant role in organizing each day's activities. It is the teacher who assigns children to working groups and who selects exercises for each group. Teachers are told to select specific exercises that emphasize the correct features of concrete-operational concepts, and they are discouraged from selecting exercises that might lead children to make errors. Specific examples of 'right' and 'wrong' exercises are given in Lavatelli's books.

Turning to the Open Framework Program, its principal distinguishing feature is that it is focused on only a single area of concrete-operational thinking, namely, classification concepts. The reason for this emphasis is Weikart's interpretation of some of Piaget and Inhelder's writings, according to which classification concepts are fundamental to most of the things that children will later be taught in the elementary grades (e.g. arithmetic and reading). Hence, the Open Framework Program consists of a series of exercises that are designed to transmit simple classificatory skills, as well as more complex classification concepts such as class inclusion. There are multiple exercises for each classification concept that Weikart deemed important. One of the readiness proposals mentioned earlier, sequentiality, is also emphasized. The order in which the exercises are introduced for individual classificatory concepts is roughly the same as the order in which children acquire these concepts in everyday life.

As in the Early Childhood Curriculum, the Open Framework teacher controls the curriculum. The teacher is instructed to select the specific exercise items, especially during the initial phases of instruction on a given concept, and explicit guidelines are provided as to which exercises should be introduced in which order. Also, the Open Framework teacher is told to observe children's performance and to ask them questions during the course of exercises.

Some evaluation data are available on both the Lavatelli and Weikart programs. When evaluating any preschool curriculum, the main question is, do children who are exposed to the curriculum show improved intellectual performance relative to children who did not attend any preschool, or relative to children who were exposed to some other preschool curriculum? Lavatelli examined this question by administering standardized intelligence tests, plus tests for certain concrete-operational concepts, to children both before they entered the program and one year later. The scores that children achieved on such tests were usually higher on the second administration than on the first, a datum that Lavatelli interpreted as showing that her curriculum was effective. Unfortunately, this conclusion does not necessarily follow. The difficulty is that Lavatelli failed to test a comparison sample of control children who were not exposed to the Early Childhood Curriculum. Normative data show that children's scores on tests of the sort that Lavatelli administered, especially the concrete-operational tests, will almost always be better after one year. For example, if we administered conservation tests to children on their fourth birthday and one year later on their fifth birthday, the latter scores will be much higher than the former. In short, without data on a control sample of children, we do not know how much of the improvement that Lavatelli observed in her children was due to the curriculum and how much was due to the spontaneous improvements that take place as children become older.

More thorough evaluation data are available on the Open Framework Program (Weikart, 1973). A sample of three- and four-year-old children attended an Open Framework classroom for several months. They attended five half-day sessions per week, and they also received a special tutorial session once a week in their homes. There were two comparison samples. The children in one of these groups, who were also three- and four-year-old retardates, received a comparable amount of instruction in a reinforcement-oriented curriculum (token economy) based on operant principles. The children in the other group received comparable exposure to a curriculum that stressed children's social and personality development rather than the acquisition of cognitive abilities.

After completion of their respective programs, three measures of curriculum impact were gathered for all three groups, namely, scores on standardized intelligence tests, teacher ratings of the children, and ratings of the children by outside experts. The surprising result was that although the three curricula were radically different, they did not differ in effectiveness; the three groups performed similarly on the three types of measures. This led Weikart to conclude that the *content* of a preschool curriculum is probably far less crucial to its effectiveness than the interest, commitment, and competence of the teachers.

Recent programs

Another round of Piagetian curriculum development began in the mid 1970s. The impetus for these second generation programs was certain conceptual criticisms of the early programs. Essentially, curricula such as the Lavatelli and Weikart programs were criticized for insufficient obeisance to the authority of Piagetian theory. They were accused, more particularly, of taking unacceptable liberties with the theory and, as a result, of not being 'truly Piagetian'.

Three of the more prominent illustrations of such criticisms are these. First, recall that both the Early Childhood Curriculum and the Open Framework Program consist of detailed instruction in concrete-operational concepts. Orthodox Piagetians are inclined to interpret this as violating the first and second readiness recommendations discussed earlier. That is, such instruction is said to involve teaching concepts that are clearly beyond preschoolers' current stage of cognitive development, and it amounts to speeding up the 'natural' rate of cognitive development. Second, recall that Early Childhood teachers and Open Framework teachers take active control of the curriculum. To orthodox Piagetians, this violates the maxim that children should learn through active self-discovery of concepts. Third, recall that Open Framework teachers comment on children's activities and help them learn by posing questions about exercises. Orthodox Piagetians believe that this violates the prescription that early-childhood instruction should not be language-based.

Criticisms such as these have led, naturally, to curricula in which the authors have sought to be as faithful as possible to Piagetian theory. The two most influential examples of such curricula are the Piagetian Preschool Education Program (Lawton, Hooper, Saunders and Roth, 1978; Bingham-Newman, 1974; Ershler, McAllister and Saunders, 1977;

Saunders, 1976) and the Piaget for Early Education program (Kamii, 1973a and b; Kamii and DeVries, 1977, 1978).

The Piagetian Preschool Education Program was developed by F. H. Hooper and several collaborators at the University of Wisconsin. When the project began, the aim was simply to determine whether it was possible to design an orthodox Piagetian curriculum. During this phase, an extensive list of recommendations was culled from Piaget's writings (see Bingham-Newman, 1974). Next, a curriculum was designed around this list, and the curriculum was eventually introduced in the University of Wisconsin's experimental preschool. The content of the curriculum was superficially similar to Lavatelli's (1970, 1971) in that it emphasized several categories of concrete-operational concepts (classification, measurement, number, seriation, space, and time). But teachers' instructional strategies were quite different.

Briefly, teachers in the Piagetian Preschool Education Program are strongly discouraged from undertaking any sort of instruction that involves direct transmission of concepts to children. Instead, they are provided with a series of classroom activities that are designed to promote self-discovery of concepts by children. As might be expected, these exercises involve the active manipulation of concrete objects by children, *but not on instructions from the teachers.* Children are free to select whatever activities they wish and, importantly, teachers are discouraged from helping children to avoid 'wrong' exercises.

Evaluation data on the Piagetian Preschool Education Program are available. The principal source of evidence consists of scores on two standardized tests of intelligence (Peabody Picture Vocabulary and Raven's Progressive Matrices) and scores on tests for various concrete-operational concepts. These tests were administered before and after children had completed two years in the program. The same tests were administered to children who had been attending preschools using non-Piagetian curricula for the same period. The results were very similar to Weikart's. On the one hand, children performed much better on all tests after two years of preschool than at the outset. However, as in the case of Lavatelli's (1970, 1971) research, it is unclear how much of this improvement is attributable to the curriculum and how much is due to spontaneous age improvements. On the other hand, there were no differences in the performance of Piagetian and non-Piagetian pupils on either the standardized measures or the concrete-operational tests.

The second example of a recent and more orthodox Piagetian curriculum is the Piaget for Early Education program. Although this curriculum has been in operation for a few years, its developers, Kamii and DeVries, have not been very specific about its content in their writings. Perhaps the most accurate thing that can be said is that the curriculum is highly unstructured in comparison to those that we have already considered. Kamii was a member of the original group that developed the Open Framework Program, and the Piaget for Early Education program was an attempt to correct what Kamii believed were misinterpretations of Piagetian theory by Weikart.

The core of the Piaget for Early Education curriculum is a list of seven guiding principles of instruction (e.g. encourage children to be independent and curious, encourage children to interact with their peers, encourage children to learn in the context of play activities). These principles resemble the list developed during the initial phase of the Wisconsin program, and there are many points of overlap. Unlike the Wisconsin program, however, the list is not translated into a 'cookbook' curriculum complete with specific exercises for specific concepts.

Essentially, no evaluation data are available on this program. Although such data could easily be gathered, they have not been for reasons that are primarily philosophical. The type of evaluation data discussed for the other three programs are what educators call *summative* evaluation. But there is another type of evaluation called *formative* evaluation. Formative evaluation is purely conceptual. It is concerned with the degree of conformity of a program to the theory that inspired it. A program receives a high formative evaluation score if it adheres closely to the parent theory and a low formative evaluation score if it takes liberties with the theory. According to Kamii, summative evaluation is distinctly unPiagetian; the proper method of evaluating a Piagetian preschool program is formative (cf. Johnson and Hooper, 1982).

To many readers, this elevation of subjective, 'construct validity' methods of evaluation over hard data may seem like a cynical avoidance of educational responsibilities, especially in view of the lack of support for Piagetian hypotheses in the literature on children's concept learning. A more charitable interpretation, one that I favor, will be familiar to students of the history of science. Experience has taught us that skepticism is the proper attitude to adopt in connection with any theory. If one is committed to the fundamental truth of some theory, it becomes possible to justify all manner of far-fetched research procedures on the ground that they produce findings that agree with the theory. More to the point, one is inclined to ignore findings that disagree with theory, as well as the procedures that produce them, in the belief that they cannot possibly be correct. Unfortunately, Piaget's work, like Freud's before him, has given birth to a circle of acolytes, particularly within education, who appear to be deeply committed to the truth of the theory. The Piaget for Early Education curriculum is only one symptom of this problem. Many others could be given.

Synopsis

In this second section, I have reviewed some aspects of how Piaget's theory has been put into practice in education, at least in North America. As we have seen, there appear to be a fairly substantial list of instructional dos and don'ts that can be derived from the theory. Some of these recommendations find support in basic research on cognitive development, but others are either poorly supported by basic research or are contradicted by it. I have also reviewed four examples of Piaget-inspired preschool curricula. These programs vary considerably in their content and in their degree of adherence to theory.

Finally, I should like to stress that the development and testing of Piagetian preschool curricula remains an active area of educational research. In addition to the two illustrations of recent curricula that were considered, there are other still more recent programs. New themes are continuing to emerge. For example, the trend away from anything resembling formal instruction that is apparent in Piaget for Early Education seems to be accelerating, and there seems to be a growing emphasis on play (cf. Johnson and Hooper, 1982). But this is essentially crystal ball gazing. It will not be possible to comment authoritatively on this matter until such trends have become more firmly established in the literature.

References

BEILIN, H. (1965) 'Learning and operational convergence in logical thought development.' *Journal of Experimental Child Psychology*, **2**, 317–39.

BEILIN, J. (1971) 'The training and acquisition of logical operations', in ROSS-KOPF, M. F., STEFFE, L. P. and TABACK, S. (eds) *Piagetian Cognitive-Developmental Research and Mathematics Education*. Washington, DC: National Council of Teachers of Mathematics.

BINGHAM-NEWMAN, A. M. (1974) 'Development of logical operations ability in early childhood: a longitudinal comparison of the effects of two preschool settings.' Unpublished doctoral dissertation, University of Wisconsin.

BOTVIN, G. J. and MURRAY, F. H. (1975) 'The efficacy of peer modeling and social conflict in the acquisition of conservation.' *Child Development*, **46**, 769–9.

BRAINERD, C. J. (1971) 'The development of the proportionality scheme in children and adolescents.' *Developmental Psychology*, **5**, 469–76.

BRAINERD, C. J. (1972a) 'Reinforcement and reversibility in quantity conservation acquisition.' *Psychonomic Science*, **27**, 114–16.

BRAINERD, C. J. (1972b) 'The age-stage issue in conservation acquisition.' *Psychonomic Science*, **27**, 115–17.

BRAINERD, C. J. (1974) 'Training and transfer of transitivity, conservation and class inclusion of length.' *Child Development*, **45**, 324–34.

BRAINERD, C. J. (1977) 'Cognitive development and concept learning: an interpretative review.' *Psychological Bulletin*, **84**, 919–39.

BRAINERD, C. J. (1978a) 'Learning research and Piagetian theory', in SIEGEL, L. S. and BRAINERD, C. J. (eds) *Alternatives to Piaget: Critical Essays on the Theory*. New York: Academic Press.

BRAINERD, C. J. (1978b) 'Cognitive development and instructional theory.' *Contemporary Educational Psychology*, **3**, 37–50.

BRAINERD, C. J. (1978c) *Piaget's Theory of Intelligence*. Englewood Cliffs, NJ: Prentice-Hall.

BRAINERD, C. J. (1979) 'Concept learning and developmental stage', in KLAUS-

MEIER, H. J. et al. *Cognitive Learning and Development: Piagetian and Information-Processing Perspectives.* Cambridge, MA: Ballinger.

BRAINERD, C. J. (1981) 'Stages II.' *Developmental Review*, **1**, 63–81.

BRAINERD, C. J. (1982a) 'Children's concept learning as rule-sampling systems with Markovian properties', in BRAINERD, C. J. (ed.) *Children's Logical and Mathematical Cognition: Progress in Cognitive Development Research.* New York: Springer.

BRAINERD, C. J. (1982b) 'The stage-learning hypothesis: strategies for instructional design.' *Contemporary Educational Psychology*, **7**, 238–56.

BRAINERD, C. J. and ALLEN, T. W. (1971a) 'Experimental inductions of the conservation of "first-order" quantitative invariants.' *Psychological Bulletin*, **75**, 128–44.

BRAINERD, C. J. and ALLEN, T. W. (1971b) 'Training and transfer of density conservation.' *Child Development*, **42**, 693–704.

BRAINERD, C. J. and BRAINERD, S. H. (1972) 'Order of acquisition of number and liquid quantity conservation.' *Child Development*, **43**, 1401–5.

BRUNER, J. S. (1964) 'The course of cognitive growth.' *American Psychologist*, **18**, 1–5.

BUCHER, B. and SCHNEIDER, R. E. (1973) 'Acquisition and generalization of conservation by pre-schoolers using operant training.' *Journal of Experimental Child Psychology*, **16**, 187–204.

CANTOR, G. N., DUNLAP, L. L. and RETTIE, C. S. (1982) 'Effects of reception and discovery instruction on kindergarteners' performance on probability tasks.' *American Educational Research Journal*, **19**, 453–63.

COLE, M. and SCRIBNER, S. (1974) *Culture and Thought.* New York: Wiley.

DENNEY, N. W. and ACTIO, M. A. (1974) 'Classification training in 2- and 3-year-old children.' *Journal of Experimental Child Psychology*, **17**, 37–48.

DENNEY, N. W., ZEYTINOGLU, S. and SELZER, S. C. (1977) 'Conservation training in 4-year-olds.' *Journal of Experimental Child Psychology*, **24**, 129–46.

DUCKWORTH, E. (1964) 'Piaget rediscovered', in RIPPLE, R. E. and ROCKCASTLE, V. N. (eds) *Piaget Rediscovered.* Ithaca, NY: Cornell University Press.

ELKIND, D. (1967) 'Piaget's conservation problems.' *Child Development*, **38**, 15–27.

EMRICK, J. A. (1967) 'The acquisition and transfer of conservation skills by 4-year-old children.' Unpublished doctoral dissertation, University of California, Los Angeles.

ERSCHLER, J., MCALLISTER, A. and SAUNDERS, R. A. (1977) 'The Piagetian derived curriculum: theoretical framework, preschool objectives and program description.' Working paper 205, Wisconsin Research and Development Center for Cognitive Learning, University of Wisconsin.

FIELD, D. (1981) 'Can preschool children really learn to conserve?' *Child Development*, **52**, 326–34.

FLAVELL, J. H. (1963) *The Developmental Psychology of Jean Piaget.* Princeton, NJ: Van Nostrand.

FORMAN, G. E. and HILL, F. (1980) *Constructive Play: Applying Piaget in the Preschool.* Monterey, CA: Brooks/Cole.

GELMAN, R. (1969) 'Conservation acquisition: a problem of learning to attend to relevant attributes.' *Journal of Experimental Child Psychology*, **7**, 167–87.

GOLDSCHMID, M. L. (1968) 'Role of experience in the acquisition of conservation.' *Proceedings of the American Psychological Association*, **76**, 361–2.

GOLDSCHMID, M. L. (1971) 'Role of experience in the rate and sequence of cognitive development', in GREEN, D. R., FORD, M. P. and FLAMER, G. B. (eds) *Measurement and Piaget.* New York: McGraw-Hill.

HALFORD, G. S. (1970) 'A classification learning set which is a possible model for conservation of quantity.' *Australian Journal of Psychology*, **22**, 11–19.

HAMEL, B. R. and RIKSEN, B. O. M. (1973) 'Identity, reversibility, verbal rule instruction and conservation.' *Developmental Psychology*, **9**, 66–72.

HATANO, G. (1971) 'A developmental approach to concept formation: a review of neo-Piagetian learning experiments.' *Dokkyo University Bulletin of Liberal Arts and Education*, **5**, 66–72.

HATANO, G. and SUGA, Y. (1969) 'Equilibration and external reinforcement in the acquisition of number conservation.' *Japanese Psychological Research*, **11**, 17–31.

INHELDER, B. (1956) 'Criteria of the stages of mental development', in TANNER, J. M. and INHELDER, B. (eds) *Discussions on Child Development, Vol. 1*. London: Tavistock.

INHELDER, B. and SINCLAIR, H. (1969) 'Learning cognitive structures', in MUSSEN, P. H., LANGER, J. and COVINGTON, M. (eds) *Trends and Issues in Developmental Psychology*. New York: Holt, Rinehart and Winston.

INHELDER, B., SINCLAIR, H. and BOVET, M. (1974) *Learning and the Development of Cognition*. Cambridge, MA: Harvard University Press.

INHELDER, B., SINCLAIR, H., BOVET, M. and SMOCK, C. (1966) 'On cognitive development.' *American Psychologist*, **21**, 160–4.

JOHNSON, J. E. and HOOPER, F. H. (1982) 'Piagetian structuralism and learning: reflections on two decades of educational application.' *Contemporary Educational Psychology*, **7**, 217–37.

KAMII, C. (1973a) 'Pedagogical principles derived from Piaget's theory: relevance for educational practice', in SCHWEBEL, M. and RAPH, J. (eds) *Piaget in the Classroom*. New York: Basic Books.

KAMII, C. (1973b) 'Piaget's interactionism and the process of teaching young children', in SCHWEBEL, M. and RAPH, J. (eds) *Piaget in the Classroom*. New York: Basic Books.

KAMII, C. and DEVRIES, R. (1977) 'Piaget for early education', in DAY, M. C. and PARKER, R. (eds) *The Preschool in Action* (2nd edn). Boston, MA: Allyn and Bacon.

KAMII, C. and DEVRIES, R. (1978) *Physical Knowledge in Preschool Education: Implications of Piagetian Theory*. Englewood Cliffs, NJ: Prentice-Hall.

LAVATELLI, C. S. (1970) *Early Childhood Curriculum. A Piagetian Program*. Boston, MA: American Science Engineering.

LAVATELLI, C. S. (1971) *Piaget's Theory Applied to an Early Childhood Curriculum*. Boston, MA: American Science and Engineering.

LAWTON, J. T., HOOPER, F. H., SAUNDERS, R. A. and ROTH, P. (1978) *A Comparison of Three Early Childhood Instructional Programs*. Technical Report 462, Wisconsin Research and Development Center for Cognitive Learning, University of Wisconsin.

MCCRAW, M. B. (1940) 'Neural maturation as exemplified in achievement of bladder control.' *Journal of Pediatrics*, **16**, 580–9.

MERMELSTEIN, E. and MEYER, E. (1969) 'Conservation training techniques and their effects on different populations.' *Child Development*, **40**, 471–90.

MURRAY, F. B. (1968) 'Cognitive conflict and reversibility training in the acquisition of length conservation.' *Journal of Educational Psychology*, **59**, 82–7.

MURRAY, F. B. (1972) 'Acquisition of conservation through social interaction.' *Developmental Psychology*, **6**, 1–6.

PIAGET, J. (1952) *The Child's Conception of Number*. New York: Humanities Press.

PIAGET, J. (1960) 'The general problems of the psychobiological development of the child', in TANNER, J. M. and INHELDER, B. (eds) *Discussions on Child Development, Vol. 4.* London: Tavistock.

PIAGET, J. (1970a) 'Piaget's theory', in MUSSEN, P. H (ed.) *Carmichael's Manual of Child Psychology.* New York: Wiley.

PIAGET, J. (1970b) 'A conversation with Jean Piaget.' *Psychology Today,* **3**, 12, 25–32.

PIAGET, J. and INHELDER, B. (1956) *The Child's Conception of Space.* London: Routledge and Kegan Paul.

PIAGET, J. and INHELDER, B. (1969) *The Psychology of the Child.* New York: Basic Books.

PIAGET, J., INHELDER, B. and SZEMINSKA, A. (1960) *The Child's Conception of Space.* New York: Harper.

ROSENTHAL, T. L. and ZIMMERMAN, B. J. (1972) 'Modeling by exemplification and instruction in training conservation.' *Developmental Psychology,* **6**, 392–401.

ROSENTHAL, T. L. and ZIMMERMAN, B. J. (1978) *Social Learning and Cognition.* New York: Academic Press.

SAUNDERS, R. Q. (1976) 'Classification abilities in young children: longitudinal effects of a Piagetian approach to a preschool program and to teacher education.' Unpublished doctoral dissertation, University of Wisconsin.

SINCLAIR, H. (1973) 'Recent Piagetian research in learning studies', in SCHWEBEL, M. and RAPH, J. (eds) *Piaget in the Classroom.* New York: Basic Books.

SKINNER, B. F. (1974) *About Behaviorism.* New York: Knopf.

SMEDSLUND, J. (1959) 'Apprentissage des notions de la conservation et de la transitivite du poids.' *Etudes d'Epistemologie Genetique,* **9**, 3–13.

SMEDSLUND, J. (1961a) 'The acquisition of conservation of substance and weight in children. I: Introduction.' *Scandinavian Journal of Psychology,* **2**, 11–20.

SMEDSLUND, J. (1961b) 'The acquisition of conservation of substance and weight in children. II: External reinforcement of conservation of weight and of the operations of addition and subtraction.' *Scandinavian Journal of Psychology,* **2**, 71–84.

SMEDSLUND, J. (1961c) 'The acquisition of conservation of substance and weight in children. III: Extinction of conservation of weight acquired "normally" and by means of empirical controls on a balance scale.' *Scandinavian Journal of Psychology,* **2**, 85–7.

SMEDSLUND, J. (1961d) 'The acquisition of conservation of substance and weight in children. IV: An attempt at extinction of the visual components of the weight concept.' *Scandinavian Journal of Psychology,* **2**, 154–5.

SMEDSLUND, J. (1961e) 'The acquisition of conservation of substance and weight in children. V: Practice in conflict situations without reinforcement.' *Scandinavian Journal of Psychology,* **2**, 156–60.

SMEDSLUND, J. (1961f) 'The acquisition of conservation of substance and weight in children. VI: Practice on continuous versus discontinuous material in conflict situations without external reinforcement.' *Scandinavian Journal of Psychology,* **2**, 203–10.

STRAUSS, S. and LANGER, J. (1970) 'Operational thought inducement.' *Child Development,* **41**, 163–75.

WALLACH, L. and SPROTT, R. L. (1964) 'Inducing number conservation in children.' *Child Development,* **35**, 1057–71.

WEIKART, D. P. (1973) 'Development of effective preschool programs: a report on the results of the High/Scope-Ypsilanti preschool projects.' Paper presented at High/Scope Educational Research Foundation Conference, Ann Arbor, Michigan.

WEIKART, D. P., ROGERS, L., ADCOCK, C. and MCCLELLAND, D. (1971) *The Cognitively Oriented Curriculum: A Framework for Preschool Teachers*. Urbana, IL: University of Illinois Press.

WOHLWILL, J. F. (1959) 'Un essai d'apprentissage dans le domaine de la conservation du nombre.' *Etudes d'Epistemologie Genetique*, **9**, 125–35.

WOHLWILL, J. F. and LOWE, R. C. (1962) 'An experimental analysis of the conservation of number.' *Child Development*, **33**, 153–67.

ZIMMERMAN, B. J. and LANARO, P. (1974) 'Acquiring and retaining conservation of length through modeling and reversibility cues.' *Merrill-Palmer Quarterly*, **20**, 145–61.

4.7   Education can compensate

A. H. Halsey

Educational budgets are now under siege all over the western world. Ministries of Education have been dominated by optimism for a century. They pursued policies of expansion in the belief that national wealth, and the reduction of social inequality, would inevitably follow.

The official ideology of liberal progress was never undisputed, but it was dominant. The consensual political middle trudged on in Britain, through the 1870, 1902 and 1944 Education Acts, slowly developing a state system of common schooling from infancy to adolescence, topped by selective and voluntary education beyond school.

Optimism reached its apogee in the easy affluence of the 1950s and early 1960s, with education steadily increasing its share of both the gross domestic product and the public purse, until at the end of the sixties it was halted. Schools and colleges now stand in the shadows, convicted of high promises and low performance.

Professor Jensen convinced many Americans that the intelligence of black children could not be boosted by pre-school programmes.[1] In Britain this abrupt reversal of fortune was rationalized mainly by the Black Paper pessimism of the right, compounded by economic depression and now by a monetarist government bent on cutting public expenditure. Nursery education – formerly and ironically a darling of Margaret Thatcher when Secretary of State – is now a prime target.

But the defences of the educational expansionists were also undermined from the left. Christopher Jencks's *Inequality* (Jencks *et al.*, 1972)[2] was a powerful American blow against what he took to be the misguided faith of the schoolmaster turned President in Lyndon Johnson's Washington:

'As long as egalitarians assume that public policy cannot contribute to economic equality directly but must proceed by ingenious manipulations of marginal institutions like the schools, progress will remain glacial. If we want to move beyond this tradition, we will have to establish political control over the economic institutions that shape our society. That is what other countries usually call socialism. Anything less will end in the same disappointment as the reforms of the 1960s.'

The most publicized 'ingenious manipulations of marginal institutions' in America in the 1960s was Headstart – a programme of preschooling. Disappointment with Headstart's early results were the starting point of Jensen's researches. All the more interesting, then, to have a study published a decade later by the American Department of Health, Educa-

Source: *New Society* (1980), 24 January, 172–3.

tion and Welfare, in which the question is elaborately asked whether there have in fact been *Lasting Effects After Preschool* from the euphoric educational reforms of the 'war on poverty'.[3]

In Britain, preschooling developed sceptically and tentatively (in the wake of Headstart) within the action research programmes of Education Priority Areas. It was greeted with hostility from both left and right. 'A research smokescreen,' declared John Barron Mays, Professor of Sociology at Liverpool. 'Nursery education has been tried in America and doesn't work,' was the crude opinion of a high-ranking Tory minister. Moreover, and unhappily, one of the most influential and deservedly respected sociologists of education, Professor Basil Bernstein, could also be involved in opposition to the Headstart idea. He entitled an influential article 'Education cannot compensate for society' (Bernstein, 1970);[4] warned against treating children as 'deficit systems'; against distracting attention from the reform of schools on to the shortcomings of parents and families; and against the sanctifying of concepts like 'cultural deprivation' as labels which would add further to the burdens of the children made to wear them.

Bernstein's were humane cautions linked to sophisticated argument. But they were easily and fatally assimilated to the holy proletarianism of a then-fashionable left, with its ideologically *a priori* rejection of the possibility that anything could be wrong with a working class child.

Those who were more concerned with practical reform than with ideological purity preferred to notice that 'deficit' could be socially created. They inferred that it could therefore be socially remedied. But, as has so often happened with Bernstein's research, the message was vulgarized by others. In the popular and political mind what stuck was his:

We should stop thinking in terms of 'compensatory education' and not the rest of the sentence, which read:
but consider, instead, most seriously and systematically the conditions and contexts of the educational environment.

The Education Priority Area (EPA) projects in London, Liverpool, Birmingham and the West Riding were well described by the neglected half of Bernstein's sentence. They also, however, contained crucial elements of 'compensatory' (even though the participants preferred to call it 'complementary') education. More precisely, the EPA researchers had been impressed by the principle of positive discrimination, put forward in the Plowden report of 1967.[5]

They tried, with resources that have to be described as miniscule by comparison with the American programme, to apply positive discrimination to the educational environment of slum children. The EPA projects – which were directed from Oxford – began when and because Anthony Crosland was Secretary of State at the Department of Education and Science, and Michael Young was chairman of the Social Science Research Council. They ended and reported when Mrs Thatcher was established at the DES and Sir Keith Joseph at the DHSS. Most precisely they recommended positive discrimination in pre-schooling.

The experience of three years in four districts had led to the conclusion 'that pre-schooling is *par excellence* a point of entry into the development of the community school as we conceive of it. It is the point at which properly understood, the networks of family and formal education can most easily be linked.' And three years of action research supported the contention 'that pre-schooling is the most effective educational instrument for applying the principle of positive discrimination and this conviction rests partly on the theory that primary and secondary educational attainment has its social foundations in the child's experience in the pre-school years, and partly on the evidence that positive discrimination at the pre-school level can have a multiplier effect on the overwhelmingly important educative influence of the family and the peer group to which the child belongs.'[6]

We can now go some way further towards testing the validity of an adherence to optimism, retained in the teeth of opposition both then and since. The new American study has been produced by a consortium of twelve research groups, carrying out studies of the *long-run* effects of the early education programmes of the 1960s (Consortium, 1978).[3] The group was led by Irving Lazar and Richard Darlington. Having pooled the data from their originally independent experiments, they collected common follow-up data in 1976–7. In this way they have assembled records of the experience and performance of 3,000 children, mostly black and all poor, who were involved in early education programmes in the 1960s, either as 'experimental' or 'control' subjects, and who by 1976–7 were between nine and 19 years old.

This is valuable and rare evidence. It would take another 15 years and millions of dollars to re-create it. Of course, it has its imperfections, quite apart from the dangers of any transatlantic passage. The original Headstart experiments were not designed to collect common information. They varied in size, starting point and content; they were, to varying degrees, experimental; and there has been a lot of attrition. Moreover, those in the Lazar–Darlington study are not just any old Headstart projects, but ones which are usable because they were properly designed and recorded. They include, for instance, the famous projects by Susan Gray in Tennessee, and by Deutsch in New York. Nevertheless, remarkable trouble has been taken in producing the final sample, and measuring its relation to the original population. Exceptionally rigorous rules have governed the testing for the long-term effects. It is, in short, an evaluation done with meticulous care.

The upshot is that the Lazar–Darlington consortium has established the existence of lasting effects from pre-schooling (i.e. nursery schooling) in four main ways.

First, they show that the beneficiaries are less likely to be assigned later to special or remedial classes. This effect of pre-schooling was shown to be there for children of the same initial IQ, sex, ethnicity, and family background. It persisted even when the comparison was controlled for IQ scores at age six.

Second, there has been the same lasting effect with respect to dropout from school, and what the Americans call 'retention in grade' – i.e. being held back to repeat a year's work because of poor performance. According to the evidence of the eight projects which had collected the relevant data, early educational experience protects against these failures. The protection holds for all poor children regardless of sex, ethnic backgrounds, early IQ and family circumstances.

Third, achievement in mathematics at age ten (fourth grade) is significantly improved by pre-schooling. The evidence also suggests a trend to better scores on reading tests at the same age.

Fourth, children from poor families who went to pre-school programmes scored higher than the 'control' children on the Stanford Binet IQ test for up to three years afterwards. In some projects, this superiority was maintained, but not among those who were aged 13 or over.

Finally, it has emerged that pre-school children retain more 'achievement orientation', and their mothers tend to develop higher vocational aspirations for them than they have for themselves – a discrepancy not found among 'control' children.

The first and second effects are shown in Table 1. Those who had the 'treatment' – i.e. went to one of these well-planned programmes, are compared with a control group of socially and racially matched children who did not. Table 1 tells us that, ordinarily, 44 per cent of children from disadvantaged homes have had to be given special remedial education, or are made to repeat a year, or have dropped out from school: but among those given pre-school education of a certain kind the proportion is reduced to 25 per cent. Altogether, if you send children to a good nursery school, they are twice as likely afterwards to stay above the minimum level of school success as a similar group of children denied the opportunity.

It is true, as I have noted, that these impressive findings come from high-quality pre-school arrangements, and not from a random sample of Headstart programmes. It is true, too, that to use avoidance of remedial classes and 'grade failure' as measures of effectiveness is to focus on the minimal aspirations of a school's work. On the other hand, these are appropriate measures from two points of view. They point to characteristic failures of the children for whom the pre-school programmes were designed – typically, the black child from a poor family. And they are measures of actual educational experience, rather than abstractions like measured intelligence, which may or may not issue in practical performance.

Educational policy makers on either side of the Atlantic may be justifiably disappointed that research has still failed to discern any particular feature of pre-schooling which accounted for success: for example, age of entry, parental involvement, type of teacher or type of

Table 1   How many under-achieving students did better after
Headstart?

Headstart project	Failure rate of project children	Failure rate of control children	Reduction in failure by attending project	Total
good experimental design	%	%	%	No.
Gordon	39.1	61.5	36.0	82
Gray	55.6	73.7	24.6	55
Palmer	24.1	44.7	46.1	221
Weikart	17.2	38.5	55.3	123
median	31.6	53.1	41.1	481
quasi-experimental design				
Beller	48.6	53.1	8.5	69
Levenstein	22.1	43.5	49.2	127
Miller	20.6	11.1	–	125
Zigler	26.6	32.3	17.6	144
overall median	25.4	44.1	36.4	920

NB: 'Failure' is defined as being placed in special education classes, and/or retained in grade, and/or dropped out of school. 'Reduction' is % control minus % project, divided by % control. Children's data were collected in different grades. The design of the Miller project permits no 'reduction' conclusion. The numbers in the total are of project children plus control children.

teaching. The programmes varied in all these respects. What they had in common was enthusiastic and careful organisation. These qualities also made them usable for comparative and retrospective research.

But what Headstart and the EPA experience do show is that a preschool programme, properly devised, can be a most economical investment for a government wishing to save money on schools. And for a government determined to relieve the handicaps of those who come from poor families, a pre-school programme discriminating in their favour seems to be one of the crucial weapons in the armoury. In that way, education *can* compensate for society.

References

1 JENSEN, A. R. (1969) 'How much can we boost IQ and scholastic achievement?' *Harvard Educational Review*, **39**, 1–123.
2 JENCKS, C., SMITH, M., ACLAND, H., BANE, M. J., COHEN, D., GINTIS, H., HEYNS, B. and MICHELSON, S. (1972) *Inequality: A Reassessment of the Effect of Family and Schooling in America*. New York: Basic Books.
3 CONSORTIUM FOR LONGITUDINAL STUDIES (1978) *Lasting Effects after*

Preschool. Department of Health Education and Welfare Publication No. [OHDS] 79–30178. Washington, DC: Government Printing Office.

4 BERNSTEIN, B. (1970) 'Education cannot compensate for society.' *New Society*, 26 February.

5 PLOWDEN REPORT (1967) *Children and their Primary Schools.* London: Central Advisory Council for Education and HM Stationery Office.

6 HALSEY, A. H. (ed.) (1972) *Educational Priority, Vol. 1: EPA Problems and Policies.* London: HM Stationery Office.

Index

Acknowledgments

The editors and publisher wish to thank the following for permission to reprint copyright material in this book:

Routledge and Kegan Paul PLC (London) for 'Children and the family' by L Stone from his *The Past and the Present*, also for 'Sources of information about the self' by Sarah E Hampson from her *The Construction of Personality*, also for 'Biological explanations of sex-role stereotypes' by John Archer from *The Sex-Role System: Psychological and Sociological Perspectives* edited by Jane Chetwynd and Oonagh Hartnett; The Menninger Foundation for permission to reprint from the *Bulletin of the Menninger Clinic*, Vol 26, No 3, pp 120–8, copyright © 1962 The Menninger Foundation; Methuen and Co Ltd for an extract (published here in two parts, 'Modifiability of cognitive development' and 'Cognitive development and the preschool') by Charles J Brainerd from *Developing Thinking* edited by S Meadows, also for 'Measurement constructs and psychological structure: psychometrics' by W E C Gillham from *Thinking in Perspective* by A Burton and J Radford; Penguin Books Ltd for chapter 24, 'The role of play in the problem-solving of children 3–5 years old' by Kathy Sylva, Jerome S Bruner, Paul Genova from *Play* edited by Bruner *et al.*, copyright © 1976 Jerome S Bruner, Alison Jolly, Kathy Sylva, also for extracts from chapter 2 (here called 'An analysis of simple learning situations') of *The Psychology of Learning* by Robert Borger and A E M Seaborne, copyright © 1966, 1982 R Borger and A E M Seaborne; North-Holland Publishing Co for 'Characteristics of maternal and paternal behavior in traditional and non-traditional Swedish families' by Lamb *et al.*, published in *International Journal of Behavioral Development*, 5, pp 131–41; Pluto Press Ltd (London) for 'The Tvind Schools', an extract taken from *The Education of the Future* by Stephen Castles and Wiebek Wustenberg; Carfax Publishing Co and Dr T M Honess for 'A teacher's implicit model of how children learn' by John M Parsons, Norman Graham and Terry Honess, published in *British Educational Research Journal* (1983) 9, pp 91–101; John Wiley & Sons Ltd (Chichester) for 'Remembering drink orders: the memory skills of cocktail waitresses' by Henry L Bennett, published in *Human Learning* (1983) 2, 157–69; Cambridge University Press for 'Conversations with children' by Catherine E Snow from *Language Acquisition* edited by P Fletcher and M Garmon; Basil Blackwell for 'Into print: reading and language growth' by Jessie F Reid from *Early Childhood Development and Education* by M Donaldson, R Grieve and C Pratt, also for 'Psychology and education' by Ann M Clarke, published in *British Journal of Education Studies* XXX, 1 February 1982; John Wiley & Sons, Inc. (New York) for 'Am I me or am I the situation?' by Lawrence A Pervin from his *Current Controversies and Issues in Personality*, pp 4–27, edited; Academic Press Inc (London) Ltd for 'The effects of teachers' behaviour on pupils' attributions: a review' by Daniel Bar-Tal from *Attributions and Psychological Change* edited by Charles Antaki and Chris Brewin, copyright © 1982 by Academic Press Inc (London) Ltd; University of London Institute of Education for 'Maladjusted children and the child guidance service' by Jack Tizard, published in *London Educational Review*, 2, 2, 1973, pp 22–37; Croom Helm Ltd for 'Withdrawal units and the psychology of problem behaviour' by Robert Daines from *Problem*

Behaviour in the Secondary School by B Gillham (1981) pp 101–12; The Open University for 'Intelligence Tests and Educational Reform in England and Wales in the 1940s' by Deborah Thom, written for this Reader, copyright © 1984 The Open University Press; Taylor and Francis Ltd and David Reynolds for 'The search for effective schools' by David Reynolds, published in *School Organization* (1982) 2, 3, 215–37; IPC Magazines Ltd (London) for 'Education can compensate' by A H Halsey, published in *New Society*, 24 January 1980 and Tony Garrett for the illustration used in that article.

Every effort has been made to trace copyright holders of material reproduced in this Reader. Any rights not acknowledged here will be acknowledged in subsequent printings if notice is given to the publisher.